The Traveling Woman

An Indispensable Guide

The Traveling Woman

An Indispensable Guide to the Pleasures and Perils of Traveling Alone, with Husbands, Friends, Lovers, Kids, for Business, Enlightenment, Sheer Joy, etc....

By DENA KAYE

Illustrations by SUSAN PERL

DOUBLEDAY & COMPANY, Inc.
Garden City, New York

For my parents
who gave me roots and wings

Immeasurable and Affectionate Thanks to:

Pamela Fiori, who started everything with a casual mention about the book as we boarded the Star Ferry in Hong Kong, for professional and sisterly steadfastness; Tara Cole for an ever-available, flawless ear and honest tongue; Stephen Golden for an unerring pencil; June Golden for unerring instincts; Adrienne Lascalere for stories; Barbara and Chip Rubinstein for the view from the table where I wrote most of the book, and to Barbara for a continuing course in life; Helen Gurley Brown for unwavering interest and faith; Randi Foreman for nimble fingers; Pamela Shaw for a cheerleader's enthusiasm, even in the face of the "I'm working" voice.

Marcie Rothman for twenty years of being there; Marie Brenner for having been there and pointing the way; Edward Weidenfeld because he's Edward and Sheila because she's Sheila; Cathy Spellman for Karmic knowledge; Gael Greene for unimpeachable counsel; Sandra Hart for teaching me how to jib the boom, or not to, as the case may be; Loraine Boyle for tolerating my typewriter and eating habits; Bob Lescher for champagne and knowing everything I don't.

Patrick Terrail for promotional savvy; ditto Bill Liss; Bugle Eye for my first lessons in how to unearth the secrets of a city; Marie Briehl and Rosetta Hurwitz, who made it possible for me to be able to express myself; Marjorie Goldstein, my friend and editor for her consummate understanding—professional and personal—A.M. espresso marathons at the Trattoria, her relatives' experiences, practical eye, impeccable taste, continuous support, and invaluable input.

Special thanks to Alison Lanier, Jacqueline Markham, Richard Kagan, David Bearinger, John Corris, Shirley Lord, Rogers & Cowan, Ila Stanger, Lillian Afrikano, Rhoda Gamson, Robert Phillips.

And my immeasurable, affectionate, and special thanks—and love—to Larry Berk.

Contents

Introduction

Without trying to recast personalities or remove impacted neuroses, I have designed this book to help you feel more comfortable, confident, curious, daring, flexible, and enthusiastic about any trip, no matter if you're traveling alone or with company, to visit relatives or faraway temples.

The Traveling Woman will take you by the hand, whether you have had a lifetime of trips with a spouse and now are going away on your own, or you are part of a younger generation starting out on an independent foot. This book addresses the specifics that can make traveling different for a woman than a man. Among other things, a woman alone in a hotel lobby is not regarded with the same indifference as a man in the same situation.

Mine is not a destination guide that tells you the cutest hotel in Provence, the chicest teahouse in Tokyo, or the latest Parisian boutique. It's a personal recipe for an approach to travel, a collection of guidelines meant to withstand the vagaries of fashion and time that cover everything from coping with your own loneliness to planning or forgetting about an itinerary; from traveling with someone who's married—but not to you—to handling kids who refuse to get cultured; from customs such as never eating with your left hand in India and the Middle East to utilizing the talents of the concierge or a travel agent.

Begin reading what interests you most, whether the topic is very practical or simply titillating. The rest will fall into place—if you let it. Just like a trip.

The Traveling Woman

An Indispensable Guide

1.
The Unedited Truth About Travel

When I was eight, I played the part of a mummy in a school play and ever since then I wanted to go to Egypt. A curiosity to see the world can begin this inadvertently, although I would have been surprised to find that not everyone walked around Cairo in queen-sized white sheets like the Egyptian citizens in our play (the pharaoh had colored ones). But we all have our illusions that are someday fulfilled or scattered to the winds by real experience. At least the spirit moves you out into the world.

Chasing those illusions is one of the purposes of travel, but you have to be willing to catch them as they exist. Your discoveries may be unexpected, they may be better than anticipated, and they may be as much about you as the places you're exploring.

A dear friend once said that to travel is to take a journey into yourself. The truths uncovered may not always be pleasant. You must face your own preferences, strengths, and quirks—and live with them (and sometimes subject others to them). Without the bunting of a daily routine and familiar faces, you almost have to find yourself in every new environment. In uncharted situations, you are forced to call on your instinct and common sense for guidance.

This utter self-reliance is precisely, if unconsciously, why there may be some ambivalence about going on a trip. You hungrily seek new experiences and the promise of adventure—intellectual, emotional, sexual, and spiritual. You want to be available for the unpredictable, to let the journey take you, rather than freeze the hand of chance. But something happens when you get away from the home routine you were trying to escape. The human and man-made treasures of a country loom ahead as dark unknowns rather than glorious new dishes.

DISPELLING OLD FEARS

Fear of the unknown is a classic, complex force that can blunt discovery and dim the possibility of satisfying one iota of your fantasy. Fear and its tributaries propel people to the nearest American-style hotel and hamburger. I certainly had pause about going into a hamam—a public bath—in Morocco when I saw the large white-tiled room, bulbs with no shades, and naked women scrubbing each other with sponges and rinsing off with water carelessly tossed from tin pails. But I managed to shelve my worst fears—like getting some disease if I sat on the floor. After all, my friends went regularly and, after one visit, so did I.

Perhaps I did take a small risk, but rewarding travel often involves *some* kind of risk, whether you hop a subway and pray you've read the map correctly, dine with a perfect stranger, or take a standby flight. In fact, the night before a trip, I never sleep well because of a combination of nerves, excitement, and knowing the many unforeseen—usually wonderful—things that await me. Sometimes, these feelings accompany me as far as my first destination, and a sour look from *anyone* makes me wonder why I voluntarily, even eagerly, left behind my comforts and friends who love me. But at journey's end, I've never been disappointed.

TRAVELING ALONE

To be perfectly realistic, women of all ages have some fears about traveling, especially traveling alone. The most basic concern stems from simple lack of experience. Sometimes the fear of not being able to handle a situation can make it more difficult than it really is, whether you're maneuvering in a language you don't speak, having a drink in a bar, or going from the airport to the hotel.

We may hesitate to go certain places because of a woman's role in that society. On a business trip to the Middle East, two friends of mine had an escort to take them from town to town. This seemingly hospitable gesture took on a different meaning when on arrival in each place they had to sign a parcel post receipt as if they were "goods delivered."

Another reality is that women alone are subject to a limitless range of approaches which have to be parried with any available means: humor; hostility; or a firm "no, thank you."

The whole feeling of being *entitled* to travel alone is relatively new, part of women's growing sense of self and self-sufficiency. At one time, "ladies" traveling alone had hired escorts who were neither friends nor lovers. On a train trip, for instance, the escorts came to buy the tickets, to raise and lower the compartment windows, and to call on the woman the following day to see how she had withstood the journey.

Today, we are comfortable having our own careers, houses, and friends, and enjoying the choices that earning money brings. Travel is one of them. While no one, let alone *this* romantic, wants to discount the possibility—and joy—of having the right man present plane tickets and say, "Darling, our trip is all arranged," *we should realize that now we don't have to wait for it.*

Traveling alone shouldn't be regarded as a second choice, an inferior alternative or a decision made by default. It isn't better or worse than traveling with a man, one or more women, en masse, or with your neighbor. It's just different, and, for just that reason, provides a bevy of new opportunities. Of course, you can sabotage the advantages. The freedom of not having to ask anyone if it's all right to spend the entire day at Elizabeth Arden is marvelous, unless you start thinking that there's no one to appreciate how wonderful you look. The point is, *you* will.

Feeling good about yourself helps you be more outgoing because you're willing to share who you are. You'll probably take more chances—have dinner at a famous restaurant, take that extra weekend trip, start a conversation with a stranger. Being responsible only for yourself is delicious, provided you're not immobilized by the feeling, "What am I doing here alone?"

ALONE IS NOT LONELY

It's important to distinguish loneliness from being alone. To me, being alone is something I associate with choice. There are many times I am content to choose my own company. I also find that a woman usually has the option of not remaining alone. For all the unshaven three-foot gremlins who appear, there is often a helpful and welcome hand. I once mentioned my interest in seeing the Taj Mahal to the bartender in a New Delhi hotel. He introduced me to people sitting at the bar who were planning to go the next day, and I joined them.

Sometimes the most overlooked camaraderie is another woman's. A conversation with a merchant in a marketplace in Martinique led to dinner with her family. The assistant manager of a hotel in Spain invited me to stay in her apartment because she felt badly that the hotel was overbooked. A waitress in a restaurant where I had lunch spent her day off showing me around Seattle.

Heaven knows, there are times when I have been just plain lonely. It comes over me in a wave, especially when I see things that are wrenchingly beautiful, or emotionally stirring. All I want to do is turn to someone and silently share the experience. I have had this feeling on a boat sailing into a sky painted fuchsia and tangerine; during a meal in a three-star restaurant in France where everyone seemed locked in romantic bliss; as twilight fell on St. Mark's Square in Venice.

Loneliness and undefinable longings are quite natural. A peculiar notion exists that the emotional swings of life do not apply on a trip. A trip is an up in itself and, like New Year's Eve, you're supposed to have a continuously rip-roaring good time. As a result, it's surprising —if not worrisome—to feel slightly depressed, lonely, or uninterested in seeing the sights. But I have a right to feel lonely when no one knows who I am, what I do, what I'm like. Not only am I unknown, I'm missing my whole support system—a familiar bed, friends a phone call away, a market that cashes my checks—and knowing the language and my way around town. I have often felt without purpose, that everything fun is better to share, that there are too many places I can't go unescorted.

There are specific antidotes for these feelings—taking a camera as a companion, or spilling your thoughts into a diary or letters to friends. But it's your basic attitude toward the trip that gives you the emotional ballast to handle such moments. A moment is just that, a moment. It passes with time. Whatever the situation, it's important to see the humor rather than the drama, to watch your own reactions and learn how to pull yourself up.

That too is part of the journey.

2.

Planning

A dependably pragmatic friend of mine recently saw a slick color ad in a magazine of a girl-next-door type floating peacefully in the azure-blue Mediterranean, with a picturesque island in the background. The ad caught her imagination because the idea behind the picture answered her pressing need to escape as well as her fantasy of how to do it. She "became" the woman in the spread and dreamed of the island off Yugoslavia's coast. Bypassing her customary and exhaustive comparison shopping, she planned to unwind for the first week of her vacation at that very spot.

The copy under the picture said that developers were transforming a fishing village into a luxury resort area, with each of the fisherman's cottages turned into individual villas. Unfortunately, the phrase "luxury" had a bigger impact than the verb tense, "were transforming." She arrived to find a half-baked establishment, with accommodations bordering on Boy Scout camp rustic, hot water running on a schedule of its own, and a staff raised on the merits of socialism rather than on gracious service. The menu featured a staggering array of international fare, but not even the fine print warned that the chef would make his own interpretation of each classic dish. "American ham and eggs," for instance, became one overly poached egg sitting in a bowl greased with butter, accompanied by a plate of lettuce strewn with diced ham.

The idea for a trip can *justifiably* be inspired by an ad, articles, postcards from friends, or locations in books and movies. And thank goodness, because the memory of what first catches your attention will get you through the tedious nights you're buried in brochures, airline schedules, and lists of "things to do before I go." My friend's problem was that she grabbed the first appealing solution.

This chapter points the way to thoughtful planning, the best method of ensuring that the nugget of a good idea translates into an equally good, if not better, reality. Planning is simply deciding what you want to do, even if it seems outrageous, and finding a way to do it within your time and budget. Nothing you discover in your research is extraneous. The more you know, the broader your alternatives. You'll only find—happily—that you are liberated rather than limited by knowledge.

FIGURING OUT WHAT YOU WANT TO DO

The first step in planning is to hold a summit meeting with yourself to decide what you really want from the trip. The crucial point is satisfying *your* needs, not the expectations of others. It's pointless to spend *your* time and *your* money going someplace you think you should, just for the plaudits of the people back home. The relationship between you and your trip is very personal, and only you can judge its value. The bottom line is that your opinion, not your mother's, counts. With these all-important facts in mind, consider the following list of possibilities gathered to help you discover the real purpose of your trip. Whether these ideas speak directly to you or whether they spark other thoughts, at least you will have a glimmer of what you'd like to do—or *not* like to do—with your time and money. One gentle note of warning: The perfect vacation is as elusive as the perfect *anything*.

1. You need to sit on a beach, a chalet terrace, in a mountain cabin with four novels, and lights out by ten. (But after three days of this, will you be ready to paint the nearest town red?)

2. There's a dentists' convention in Düsseldorf . . . Let's be frank. You want to meet a nice doctor.

3. This trip is the splurge of the year. You'd like to be cosseted by a smiling staff, preferably French or Italian.

4. It's time to get your body back in shape at a spa.

5. Your hobbies call: Romanesque architecture, wines, London theater, Mexican pottery, Renaissance sculpture, Bolognese cooking.

6. You'll find the cheapest airfare to India, Europe, California, etc., and take it from there.

7. You are ready for Mother Nature: camping, canoeing, a dude ranch, hiking, backpacking. (Is there a hidden condition that room service is available?)

8. Only a rip-roaring social life will do. A ski resort, a Club Med, anyplace with a built-in crowd.

9. You decide to come home rested, but more skilled, so you look for a tennis camp, or a cooking, sailing, scuba diving, weaving, or painting school.

10. All you know is that you have to get away, so you'll listen to whoever has the best idea for under $1,000.

Next, begin the information-gathering process—a treasure hunt for the facts in which you simultaneously play a detective, an investigative reporter, a consumer advocate, and a dreamer. My resources fall loosely into two categories: official and unofficial, or, put another way, paid and unpaid. The official/paid first group includes the national tourist offices of foreign countries and American states, national airline carriers, consulates and embassies, and guidebooks. The unofficial or unpaid resources are the people you know: friends who have been where you're going, friends of friends who have been there, and friends of friends of friends, etc. (See Contacts in this chapter.)

SOURCES OF INFORMATION: HOW TO USE THEM

National tourist organizations are official arms of foreign governments and usually headquartered in New York, with branch offices in such major cities across the country as Los Angeles, Chicago, Boston, Atlanta, San Francisco, or Houston. These bureaus are rich sources of free information, but their function should not be confused with travel agencies, whose agents can do everything from planning your itinerary to notifying the hotel you'd like a board under your bed. (See Travel Agents in this chapter.) Some tourist offices provide more helpful literature than others. I have seen everything from seductive color brochures that give no specifics, to plain xeroxed sheets with detailed walking tours. Some countries just know how to sell what they've got. The French recognize that we go to France to eat, so they have myriad restaurant guides for all price ranges. Although the word "bargain" should be excised from almost every country's vocabulary, Hong Kong still offers good buys. Logically, Hong Kong's tourist bureau offers a comprehensive shopping guide. The Italians push their history and, among other items, have a first-rate map to Rome's historical monuments, museums, and catacombs, with extensive historical notes.

The material you receive will vary according to what is available and, equally important, *how you ask for it*. The ideal method is to talk with a representative in person. If you are researching via the mail, write early and give a deadline by which you need the information. Most of the travel literature you will receive is sent third class, so you want your request in the "action pile," not the "futures" department.

Because there is nothing quite so confusing as getting an avalanche of generalizations, make your questions as specific as possible when you write, call, or go in to seek information. Instead of asking for hotels in Paris, for instance, indicate how much you want to spend, if you want a breakfast-included arrangement, if you prefer small, family-run establishments or large modern quarters. Ask for information about special events. Many countries have year-long celebrations for the birth—or death—of musicians, saints, philosophers, war heroes, etc., and if the trend to turn chefs into national heroes continues, we may see national holidays for Escoffier or Paul Bocuse. Fetes mark the anniversary of the founding, liberating, or destruction of a city, the building of a famous church. If you are traveling with children, request information on activities or places of special interest. Some countries—Denmark and Ireland, for example—have farm vacations which are particularly suited to kids, and others have guides specializing in sight-seeing for kids so you can have a two-hour meal without a hamburger in sight. (See the chapter, "Traveling with Children.")

The airlines also have a windfall of free or low-cost information. Call your local reservations office and ask what is available. They might suggest that you contact their tour department, write to the main office, or they may take your name and address and send booklets to you directly. Some airlines, like Pan American, have small guidebooks to capital cities and the environs. Japan Airlines, for instance, puts out "Business in Japan" and "The Woman's Guide to the Orient." Air India will even tell you how to wrap a sari.

After the story of the island off the Yugoslavian coast it would be incontinent to think that ads, official brochures, booklets, etc., give an unbiased picture. While plowing through this "helpful propaganda" remember that ad agencies and public relations companies have spent billions to seduce you with words and pictures. Rarely will you find any critical evaluations. Have you ever seen a picture of a tourist with third-degree burns from lying in the sun? You must read the fine print, note the asterisks, and ask as many questions as you think necessary. Be wary of the possible hidden meaning of these adjectives: pleasant (without character); comfortable (worn); colorful (teeming); peaceful (boring). Is the work *completed* on the newly remodeled wing, or will you be lodged in the old, crumbling section? Is the balcony more than a window ledge? Do you have to contort your body to see the water in an ocean- or lake-view room? Does "extensive convention facilities" mean you will be sandwiched between the five hundred cash-register salesmen wearing badges? Is the special children's program more than just hamburgers on the menu? What does "year-round sunshine" or "occasional showers" mean?

THE TRAVEL AGENT

Even if you were the world's most assiduous researcher, it's unlikely that you could ever amass and *evaluate* all the information about your trip as well as the skilled travel agent with his constant access to travel industry literature and "fam trips"—familiarization trips—that provide firsthand experience. The operative word here, however, is *skilled*. The field of travel agents attracts as many hucksters and opportunists as the health food business. Some of the most common "nonprofessionals" are businessmen using the agency for tax benefits and free trips; people selling paradise cheap, with only a box office number for identification; or "outside travel agency salesmen" who trade in stolen tickets. Those types *are* a minority, but awareness that they do exist is part of your self-protection.

The bona fide professional belongs to the American Society of Travel Agents. The elite travel agent will also have CTC, or "Certified Travel Counselor," after his name, which means he has completed the two-year course of the Institute of Certified Travel Agents. If you have any suspicions about the agency you are considering, ask if the local Better Business Bureau has any complaints on file, or write to the American Society of Travel Agents, Consumer Affairs Department, 711 Fifth Avenue, New York, N.Y. 10022. You're being intelligent, not snoopy.

A satisfied customer is the most comforting and reliable recommendation you can get for an agent. Ask friends who have returned from a good trip for the name of their agency, and specifically who handled the planning. (An unsuccessful trip is also a recommendation of who to avoid.) The quality of agents within a company can vary. The next step is to call the agency and make an appointment. Since time is money for an agent, he will always appreciate someone who considers both parties' schedules. If you know what you want to do—a cruise, visiting the Mayan ruins in Mexico, etc.—ask to see someone with expertise in that field.

Rapport with a travel agent is as important and personal as rapport with your gynecologist or lawyer. Don't be embarrassed to "interview" the prospective agent. However, you can't expect a mind reader. What you want is someone who can translate your ideas—as vague as they may be—into concrete plans. Does he/she seem to understand your particular needs? Does he/she seem willing to take enough time to ask you the important questions: your interests, your budget, your anxieties, if any, about food, types of accommodations, customs relating to women, or political situations in certain parts of the world? Anyone who minimizes the differences between travel agents on the grounds that they all get the same kind of information is taking the easy way out. But even the best agents aren't miracle workers. Each piece of information you provide will help them come up with the right trip for you. A travel agent, like an interior designer, works best when he has all the pertinent information. In order to make a bedroom function most effectively, for instance, your designer would have to know if you read in bed in order to have a good reading light, or if you pile magazines, books, a radio, phone, flowers, by your bed in order to give you a large-enough table. I would recommend you divulge the following to your travel agent:

1. Tell him/her the purpose of your trip. Try to list *all* the elements you'd like to have. You may be doing yourself a disservice by stressing the importance of a secluded beach and neglecting to say you're passionate about gambling, that you care about good food, or that you feel uncomfortable unless you speak the language and you're only fluent in English.

2. Outline your budget, and how you want to apportion the funds.

3. Explain what *you* mean by a "one-star" hotel. Hotel classifications are so diverse that first class in one country might be the equivalent of third class in another. The agent also has *his* own interpretation of such terms as luxury, standard, budget, old, charming, etc. (See the chapter, "Hotels.")

4. Several destinations may suit your needs. Listen to all the possibilities, and be flexible enough to consider a new idea. No one would go so far afield as to suggest ice fishing in Newfoundland when you've asked for ancient temples.

5. What does the price of the tour or package arrangements include: tips, taxes, admission fees to museums, transfers from airports to hotels, sightseeing, meals? You don't want to find out after you get there that dinner is "an extra."

6. Go over any cancellation clauses in package plans and ask your agent to translate from "legalese."

7. Inexpensive air fares often require advance booking so talk to an agent early enough to take advantage of them.

It won't cost you anything to use a travel agent—with a few stipulations. A travel agent is paid on a commission basis from airlines, hotels, and large tour operators. There is a set commission fee, for example, on domestic and international flights, so you needn't worry that he'll book you on an airline managed by his cousin Morris who gives him a higher fee. You can even have a travel agent book you a flight from New York to California and nothing more—at no cost—although some agents prefer not to do it because of the small commission rate. On any kind of booking, you may be charged for long-distance telephone calls or cables.

An agent usually has one self-protection rule. If you ask the agent to plot an individualized itinerary for you, he may ask for a nonrefundable deposit, perhaps 10–15 percent of the estimated cost, to be applied to the cost of the tour. He's protecting himself against the client who takes the professionally planned itinerary and books the trip himself, meaning the agent will not receive any commissions, and in essence has planned the trip for free. The deposit also helps separate the people who realize they are paying for an agent's expertise from those just looking for general information or an "armchair" trip.

How a Travel Agent Usually Works

1. You talk, sketch out and decide on an individual itinerary or a package tour.

2. When you pay the agent a deposit on the total amount, you are given a receipt and an invoice telling you when the remaining balance is due.

3. A few days later the agent will show you a completed itinerary, and if it suits you, he will then check the availability of hotels and transportation—and make the bookings. In the event of space problems he will consult you and suggest alternatives.

4. The arrangements are made through a tour operator, companies that specialize in putting together transportation and land arrangements, a corresponding travel agent at the destination, or with personal contacts at hotels.

5. He will inform you if visas are necessary and process the forms for you through a visa service.

6. He will tell you what shots are required, if any; have passport forms on hand to show you how to fill them out, and usually will collect information about your destination from the tourist offices.

When you leave the office for your trip, your travel folder should include:

1. A detailed itinerary.

2. Airline, rail, cruise tickets.

3. Original vouchers for you, copies to the corresponding agent (you will have the phone number and an agency contact), and copies to the reservations manager at the hotel. The voucher, in fact, is a replacement for the money you have paid to the travel agent at home, and it will be marked "prepaid" with the exact amount in dollars. It will specify what you are entitled to; if you will be met at the airport in a motor coach or limousine; the kind of room accommodations you will have; if breakfast is included; sightseeing tours and any special requests, whether it's a particular interest like jewelry auctions or having kosher or vegetarian meals. If you don't know how long you want to stay in a hotel, the agent will usually give you a voucher for one night, and notify the hotel that if you decide to stay on you will pay the additional cost on departure.

4. Travel and baggage insurance forms to fill out and mail back to the agent. Baggage insurance covers lost luggage. But let's say you have an airline ticket with specific departure and return dates. If for some "good" reason you have to return early, or postpone the trip, you forfeit the cheaper fare. Your travel agent can sell you a policy that will cover the additional cost of the ticket. Ask the agent what the insurance company considers a "good" reason—illness, a death in the family, etc.

BUDGETS AND COSTS

A foodnik friend of mine decided that eating in three-star restaurants was the most important part of her trip to France. To save money, she combined her transportation and lodging costs by traveling overnight by train from city to city. She chose lunch, instead of dinner. She spent afternoons exploring the towns and if a dinner invitation was not forthcoming, she had "un sandwich" in a cafe for supper and caught the train to the next restaurant. As it happened, she had many invitations, some from the restaurant owners themselves who were intrigued by an American girl on a gastronomic tour by herself.

Planning a budget for your trip is rather like counting calories. You can parcel out the amount any way you choose. You can juggle the fixed costs of hotel, food, and transportation just to your taste if you're traveling alone, or with the consent of your traveling companion. (See the chapter, "Traveling Companions.") Some people include shopping as a fixed cost. You can spend the weekend at the Ritz and then stay in budget hotels the following week. You can scrimp on everything just to buy a designer dress, or take a side trip. In any case, you should allot a daily sum for entertainment, whether that includes theater, hairdressers, or concerts, and an amount for local transportation.

It is foolhardy to make a blueprint for the cost of your trip because not every factor is predictable. In the past several years, for instance, the airfares have become the most affordable expense, with Freddy Laker's SkyTrain and the innumerable special discount fares available on scheduled airlines. (More about this in the chapter, "Transportation.") There's no need to pretend you've been a member in good standing of a nonexistent garden club in order to take advantage of inexpensive charter airfares. Countries such as Spain, Portugal, and Yugoslavia have been considered good travel value, but when Portugal erupted in a revolution, bargain prices became irrelevant. World politics and the health of the dollar are mercurial but ever-present influences in the travel picture. In addition, the internal structure of the tourism industry itself can affect the cost of your trip. Take the case of "seasons."

Seasons in the travel business are called "high season," "shoulder" (in between high and low), and "low" or "off season." In this context "high" or "in" season is the most desirable time to be someplace to get the maximum benefit from the weather (hot or cold) and the activities that usually depend upon it. Ironically, the Caribbean is considered a winter resort, while, in fact, summer temperatures are only a few degrees higher than winter, but the price still reflects the "season," and the winter rates are practically double the summer rates. July and particularly August are "in" season in the South of France, the Greek Islands, and most beach resorts. Thanks to extensive media coverage, we hear tales of the jet set and who was last seen with whom at the disco/port/bar/bistro, etc. Half the fun is to see the colorful and eccentric people, clothes, and behavior at these places during the "high" season.

Part of the lure of "off-season" is economic because the airlines and hotels have lower fares and rates. But I find that in "off" season, you will probably have a chance to meet more locals. Shopkeepers and waiters will have more time, and you won't have the in-season crush. Each locale is so different that you should discuss the merits of each season—and how they fit into your expectations about the trip—with your travel agent and tourist bureau.

ORGANIZING THE TRIP

How you organize your trip also affects the cost: It costs more to travel alone. The travel business benignly calls the added cost "the single supplement," a surcharge that you pay whether you are completely on your own, or with an escorted tour or group. You're not being docked for unsociability—the explanation is simple arithmetic. Hotels and tour operators determine their rates and prices on double occupancy, or two people in a room. (Two people also eat and drink more than one.) In their view, one person in a room means giving up potential income, so the single rate is always slightly higher than half the double rate. The increase in the price depends of course, on the length of your stay and the type of accommodations. The cruise business, for instance, has made some concession with so-called standby plans. You are notified within thirty days of sailing if a single accommodation is available and sometimes, to fill space, you might even get a double room at the regular double rate.

GROUP TRAVEL

Group travel these days has taken on a much broader meaning than the picture of twenty-five people religiously following the

leader. After two trips to Europe en masse, I developed a phobia of being whizzed past the Mona Lisa, eating a programmed meal in a restaurant while others nibbled the specialty of the house. I decided there must be a better way. Fortunately there are many different kinds of package tours that combine transportation and land arrangements, such as cars and hotels, or trains and cruises, or fly and drive. These packages can make your trip less expensive than if you bought a separate plane ticket and made your own independent reservations, and you're not necessarily chained to a tour group.

Fortunately, the word "group" has become very flexible. A "group tour" may be as painless as sitting on the plane with a collection of people who have bought into the same airfare and hotel plan but have no further obligation to each other, and will only meet in passing in the lobby. On an "airfare-only" arrangement you won't even know the other members of the group. Many airlines offer such "air and land" packages so you can conveniently make all the bookings in one phone call. You can also use a travel agent.

To make the picture clearer, let's say that Air France is offering a week-long package at a deluxe hotel in Paris; rooms with private bath and shower, breakfast included, and a half-day sightseeing tour. You call Air France reservations, and they transfer you to their tour department (as would any airline with similar packages). The tour department then makes your plane and hotel booking. They will accept payment by personal check, bank money order, or certified check. If you pay by personal check, do so far enough in advance so the check can clear. You can pay by credit cards only if you go in person to a travel agent or Air France reservations office. The airline then sends you the travel documents: the airline tickets, voucher for the hotel, stating you have confirmed a single room with bath, and breakfast (or whatever) with an additional voucher for a half-day sightseeing tour.

Group Tours with a Purpose

I am wholeheartedly enthusiastic about the trend in group travel to organize around a common interest. It is travel industry lore that Thomas Cook, the Englishman credited with the invention of group travel, planned his first mass movement in 1841, chartering trains, carriages, and coaches, to carry teetotalers to a temperance convention. I joined a group who shared a passion of quite a different character: cooking. We enrolled in a cooking school in Bologna and for a week did nothing but savor the cuisine and wines of the region. My only complaint, unfortunately all too short-lived, was that I never wanted to see food again.

I think that interest-oriented group trips are particularly suited to women. The awkwardness you may feel as a woman alone is dissipated by the fact that you're there to learn something. It helps amend the unwritten axiom that says women traveling alone never want to remain alone. At the cooking school, for instance, conversations began easily because we could bypass the agonizing getting-to-know-you preliminaries and debate the virtues of hand-rolled versus machine-rolled pasta, go shopping for espresso machines, and try to restrain each other from our third Italian ice.

Club Med is another version of the group tour with a purpose. Each club has a different personality. Most of them emphasize sports activities, and every single second of your day can be filled with tennis, swimming, riding, scuba, and snorkeling. But at this camp for adults you can also be a bohemian or a bookworm. The club is particularly appropriate if you want to go someplace exotic but are reluctant to stay in local hotels and make your way through the city. You can live in a "protected" environment (the club isn't open to nonmembers), and club people, called "gentils organisateurs," are well meaning, nice counselors who will show you the sights. My two reservations about the club are that if you come alone, you automatically get a roommate, although if you have any complaints you can request a change, and some clubs are principally French-speaking. On the special plus side, some clubs have minicamps for children. And I don't mean children over forty-five.

HOW TO PLAN ITINERARIES

I never even heard the word "itinerary" until I left home to go to college, having grown up in a family that championed spontaneity and playing everything by ear, whether it was a dinner menu or a trip. I realized as I got older, however, that my mother often made plans for us as unobtrusively as possible. My father did things differently. It always seemed to me that while some fathers had date books, read—and answered—the day's mail, promptly returned phone calls, and prided themselves on being highly organized, my father considered this behavior highly neurotic. He reveled in saying things like, "How can I know in January what to do this summer if I don't know what I'll feel like doing next week?"

Everything changed when he started to cook. He constructed each menu with the care due a presidential dinner, kept a record in a looseleaf notebook of who had eaten what (and when) so no one would ever get the same thing twice, to the disappointment of many guests who developed favorites. As a result of such planning he was forced to think ahead and organize shopping for all the ingredients. He now plots out when he'll go to the duck store so it doesn't interfere with getting the fresh fish on the other side of town. He calls the poultry man in time for him to prepare the order, and if it's not ready, he may spend extra time discussing the merits of a particular fruit with the green grocer. All I can tell you is that on the last trip I made with him, we had a typed-out itinerary of flights and hotels.

Basically, an itinerary is the outline for your trip. It can be as informal as knowing in your head that you'll leave Los Angeles next Thursday, and arrive in Seattle two weeks later. (There is a restaurant on Highway 1 where you would like to stop for a meal, but that's your most definite plan.) This absence of structure unnerves many people, who require a detailed itinerary that tells them how, where, and when they will be spending their time. Happily, there are no rights and wrongs about charting your course. The form and style will depend on your priorities and, strangely enough, your emotional needs. I have a close friend who went to Europe for the first time on her own and told me it was reassuring to have life typed out on crisp white stationery. The point is, an itinerary can be a comfortable framework but should never be a corset that makes breathing difficult.

It is very tempting to schedule every moment, to cut corners on leisure or unprogrammed time and forget you are a human being. It may undermine your dedication to getting the most for your time and money, but you'll be kinder to yourself the moment you accept the terrible truth that there will always be more to see and do than time permits. To be honest, I have never planned an itinerary that didn't change because I met people, fell in love with a city—or had to leave immediately—or felt like wandering aimlessly rather than doing what I had planned. The most important thing to decide is what matters most to *you*. You may not know until the third day of the trip. And each day may bring a new decision.

As you sit with your maps, brochures, suggestions from friends, travel agent, or companions, struggling to decide whether to see "a little bit" of Venice, or none at all, here are some thoughts to consider:

1. The question is: How much time to give to each interest? What is there to see, and what do you *care* about seeing?

2. Don't plan a whole day of museums, or churches, or any one thing. Balance the day with a different rhythm of activity during the morning and afternoon.

3. Find out how long it *really* takes to get from one part of the city to another, particularly if you have business appointments.

4. If you are going by car, read up-to-date maps carefully and note the conditions of the road. You may allow one hour's driving time on a road in good condition, when it's actually being repaired, or reduced to one lane, and you need several hours. Look for an alternate route; know approximately when it gets dark so you're not caught on a winding mountain pass or arrive in town and have difficulty finding your way, possibly in a strange language. Not every town has a landmark that's easily visible at night like the Eiffel Tower. Do not drive in the hottest part of the day. Have lunch. (See Cars in the chapter, "Transportation.")

5. Don't plan anything for the first few hours after you arrive anywhere. It may seem like a great idea at home but won't be when you get there. (See Organizing Each Day in the chapter, "Meeting a City.")

6. LEAVE TIME TO DO NOTHING.

MONEY: NEVER LEAVE HOME WITHOUT IT

The amount of money you should take with you depends on several factors:

1. How much of your trip has been prepaid; what fixed costs, i.e. lodging, transportation, and food, will you cover en route?

2. How much "mad money" can you afford for whatever you consider extras and entertainment?

3. How much should you bring so you will feel able to take care of yourself financially? Knowing you have enough money is important psychologically because it means you are in charge of yourself, that your decisions will be made in your best interests, and not out of default because you can't afford the choice.

What you will *get* for your money is less predictable. The fluctuating world money market means that how much the dollar can be exchanged for in other currencies may vary from day to day. Each time the dollar is devalued, you get less for each dollar. Dollars used to work magic everywhere. Now, they're sometimes refused, or given an unfavorable rate of exchange.

Cash

It's often easy to treat foreign money more casually than dollars. It looks different, has different names and denominations, and never seems to be the right size for *any* wallet. Before I leave home, I always get about $50 worth of the currency I'll need at my first stop to familiarize myself with it or pay for any ground transport if I arrive when the banks are closed. I also carry $25 in one-dollar denominations for tipping purposes. When I have no idea what is appropriate, and no time to figure it out gracefully, dollar bills are very convenient. (See Tipping in the chapter, "Etc.")

Traveler's Checks

I feel the most comfortable with traveler's checks because by contacting the proper sources I can get an immediate refund if they are lost or stolen. There are several different "brands" of traveler's checks on the market. You should decide to buy one or the other on the basis of these factors: Where are they sold (is it convenient to you)? Is there a charge for issuing the checks? What is the refund policy? Is there a booklet or listing of the worldwide offices so that you can report stolen checks?

Traveler's checks look almost like regular bank checks, with a place for the date, and a "payable to" line, except that there are two places for your signature. When you buy the checks, you sign your name on the top left-hand corner of each check. When you pay with the check, you countersign in front of whoever is cashing it, as a protection that the check belongs to you. Checks are available in denominations of $10 to $5,000 (and more), but I always get tens, twenties, and fifties depending on how much I am taking. The smaller amounts are particularly important in foreign countries because you usually get the change in local currency. I once cashed a large check to pay my last dinner bill in Paris, and found myself the next day in Italy with $80 worth of French francs I couldn't use. Just don't get *so* frugal you find yourself in a delightful, but backwoods place over the weekend or holiday, where you can't cash a check.

You can buy traveler's checks from your bank, or such agencies as American Express, Perera, the largest foreign currency exchange company in the world, Barclays or Thomas Cook. Cook himself invented the first traveler's checks in 1874, and called them circular notes. He personally went to Europe and through the states to arrange that banks accepted the checks as legal tender.

Traveler's checks are sold in foreign currencies as well as dollars. The advantage of the former is that you are hedging against the falling value of the dollar, and you can cash checks anywhere without being concerned where you'll get the best rate.

On the other hand, you will have to make a more careful estimate of what you will spend, particularly if you're going to several different countries. If you have money left over, you'll have to convert the checks back to dollars when you get home, and perhaps lose on the transaction. If you have dollars or traveler's checks in dollars, always change them in a bank. Hotels, restaurants, and many shops will accept them, but you will pay for the convenience by getting a lower rate of exchange.

I would never encourage anyone to change money on the black market. Some friends of mine do it nonchalantly, and recount how people appear magically outside your hotel the moment you walk out and say things like, "My uncle has a store with beautiful perfume," then he'll look at you meaningfully and say in hushed tones, "and he'll give you a *very* good rate of exchange."

Credit Cards

A *major* credit card is valuable for several reasons, especially if it is in your own name—as in "Joan Smith," rather than "Mrs. Ralph Smith"—because it's a means of identification. With credit cards you can pay bills and have official receipts for your personal records or tax purposes, while saving as much cash as possible. (Keep in mind that many small inns and restaurants don't take credit cards.) Just be sure to make a note of how much you're charging so you don't get home and find that the accumulated bills have null-and-voided your projected trip budget. If you have an American Express card, an American Express office anywhere in the world will issue you a certain amount of cash on your card. A card is also an important form of ID for cashing personal checks. Before you go, find out the company policy on lost or stolen cards.

The only possible drawback in using a card, unless your card expires midway through the trip, is that when you receive the bill weeks later you may find you're paying more than you expected. What has happened is that you are paying the rate of exchange in effect the day the bill *arrived* at the local offices of the credit card company. You may have left ten days earlier, when the rate was better. It could also happen to your advantage. In either case, you can negotiate with the company that issued the card.

If You Run Out of Money

1. Use your credit card to get cash, as explained above.

2. Always take personal checks. It's surprising how many places will accept them with some identification. I remember a hotel cashier in Italy who was slightly bewildered, although amused, by my checks from The First Women's Bank in New York. The idea of a bank for women only, which is what the title erroneously implies, hardly fits the Italian mentality. But he passed it off with a shrug and a smile and merely said, "Those American women."

3. Call or cable a friend at home to take cash or a certified check to a bank and wire it to you at a corresponding bank. Bring your passport to the bank as identification in order to claim the money. American Express will also wire money.

4. I always stash about $300 in traveler's checks or cash in my passport case and promise myself I will ignore it unless there is an emergency. (Clothes absolutely do not qualify!)

5. If someone *else* runs out of money and comes to you for a loan, think about it for a long time, unless it's for your next of kin or

the equivalent. I learned the hard way. I once met an actor in Spain who was making a low-budget picture. He knew the area well, and included me in social goings-on as often as possible. He had to leave unexpectedly, and said he had no cash. Could I lend him $300? It never occurred to me to suggest his producer advance him money. I lent him the $300, and he gave me an I.O.U., and his address—a bar in Los Angeles. It is now hard to imagine that I ever thought he would pay me back.

HOW TO ORGANIZE YOURSELF BEFORE YOU GO

The only way I get anything done is to make lists, so I divide my chores into two categories: trip-related and household-related; and I write all the items down on a legal pad. I get out my daily calendar and plot out what I can do each day. I usually allow a few weeks so I am never undone by running around madly at the last minute. You shouldn't have to plan any further in advance unless you're going someplace that requires a series of shots, and a certain time in between each inoculation. If necessary you can get your passport the day you leave, if you show an airplane or cruise ticket as proof of departure. (See the chapter, "Etc.")

The Trip-Related List

1. Call the public health official and find out what vaccinations are required (if any). If you have shots be sure to get a certificate of vaccination. (See the chapter, "Etc.")

2. Get your passport, tourist cards, international driver's license (see the chapter, "Transportation"), visas. (Register cameras, jewelry with customs—at airport—so you won't have to pay duty when you return on things you already own.) Take a Xerox copy of your passport, or an expired passport. (See the chapter, "Etc.")

3. Buy traveler's checks.

4. Make a list (and several copies) for a reliable friend, with your passport number, traveler's checks numbers, and itinerary. Even if you want to disappear completely, it's a wise idea to tell one person where to find you in case of a *real* emergency. And specify just what you mean by emergency.

5. Find out if your medical insurance covers you while you're traveling. Are your dependents covered? Do you want to get special luggage, or life insurance, etc.?

6. Get business cards with your name, address, and job description if it applies. If you're going to Asia, be sure to have them printed in the appropriate local language on the reverse side. Even if you're not *in* business per se, having cards implies a certain self-esteem, and in most cases you'll be treated accordingly.

7. Make a "trip" phone book, and list names of contacts under each country, as well as important names and numbers of friends and family at home. NEVER take the only phone book you own unless you have a duplicate. One easy trick is to address self-adhesive labels for people to whom you know you'll be writing and put them in an envelope.

8. Reduce your clipping file to the essentials by putting information on index cards. For example, one card lists restaurants open for brunch on Sunday in New York, the plays you want to see in London, the dishes you'd like to order in Italy, places for morning tea in Japan, etc. (See Appendix, "Indispensable Reading.")

9. Get prescriptions for necessary drugs, extra glasses, cosmetic items, etc. (See the chapter, "Packing.")

CONTACTS

Swallow your reservations, shyness, ignore the the quickened pulse rate. Be unhesitant and resourceful about asking everyone you know for names of people to contact wherever you're going. You have many ways to go:

1. Ask your close friends to write a note so that when you call, you'll be saved giving your résumé. And you'll feel more comfortable.

2. Get letters of introduction from business associates, club managers with affiliate clubs in other cities, etc.

3. Find out if your church, temple, professional association, college group, alumni association, women's clubs, or whatever group you belong to has an affiliate organization, or an informal representative in other cities. The American Women's Club, for instance, with headquarters in Washington, has clubs all over

the world. A friend of mine who now lives in Brussels showed me the material the club provides, including shopping and restaurant suggestions. You pay a small membership fee.

4. Do you have any hobbies or vocational interests that translate into other cultures? Ask your local art dealer or gourmet shop owner for their favorite places, or names of suppliers. You might wind up, as I did, in a bakery in Paris, with a personal tour from the owner.

5. Ask your doctor, dentist, or even your hairdresser to recommend people in case of any "real" need, but also as a social contact. My dentist once wrote to a patient of his on my behalf. This patient turned out to be a pivotal figure in the social life of Newport, Rhode Island. You never know. I have one friend who asked the waiter at her favorite Italian restaurant if he still had family in Italy. She stayed a week with his parents on their farm in Sicily.

LANGUAGE

I once spent a summer in a small town in Italy with a family who spoke no English, and my Italian was limited to what I had learned in five lessons at Berlitz. How far could I get on "This is a pencil"? I also knew from my mother's experience that it was useless trying to enlarge my vocabulary with musical terms in Italian. In an effort to get a taxi driver in Rome to go faster, she said, "Allegro! Allegro!" the term for "fast" in music. The driver responded by turning around, nodding, smiling, and looking generally pleased. She kept trying, "Allegro! Allegro!" He smiled more broadly. No wonder. Allegro in everyday Italian means "lively, gay, and spirited."

I discovered how much we all take being able to communicate for granted. That summer I had to resort to a combination of sign language, pointing, and using pictures in books to make myself understood. I had raging headaches the first few nights from the frustration of not understanding, and thinking that any minute now everything would make sense. What helped me the most was that I overlooked my gross ineptness at the language, making mistakes, malaprops left and right. I realized the idea was to communicate any way I could, not to have perfect grammar and vocabulary.

Needless to say, your trip is immeasurably enriched if you do speak the language—by exchanges with merchants, listening to conversations, and being able to meet more people. I would do everything possible—and practical—to brief yourself before you go. Get Berlitz phrase books, language lesson cassettes, take lessons if you have enough time to get beyond "This is a pencil."

The House-Related List

1. If you live alone, make sure your house or apartment doesn't look abandoned. Get timers that turn lights on and off automatically. Suspend your newspaper delivery. If you normally get an avalanche of mail, check with the post office to see if you can rent a box for the period of your trip, ask a neighbor to pick up the mail, or have your mail stopped.

2. Pay as many bills as you can in advance. Leave checks made out for the phone company, or from your credit cards with the same friend who is picking up your mail. Nothing is worse than coming home to find your electricity or phone has been turned off because of unpaid bills.

3. I have a friend who always leaves me with the silver service she inherited from her mother. You might consider leaving valuables in a safety deposit box at a bank, or with a friend who doesn't mind the responsibility.

4. Concerning plants and gardens, I've heard that if I wrapped all my plants in plastic bags to keep in the moisture, I wouldn't have to impose on anyone to water them. Because I am convinced the plants will die, I've never tried it. I rely on neighbors.

5. University students make inexpensive housesitters if you hesitate to leave your house or apartment unattended, especially if you have pets and prefer not to put them in a kennel. If you leave your pets with a friend, be sure that they won't try to follow you, or that your dog or cat won't come into heat. This is particularly disruptive if there are any other animals around.

6. Neither children, husbands, nor lovers like to feel they've been abandoned. How you handle the children will depend on their age. You may ask a relative to stay with them, or a trusted housekeeper, or a neighbor. Your kids might be able to stay with a friend, provided the parents agree, and you are prepared to return the favor.

On the other hand, hiring a professional sitter may be your only choice. If one of your children has an important occasion while you'll be away—a play, a recital—call or send a telegram. Young children sometimes have difficulty understanding why you've gone away, even if it's overnight on business. It seems to them that they've been left or forgotten. Explain where you're going, what you'll be doing, and even show them on a map where you'll be so they won't feel you have disappeared.

How you deal with the man in your life is a very personal issue. I assume that in some cases you'll want to leave wonderful things in the refrigerator or freezer for him to eat. On the other hand, you may announce that the time apart will be "constructive separation."

7. Lock the front door behind you.

3.

Packing

THE PSYCHOLOGY OF PACKING: THE WHAT IFS

It's doubtful that anyone loves packing. In fact, I know people who think packing is the *worst* part of the trip. It's a true chore, joyless and anxiety-producing. The problem is compounded by the fact that you're not only concerned about taking the right things for snow or the tropics, a black-tie dinner, and a working lunch, but are dealing with the issue that clothes become your most personal statement. People notice *how* you look because that's the first information available.

Complicating your packing problem may be your hope that this trip will reveal the "new" you. You want to go from turtlenecks to décolletage. No wonder you can't decide what to take. The final trauma usually strikes when you've got everything laid out on the bed and are in agony over what to eliminate. It's called the "what if" syndrome, which is a first cousin of the "you never know" syndrome. You feel compelled to prepare for any eventuality. Someplace in your mind, as you throw in forty-nine pairs of panty hose, you are envisioning a blizzard in Hawaii, one of the likely cataclysms certain to occur if you dare to travel light.

The "what ifs" are fanned by the wish that some of your fantasies will materialize. And so, in the quiet of your bedroom, you plan your wardrobe accordingly. The reality is that you can make do with whatever you've got. If not, borrow, buy, or rent the necessary item. Even if you are going to camp out in a remote tent in the desert, you'll pass through some sort of commercial center in order to pick up your camel and other "necessities." This chapter tackles the "what ifs" and all other "ifs" to try to point you in a sensible direction.

HOW TO DECIDE WHAT IS APPROPRIATE

A number of factors, ranging from the weather to a respect for the traditions of a country, will determine which items actually make it into the suitcase—and remain there. (See sample lists, in this chapter, of what to take.)

1. *Weather*—Climate is your first concern. Usually, you will need either a summer (lightweight) wardrobe, or a winter (warm) wardrobe. Occasionally you may need both. Find out some specifics and carefully read "Around the World Weather Guide" in the Appendix. If you are going to a warm climate, is it dry desert heat all day that cools off in the evening when the sun goes down, or the tropics where it's hot and humid and rain showers are frequent? Will you be in and out of air-conditioned environments?

Consider the altitude. To take one example, many people think Santa Fe, New Mexico, is arid desert all year round. Actually, Santa Fe sits at seven thousand feet, as high as some of the big ski resorts in Colorado. Consequently Santa Fe is toasty in summer but gets its fair share of winter snow.

2. *How you plan to spend your time*—Based on your itinerary, your interests, and the purpose of the trip, imagine what you are likely to be doing during the days and the evenings. (Watch out for the "what ifs" and the "you never knows.") Do you always go to high-style restaurants, operas, theater and gallery openings? If so, plan accordingly, with the understanding that you *are* traveling, you have limited luggage space, and a pretty black shawl wrapped around your shoulders can probably get you through a theater lobby where everyone else is in black tie. Will you be climbing through ancient ruins or sitting on a beach? Playing tennis, taking cooking lessons (bring loose-fitting clothes or styles with expandable waists), or

painting the landscapes? (See Packing in the chapter, "Business Travel" for special considerations.)

3. *The length of the trip*—It is simply not true that the amount of clothes you take should be proportionate to the length of your trip. You'll be surprised how little you really need. I learned my lesson about how much *not* to take on my first trip to Europe. I was seventeen, and going to live with a family in Italy on a program sponsored by the Experiment in International Living. We had a week of orientation at Experiment headquarters in Vermont, and one of the "packing" exercises was to put on our traveling clothes and walk around the tennis court three times, with our luggage in hand. Presumably, the combined effect of carrying our own bags, and knowing porters were rare would cure us of overpacking. In fact, I sent one suitcase home. You can pack for one week and be gone three. The key consideration is that you *feel* clean and attractive, and, contrary to popular belief, the size of your wardrobe is less important than how you feel about yourself.

4. *Maintaining the clothes en route*—On vacation you don't want to worry about expensive laundry bills, or whether you'll get things back on time, and in wearable shape. It is true that many deluxe and first-class hotels have very efficient laundry and valet services, although I have seen shirts that look like they were washed in an abrasive. Take fabrics that travel and wash well. Cotton blends, polyesters that look like silk, and knits all launder in cold water, wash and dry without pressing, ready to wear. Cotton is particularly good for warm climates. Unlike many synthetics, it doesn't "hold" the heat.

5. *Big city, small city, resort*—With the spread of Western culture and communications, or what could be called the Coca-Cola-ization of the world, a certain level of sophistication in dress has become standard almost anywhere you go. To make a distinction between what is appropriate in France, as opposed to Japan as opposed to Australia is less helpful today than it is to think in terms of the major cities, the smaller cities, and the resorts. Each has a different style of life and pace which determines appropriateness.

- *The Big Cities*—Here a general awareness of what is "fashionable" exists. If there were any place to wear the current styles (within reasonable taste), it's in the big city. (A "big city" could be a nation's capital, or simply a large population center with thriving industry and night life.) I tend to use what would be right in New York as a model and I wear my "transcultural uniform" of black silk pants and white silk shirt (or vice versa) augmented with a vest, shawl, blazer, or scarf, to the fanciest restaurants, operas, and theaters in Hong Kong, New Delhi, Paris, London, and Los Angeles.

■ *The Smaller Cities (or the countryside)*—Change on every level of life comes more slowly. Women still marry younger, and fashions are more conservative. In this context, the "small cities" label applies to rural areas, places removed from out-of-town business traffic, or without international cross-pollination. Some cities may have a famous attraction so that the residents are used to seeing tourists, but this conditioning shouldn't make you any less sensitive to what is appropriate.

■ *The Resorts: Sea and Ski*—The whole point of a resort is relaxation in an easygoing, playful, even permissive atmosphere. Half the game at a beach resort is to show as much skin as possible (if you're made right). You might wrap yourself in a length of brightly printed fabric that is equally suitable as a beach cover-up or evening attire. You have much more latitude because there is no specific piece of clothing for women that translates as "black tie." Patio or at-home dresses, silk pants and shirts (or a polyester that looks like silk), and the trendiest styles are all appropriate at beach resorts from Greece to the Caribbean. I've seen outfits—should I say costumes?—as diverse as one-piece bathing suits worn with gold jewelry, to long white muslin peasant dresses with shell necklaces and matching earrings. Bear in mind that private clubs in certain resorts, like Newport, Rhode Island, are "old guard" and formal, and you should bring a shawl to cover up your plunging neckline or bare back.

Après-ski in Europe tends to be more dressy than in Vermont, Colorado, or California. In places like Aspen, which is a combination of college fraternity/Disneyland/restored western town, jeans and a clean shirt pass in the fanciest restaurant. In the more jet-set haunts of Switzerland, add some jewelry and a silk shirt, and don't be surprised to see that many people do dress to the nines.

6. *A cruise*—On a cruise ship you can indulge yourself and take every last item. You need a little bit of everything. Daytime wear is

the same as a resort: bathing suits and white pants (see lists in this chapter), but you do have to be dressed to go in the dining room. Usually there is a more informal area for lunch, where bathing suits with cover-ups suffice. Cotton caftans are just dandy on deck, to sleep in, and, with the right jewelry, to wear to dinner. In the salad days of cruise travel, every night was serious black tie, but today the most formal events are the captain's welcome-aboard cocktail party and the captain's dinner. A long, noncrushable matte jersey dress, or pants and shirt in a fine material, will do.

7. *Car, plane, train travel*—THINK COMFORT. You'll be sitting for long periods of time, and eventually curl up to sleep, so your clothes should be loose-fitting, relatively wrinkle-free, with expandable or no waists, and in layers to adapt to temperature changes, particularly important when you are flying from snow to sunshine or vice versa. Jeans rate for informality, but a wraparound skirt gives you more room to move. Your feet tend to swell if you sit a long time, so boots are impractical.

8. Leave anything of irreplaceable sentimental or material value at home.

9. *Customs of a country or area*—In ancient times the line between right and wrong, appropriate and gauche, was clearly defined. In China, for instance, colors had meaning and symbolism. Yellow was the national color, sacred to the Emperor and worn only by his descendants; purple was the color of the literati and the educated; white was the color of mourning, and red the emblem of joy. Red, in fact, is still the color of the bride's dress in traditional Chinese weddings.

Customs are less precise today because much of the world is in social transition. But as a foreigner in some parts of the world—particularly in underdeveloped, Third World countries or places relatively unexposed to tourists—you are a natural point of curiosity. As an unaccompanied woman, you are an oddity, and for that reason, if no other, you can become the center of attention.

In areas such as the Middle East, the role and behavior of women in society has been decreed by centuries of tradition, custom, and religion. Obviously, you are not bound by their code, either as a woman or as a foreigner, but *as* a woman and a foreigner, you will

automatically be set apart, and judged by your dress and behavior according to *their* standards, and *their* perceptions of the West and Western woman. Friendly chitchat at a hotel bar can be interpreted as an invitation; a short-sleeved T-shirt may seem perfectly fine to you and "overexposed" to them. The genesis of this point of view will make the suggestion to dress conservatively seem less arbitrary.

Given that generalities are flawed by definition, let me take the Middle East as an example. Every country in this vast area has an individual personality, but it is safe to say there are "hard-core," more conservative places, such as Saudi Arabia and the Gulf States; others have kept less to themselves, like Egypt and Lebanon and Jordan, which are geographically nearer and more influenced by the West. What they all have in common is that they are Arabs and followers of Islam. The precepts of the Koran and the family form the cornerstone of their lives.

Islam "apologists" will say it is a liberal religion for women and quote chapter and verse to support this viewpoint. They claim that many of the customs that might be considered "oppressive," like the veil, are not imposed by the Koran but were brought in with the Byzantine conquests. (The veil originally distinguished the women of breeding from the slaves, who were sold with their faces naked.) Women today are not exposed in any way (although girls in Saudi Arabia have been known to wear mini skirts under their long robes). As a rule, women don't go out with their husbands. In some countries they aren't permitted to drive a car and only recently have been allowed into the universities. The rationale is that the women are treasures and must be guarded against any contaminating influence. The sub-rosa explanation is that the Arabs believe women are torridly sexual and mustn't be "left to wander, exposed and free." What complicates matters is that the family honor rests with the women. It is a far more heinous crime for a daughter to be an adulterer than for a son to be a thief.

For these people, there are only two kinds of women: the good and the bad. Good women are at home, and veiled when they go out.

Then there are the others. You may qualify unintentionally. I know an English woman who had been doing business successfully in the United Arab Emirates for a number of years. She arrived at the office of the secretary, who, as is customary, called the porter to take her into the meeting. He came, saw her outfit of jeans and a spaghetti-strap T-shirt, which to his mind was that of a "bad" woman. He absolutely refused to escort her because it would have been a slur on his character to be seen publicly with such a person.

As much as many of these countries have imported our education, technology, music, and blue jeans, they are selective about the westernization of mores. They don't want the family unit to break down, as seems evident in parts of the West. This "disintegration" of the family is usually associated with the liberation of women. To them, this is a modern-day rationale for continuing the philosophy that their women are treasures. The spill-over effect can be that others are fair game. As one American friend who lived in the Middle East told me, "Pack defensively, dress defensively, act defensively, and you'll have a good time."

THE DON'TS: EXPLODING THE MYTHS OF A TRAVEL WARDROBE

1. *Don't buy an entire, new wardrobe for a trip.* Clothes for traveling should be tried, comfortable, and successfully washable. You might get the odd shirt, a basic pair of pants, a bathing suit, but you can always buy where you're going. The business trip is an exception. Stopping for extras or necessities isn't a diversion but a dissipation of precious time. (See Packing in the chapter "Business Travel.")

2. Don't pack the outfit that's really "not you." The trip would be the wrong time to try it out. My personal style is clean cut, straight lines, no pleats, very classic. But for two years on every trip I diligently packed a ruffled skirt and matching halter top. Whenever I got dressed I'd pick something I felt good in. I finally gave the ruffled skirt and top away.

3. Don't assume that clothes for a trip have to be so practical that you sacrifice style.

4. Don't take those "good" walking shoes without really walking in them for a few weeks. One turn around a shoe shop is not ade-

quate. You might find sandals or espadrilles more comfortable. I do suggest you keep your high heels for evening, especially if you plan to climb ruins, walk on cobblestones, etc.

5. Don't take clothes that need pressing. Travel irons are unnecessary baggage. Use a hotel valet service if necessary.

6. Don't plan to steam things in the shower. "Showers" are often just a shower head in a corner of the bathroom with no curtain and a drain in the floor.

7. Don't take an oversized purse. When I first went to Europe, I took a small suitcase that I euphemistically called my "travel purse." A "travel purse" was something I'd always heard was an essential. I was never sure what was different except that you carried your passport case, traveler's checks, and a city map. It had special pockets, zippered cases, and sundry nooks and crannies, which I carefully filled so that I was practically lugging my entire life around. In self-defense I finally sat down to figure out exactly what I needed with me at all times. To my astonishment I discovered the essentials would fit into a small shoulder bag. They are: my passport, traveler's checks, notebook and pen, lip gloss, and tissues. I carry my camera on my shoulder, and use paperback guidebooks. Occasionally I tear out the section I need that day.

THE IDEAL WARDROBE

Your goal is to look and feel good with maximum comfort, flexibility, and minimum maintenance. (This means take half of what you had originally planned.)

1. *Crossover Clothes:* Plan a wardrobe around separates—sweaters, blazers, vests, skirts, and pants—so you can make many outfits out of a few pieces.

2. *Double-duty Clothes:* Try to make each piece do as much as possible. For instance, in cold climates I take a long-sleeved, floor-length T-shirt as a nightgown *and* robe. In warm weather a light-weight bathrobe doubles as a beach robe.

3. *Keep colors to a minimum:* Pick one basic color, or two that mix well. My favorites are black, gray, brown, burgundy in winter; burgundy, khaki, white, and black in summer. Your accessories, such as T-shirts, shirts, and scarves, provide the complementary or accent colors. I avoid prints as a basic "color" because they are not good building blocks. (I do take thin-striped T-shirts and turtlenecks.)

4. *Jeans are universally accepted:* In warm climates I like jean skirts because they're equally informal and are cooler than pants. A well-cut pair of jeans, a silk (or polyester) shirt and scarf will take you almost anywhere. One of my most comfortable, workable outfits is a pair of jeans (in classic dark blue) with a matching jean jacket.

5. *Scarf-dressing:* Scarves can be your most important accessory for making the same pair of pants and shirt look different. Take various shapes: the two-foot-long, thin scarves work as a belt and a turban; the large squares make shawls (more for color than warmth), and "aprons" for a skirt; smaller squares make purses, necklaces, bandeaux (halters), and, of course, babushkas.

6. *Underwear is the only area where I overdo it:* I know people who travel for an entire summer on one pair of underpants and one bra and wash them out every night. Others save once-worn underwear for the next day's tennis game. I take enough for five days of clean changes without doing laundry, especially panty hose, one item you may not find even in the most sophisticated cities abroad.

7. *Raingear:* First you must gauge what *kind* of rain you will be in. Summer thunder showers? Tropical or monsoon country? If possible, take the lightest-weight rain poncho. You don't want your raincoat to hold in the heat. In cold climates, where you'd need a warm coat in any case, take a trench coat with a zip-in lining, or a trench coat worn with layers of sweaters underneath for warmth. If you anticipate—or love—walking in the rain, bring small rubber boots that will fit over your shoe (and height of the heel), and a collapsible umbrella. Have your nonrubber boots and shoes waterproofed with silicone. Take a vinyl rainhat.

8. *Coats:* Cool climates pose the problem of a suitable coat for daytime and evening. I like to bring a water-repellent black or khaki coat with a zip-out lining in case the temperature changes. I avoid

the "classic" trench coats, with epaulettes or double-breasted collars, because they tend to look too sporty for evening. Needless to say, it's entirely possible that dressiness is unimportant for your kind of trip. Warm weather is less of a problem because you can make do with a shawl or dressy long sweater that will match your entire wardrobe.

9. If you are going to both warm and cool climates, take heavier-weight sweaters and blouses, and wear the same pants or jeans with panty hose. There's no way of getting around the coat problem. You'll just have to carry it along

10. LEAVE YOUR STRAW HAT AT HOME! It is awkward to pack; and it is almost impossible to keep the original shape. Buy an inexpensive one wherever you go and consider *leaving* it there.

MY FAVORITE TRAVEL WARDROBES

Here's an example of what I took to Europe for a three-week summer trip. I planned for black-tie affairs, extensive car travel, and basic resort life. I decided to take black and white only, and use primary colors for accents. I never got bored, and deciding what to wear became much simpler. If I felt the slightest twinge of *"that thing again?"* I bought some inexpensive additions: a few colorful T-shirts, jewelry from a streetside stall, a black straw bag, a scarf to use as a belt, and of course a straw hat. If you have the basic bottoms, the tops will cross over for day or night.

1 pair white cotton pants (to wear at night)
1 pair white cotton jeans
1 pair black cotton pants
1 pair black crepe pants
1 dark-blue jean skirt

1 red short-sleeve, V-neck T-shirt
1 yellow long-sleeve, round or turtleneck T-shirt
1 black, green, red, and blue short-sleeve striped shirt
1 black cardigan sweater (jet lag and travel make
    you more sensitive to temperature changes. I throw
    it in my purse to take to theaters or restaurants
    with air conditioning)
1 short cotton jacket for day or evening
1 Kelly green, long-sleeve cardigan, cotton top
1 long-sleeve, buttons-down-the-front, black cotton
    shirt (doubled as jacket)
1 black silk shirt
1 black short-sleeve, V-neck cotton shirt
1 long noncrushable black jersey dress

1 pair black espadrilles
1 pair black patent-leather sandals (high heels for evening)
1 pair white sandals (medium heel)

1 navy, 1 brown bathing suit
1 long yellow thin cotton caftan (robe and beach cover)
1 nightgown (I prefer men's nightshirts)
1 pair folding slippers

1 large square red and white cotton scarf
1 medium size (to fit around the neck) black and
   white print cotton scarf
1 red silk scarf (long and rectangular, belt, shawl)
1 red, 1 black, and 1 white cotton scarf
1 large black shawl

Here is a wardrobe I have used for cold climate:

1 pair black wool pants
1 pair blue jeans
1 pair burgundy (or gray) wool pants
1 pair black silk pants and matching top (for evening)
black sweater set—turtleneck and cardigan (I tuck
   bright-colored scarves *inside* turtlenecks)
1 red turtleneck sweater
1 purple turtleneck sweater
1 long black oversweater (cardigan)
1 white silk blouse
1 black silk blouse
1 burgundy oversweater
1 long-sleeve black T-shirt
1 long-sleeve yellow T-shirt (or sweater)
1 floor-length T-shirt—to sleep in, doubles as robe

burgundy or black boots (waterproofed) (wear them
   when you travel; don't try to pack them)
1 pair black loafer-style shoes
1 pair evening sandals

1 long black jersey dress
1 black shawl/an assortment of scarves
1 black wool cap
1 trench coat with zip-out lining (not the plastic variety
   that holds the heat like a Finnish sauna)

COSMETICS

Start out with your favorite products. If you run out, you'll undoubtedly find either your brand or an adequate substitute. Unless, of course, you are going on safari, trekking, etc. Then estimate the amounts used daily. Multiply by the number of days on the trip and add three days more for emergency or miscalculation. I keep duplicates of my basic list so I can check off the items each time I take a trip. I pack everything in the cosmetic bags that open like a book because you can see everything in a glance, instead of rummaging through with your hand and trying to find what you need by feel. I buy shampoo, conditioners, etc. in plastic bottles or tubes and what comes in a glass bottle I transfer to plastic bottles (preferably without the nozzle tops, because they leak) and wrap in a plastic bag for extra protection. (See the chapter, "Beauty and Health on the Road" for the Pursepac.)

CHECKLIST

cleansing oil/moisturizer/astringent
cotton balls/cotton swabs
sunscreen/cream to relieve sunburn
deodorant/perfume/cologne
hand and body lotion
rubberbands
nail polish/nail polish remover (pads)/emery board
tissues
toothbrush/toothpaste/toothpick
brush, comb
hairspray—non-aerosol in small, refillable bottle
electric curlers or blow dryer—plugs if needed
shampoo/conditioner/setting lotion/hair clips
folding scissors/sewing box
soap (Bring the perfumed soaps home from the hotel
    to use as gifts. Your own soap is important be-
    cause there are so many changes in climate and
    food that you don't need to add one more
    strange element.)
pen/pad
razor and extra blades

tweezers
bath oil
panty shields/tampons
small packets of cold-water wash
small packets of spot remover
eye shades
shower cap
small collapsible plastic cup
travel mirror—magnifying on one side
take an extra pair of prescription glasses—and keep a
    copy of the prescription in your wallet

THE TRAVELING MEDICINE CABINET

When it comes to medicines, my philosophy is the absolute opposite of clothes: the "what ifs" and the "you never knows" are my
guiding lights. I pack with the idea that if I wake up in the middle of
the night I'll have whatever I need. Suppose there is no "all-night
drugstore" (known in many parts of the world as pharmacy or chem-
ist), not to mention a doctor available to write a prescription. An unexpected plus, however, is that outside the United States you can
often buy certain medicines over the counter, such as tranquilizers or
antibiotics, that would ordinarily require a prescription. On the other
hand, I once needed a prescription for a routine nasal spray.

You might even find an alternate kind of treatment. In the Far
East, it's possible that a doctor might prescribe herbal medicine. The
herbs can be steeped in tea or, as one package suggests, "cooked in
chicken broth." In addition to herbs, herb stores are the pharmacies
of Chinese medicine and dispense other remedies, including many
varieties of deer antlers from the Manchurian forest, sea horses from
the Gulf of Tonkin, bear's entrails from the Tibetan highlands, and
unfamiliar cures for, among other ailments, "soft feet" and "hidden
women's diseases."

But first, here's my "conventional" list. (Eliminate at your discre-
tion.) All medicines should be kept separate from the cosmetics; take
another zippered, plastic case, and label it DRUGS. Medicines should
be kept in plastic bottles. If the bottles aren't labeled from the drugstore, label everything with a label gun. If you put two pills in one
bottle to save space, then label accordingly: yellow is sleeping pill;

white is antacid, etc. Don't rely on remembering the color code at 3 A.M.

CHECKLIST

antacid tablets
aspirin or Bufferin/sleeping pills
peridium—for bladder infection
Valium—even if you've never taken one in your life,
    have your doctor prescribe the lowest dosage possible
single-use enema
glycerine suppositories or other laxatives
antihistamines—good for any allergic reactions, bee stings
    and particularly itching and stuffy noses. (Especially
    important to combat itching from mosquito bites.)
diarrhea medicine
any antibiotic (and refill prescription)
antiseptic—for surface skin irritations
thermometer
vitamins
analgesic, anesthetic gel for bites, scratches, sunburn
Band-Aids—a few of all sizes. Remember, you might
    get blisters on the backs of your heels from walking.
acne cream
any prescription medication taken regularly and the
    prescription for any drug that's a narcotic
birth control—diaphragm, jelly, foam, condoms. Yes, condoms.
calamine lotion
eyecup/eyedrops
foot powder
nasal spray

I have a small list of items that fit in neither category but are equally important to either my health or peace of mind.

CHECKLIST

small packets of instant soup, coffee, and tea bags
an immersion heater and cup (with the correct voltage plug)
Swiss army knife
sugarless gum
alarm clock—I don't like to be up half the night wor-
    rying the operator will forget my wake-up call

felt-tip pens/envelopes (letter size)
can opener/bottle opener/corkscrew
camera (see Cameras in the chapter, "Etc.")/film
opera glasses or binoculars.

LUGGAGE

The luggage most suitable for you will depend on the length of your trip, and how much you mind carrying your own, or waiting for it at airports. I have a variety of shapes and sizes of suitcases:

1. *Canvas duffle*—Good for sweaters, nonwrinkle items, makeup, shoes, underwear, etc.

2. *Collapsible canvas bag*—I always pack it *inside* a suitcase for unexpected purchases, or weekend trips when I want to leave most things behind. (If you don't want to pay for an empty room, ask your hotel to check your big bag in the package room. Just get a baggage check.)

3. *Metal frame, canvas hanging bag*—For longer trips, I pack dresses, suits, pants on hangers, put shoes in the bottom, and lightweight items in zippered compartments. The great advantage is that you have little unpacking to do.

4. *Large shoulder bag*—This bag is with me at all times, and in it I pack anything I can't live without. Makeup, jewelry, my work, all my medicines. Never, never check your drug kit (or your jewelry). The luggage could be lost.

5. *Large, rectangular canvas case that expands*—I only take this on trips when I am going to stay put, because when I'm moving from place to place I never unpack, things get terribly creased, and the clothes seem to take up more room than when I first packed.

THE ACTUAL PACKING PROCESS

I pack the day before I leave. I lay out the separates on the bed (or the dining room table, couch, or a coat rack) and put all the accessories, shirts, shoes, bags on a card table (or on the bed or couch) so that I can see all the possible combinations, and exactly what I need to add or eliminate.

You need three things to be a successful packer: common sense, restraint, and a dash of inventiveness. When I pack, I think about unpacking as well. How can I make both steps quick, painless, and least damaging to the clothes? To this end, I have several, compartmentalized plastic cases. I can see everything and the bags go from the suitcase to the drawer (and back) in one motion. I use them for all my lingerie, scarves, bathing suits, underwear, nightgowns, T-shirts, socks, stockings. I tuck in a piece of cotton scented with oil (cologne evaporates) to keep them fragrant. I pack dresses, pants, skirts, etc., according to use, not fragility. You never know what side of your suitcase is up in a baggage compartment.

Everyone has a surefire how-to-pack-and-avoid-wrinkling technique, from folding things inside out, rolling them in a ball and putting them inside stockings, to the more familiar methods of tissue paper or plastic bags from the cleaner. I like plastic bags because they don't wrinkle in packing and repacking, like tissue paper. The air trapped inside acts as a cushion and keeps creasing to a minimum. I crumple up tissue paper to put inside sleeves and collars, and inside shoes and boots to help keep the shape. Socks and stockings are equally effective.

THE "INDISPENSABLES"

I've always thought my mother was wonderfully eccentric, but she is clearly runner-up to one woman I know who takes black satin sheets made up into curtains with hooks to put under the regular hotel curtains to block the early morning sun. She also takes her regular bed pillows, because she can't stand the smell of cigarette smoke that gets into the bed pillows in hotels.

I have another friend who takes ginger to disguise the taste of food in certain countries, and cardamom seeds to sweeten the breath and aid digestion; another who packs a one-burner hot plate, a one-cup espresso pot, and a can of Italian espresso coffee (she hates instant). First prize in the gadget department goes to my friend who takes a small juicer so he can buy oranges on the roadside and make juice.

But without question the gold medal goes to my friend Pat, who with her husband runs the neighborhood market. She lines the bottom of her suitcase with airtight specially sealed plastic bags, filled with martinis made according to her favorite recipe.

4.

Transportation

Sometimes you wish you could just *be* there. Just thinking about the inevitable reservations, airports, train terminals, and luggage seems overwhelming. You'd like to be beamed directly from your favorite spot at home to a talcum powder beach, an awesome cathedral, or a canopy bed in a castle.

This chapter will walk you through a passel of routines, problems, and the bright spots of getting there—on land, air, or sea—and unscramble airline and shipboard jargon, unleash the secrets of how to outsmart airport chaos, and provide surprisingly important details, like what food *not* to take on a bus trip.

AIRPLANES

It's not just because my birthday happens to be a landmark date in aviation history that I love flying. (December 17 was the Wright Brothers' first flight on the *Kitty Hawk* back in 1903.) My mother says I was crazy about my first flight. I was three months old and it took us eighteen hours to go from New York to Los Angeles. She proudly tells me that I didn't cry and looked wide-eyed at everything. The only snag was running out of diapers, a problem she solved at a stopover in Dallas with an adequate, if original, solution: linen napkins from the airport restaurant.

I have more vivid memories of the flights on the Superconstellations, the airplanes that had berths for the transcontinental hops. Sleeping in a bed in the sky was delicious adventure for an eight-year-old, and I remember my mother tucking me in the sheets and covering me with her coat, thinking that something of hers would make me feel safe in a strange bed. Berths are history now, although one airline did bring them back for a time by putting beds in the upstairs lounge on 747s. This service was discontinued after the stewardesses went on strike because passengers dressed and behaved immodestly.

I did hear of one woman who took the situation in her own hands. She so regretted the demise of luxury steamship travel from London to Capetown (South Africa) that she bought the entire upstairs lounge on the aircraft for herself, and had a double bed installed. She paid $20,000 for her sleeping quarters. One way.

My devotion to air travel added an unexpected dimension when I was about fifteen. My father decided he was going to learn how to fly. After promising me and my mother that he'd never take chances, he took flying lessons and went to ground school with unmitigated zeal. The man who prided himself on not being able to do long division was suddenly using a slide rule. We couldn't eat in the dining room for months because the table was covered with charts, compasses, maps, etc. Pilot lingo crept into our everyday lives. Instead of asking me when I'd be home from school, he'd say, "What's your ETA?"—my estimated time of arrival, of course. I still wonder if my father has ever *really* gotten over the first time I flew with him. I threw up.

No matter. I love air travel today as much as I did when I was a kid. Of course, during the intervening years the airline industry has become more sophisticated, from the aircraft available to the services offered. The Concorde made it possible to have breakfast in London and a coffeebreak that same morning in New York. On the other end of the scale, Freddy Laker's SkyTrain and the standby fares offered by the scheduled carriers have practically made air travel another type of mass transit.

Airlines have also changed their selling tactics. After luring potential passengers with stewardesses in Pucci outfits, menus composed by three-star French chefs, lounges with piano bars (and sing-along song sheets), the emphasis switched to what was called "no frills." The message was clear, even if that particular ad campaign was short-lived: you're paying to get from one point to another, not for the extras. Brownbagging it and sharing your tuna on rye with a neighbor became the only way to go. Then ads began appearing that extolled the benefits of flying full fare. What next?

Since Madison Avenue will continue to find new ways to seduce potential passengers for their airline clients, how on earth are you supposed to know which airline to choose?

CHOOSING AN AIRLINE

We all know people who swear by one particular airline. When you really pin them down, it's usually because the flight attendant refilled the wineglass without being prompted (and remembered it was red not white); they didn't have to hang on the phone ten minutes, listening to music; or their bags were first out. By the same token, there are people who've said, "Our flight was two hours late," or, "The food was terrible, I'm *never* flying *that* airline again." The whole point is that you can be devoted to, or ignore, an airline on the basis of one incident. This kind of judgment is as unfair as deciding whether or not you like a city by the character of the taxi driver who picked you up at the airport. For the most part, you should take an airline because it flies where you want to go, at the right time, at the right price.

Naturally, there are exceptions. If you are going to, or even through, a country with a national airline, it may be worth taking it at least one way. The chances of meeting people who live in those countries are greater (though not guaranteed!) and I've gotten some of my best inside information flying the country's carriers. Some even attempt to serve food that is part of the national cuisine, and not just in first class. On one Air India flight I had vegetable curry (which they always have on board for vegetarians), lamb curry, and a dessert called shahitukra, made of white bread, nuts, milk, and saffron. It was dusted with bits of silver, which I logically deduced were remnants of a tinfoil cover the stewardess neglected to remove. It turned out to be *vark,* Kleenex-thin shreds of real silver (or gold) frequently used to garnish desserts.

Assuming that you're not like a relative of mine whose first two
questions are "Is it a 747?" and "What's the movie?" many airlines
will suit your needs. The problem is that few things seem as bewil-
dering as all the possibilities, especially with so many different fares.
Call the airline and pray you get a patient person. I've sometimes
called back several times until I got a satisfactory answer. Your other
choice is to ask the nearest travel agent. They have what is known in
the travel industry as the OAG, the Official Airline Guide (constantly updated), that lists who flies where, when, all over the world.
The travel agent will also know about special packages featured by
every airline, and offerings like how much you save by going after
midnight, or, by making three stops. (See The Travel Agent in the
chapter, "Planning.")

Here is basically what you will be getting for your money on the
most standard-fare structures:

- *First class*—Normally there will be a separate check-in line at
  the airport, and possibly a first-class lounge area, which should
  not be confused with clubs sponsored by airlines. You may
  get VIP treatment, like boarding early. On the aircraft the
  first-class section is usually in the front of the plane, and on
  747s it may include the upstairs lounge with its small chairs
  and no restrictions on smoking. In fact, before you're barely
  in your seat, someone is offering you champagne (you don't
  pay for liquor), wet (overperfumed) towels and little bathroom kits with toothpaste and toothbrush and aftershave,
  and knit slippers and headsets. The seats are generally wider
  than in economy class, and only two across.

  Presumably the food is better in first class. You get linen
  napery, at least three forks, two wineglasses, and each course
  is served from a trolley. You have a choice of hors d'oeuvres
  and entree, which are described in titillating but not always in-
  formative menu-ese: tender points of beef filets, roasted just to
  your liking, with savory garnishes; fish from the gulf (both unnamed) lightly poached in a white wine sauce; cannelloni with
  delicious bits of cheese and meat. Translation: meat, fish, or
  pasta. Desserts are invariably gooey and fattening—ice cream
  sundaes with everything on them—cakes with the option of
  putting everything on them.

  If you can afford first class, choose it on the basis that you
  have more room, a particular bonus on a sold-out, overseas

flight. To be honest, sometimes first class makes you feel good, unless the price makes the pleasure irrelevant.

■ *Economy or coach*—This section is located in back of first class. Some airlines feature special classes within economy— such as Pan American's "frequent traveler" status that is available to anyone who flies Pan Am a specified number of times each year. This status entitles you to sit in the section directly behind first class, and you can use the first-class lounge at the airport. Economy sections have two, three, or four seats together, depending on the aircraft. (When you check in, ask the agent if the plane is fully booked, and, if not, could he possibly "block out" four seats for you. It's worth trying.) If you can get four across, remove the armrests and stretch out. As for the food, you probably don't get a choice of entree, and drinks and headsets are on you.

■ *Excursion fares*—These are reduced economy class fares calculated on the number of days you are gone and sometimes what day of the week you leave and return. The longer you stay away, the cheaper the price. Time periods generally range from 14 to 21 days, and 21 to 45 days. You can generally book this kind of ticket at the last minute, although some excursion fares require advance booking by a predetermined date and a nonrefundable deposit. Several airlines have had special rates for "married" couples. One pays full fare, and the spouse gets a hefty discount. When one airline wrote notes to the "wives" thanking them, many husbands had a lot of explaining to do. (The fare was eventually discontinued.)

■ *Standby fares*—Presumably this is the cheapest way to go. (How much do you mind waiting around airports?) It is not recommended if you are traveling with children, who will get extremely fidgety milling around for an entire day. Come to think of it, so do most adults. To take a hypothetical example: Let's say there are three flights a day from New York to London on one airline. About a week before your departure date, the reservations department can indicate your chances of getting on the desired flight as a standby. You buy your ticket at an airline office and go out to the airport, usually a minimum of three hours before the first flight to your destination. (You can also buy a ticket at the airport, but I'd advise against it under the best circumstances.) Your vigil may begin at five A.M. with no guarantee you won't be standing by a day later.

■ *Stopover privileges*—This feature is most applicable on international flights. Your fare is based on air miles to the farthest point. If you have a full fare excursion ticket, you have unlimited stopovers. If you are going to Tel Aviv, for instance, you can stop off as many places as you want—Rome, London, etc. —between your point of departure and Tel Aviv without paying anything extra. If you have a 14–21-day ticket or a 21–45-day ticket you may be limited to two stops outbound, and two stops coming home.

MAKING RESERVATIONS

Unless you work with a travel agent, you make your reservations over the telephone with a particular airline or in person at the local ticket office. Explain where you would like to go, and approximately what date. The airline agent will check your request, and ask if you want to travel first class or coach. At this point, ask about special fares that might save you money. If one airline is unable to accommodate you, ask what other lines are available. How helpful the agent will be about another airline will depend almost entirely on the individual.

The agent making your reservations will need your home and business phone to be able to notify you in case the plane is substantially delayed or late. (I always call a few hours before flight time myself.) Airlines that have tie-ins with hotels and car rental agencies will offer to make reservations.

Your other area of choice includes the smoking or the nonsmoking section. As a nonsmoker I've always found "nonsmoking" highly ironic because in the enclosed space, smoke from only a few rows away eventually curls my way. You can also request a special meal. The variety is quite astounding. Most airlines offer: a Weight-Watchers-approved meal; soul food, described as "home cooking with hot sauce"; oriental style, mainly stir-fried and (hopefully) undercooked vegetables; Kosher, usually beef or chicken or a dairy plate; vegetarian, mostly overcooked vegetables and salads; and diabetic, without sugar.

An alternative is to bring your own food. My mother usually takes broiled chicken and potato salad. I was slightly embarrassed the first time but the food was so superior I got used to it.

Sometimes reservations agents forget to tell you important details about changing planes or changing airports. If you are making a connecting flight, check to see you arrive and depart from the same place. In Europe, many cities have separate terminals or separate airports for domestic and international travel. Your baggage is usually checked through to your final destination. I'm always dubious that my bags will arrive when I do, at the right place. If you are a dedicated disbeliever, you can check them to each destination separately, but I have only done this in small airports in Asia and Africa, not in international cities accustomed to the procedure.

Airlines have their own lingo. Here are some terms you might hear while making your reservation:

- *Wait list*—If the plane is sold out, you may be put on a wait list. The agent will take your phone number and call you if space opens up. The agent can sometimes give you the odds on the basis of the flight's normal bookings. During peak travel seasons the wait list may be closed.

- *Standby*—You're gambling and taking your chances by going out to the airport, even if the wait list is closed. You give your name to the check-in counter at the departure gate, and wait to see if your name is called.

- *Upgrading*—You change from economy to first class (and pay the difference). When the airlines overbook, flight passengers ticketed for economy will sometimes be put into first class at no added cost.

- *Reconfirmation*—A phone call to an airline to confirm you are using your reservation. This is particularly important during holiday and peak travel seasons—holidays, school vacations, etc. It is equally important to call and cancel reservations.

- *Direct vs. nonstop*—Nonstop means no stops; direct means there may be one or more stops, but you don't have to change aircraft.

PAYING FOR THE TICKET

There are various ways of paying for your ticket. The agent will ask if you are picking up the ticket and paying for it at the airport. I don't suggest this method under any circumstances unless you are taking a shuttle flight where you actually buy tickets on board (or, if you make a spur-of-the-moment decision to get away). Airlines will accept all major credit cards, or personal checks with sufficient identification. The airline will mail you the tickets (with enough advance time), or you can pick them up at the reservations office.

In some cities, the reservations office can also give you your boarding pass, so that when you get to the airport you just have to give your bags to the porter for curbside check-in and proceed to the gate. If you are doing the transaction by phone, the agent will probably say that you have to purchase the tickets by a certain date, or the computer will automatically cancel your reservations. I always ask for the latest possible pick-up date.

THE AIRPORT

You are entering the battle zone. However you get to the airport—hotel limousine, taxi, friends, husbands, children, neighbors, or your own car you plan to leave in the long-term garage at the airport—GET THERE EARLY.

Airports can be the most distressing part of air travel. Medical monographs have been written about "Airport Panic," a condition defined in medical-ese as "high anxiety levels due to very impersonal environments that lead to temporary emotional instability." It's supposed to get worse when you have a connecting flight. Granted, not all airports are a hybrid of Ellis Island and Grand Central Station, but I still like to arrive with plenty of time so I can calmly handle the unforeseen, or just relax. (Remember to allow time to go through the security check.)

Many airports have curbside check-in. A porter takes your bag, gives you the baggage tickets (which you have to show to security at the other end to claim your bags), and you proceed inside the terminal. Counters are marked "Passengers with Tickets," "Without Tickets" "With Baggage," "No Baggage," and sometimes there is a special line for first class, and charter flights. You make a seat selection here, although this may be done right at the gate. Where you sit is a matter of personal preference, smoking, nonsmoking, aisle or window. I make sure I can see the movie from my seat, and prefer aisle seats because I make a point of getting up and walking around.

You will get a boarding pass, and a departure card in most overseas countries. Out of the United States, keep a few dollars in the local currency in case you have to pay an airport departure tax, although dollars are usually accepted.

Depending on the organization of the airport, you must go through a security check, a procedure with different incarnations in each country, some being more thorough than others. Generally, all hand luggage, including purses, are put on a conveyor belt and pass through an X-ray machine. (See Cameras in the chapter, "Etc.") The contents appear on a TV screen. You then walk through what looks like a doorframe, equipped with metal detectors. Innocuous items like house keys can set off the beep. I will never forget the time my father was taking three large Chinese cleavers to a chef in Europe. He told security in advance, who thought he was making a joke, until he pulled gleaming specimens out of the shopping bag. "Gee, Mr. Kaye," the chief of security said sheepishly, "I'm afraid we'll have to keep those for you in the cockpit, and return them after you've deplaned."

In many countries with tight security, there are booths for men and women where someone of the appropriate gender runs a metal detector swiftly over your whole body. Some of the more elaborate security checks occur when you go in and out of the Middle East. On a flight from Zurich to Tel Aviv, not only were we personally checked, but we were taken by bus to a hangar in the middle of the field where we had to identify our luggage, and open each bag for a complete inspection.

Services Available at Most Airports

Passenger service representatives—Airlines are a service business. You should feel free to ask the customer service representative to help you on any matter. Never forget you have paid for the seat. The airline isn't doing you a favor. You are entitled to as much service as you can get; it's not just reserved for "VIPs." I once found myself in the astonishing position of arriving at the airport for a flight to London, realizing I had left my passport back at the hotel. For a number of complex reasons, I *had* to be on that particular flight. I found the head of customer services and explained my dilemma. He decided the best approach was to wire the service representative in London, saying that they had found my passport in the departure lounge, and would send it on the next flight. I arrived, and was met by the representative with just that message. (Actually, my aunt brought my passport out to the airport and the airline flew it over to London.) To this day, I am surprised that U.K. immigration let me through with just that note. My passport *did* arrive the next day.

Airline clubs—Most major airlines have a private club at major destinations that you can join for a modest annual fee. (Applications are available through each airline.) You can wait for your flight in relatively peaceful surroundings, make local phone calls, have coffee in china cups, work at a desk, and avoid the crush of the airport. It's also a relaxed situation for meeting people. Just be sure to not miss the boarding call. The clubs are a lifesaver if your plane is delayed.

Paging system—This is how you reunite panicked parents with lost children, bring together arriving passengers and people meeting them, and how the police locate you if you've left your car unattended in front of the baggage claim area. When you hear your name paged, you will usually be asked to go to a courtesy phone, an information counter, or a specific airline agent who will transmit the message.

Kiosks—Many airports have some form of kiosk or bulletin board near the baggage claim or customs area with boxes or "pockets" arranged alphabetically so that you can leave messages for arriving passengers. Check under your first and last name.

Duty-free shops—If you have time and money left, these shops can *sometimes* offer good buys. (See the chapter, "Shopping".)

WHAT HAPPENS IF YOUR FLIGHT IS CANCELED, DELAYED, DIVERTED, ETC.

Aside from getting tired and irritated, you also get what airline folks call the "amenities," the services provided if for any reason your flight is interrupted. The "amenities" are listed in the official operating tariffs of each airline, and may vary with the individual carrier. First class or standby, you get the same treatment.

First, you will be fed. You might get cash or a voucher for a specific amount of money, relative to the cost of living in that particular city. (You'd get more in New York than you would in Kansas City.) You can make a long-distance phone call, send a cable, or ask the airline to telex their offices to inform family, friends, etc. You will be given a hotel room (if available) if the delay exceeds a specified number of hours, between certain hours at night. Provisions are also made for transportation back home, or to a hotel in the nearest city. If you are bumped *involuntarily* (sometimes you'll be offered money to give up your seat) there is remuneration, depending on the price of your ticket and the number of hours you are inconvenienced waiting for another flight.

ON BOARD

There are several important points to remember: wear something comfortable, loose-waisted, and layered so you can adjust to the temperature fluctuations in the cabin. Consider climate changes. If you are going from a snowstorm to the tropics, make sure you have either a lightweight blouse, an easily packed cotton jumpsuit, or jeans in your hand luggage. Change on board or on arrival in the ladies' room at the airport. If you have any kind of sinus condition or head cold check with your doctor before flying. A stuffy nose can lead to severe ear infection. Keep your nasal passages open with a nose spray (a half hour before takeoff—and as needed during the flight). To help fight fatigue and jet lag, keep your ears open by chewing gum, or sucking on a hard candy, and keep swallowing; walk around if possible so your feet won't swell, and never, never eat or drink too much, even if it does *seem* like the only way to make the flight go faster. Instead, bring books, writing paper, magazines—which are also helpful in case you want to deflect an overeager seatmate.

ON ARRIVAL

Finally. But don't be surprised if you feel dazed, especially after a long trip. On international flights, you won't see a familiar face until you've cleared customs. First, you go through passport control (and if applicable, health and immunization control). More often than not, you are asked the purpose of your visit, and your proposed length of stay. Then you proceed to the baggage area, claim yours and if you have no purchases to declare, you head for transportation to take you into town.

On a domestic flight, you deplane into the gate area to face crowds peering expectantly at you, through you, and beyond you, searching for familiar faces. You thread through reunited lovers and families to the baggage claim area where you wait, secretly convinced your luggage will be missing. If, in fact, you don't see your bags, contact the nearest airline representative. He will direct you to either lost and found, or the lost baggage claims area where you will probably fill out a form with your name, address (local—i.e., the hotel or friends), and a description of the bag. Usually the airline is responsible for getting the luggage to you. If it apparently is lost forever you make an estimated value of the contents and the airline is legally bound to reimburse you for some if not all the claim. Always carry jewelry and other important or expensive items in your carry-on luggage.

Getting into Town

Generally there is a choice of taxi, bus, or a limousine service provided by some hotels or an independent company. The price is usually reasonable. After a certain hour, however, the schedule may be infrequent and taking a taxi (or sharing one) is the safest and most practical solution. Often there are airport buses to a central downtown location and you can take a taxi from there to your hotel. Group tours are usually met by a company representative who waits in the baggage claim area holding a sign with the name of the tour written in big block letters. Bus drivers and taxi drivers who don't speak English usually know the names of the big hotels, and if you are concerned, ask a passenger service agent to write down the name and address in the local language.

TRAINS

I was nine the first time I left home for longer than a slumber party. I was going to overnight camp in Vermont, and I was taking the train. Everyone was supposed to meet under the big clock in Grand Central Station in New York. I stood tearfully by my mother's side and watched the old-timers happily abandon their parents to renew summer friendships. The time came for final good-byes, and my mother gave me a white lace handkerchief, starting the tradition of giving me something of hers each time I left home. (I had worked up to nightgowns by the time I went to college.) Sniffling and looking back at my mother through a scrim of tears, I made my way to the train and the beginning of what I considered my sentence of summer camp.

That overnight ride to camp was memorable for two reasons: it was the only time in the next two weeks that I wasn't homesick, and I discovered one of the commandments about train travel . . . bring plenty of food and you'll make friends. We all had berths that lined the corridor like bunk beds, and after much giggling and swinging from one top bunk to another, we changed into pajamas. Five of us jammed into the berth of a girl whose mother must have feared she wouldn't get enough to eat for the rest of the summer. Over fried chicken, cole slaw, pickles, cream cheese on raisin bread, turkey legs and Mallomars, the old-timers told me about the glories of camp, uppermost of which seemed to be the bittersweet chocolate bars you got with lunch on hike days.

I have never managed to duplicate that particular picnic, but in my train travels as an adult, an ample supply of crusty bread, cheese, and red wine have had equally socializing effects. It is highly probable that on a train you will eat with your fingers, drink out of the bottle, toast adventures past and future, tell dark secrets to strangers, and enthusiastically exchange phone numbers and addresses you will never use. But that doesn't really matter. It's part of the fleeting, but intense sense of community that seems to exist only in a train compartment. "Anything is possible on a train," wrote Paul Theroux in *The Great Railway Bazaar,* "a great meal, a binge, a visit from card players, an intrigue, a good night's sleep, and strangers' monologues framed like Russian short stories."

Perhaps more than any other mode of transportation, a train has intrinsic mystery, a romance of speed and distance that has enhanced our literature and our movies. Part of the allure has been such evocative names as the Orient Express, the Golden Star, or the Night Mail.

My own favorite is His Exalted Highness the Nizam's Guaranteed State Railway, which belonged to the Nizam of Hyderabad, one of India's richest maharajas. These trains were appointed with great finery: mahogany chairs, marquetry on the berths, polished brass oil lamps, and Louis XVI chairs in the club cars. The linen, silverware, and crockery were made to order and there were male-only club cars with barber shops. The famous Trans-Siberian Express had an instruction booklet for the crew that not only detailed *what* to dust, but in what order.

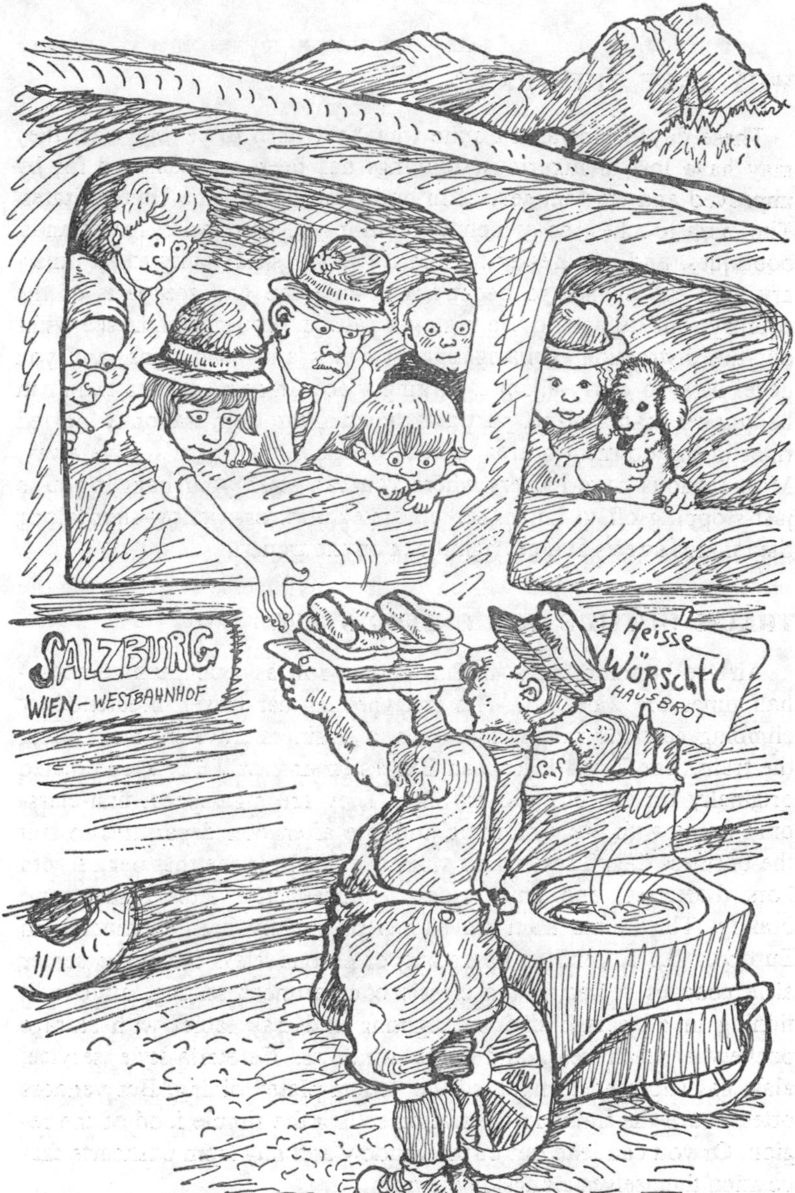
SALZBURG
WIEN-WESTBAHNHOF
Heisse
Würschtl
HAUSBROT
Senf

WHY TAKE THE TRAIN?

These days trains aren't quite what they used to be, but what they may have lost in luxurious trappings has been compensated for by improved and efficient service in both Europe and the United States. The extra touches today include multilingual secretaries, newsstands, boutiques, and hairdressers. Train travel gives flexibility to an itinerary, and the chance to backtrack or sidestep and see parts of the country that lie behind the highway façade. You can sight-see without the distraction of navigating by maps and road signs, and you never have to worry about a parking space. In some cases a train can be quicker than a plane, particularly when the train station is located right in the downtown area, and the airport is an hour's drive away. Most stations have lockers where you can stash your bags if you're just stopping off to lunch, see an art exhibit, or window-shop along the famous streets and get right back on the train.

TRAINS OUTSIDE THE UNITED STATES

Airfare between cities in Europe can run as much as two-and-a-half times the train tab. With freewheeling car travel threatened by climbing gasoline prices, tourists and business travelers may prefer the train. The Trans-European Express trains, or TEE, were created originally for the business traveler. They are high-speed, first-class-only trains with early morning and late afternoon departures to suit the business day. These trains still have meal service that begins with hors d'oeuvres, and finishes four courses later after dessert and brandy. Third-class train travel has practically been eliminated in Europe, with a trend to upgrading of second class including center aisle coaches replacing the classic compartment seating, air conditioning in all cars, individual lighting and tray tables with storage pockets at each seat, and large windows. Cafeteria-style service, alas, has superseded much of the "china-plate" dining. But vendors often board the trains in the station selling the simple food of the region. Or you can lean out of the window and buy from pushcarts that position themselves alongside the train.

In Japan, for instance, where the island geography makes rail travel the only sensible mode of transportation and the famous Bullet trains leave as regularly as a subway, you can buy a *bento,* or Japanese lunch box, that might contain seasoned rice, cold, deep-fried fish, vegetables, and Japanese green tea which comes in ceramic teapots with a cap that doubles as a cup. On one of Mexico's most scenic routes, the Railway in the Sky, that runs through the Sierra Madre Mountains in the north, you can buy tacos and tortillas made by the Tarahumara Indians. This tribe still lives in caves and subsists on the corn they grow, except for those who have set up houses for this short-order food operation in the abandoned cars along the railroad sidings.

Trains offer unique opportunities for sight-seeing. Possibly the most unusual trip of this kind I have ever heard of is the Polar Bear Express that flashes its way into the Hudson Bay area of Canada so passengers can take in the migration of the polar bears. It is quite a sight to see the polar bears walking right down the main drag. It seems, however, they are not as friendly as one would hope. The police frequently issue "polar bear alerts" that warn people to watch the migration from a protected area. One gentleman chose the nearest telephone booth. Clearly he never figured on being trapped inside by a curious polar bear who planted himself at the door. At least the man had the intelligence to call the police, who dutifully arrived with a tranquilizer shot for the polar bear.

TRAINS IN THE UNITED STATES

Amtrak is a quasi-public corporation that took over operation of most American passenger trains in 1971. Like many of the national railroads of Europe, Amtrak is trying to make the schedules more appealing to business people as well as pleasure travelers with a number of package tours, discount fares, and arrangements with cruise lines, hotels, and rental car companies. You can still cross the country by sleeper train, and sit in a bubble dome to watch the passing scene, and, on a few select routes, take your own car along. There are even package tours with guides for sight-seeing trips.

Information and Reservations: Some Helpful Hints

Amtrak sales office—The Amtrak sales office often can provide information, and discuss routes, but they cannot sell you a ticket. Ask the 800 number Amtrak operator for the address of the nearest sales office.

The Amtrak 800 number—Operators at the toll-free number throughout the country will not discuss the *merits* of train travel but will mail you Amtrak literature. The 800 operators give you information, timetables, will book seats, take special requests for meals, or equipment for the handicapped. You can also ask for "station profiles" that will tell you what services to expect at your destination: taxis, bus, restaurant, etc. For instance, some railroad stations don't even have a ticket office. These stations are called "flagstops," and are preceded by an "f" in the official railway guide, which means the train stops here by passenger request only. If you ever find yourself at such a station and your train is long overdue, find the nearest phone booth and call the 800 number. Explain what train you are waiting for, and the scheduled arrival time, and the operator can check the computer to tell you when the train left its last stop and give an approximate arrival time.

Reservations—Amtrak surveys show that in America most people buy their tickets at the station, where credit cards, cash, and personal checks—with two kinds of identification—are accepted. If you plan enough in advance you can also give your credit card number over the phone to the 800 operator, who will ask for another reference and mail your tickets to you or to your travel agent.

The Official Railway Guide—This book includes information about schedules in all of North America, and a condensed schedule of the most popular, international tourist routes.

TRAINS IN EUROPE

In Europe, reservations are mandatory only on TEE services and for sleeper (called couchette) accommodations. Most times of the year it is possible to board almost any train (except a TEE) without advance booking; not, of course, at the peak of the summer season or on a holiday. Rail reservations in most European countries are now processed by the computers of the various national railway systems. The result is that small "teleprinted" tickets are placed above each seat and at the entrance of every compartment before the train leaves the station. The computers of the different national railroads are connected throughout the many stations and travel agents in Europe. This makes it possible to make reservations on trains in several countries.

The problem with overseas train reservations, however, begins when the railroads are slow in answering the phone—frustrating if you are planning your itinerary on a day-to-day basis. I have discovered that even if you do speak the language, communicating over the phone is somehow more difficult. (Your facial expressions can't keep them occupied while you're busy searching for the right words.) Unless you feel truly comfortable in a language, ask the hotel concierge for assistance, or go to a local travel agent. In big cities rely on the large international agencies like American Express or Thomas Cook. The station can be another problem area. Your first stop should be the information counter because the clerk is more likely to speak English than anyone else. Guidance is particularly important in a large station when ticket and reservation offices are located separately. Sometimes there are special windows to book for different parts of the same country.

Offices of the national railway companies—Many countries have branch offices in major American cities that can provide timetables, make reservations, answer specific questions. One official told me he once got a letter asking if there were any stops between Paris and Marseille because the client had a dog to walk. Another asked about maximum altitude because of a sensitivity to heights.

Travel agents—First and foremost, ask for the person in your travel agency who knows the most about trains. Discuss itineraries and the merits of one route over another; compare the price, speed, and value to other kinds of transport; rail ticket passes offered by most European national railroads, and Eurailpass (see Eurailpass section). The travel agent will probably not make an isolated reservation for you on European trains (unless he's doing your whole itinerary) because it's not worth his time in relation to the paperwork, phone calls or cables. He will suggest that you go to the train station in the city of your departure, get the up-to-the-minute schedules and book the train at the station. Your other alternative is asking the hotel porter to handle your reservations. With enough notice, the hotel can have the tickets picked up.

The Thomas Cook International Timetable—"A simple guide to the principal rail services of Europe, Africa, America, Asia and Australia," the front page states. And with a little study time following the detailed instruction page, the timetable can be invaluable to everyone. Published twelve times a year, the timetable also has the visa requirements of each country, and lists holidays, which is very helpful when your travel agent may say, "No reservations are necessary except on all TEE trains, and on major holidays." The crucial point often omitted is that holidays vary from country to country.

RAIL TRAVEL TERMS

Car-sleeper express service—This combination of train and car travel is most refined in Europe. It has evolved primarily on medium- to long-distance services. You take your car to the auto-rail terminal, usually within the main passenger terminal (if not, the railroad usually provides a shuttle bus between the two), and the car is normally loaded by railway employees onto bi-level railroad flat cars. The cars are delivered to passengers at the destination, within an hour of arrival. Sometimes the railroad will provide a continental breakfast at the station restaurant. You must make a reservation through the railway or travel agent for both yourself and your car.

As a variation, some countries have an "auto-express," or express car service. In this case, your car travels on a completely different train. You can take any regularly scheduled night or day train, and find the car waiting at your destination.

Car-ferry services—You drive your car aboard a special train of single level flat cars, and remain in the car for the duration of the trip. This service is usually offered in winter by certain European railways to transport cars and their occupants through snowbound or potentially treacherous mountain passes.

Clubcar—Generally the hub of a train's social life, open to both first and second class. It's one of the few "bar" situations I know that is relatively free of the predatory atmosphere of many conventional bars.

Conductor—The captain of the ship, the man in charge. But the car attendant is the most likely one to answer your questions, i.e.: "How long is this stop?" "Can I get coffee in my sleeper at 9 A.M.?"

Couchette—The word actually means bunk or berth in French, but in train lingo, a couchette is a regular compartment that can be converted using pillows and blankets to sleep four in first class or six in second class. "You're not *supposed* to undress," as one railway official put it, "but most people do." Since it's entirely possible that you may be the only woman, wear something that you can sleep in. (My memories of couchettes are not the most encouraging: all-night whisperers, smokers, tipplers, snorers.) Since you will be sitting with the same people before the couchettes are made up, you'll have a general idea of your sleeping companions' habits. No one I know has ever reported any awkward or forceful propositions. If you are at all concerned, try to make friends with one person you could call on, and—for the extreme case—note the location of the emergency brakes for the train.

Eurailpass—A Eurailpass gives you unlimited first-class travel throughout most European countries. Eurailpasses are available for different lengths of time, for fifteen days to three months. The Eurailpass will also get you discounts on some steamer and bus lines. It is not available in Europe, and so must be purchased from a travel agent in the United States. Before you embark on your first train ride, you must have the Eurailpass validated to mark the starting and expiration dates. One of the chief advantages is that you don't need individual tickets. If you are planning to travel around Europe, rather than stay in one city, a Eurailpass is probably the least expensive way to travel, next to hitchhiking. Eurail Youthpass offers two months of unlimited second-class travel for people under twenty-six.

Redcap—In the States, the redcap is a fully salaried employee of Amtrak (and not supposed to take tips, but it never hurts) who will take your bags onto the train, put them in the overhead baggage racks, or check them in the baggage car.

Sleepers—Most people still call them Pullmans, named after the company that originated the sleeping cars. A sleeper is a small compartment with one or two beds, and a wash basin, and usually a private toilet. The compartments are still as small as they used to be when I was a little girl. I remember my father had to contort himself into an advanced yoga posture in order to play jacks with me on the compartment floor. On Amtrak, the sleepers are the last car on the train so noisy passengers won't come marauding through at 3 A.M.

Supplement—An additional amount that is paid over and above the price of a ticket, usually for couchettes, sleepers, or TEE trains. Be forewarned that conductors may ask you for a supplement that is totally unnecessary—except to fatten their wallets.

GENERAL TIPS FOR TRAIN TRAVEL

Travel light. Although there is no limit on luggage, redcaps and porters are often scarce. I once had two large bags stashed in the overhead luggage rack that were so heavy that the train left my stop before I even got them into the corridor. If you can't help taking a lot of luggage (or a bicycle) it is advisable to check it in the luggage car whenever international border crossings or railroad regulations permit.

The timetables are often written on the twenty-four-hour clock, so that 17:00 would be 5:00 in the afternoon. If the number is larger than 12:00, just subtract 12:00 from the number and you get "regular" time.

If you don't immediately recognize that a sign saying *bahnhofswirtshaft* means station restaurant, never fear. Almost every major station throughout Europe has overcome the language barrier by using standardized pictograms. These are easily recognizable symbols that will identify everything from a restaurant/buffet, to a barber/beauty parlor, to an indication that reservations are required. This setup has been organized by the International Union of Railways, a sort of "United Nations" for many of the world's railways. Some other UIC programs of participating railroads include staffs of multilingual information personnel at most major stations; standardized arrival and departure boards showing arrivals on yellow background and departures on white, with red letters for express trains and black for ordinary service. Departures and arrivals are announced over a loudspeaker system in several languages, but they all seem to run together if you don't speak the languages.

Some cities have several train stations; each serves different regions of the country. Be sure you are at the right one.

Not only do you have to find the right station, you must get on the right car. It sounds tricky but it's not. Long-distance international trains in particular are really a composite of cars that each has its own destination. At a predetermined stop, a car may be switched over to another train. When you have the proper track, walk down the platform to the train and you will see that each car has an identification tablet on the side. The very top might be the name of that particular train; the next line will be the name of the city of origin and the name of the train station; on the bottom, the name of the city where that car will terminate its route, and, in between, the names of the most important stops en route. The other important marker is the yellow band just under the roof of the car indicating it is a first-class car. If you get off for a short stop, be sure you get back in the correct car. The longer station waits usually mean some cars are being switched to different rails and routes.

Immigration officers will normally board the train and inspect your passport or visa while the train crosses border points. It is possible that your luggage will be inspected by customs officers except between Common Market member countries where there are no customs formalities.

If you are using the train as a "hotel" each night, major terminals often have shower or tub facilities where you can rent clean towels, soap, slippers, washcloth, and a bathmat. Many railroad stations in fact are mini-cities, featuring banks, restaurants, post office, boutiques, and a branch of the local tourist office or welcome services that have lists of all the hotels/pensions in the city. Most of the bureaus are open late, but generally not past midnight. They will call to book hotel rooms for you once you've indicated your price range.

Unlike the airlines, food is not included in the price of even the most posh train accommodations. The TEE trains and many long-distance trains in both Europe and America have dining cars. The food ranges from made-from-scratch, to the prepackaged, frozen, and microwave-cooked variety. In most cases the price is not a bargain. You can't book a table in advance, so just simply make your reservation with the attendant when he comes by your compartment to announce the opening of the dining car. The attendants usually prefer you to pay for the meal (and tip) in the local currency.

In some countries, meals are brought to your seat. I once dined on the Taj Express, which sped along the Indian flatlands from Agra, home of the Taj Mahal, back to Delhi in three hours. Our seats reclined to induce horizontal reverie, a steward in a beige silk jacket served us chicken korma (a regional chicken curry) on china plates, followed by fresh mangoes for dessert and tea brewed black as onyx. You can buy sandwiches and drinks inside most stations, or lean out the train window when the train pulls into a station and buy whatever the vendors hold up for your perusal, from ham and cheese sandwiches (no guarantee they're fresh) to pasta in Italy. Sandwich carts or mini bars roll up and down the aisles of some trains with regularity.

If I'm not going to eat in the dining car I like to bring my own pickings, and even on short hops I bring something to drink, like bottled water, since tap water on all trains is undrinkable. I still haven't forgotten how much those Mallomars and turkey legs on my first train ride to camp improved the trip and fostered camaraderie.

CARS

Growing up in Southern California, I always felt it was incumbent on me to be crazy about things like tennis, blond hair, health, and cars. Especially cars. This was such a highly developed car culture that many businesses tailored their services so customers wouldn't have to bother getting out of the driver's seat. There were drive-in movies, drive-in banks, drive-in cleaners, drive-in restaurants, and the ultimate, drive-*through* restaurants, where you ordered through a speaker phone at the entrance and picked up the inevitable hamburger at the exit. I'm sure that nine out of ten cars in California have catsup going to seed in the carpet.

In my view, having a car was not only sensible, but considerate of my family. After weeks of systematic persuasion following my sixteenth birthday, my parents relented and my father and I went shopping. What we found was the "cutest, most darling little car," as I said to my mother in my state of euphoria. I christened it the Root Beer Float because it was brown with a white roof.

The Root Beer Float has long since gone to the Great Parking Lot in the Sky, and since I no longer live in a car culture, I rent or borrow cars from friends. But my enthusiasm is undampened. In fact, my appreciation has broadened now that my life with cars is more related to taking trips on the road. Unlike other forms of transportation, cars give you every option: a means of getting from one place to another, and a creative vehicle that lets you—and in fact forces you—to take total responsibility for yourself.

I like having the flexibility to change plans; the serendipity that leads to the discovery of a tiny restaurant, a village unravaged by tourist buses, a roadside stand selling freshly picked oranges. I like the personal feeling you get from driving around a country that may only be exceeded by bicycling; the choice of either the quickest or the most scenic route depending on your mood and purpose. I even like the fact that my penchant for shopping at local food markets always seems to leave the faint aroma of the area's specialty in my car, whether it's garlicky sausage in France, a freshly cracked coconut in Martinique, catsup and french fries right here at home.

Needless to say, there are factors that may reduce the appeal and practicality of going by car. First of all, do you *enjoy* driving? Are you a *confident* driver? You will encounter different road conditions and different kinds of cars, not to mention diverse driving habits of some nationalities that reveal as much about their national character as the cuisine. I had always thought that driving in California and a few years' combat practice with Manhattan's taxi drivers was adequate preparation for any situation, but five minutes on Italy's autostrade proved me incorrect.

I deduced that Italians must believe if they get killed driving a car, they'll go to a special place in heaven. Even though the myth of the Latin lover has finally died in the bedroom, its greatest perpetrators (the Italian men themselves) are trying to keep it alive on the highways. The need for prowess behind the wheel is as Italian as being umbilically tied to Mama for life, devoted to the wife and family but still having a mistress, and having pasta every day.

Being a good driver, it turns out, has nothing to do with following the law. The manly skill is in *not* following the law, and *not* getting caught. I will never forget one episode in a car with an Italian man who had lived in "the States" for years. On a trip to Italy together, we came to an intersection where an arrow directed our line of traffic to turn right. He continued straight ahead. Not surprisingly, a car with the right of way hit us. A crowd gathered as it always does in Italy at the slightest provocation and opinions flew back and forth between the involved parties, witnesses, and people who had probably been two blocks away at the time of the incident.

Finally, it was settled. We drove in silence through several towns, and then my friend said with great indignation, "That SOB said it was my fault!" I calmly pointed out that the other person *did* have the right of way. No response. Just more miles of silence. Then in a hurt, almost petulant tone of voice he said, "Well, maybe. But that son of a bitch saw me coming. Why did he have to hit me?"

Aside from the cultural considerations, which should enlighten, not dissuade you, you must decide if going by car suits the purpose of the trip. Is it appropriate for the weather and topography of the country? Are astronomic gas prices a deterrent? Is it important for you to spend all your time in one or two places and leave what's in between for the next trip? If so, a car may not be the most practical solution. You should also consider the layout of a particular city. Traffic and parking make a car a burden in Paris or New York, but in Los Angeles, where distances are calculated in driving time, not miles, cars are essential.

Many resorts are self-contained so that what you want to do is within walking, bicycling, or boating distance, but it's wise to double-check when you're making reservations. I stayed in one resort where everything was just beyond reasonable foot distance, there was no public transportation, hotels didn't provide shuttle service, and the bus schedule was as freewheeling as the wind. A car was indispensable.

If your final concern has anything to do with getting lost, or not being able to ask directions in the language, I assure you the problem is never as grave as it seems. Maps and pointing are surprisingly efficient means of communication.

LEGALITIES BEFORE YOU GO

Driver's license—In most Western European countries, your current United States driver's license can be used. (Just make sure it doesn't expire midway through the trip.) Some countries require an International Driving Permit that, conveniently, is written in at least nine languages, from Arabic to French. I would recommend it for no other reason than should you get stopped, or asked for your license by non-English speaking officials, they will understand at least *one* language on the International Permit. And when officials cannot understand legal documents, you invariably face delays, questions, and inconvenience. (The smaller the town, the worse it seems to get.)

Insurance—Check the provisions of your own insurance for public liability and property coverage which are compulsory in many countries. Find out if your insurance is valid outside the state in which you live. Are you covered if someone else drives a car that you have rented, bought, leased, etc.? Do you have personal accident, baggage, and personal effects insurance that will also cover personal items stolen from the car? The American Automobile Association (AAA) will issue insurance policies, as well as issue an International Motor Insurance Green Card that is proof your insurance complies with the local insurance laws.

AAA membership—In addition to all the services the AAA provides on our own highways—information and arrangements about renting, buying, and leasing cars abroad, with specific country by country information, including maps—the AAA membership card can serve as an introduction to the various affiliated automobile clubs all over the world. Most countries have some kind of automobile club, and you should have the address and phone number with you in case of emergencies. If the clubs don't provide on-the-scene rescues, ask them to recommend garages in the areas where you'll be traveling.

GETTING A CAR

You can rent, buy and resell, buy and ship home, lease, or even ship your own car to almost any place in the world. For all the nonrental alternatives the two main considerations should be: 1) will the cost of shipping offset any savings? 2) will you be driving for a long-enough period of time so you'd save in comparison to renting a car or other kinds of transportation?

Buy and ship home—It isn't the bargain of yesteryear, but what is? If you need a new car, if your trip is long and involves a lot of driving, buying and shipping home may be worth it. I did hear of one case where the motive was pure romance. A friend of mine and her husband honeymooned in France many years ago, and drove from Paris to the South of France in a Citröen. She says it's the only car he's ever coveted. So for their twenty-fifth anniversary, she stopped in Paris on her way home from a business trip in Europe, and bought a twenty-five-year-old Citröen and had it shipped home. Her only complaint was that customs practically ripped it apart looking for contraband. But her husband hardly noticed the damage. He was busy enjoying a rediscovered treasure.

The normal procedure for buying overseas is to contact an authorized foreign car dealer for information. Do you pay a factory price? Is there duty? How much is the saving? Where will you pick up the car? Will the manufacturer deliver to where you're going, or will you have to change your plans? What safety standards must the car have to get back into the United States? Do cars purchased in Europe have the smog control devices? What are the customs requirements? How will you ship it home? What insurance is necessary? Ask about marine insurance, which usually covers the car against loss or damage, including scratching, denting, etc. (Sometimes cars are kept on deck and the paint job takes a beating.) The policy begins when the car is delivered to the steamship line for shipping to the port of entry and remains effective seventy-two hours after arrival. Will the steamship line arrange for the steam-spraying and cleaning required by the Department of Agriculture? What are the service and warranty guarantees? Will they be handled through the dealer? Be sure you have clear answers before you proceed.

Buy and resell—You buy the car from a manufacturer, and he agrees to repurchase it at a set figure, minus the depreciation. The most customary arrangement is that you will get a refund check after the car is returned to the manufacturer. I would not recommend the favorite method of students, which is to buy a second-hand car abroad, and hope to resell it *somehow*. Your resale chances are uncertain, and if you don't have time to place ads in newspapers, you may be saddled with an unwanted car, and a time-and-money consuming responsibility.

Shipping your own car—You might make this choice if you are taking an inordinately long trip or plan to live elsewhere. Keep in mind that if you are shipping an American car to Greece, for example, the mechanics aren't going to be quite as familiar with your car and may not stock the right parts. Major steamship lines will take cars as long as you're going along, too. It's called "accompanied" baggage, and there's no extra charge. Just book space early for the two of you. This is probably the one time you'll want to have as little gasoline as possible. The gas tanks are drained before boarding as a safety precaution. If you want to fly on ahead, the car can be shipped as freight. Cost is based on a per cubic measurement and may vary with the port of entry and departure. At a small charge, a shipping agent will handle the procedure and provide information about the necessary documents.

Leasing—This alternative is a good idea if you would like a new car in Europe but don't want resale problems, if you don't need a new car at home and will need the car for a long-enough period of time to make leasing more economical than renting. You will get a new factory car with unlimited mileage. The minimum lease is usually thirty days, and can be extended up to six months. There is a depreciation fee which you must pay before leaving Europe, and you must sign a promissory note for the balance of the sale price, which is canceled upon return of the car to the manufacturer.

Renting a car—It's most likely that if you are going to travel by car, you will rent one. Major American companies like Hertz and Avis have offices around the world. Outside the United States, the cars are often not automatic, few have air conditioning, and most are foreign made. Commonwealth countries, of course, have right-hand drive cars. Most countries have local rental agencies, some of which have banded together to form Europacar. The rates are sometimes less expensive than the better known agencies, but you may be sacrificing service and convenience, depending on where you're renting the car, and where you will leave it.

TIPS ON RENTING CARS

Most of these tips are for international travel but should be thought about even if you're going from Denver to St. Louis.

1. Before you decide on one rental company or another, ask if there are offices in the locations where you'll be traveling. This is especially important if you have mechanical problems with the car.

2. Each company has a different "drop-off" policy. In some cases, there is a charge if you don't return the car to an office in the same country. If you rent in Italy and want to drive to Paris and fly home, you might have to pay a drop-off charge for this convenience. In general, the smaller the car, and the longer you keep it, the better chance the fee will be waived.

3. What does the insurance cover that comes with the car? In some countries there is a surcharge for people under twenty-five, or twenty-one.

4. Stick-shift cars generally get a better rate of mileage and are less expensive. Just make sure you are comfortable driving one.

5. Check the value-added tax in the countries you're planning to visit. In some cases, you get substantial savings if you rent in one country, and then drive it in another. Some countries just have cheaper rates than others. Your itinerary should be flexible enough to benefit from the potential savings.

6. You can pay with a major credit card when you rent the car, and the total will be computed when you return the car. If you pay cash, you must pay the estimated total amount, *plus* a certain percentage of that amount to cover mileage and time not covered in the initial policy. The unused portion of this percentage will be returned to you when you turn in the car at your final destination.

7. You can reserve a car abroad through the toll-free number of Hertz or Avis, and pick it up at an airport or an in-town office. If you are arriving at night, or during a rush hour, it might be wiser to take local transport to your hotel, and get the car downtown.

8. In addition to asking the rental agent for maps, driving regulations, and any other pertinent information, ask *how* the car works. I once rented a car in Italy and noticed there were two keys on the key chain. I assumed one was for the trunk, and the other for the ignition. Quite naturally, I put one in the ignition which instantly set off the car's very loud burglar alarm. Remember, this was Italy, and so the proverbial crowd gathered. Thank goodness. Someone showed me that I had to put one key under the dashboard first to deactivate the alarm, and *then* I could start the car. Quietly.

Make sure you know the whereabouts of the headlights, bright lights, and window wipers. Some models have them attached to the turn signals and gear shifts, and it's a matter of turning, pushing, or pulling. I drove around for an entire week in an American car thinking the radio didn't work because I pushed instead of turned the knob. Ask about changing the tires. Is there a spare tire, and the equivalent of a jack in the trunk? How does the trunk open? Is there a special key for the fuel tank?

EN ROUTE

Sit in your car ten minutes before going anywhere and read the map. Familiarize yourself with the names of the major streets and important landmarks, even if it's only the corner drugstore. Take a pen with a color of ink that will stand out from the lines on the map and trace your route. With all the one-way streets in many towns, you might go by the same spot every ten minutes. Maps made by the Michelin Company and the AAA are excellent. A language of international symbols for highway travel solves the problem of having to know highway terminology in every country.

Never hesitate to ask. Ask and ask again. If you don't speak the language, at least be sure to have the name of the street or destination in the native tongue. Keep a pen and paper handy in case you find a budding cartographer, whose drawing can help avoid having to know the words for "left," "right," "straight ahead," or "two blocks down by the Victorian building with the red roof."

Gas stations are sources of information. Some are mini shopping centers with markets, toy stores, cafeterias and restaurants. Many European countries have discount gas coupons that must be purchased outside the country or at the border. You can exchange unused coupons for cash when you leave the country. Always keep your tank as full as possible, especially outside the major cities. Stations may close for special holidays, and with the ongoing oil crunch, some countries have legal restrictions and many stations informally ration their supplies. You will recognize the brands of gasoline, but U.S. oil company credit cards are not honored at stations in Europe. Some countries will take "major" American credit cards.

The metric system of weights and measures is used in most parts of the world. Speed limits, when indicated, are given in kilometers which will correspond to your speedometer unless you have an American or English car. In this case, just make the approximate conversion for several speeds (60 MPH is about 100 KPH, etc.).

Finding your way on the highway can be very disconcerting. One mistake and, zap, you're on the wrong cloverleaf. What kind of civil engineers place large signs with arrows indicating a route number, and abandon you at the turnoff where the road forks? My pet peeve is not knowing what lane to take when neither of the city choices is where I want to go. I prepare myself for this lapse of logic on the part of the sign makers, and familiarize myself with the names of the points along my route, and even those beyond my destination.

A white flag (or restaurant napkin, towel, or T-shirt as long as it's white) tied to the antenna is an international sign of distress. If you are on a highway, you can hope a policeman will pass by or you might have to hitchhike to the nearest town. The first step if you have car trouble is to find out if there is a local branch of the agency from which you've rented the car. If not, try the local mechanic.

I have two friends who came out of a restaurant in the Greek countryside to find their battery was dead. Neither one of them spoke Greek, so they went back into the taverna and found a waiter who spoke some English. He took them to a garage and explained the problem. (No matter how fluent you are in a language, the phrase for "My fan belt is broken," assuming you *even know* what the problem is, may not be on the tip of your tongue.) The waiter also called the original renting agent, who told my friends to pay the bill, keep the receipt, and eventually they were reimbursed.

Horn blowing is not allowed in many major cities. Blink your headlights if you want to pass. Parking lights are generally used for night driving, but use your common sense—and your bright lights— especially on country roads. Good tires are essential, particularly on country roads that are eroded by weather. Check for worn-down treads. Do you need snow tires?

Even though in many countries it seems as if there is no speed limit—from the way most people drive—there probably is, although they're often not posted as visibly as in this country. Ask a policeman. I got a speeding ticket in Spain once, and although I was doing some 5 km over the speed limit, I paid the fine without question. I make it a practice not to argue with the law.

Plan your itinerary so you don't arrive at 3 A.M. hoping to find a hotel room. Book ahead, or arrive early enough. Personally, I like to do the longest stretch of driving in the early morning, get to the hotel about noon, or check-in time, and have the entire afternoon and evening.

What to take in your car: tissues, moist towels, a good-sized flashlight, sunglasses, a roll of toilet paper (you never know about gas station restrooms, or bathrooms in restaurants), glass cleaner and rags to keep windshield clean, a bottle opener, a small knife, some kind of liquid—bottled water or individual cans of juice—and a few snacks—fruit, cheese, yogurt, nuts, raisins, gum, hard candy. When you buy fruit along the way, ask if there is running water to wash it off.

If You're Going Alone

In addition to all the above:

1. Give someone the license number and description of your car. In an emergency, this would help police find you.

2. Take a cassette player so you have "company" and stay awake. Open the windows regularly, especially if you smoke.

3. Don't pick up hitchhikers.

4. If possible, avoid driving at night unless you know the area very well.

5. Get a CB if you are in the United States.

If You're Going with Another or Several People

A trip is no time for a beginner to practice, or for a self-designated Indy 500 contestant to make the route his personal racecourse. I speak up if I feel that I am the best driver. You may be faced with gently persuading someone who has had too much to drink at dinner, or who is overtired, to relinquish the wheel. It's worth your life to be insistent.

OTHER POSSIBILITIES WITH CARS

Auto-Express Train. (See Trains in this chapter.)

Car ferries—The word "ferry" can be as ambiguous as the word "hotel." Ferry may mean a commuter's route from New York to Staten Island, Sausalito to San Francisco, Bainbridge Island to Seattle, or an overnight trip. Basically, you take your car with you and there are several advantages: you may cut driving time, save gasoline, and eliminate hotel expense on overnight trips. Some ferries even have cabins, restaurants, hairdressers, nurseries, gambling, and —in international waters—duty-free shopping. I had friends who used to take the Copenhagen–Malmö run just to buy cigarettes and chocolate. Reservations are always helpful, and essential on highly traveled routes in high season. Get to the loading area with time to spare, particularly if you have no reservation. If you are going from one country to another you have to present your passport and the papers for the car, including the International Motor Insurance Green Card and the registration or the rental policy. If you are on a tight schedule, allow plenty of time for the customs formalities.

I will never forget my trip by ferry from Spain to Morocco. We had to fill out "landing cards" for arrival in Tangier, and, as always, there was an entry for occupation where I wrote "journalist." Later on I thought I heard my name over the loudspeaker on the ferry. I turned to my friends and said, "Don't you hear someone calling my name?" They thought I was being funny. Then I heard it again, this time with the added fillip requesting I report to the police. I couldn't imagine the problem. It turned out the word "journalist" caused the problem. They wanted to know my exact purposes, what I was photographing with my camera, what I was planning to do, whom I was planning to see. I wasn't comfortable answering so many questions, so my replies were truthful but vague. I was simply visiting friends. They let me go, but on the way back I filled in the occupation blank, "teacher."

Cars with drivers—I'm not suggesting that you hire a limousine with darkened windows, a wet bar, and a driver in complete chauffeur's regalia. A "simple" car and driver may be less expensive, and more practical, than you might think, especially if you have limited time. Ask your hotel or the local tourist office. You can rent a car with a driver who simply takes you from place to place doing errands or sight-seeing within a city, or one who drives you to another city and back. (You can sometimes hire taxis for this purpose.) Another alternative is to have a car with a driver who is also a guide.

In any case, agree on the price first. Tipping is customary (about 10 percent of the fee). In many countries, the government tourist office will license the "driver-guides" so that you know the person is qualified. This is not to say that they won't have personal prejudices about what you should see. But you have the opportunity to discuss the country on an informal basis with an informed resident, even though in some cases you may be getting the party line. My only complaint over the years are the drivers who turn to talk to you in the back seat, predictably at the moment you're going around a hairpin turn.

Most of the driver-guides speak English, although you should make that a specific request. I remember arriving by boat on the Greek island of Patmos, famous for the cave where St. John is said to have written his doctrine on Love. I had never heard of it, but as the cave was the only attraction, my friend and I decided to go. We got a taxi driver who had a battered four-door American Pontiac that looked strange because it was out of scale for such a small island. (And where did he get it?) Anyhow, he only spoke Greek, so we pointed to a picture of the cave in the guidebook. He smiled broadly, revealing a pair of gold front teeth, and "talked" to us by whistling various birdcalls as we drove along.

The most clever solution I ever heard about a language problem involved a great friend of mine who had only one day to see the city of Kyoto, Japan. She arrived at the railway station and asked the travel service for a car and driver. The only driver available spoke no English. She spoke no Japanese. So the travel service made out lists of what she wanted to see, one for the driver in the Japanese characters, and one for her in English. Each sight had a number. She sat in the front seat, and at each sight they would point to their respective lists to make sure that she wasn't busy appreciating number 3, when they were actually in front of number 5. The last number on the list was a teahouse, and she invited the driver to join her. They shared fragrant Japanese tea in silence, somehow a fitting close to the day.

BUSES

"Zee ALPES! Stewdents! WACK UP! *WACK UP!*" exhorted my high school French teacher as she stood at the head of the bus, surveying her twenty-five star pupils, who were busy sleeping off the wine they had had at lunch on their first trip to Europe. We spent almost two weeks traveling by bus, listening to her periodic "wack up" calls, from Paris through France into Austria, Switzerland, and Italy. I quickly learned the whys and wherefores of bus travel. So a year later, when I was a student living in Italy, and wanted to make the most of my free time for the least amount of money, I engaged in a constant comparison of buses and trains.

The principal advantage of the bus is that it may be the only way of getting where you are going. I have a friend whose mother lives in a small town in Pennsylvania. The nearest train station is three towns away; she is 135 miles from one airport, and 40 miles over a mountain road from the other. She doesn't drive, the cost of taxis to and from the airport would be exorbitant, and you really can't make a habit of asking your neighbor. So the bus is her only choice when she wants to come to New York to visit her daughter.

Commuters in Switzerland depend on the famous Post-Alpine buses, which originated as "Go-to-every-village," horse-drawn mail coaches in the 1920s. Today the easily recognizable yellow coaches are used as mass transit by the Swiss and by tourists who want to visit the off-trail Swiss villages, or find untrammeled hiking and fishing areas. The Swiss Railways can give you the bus schedules. If you're told that the driver is multilingual, be sure to ask if English is one of the languages. It may refer to French, German, Italian, or Swiss-German, the four main languages of Switzerland.

The second plus to bus travel is economic, although it may be a qualified plus. You must figure out how much you are spending—and saving—and weigh it against personal and physical cost to you. Is the saving great enough to make up for lost time and the discomfort of bus travel, especially on long trips? Not all buses have air conditioning and comfortable seats. If you are planning an overnight trip, you must realistically consider how much sleep you need. Will you be getting your money's worth if you are semiconscious on arrival? If you're going to visit relatives or friends and can make up a few hours' sleep it may not matter. I have found that I really need my energy—if only to enjoy myself—on a sight-seeing trip.

Since a bus is clearly not the fastest way of getting from one point to another, consider how much time you'll be spending in transit compared with how and where you *really* want to be spending your time and money. In addition to the regular travel time, such unexpected factors as traffic and weather might prolong the trip. Unlike having your own car (which is subject to exactly the same elements), you can't just change your mind: pull off the road and snooze; find an alternate route; change your itinerary; or wait for the roads to clear while you work your way through two hot fudge sundaes at the nearest bar and grill.

INFORMATION AND RESERVATIONS AND BUS STATIONS

In the United States, the quickest line for up-to-date schedules is to look in the Yellow Pages under the two major bus lines, Trailways or Greyhound, and call for information. Outside the larger cities, you are likely to be talking to the owner of a diner or gas station who is also the agent for the company. This establishment is usually the town's "bus depot" as well. Understandably, this person won't have the time to give you much more than the essential information, and will probably be interrupted by customers wanting scrambled eggs or a full tank of gas.

There is no first or second class on a bus. One bus company spokesman said, "Ma'am, we don't have classes. We just have people." There are no reserved seats but there are smoking and non-smoking sections, and you are guaranteed a seat. If the bus is full, they have to add an extra bus just for you. You have to be at the bus station about half an hour before departure. Some stations have shopping arcades like New York's Port Authority, with a maze of gourmet food shops and high-fashion boutiques.

The major terminals will accept credit cards and cash, not personal checks. You are allowed to check two suitcases for a total of a certain number of pounds. Call to verify the amount. Just weigh them on your bathroom scale. If someone is picking you up at the depot, make sure that you have its "newest" name. A friend of mine was taking the bus out to Long Island to meet me one weekend, and she said the bus would stop at the Eastbrook Diner. Luckily I had asked in the gas station for directions and the attendant told me that even though it was still a diner and at the same location, it was now called Ruth's Place. If you are making your own way from the depot, particularly late at night, ask the bus driver if it is convenient to stop at a bar or restaurant so you can call a taxi.

Pets are not allowed to travel by bus.

The most efficient way to find out about bus services abroad is through the tourist office. (Bus *tours* are covered in the chapter "Meeting a City and the People.") It has been my experience that they will suggest you wait until you get to the country and ask the local tourist office, or go directly to the bus station.

Perhaps the most organized bus system in Europe is Europabus, even though the tour department is more extensive than the straight transport sources. Europabus is the international bus network that is really a part of the European railways. Travel agents are familiar with Europabus. Also, you can write them directly.

HOW TO MAKE YOUR TRIP MORE COMFORTABLE

Yes, there are bathrooms on buses. I had two friends from England who bought a pass for bus travel all around the country and planned to sleep at night in the bus. When the driver announced that there were "restrooms" at the rear, they were overjoyed! They thought it meant an area with cots to stretch out, and rest, of course. Even so, the bus *will* stop someplace with restroom facilities about every four hours.

Bring a neck pillow, even though many buses have reclining seats.

Don't leave home without earplugs. It could be just your luck to sit in front or behind someone telling his life story, or someone who snores.

Take a small transistor radio with earphone attachments.

Reading material is great—if you can read without getting motion sickness.

The food along the way is often overpriced and not really what you'd like to eat, especially if you're faced with a room full of vending machines dispensing candy, ice cream, and soft drinks. The most practical idea is to bring your own: peanut butter and jelly sandwiches (they last overnight); hunks of cheese in a Baggie; single-portion containers of fruit juice (can openers if necessary); crackers, cookies; yogurt (it will keep for the first few hours of the trip); nuts, raisins, dried fruits; fresh fruits like apples, pears, oranges, but as my friend's mother advised, "Don't take bananas—they smell."

CRUISES, FREIGHTERS, YACHTS

In the old days, the glamour of shipboard life began before you even left the harbor. There were bon voyage parties in the stateroom with mounds of caviar and fountains of champagne, good-byes shouted from the deck, and swirls of confetti thrown by well-wishers. The mood continued with show-stopping entrances by the ladies in formal attire who came down a staircase fanning into the dining room. Every morning at eleven a steward brought a cup of hot bouillon to your deck chair, where you lay encased in a plaid blanket, and the haute cuisine had little touches like baskets of petits fours tied with large pink and orange ribbons, made of glistening strips of boiled sugar pulled like taffy. My mother says it was like traveling on the Waldorf-Astoria.

I knew all about this, of course, from novels, the movies, newsreels, and television. The way they told it, life on board was glamorous and wildly romantic—lots of sunsets and leaning over the rail to contemplate the sea below. (Even my mother was fooled by this last part. She said all she could see was the deck below.) If life wasn't searingly romantic, then it was a total disaster. You were hurled either into the eager arms of the captain, or ashore by a tidal wave. If people were ill, it was never anything mundane, and always reached epidemic proportions.

I have long since realized that these calamities generally strike characters in Robert Louis Stevenson's novels. The reality is that the passing years have not dealt kindly with luxury ship travel. The cruise business is thriving because it has successfully adapted its offerings to an era dedicated to making the world available to more people at a reasonable price. Naturally, you can still buy a deluxe cabin on a transatlantic crossing for an unconscionable amount (no limits on the caviar), although tight security precludes bon voyage parties in the stateroom.

The cruise business has shifted the emphasis from "crossings," as in the Atlantic, to a kind of "touring," in smaller ponds like the Caribbean. You still get the good parts: a cruise is probably the only kind of affordable vacation where you feel pampered. A resort may run a close second, but there's an added something about being in a contained environment supported by the sea; the feeling of a no-hassle vacation that starts the moment you step on board; no concern about bringing too much luggage, unless you're planning to go on after debarkation; social activities from backgammon tournaments and dance contests to shuffleboard and pools; decisions about meals that are only as serious as deciding to take the first or the second sitting; and knowing in advance how much your trip will cost.

Most cruise lines have a bundle of alluring programs, and themed voyages have proliferated. You can go on a music cruise with famous musicians and opera stars giving concerts; archeological cruises with college professors lecturing on the sights you will stop and visit; beauty cruises with experts on nutrition; even cruises in the nude—clothing optional.

Don't unintentionally sabotage your good time by expecting to fall in love on the first moonlit night. You can, however, increase your chances of meeting a lively crowd on the "themed" cruises. These shorter jaunts to sunny climates attract a broader swatch of people than extended cruises for those who have the time and the money. The added appeal of a theme cruise for women is that being friendly is not automatically interpreted as an invitation. Small flirtations are the order of the day.

In any case, ship travel is not unlike being on a group tour. The passengers will quickly divide into subsets characterized by a particular interest. You can choose your crowd. The Drinkers will ignore the meals except for an occasional potato chip and spend most of the trip on a barstool. The Eaters will down an entire year's caloric allotment during the cruise. The Jocks will run around the decks faithfully at six-thirty every morning. The Resters will be supine for the whole trip, except possibly for meals, and the Swingers will wake up for the second sitting for lunch. Somewhere in the crowd you'll find a kindred soul. It may be the swashbuckler, a couple, or another woman.

HOW TO PICK A CRUISE

1. *The itinerary*—First and foremost, does the ship go where you want to go? Do you want more time in port, or more time at sea? Some people like to take the "six ports in seven days Caribbean cruise" because they will come home and feel that they've seen a lot. This pace will exhaust other travelers. Some people I know prefer more port time because they need the contact with land and a daily newspaper. Keep in mind that when the focus is on the ports, the ship is only serving as a floating hotel. It is only at sea that a ship really comes to life.

2. *Season*—Does the ship go *when* you want to go? Is the sea relatively calm? In Greece, for instance, there is a strong wind called the *meltemi* that gusts around some of the Greek islands in the height of the summer season. You might want to visit the groups of islands undisturbed by the *meltemi*.

3. *Price*—Some lines have off-season discount prices, or combination fly-sail packages. You sail one way, they pay your airfare home. Airlines also offer these packages (transatlantic crossings only). Some ships have first-class accommodations only, and if you are traveling alone there may be an additional charge for the privilege of privacy. Side trips ashore and booze are always extra. At your request, the cruise line will pair you with a roommate (your gender) or you can ask about the standby programs that, a certain number of days before sailing, will give unoccupied double cabins to single travelers at no extra cost. If you are traveling in tourist class, find out if all the facilities on the ship are available to you.

The location of your cabin is largely a matter of personal preference. Actually the word "posh" was originally a term that referred to cabin location. In the days when the sun never set on the British Empire, and people were forever sailing away to check on the colonies, they would request a cabin or stateroom "*P*ort *O*ut, *S*tarboard *H*ome" because that way they were always on the sunny side of the ship, considered the most luxurious.

Some people insist on a porthole, even though it's always sealed airtight and the view may be blocked by suspended lifeboats. All cabins have air conditioning. (The upper deck suites have regular windows.) Other people prefer the feeling of being in a cave. You should avoid a cabin located anywhere in the vicinity of the engine room, or any noise-making operations that might rumble on through the night. A cabin dead center usually has the smoothest ride.

4. *Nationality of the cruise line*—Cruise lines not based in the United States are sometimes called "foreign-flag carriers." Don't confuse this term with the flag the ship actually flies, which is called a flag of convenience and is usually from the country where the ship is *registered*, unlikely spots like Monrovia, Libya, Panama, Lichtenstein. (These countries are chosen for the same business purposes that make people have Swiss bank accounts and companies in the Bahamas.) You should take note of the nationality of the cruise line and the crew, because the national character is usually reflected in the atmosphere, cuisine, and activities on board. The following are generalizations, but it's a start.

- *The Greeks*—There is no word for stranger in the Greek language. The word "stranos" means guest. A Greek crew will kill themselves to serve you, but it's with the feeling that you're a welcome guest in their house. Smile and appreciate them. There is always an electricity and energy when you're on a Greek ship. You will probably have some Greek food—moussaka, roast lamb, the mezedakia, or hors d'oeuvres—and a night of bouzouki music and dancing and entertainment by the crew.

- *The Italians*—Their reputation is for fawning, almost obsequious service. No woman of any age is neglected on an Italian ship. You may feel pampered, even resentful at all the attempts to ensure your comfort. It's not unlikely to have pasta and an Italian night of singing and dancing.

- *The Scandinavians*—The crew isn't terribly gregarious, and is noted for cool, formal, impeccable service.

- *The French*—There will be great emphasis on the food, served with arm's length charm. Some lines have meals that reflect the culinary specialties of the regions of France.

- *The English*—The crew is usually quiet, invisible, and almost telepathic in meeting your needs. The Cunard Line features a mainly French menu, although there are some dishes from the British cuisine, a phrase which is sometimes considered a contradiction in terms.

■ *"The Florida ships"*—A general, cruise industry term for the ships that sail out of Florida into the Caribbean. Devoted to fun, food, and sun, these cruises may be staffed by many different nationalities.

ON BOARD

Get yourself organized in the dining room. Your travel agent or the cruise line probably requested a table for you when the reservation was made, but since you generally have the same table for the entire trip, it's worth the effort to check on the location when you first board. If you're traveling alone, ask for a table with more, rather than less people. There are usually two sittings. The second, later sitting gets a livelier crowd.

If you are at all interested in the ship's activities, make an effort to meet the cruise director. Personal attention never hurts. Getting to know the crew is also helpful, particularly when you are stopping in many ports. They probably have been there before and can give you tips on restaurants and shopping. Besides, familiar faces that you know by name, and know you, will make the ship feel more like home. One friend of mine always says you get the real dirt about shipboard life from the masseur/masseuse or the hairdresser.

When you unpack, be careful to place things in secure positions so that unexpected rough seas in the middle of the night won't start an avalanche.

Toilets on a cruise ship are flush toilets.

Tipping is always a puzzle. You should tip *the waiter* $3.50 to $5.00 a day. The waiter will then tip the bus boy. If not, the bus boy won't clear the table, which will affect the waiter's service, and *he* won't get such a healthy tip. The waiter is your lifeline to the kitchen. He will also arrange special requests and will make sure you eat quickly if you are leaving the ship on a shore excursion. Tip at the end of the trip. Put the money in an envelope with his name on it, and yours with the cabin number. Tip in dollars: *the room steward*—he/she functions like a maid in a hotel, and should also get $3.50 to $5.00 a day (per person); *the wine steward*—if you have wine at every meal, and he takes special care making selections for you, tip $3.50 a day; *the bartender*—as you would in a restaurant, usually 15 percent of the bill.

Getting seasick. Up to now, only my closest friends have known that my record as a sailor is abysmal. I have actually turned green on ships securely anchored in a quiet harbor. I once got off a ship because the sea was too rough and flew to the next port of call. I spent an entire crossing from Norway to Copenhagen practically strapped in a deck chair, trying to take in the "refreshing" sea air. Chances are that on a large ship you won't feel seasick. If you are at all concerned, ask your doctor to recommend a motion-sickness pill, preferably one that won't make you sleepy. Don't wait until you feel nauseous to take it. (The ship always has pills on board.) When you do feel queasy, SAY SO. There is absolutely no point in being heroic. Your condition is a common fact of life at sea, and I have always found people to be most sympathetic and helpful. If possible, stay in the fresh air, especially on sailing yachts where the cabins are probably not air-conditioned. Put cold towels on the back of your neck and forehead. Undo tight belts or garments. If necessary, triumph over the need to throw up in the privacy of your bathroom. You may not make it that far, anyway.

FREIGHTERS

Freighter travel could be considered the "roughing it" aspect of cruising. There are no social directors, no printed menus, no bars and discos, certainly no shuffleboard, and cargo may take up most of the available deck space. You are tossing in your lot with a dozen or so other passengers (there may be as many as fifty) to take potluck on how long you'll be gone, and your ports of call. When you opt for a freighter, you have no choice but to follow John Steinbeck's exhortation that "the journey must take the traveler." All you get is a confirmation of space from the particular freighter line, and an idea of approximately how long you'll be at sea. On some ships there is a "first class," which means private baths and showers, and tourist class, which has communal facilities. All towels, sheets, soaps, etc. are provided. There may be separate dining rooms if deck space is short, but there is one lounge. There are waiters and stewards as on regular cruise ships and tipping 5 percent of your total ticket cost to each is customary. A doctor is also on board.

You must provide your own entertainment, but people have told me that watching the cargo being loaded and unloaded in port is a riveting pastime. A stay in port may vary from one to three days, and a travel agent will usually come on board (prearranged by the freighter) to suggest side trips by bus and train for the passengers. If you are in Genoa, for example, you can take the train and spend the day in Venice. Sometimes the shipping line will put you up in a hotel, but there is no set pattern to any cruise on a freighter. That's half the appeal.

YACHTS

There are just no better words for it: when you're on a yacht with a professional crew, YOU FEEL RICH. The nicest part of yachting is that you don't actually have to *be* rich in order to have that feeling. There is a yacht to fit every pocketbook, as long as you don't have your heart set on teak paneling throughout, brass fittings, and a master bathroom with Carrara marble tubs. You can still have cold lobster lunches on deck under a blue awning, and tangerine-colored sunrises.

Yacht owners, like actors or sports figures, have agents or brokers who handle all the bookings. The agent will have the information and specifications about each yacht on file—the size, the price, the accommodations, its home port, and generally where it goes. BE SURE YOU ARE DEALING WITH THE HANDFUL OF BROKERS WHO INSPECT THE YACHTS EACH YEAR AND KNOW THE YACHTS AND PERSONNEL ON A FIRST-NAME BASIS. I can't make this point too emphatically. Chartering a yacht is a very personal business. Layout is important because you will want to feel like the yacht is your home. If you are traveling with other couples, which makes chartering affordable, is there one master suite and two tiny bedrooms? How will they be divided? Do you want a yacht that is built for speed or for comfort? The captain and the crew are part of the commune at sea, so personalities are important.

Yachts are sometimes owned by the captains themselves, and they are called "owner-captains," or the captain works for the owner, who is rarely there. The charter yacht captain is a special breed. He is devoted first and foremost to his ship. She is his mistress. The women in his life are always second fiddle, although there are usually many of them. Captains are independent, resilient, tough, weather-beaten, unafraid of nature, and take life each day at a time. And they appreciate people who make an attempt to understand sailing and the sea.

One word of caution: there is a kind of chartering called "bareboating," which means all you get is the boat. No crew, no provisions, nothing except the vessel. It may sound romantic, and cost less than a yacht with a professional crew, but unless you or your companions are really seasoned sailors and *know the waters,* don't even entertain the idea. While running the yacht itself may be fairly straightforward business, navigation is another story. In the Caribbean, for instance, navigation is done according to the British Admiralty Charts, which are excellent, but they were drawn up in the 1800s. Sandbars, shoals, the geologic formation around certain harbors have indubitably changed in the last hundred years. In addition, you may spend half the time provisioning the boat. A professional crew knows where to shop for the best price.

What Makes a Yacht Different from a Cruise Ship

The toilets, for one thing. You don't flush them. You turn a small knob that releases the running water, and then pump a small foot pedal at the base of the toilet that flushes the water through. When the toilet bowl has just a small amount of water, close off the supply by turning the small knob in the reverse direction.

Your itinerary may be set in lead before you go, but it is always subject to change because of weather conditions, and the final decision always rests with the captain.

Fresh water is precious, hence the expression "shower with a friend." On one Greek island we used to take showers in a barber shop to conserve the water on the ship.

A yacht is informal. Unlike cruise ships, where the protocol about clothes is the same as a well-heeled resort, clean white pants is "dressed up." Bathing suits, cover-ups, jeans and T-shirts are standard dress, unless you are going to a fancy restaurant in port. (Most seaside restaurants are casual.) You can usually get away with white pants and a halter top, or a long anything. Pack in a soft-sided suitcase that will crush nicely under the bed or in a closet. Space is not at a premium.

You can bring hair dryers and electric rollers. The captain usually has a converter.

Never wear shoes on board. This custom comes from the days when the decks were always finely polished wood, and scuff marks were anathema. No shoes is more of a tradition, and in the boating world, tradition is ever important.

The cost of the trip includes the food but not the booze. You can also arrange to pay by the meal so you can eat ashore at no extra cost. You can request the kind of food you'd like when you make the reservation with the broker. But the provisions also depend on what's available in the local markets. I've seen captains shake their heads at requests for peanut butter and jelly. (I have also known people to ask for caviar at every port.) In the French islands in the Caribbean, for instance, you can count on excellent wines, cheese, and pâtés, since most everything is imported from France. Ask the cook what he/she would recommend. The only problem is that sometimes the cook is the current live-in friend of the captain who only coincidentally, and sometimes just barely, can throw a meal together. But haute cuisine is not the most important consideration on a yacht. It's the incomparable feeling of discovering secluded coves, sunsets, and diving off the railing into a clear-blue sea.

GLOSSARY OF NAUTICAL TERMS

I have always felt that not knowing the language of a particular world can be frustrating, intimidating, and add to my feeling of "Why did I come *here?*" Even if you yourself never utter any of the following terms out loud, when someone else does they will have a familiar ring, and help to make you more comfortable in a sailor's world.

On a Cruise Ship

- *Master captain*—He is in charge of the operation of the vessel. Depending on the ship's size, there may be several captains. The *staff captain* is usually the second in command, although he is fully qualified to take charge. When you are invited to the "captain's dinner," the master captain is your host.

- *Chief purser*—Originally in charge of the ship's purse or finances, he was really a glorified accountant. Today, he is considered the "hotel manager" of the ship who is responsible for the smooth operation of the living areas, the staterooms, and the cabin staff. He will handle all your special requests, such as arranging for people to come on board as your guests for lunch or dinner. You will usually find him at the reception area of the ship.

- *Chief steward*—Responsible for the dining room, and in charge of the stewards in the dining room.

- *Cruise director*—In charge of all the social activities, from backgammon tournaments to special requests.

- *Steward*—Originally a biblical term for "someone who served." You have a dining room steward or waiter, and a wine steward. The bedroom steward takes care of your cabin. If the hot water doesn't work, if you need more blankets, ask him/her.

- *Shore excursion manager*—He/she will expedite all the land arrangements, which will have been prearranged by a staff on shore. When the shore excursions are extensive, you can occasionally purchase them as a package in advance. You may get a discount rate when you prepurchase because you are giving the company cash to make the arrangements.

On a Yacht

- *Yacht*—A vessel having a bowsprit, the long pointy stick at the end of the front section that is meant to guard against ramming head on into something, and at least three masts. Yacht does not necessarily mean a vessel with sails; there are also power yachts, which the sailing community refers to as "stink pots."

- *Yawl, ketch, sloop*—Different kinds of sailing yachts. The name is determined by the cut or shape of the sails, how many there are, and where they are "rigged" or put up. I have a friend who's a boat maven, and *she* has to think twice about which is which.

- *Boat*—In the sailing world, you really never use the term, although in old navy terms a boat is something carried on a ship.

- *Tender or launch*—These smaller craft are attached to or kept on board a ship and used to transport passengers and light cargo between shore and the ship. The two most popular types are a Zodiac, a heavy rubber inflatable raft with an outboard motor, and a Boston Whaler, a fiberglass or wooden launch. Sometimes Zodiac and Boston Whaler are used to refer to any number of smaller craft, much like the word Xerox has gone beyond being the name of a company, and come into the language as a verb that means, "to make a duplicate copy."

- *Port*—Left side of the vessel when you are facing the fore, or front part. Remember that port and left have the same number of letters.

- *Starboard*—The right side.

- *Midships*—The center of the ship, and the most stable area.

- *Aft*—The back part of the ship.

- *Galley*—The kitchen area, usually as big as a closet.

- *Salon*—As opposed to "saloon," where food and drinks are served.

- *Head*—The bathroom. The whole thing: john and shower, which might just be a shower head and a drain in the floor.

- *Mainsail* (*pronounced mains'l*)—Usually the largest sail.

- *Mizzen*—Usually the last sail to aft.

- *Jib*—A sail. There are three different kinds: the flying, inner, and outer jib.

- *Spinnaker*—The prettiest sail (usually bright-colored), which balloons out in front of the ship; used mostly in light wind conditions.

- *Sheet*—Another word for sail.

- *Line*—A rope, but for God's sake, don't call it that.

- *Heel*—To list or lean at an angle.

- *Below*—Anything below deck.

- *Coffeegrinder*—Large winches used to pull the lines in or out. (The lines hold the sails.)

- *Captain*—A ship is not a democracy; he is the sole head.

- *First officer*—The second in command.

- *Boatswain* (*pronounced "bosun"*)—He is in charge of the entire deck crew.

- *Foc'sle*—The crew's quarters. Off limits unless specifically invited.

- *Anchoring off*—Dropping anchor a fair distance from shore, usually because the water is deep enough for the size of the ship.

- *Come alongside*—Coming next to another craft, or coming alongside a pier, dock, or jetty for the purpose of taking on water, fuel, passengers, baggage, or anything impossible to move by launch.

- *Aground*—The captain will be purple, and the ship will be stationary—probably stuck on a sandbar.

- *Squall*—Rain clouds moving fast, usually in your direction.

- *Foul weather gear*—What you wear in a squall if you're on deck. Usually bright-colored, rubberized rain jackets, pants, and boots.

- *Ship to shore radio*—Several frequencies by which vessels at sea maintain communication to shore-based operations, and place and receive phone calls from all parts of the world (that is, if it's working and there isn't a mountain range in the way).

- *Fire stations*—Deck stations assigned according to cabin number in case of emergency.

- *Abandon ship*—Swim, or walk on water, but get off. She's sinking.

5.

Hotels

A VERY BRIEF HISTORY

A bare plot of land near a spring is a far cry from today's Hilton where each number on the telephone will put you in touch with a different hotel service. Gradually, those little plots of land where people on the trade routes into Asia stopped to rest were enclosed by walls and roofs to insure the traveler's comfort and safety. It is said that the information exchanged in these first "hotels" was the basis of the earliest recorded history.

Some of the words meaning "inn" or "hotel" reflect the development of transportation and the purpose of travel. Inns in Western Asia were known as *manzils,* which meant "the place where the traveler descends." Persia had Caravan Serai (later caravansary) or "House of the Caravans." During the pilgrimages to the Holy Land, monks in southern and eastern Europe provided lodging at their monasteries, many of which have now been converted into hotels. In France they were identified as "cabaret," "gargote," and "hôtellerie." Lodgings in Italy during the Middle Ages were called "locandas," and the income from those in northern Italy bolstered the Medici fortune. A friend of mine once explained that getting a hotel room in Italy was never a problem. "They have a chain that must be as big as Hilton, maybe bigger," he said. "No matter how small the town, they have an Albergo." We gently broke it to him that *albergo* means hotel in Italian.

The development of hotels was slower in countries where hospitality was a way of life. In ancient Greece, for instance, every traveler who knocked at the door of a residence was welcomed with compassion. It was believed only ill fortune took one far from home. No questions were asked until the guest had been entertained, for he was protected by Zeus Xenios, the guardian of the guest.

Hotels today could learn from this philosophy, especially in their treatment of women guests. Single women of all ages seem to engender a certain curiosity and suspicion although some hoteliers are beginning to address themselves to the particular needs of women. I once was invited to address the Hotel Executives Club of New York to suggest how to service the growing women's market. I mentioned obvious things like having enough of the right kind of hangers, hair dryers, a beauty salon open early (and late) enough to accommodate business women, good lighting in the bathroom, and, most important, a staff that would treat women as respected guests, not intruders.

Personally, I love hotels. This "condition" may stem from the days when I was "Eloise" at the hotel *across* the street from the Plaza, although I didn't throw water down the mail chute, or call room service with outlandish orders. My affection for hotels grew with memories of pink bougainvillea creeping in a grillwork window in Tunis, shutters opening up to a view of a harbor and ocher-colored roofs in the South of France, or cacti flowering in the New Mexico desert.

Or maybe it's because I think one of life's great luxuries is breakfast in bed. I love charming, side-street pensions where Madame offers oven-fresh croissants and steaming café au lait. Breakfast in grand style means the waiter silently sets a tray at your bedside with fresh orange juice, a basket of toast, blueberry muffins and brioche, coddled eggs in porcelain cups, and orange marmalade.

This chapter will try to lead you over to my weakness for hotel living. It's easy to fantasize about the romance of a hotel but the actual choice must be practical as well as soul-satisfying. The French reputedly pick hotels on the basis of the view, the tranquility, and the croissant, but you must consider location, price, reputation, safety, meal plan, and the variety of the hotel services—unless you're French.

HOW TO CHOOSE A HOTEL

Location

Some thought—and research—about what you want to see in a city can help choose where to stay. The research can be as simple as leafing through guidebooks and looking at a city map to decide—more or less—what areas and sights intrigue you. For example, if you like the chic bohemia of Paris' St. Germain district, with the funky shops, art galleries, bistros, etc., then a hotel on the Left Bank is the

most practical. You will always do more if your hotel is conveniently located and you reduce the frustration, expense, and time of taking local transport *everywhere*.

Even when a resort is the focal point of your activity, location is important. I stayed in a hotel in Sardinia that was a ten-minute drive from the main piazza where the shops, restaurants, and the port were located. I had to rent a car because the hotel didn't have shuttle service and, in retrospect, I would have been better off spending more on the hotel in town to avoid having to rent a car.

Location can mean conveniences, but it can also mean security, although problems exist in hotels with the most elaborate security systems: the twenty-four-hour guards, the mechanical precautions like closed circuit television and sonar alarms. What matters is that you *feel* you are relatively safe. Naturally the locations vary from city to city and the best sources of information are the tourist offices and your travel agent. Just remember that the tourist office isn't in business to tell you about crime and red-light districts, so you should point out that you are somewhat apprehensive about being on your own in an unfamiliar place.

Big vs. Small and Charming

Large hotels with their plethora of amenities should not be summarily dismissed for lack of "character." The lure may be an acupressure massage treatment, bilingual secretaries, or something as simple as air conditioning. On humid days, an air-conditioned closet has more appeal than a royal suite warm and moist enough to keep cigars fresh.

Large hotels are usually located near shopping areas, restaurants, and entertainment centers, but the in-house services themselves can be extensive: drugstores, bookstores, airline representatives, shops, and restaurants often make the hotel more like a mini-village. (The first service offered in a hotel was back in the tenth century when monks kept St. Bernard dogs to track down travelers lost in the Alpine snows.) Some of the best buys I found in India were at the hotel boutiques; the best tailors were at the major Hong Kong hotels.

One of the least utilized hotel privileges—particularly valuable for women—is the reciprocity arrangements to use the facilities of other hotels, beach clubs, tennis and riding clubs. Sport activities are convenient and casual ways of meeting people. I play tennis, so in resort areas I like to take a lesson from the pro, and then ask him to arrange a game, preferably with someone who lives in that city. It's another way to discover a city's secrets.

When I'm staying in a good hotel, I always go to the beauty shop, to eavesdrop on the local gossip and cross-examine the manicurist, masseuse, or hairdresser. They always hear their clients discuss what's going on in town. Conversation is easy because the formalities of meeting new people disappear. How proper can you be with a wet head and your hands in a bowl of cuticle lotion?

Most of us share the rather romantic belief that all small hotels have four-poster beds, stone fireplaces, and charm galore. Some *do*. Elsewhere, the personnel may not speak English (and you don't speak whatever-it-is), the night clerk is always on a break in the back room or resting his head on the reservation book, and the chambermaid's attitude can charitably be described as "casual." In sum, a small hotel can have the best and worst aspects of staying with your relatives.

Such establishments are often family-run pensions where the wife cooks for all the guests. In some European countries pensions are graded on a national system that assures certain standards. A general rule of thumb is to compare a first-class pension to a second-class hotel. In pensions you are expected to arrive for specific mealtimes, and you may eat around the family table. The owner might even ask how late you'll be coming in at night, an inquiry that usually reflects concern, not officiousness. It's common in small pensions to lock the door after a certain hour. Just find out if there's a night bell or a key.

One of the most colorful, slightly offbeat little hotels I've ever found was in the desert oasis of Taroudant, Morocco. The Hotel Taroudant had no front desk. You entered through the bar, a bright yellow room with a wooden bar the length of the room, barstools, and an obliging bartender who took requests for both drinks and rooms. At this hotel, like many small, off-track hostelries, you take the chance that no one speaks English. Morocco is a former French protectorate so a smattering of French will do. Failing that, it would still be fairly easy to communicate with simple gestures that you wanted a room for the night. I got a room on the second floor, with a small sink and two beds overlooking a garden overgrown like a Rousseau painting. The toilet (with a wooden seat) was at the end of the balcony in a small room with a screened-in window.

Breakfast featured freshly baked and toasted slices of a baguette, one of those long wands of French bread, with ample honey and jam and pots of tea, all served in the dining room that had a Scotch plaid carpet, and a TV that always seemed to be on. The grand total for room and breakfast was $7.00, an account one settled, of course, with the bartender.

Price

The custom for room rates in German inns during the Middle Ages was that departing guests put the amount of money they felt was appropriate for their lodging in a dish. The colonists in America set fixed tariffs as a response to the exploitation of the public by the English innkeeper. Today, of course, room rates are determined by a number of factors: the type, size, and location of both the hotel and the room. A larger room will cost more than a smaller one; a room on a high floor is more expensive than the same room on a lower floor. If one person occupies a room, regardless of the size or the number of beds, it's billed at a "single" rate. Two people pay a "double" rate. The single rate is slightly more than half the double rate because hotelmen figure they lose money when only one person occupies a room with two beds, not to mention that one eats and drinks less than two. In most hotels children can sleep on rollaway beds or cots for a small additional charge, and children under a certain age are free. (See the chapter "Traveling with Children.")

One way of saving money is to get a room without a bath, a setup more common outside the United States. The expression "without bath" usually means your room has a sink but the toilet and shower/bath are down the hall. In rural areas, the facilities may be unisex. I love "without" bath in countries where the general cleanliness allows it: Germany, Switzerland, Austria, Scandinavia, France, Italy, and England. Most big, older hotels have many rooms without private bath. One friend of mine still talks about a hotel in Vienna where the chambermaid drew the bath in a huge old-fashioned tub (with legs) and provided oversized towels, all for fifty cents. (See Bathrooms in the chapter "Etc.")

Whether or not meals are included also affects the price. In colonial times American inns offered a bed, food, and drink for one price —the origin of the term "American Plan" that today indicates all meals are included. It may be a result of this custom that the French word "hôtel," came to mean a place of lodging. It is said that the chefs in the "hôtels," or mansions, of France, fled the revolution, came to this country, and found jobs cooking in the tavern, except they kept referring to "tavern" as "hôtel."

Many resorts and vacation-oriented hotels offer the American plan. Modified American plan, or MAP, includes the room and two meals (usually breakfast and dinner). European plan, or EP, covers the room only. CP, or Continental plan, means the room comes with continental breakfast of rolls, bread, jam, and coffee.

WHAT'S WHAT

Every industry has its own jargon and hotels are no different. The terminology may be self-explanatory, but here is a quick reference:

- *Single room*—a room rented to one person. It may have one or two twin, or double beds, but usually the rate is based on single occupancy. (There were no single rooms in America until 1838. Prior to that, guests slept on the floor of a long room, alongside a dozen or so other people of both sexes, with feet turned toward the fireplace, and one's head resting on a rolled-up coat.)

- *Double room*—a room occupied by two people. It may have one or two beds, each big enough for two people, but the double-room rate is based on occupancy by two people.

- *Twin room*—furnished with two separate "twin" or single beds. Twins can accommodate two adults. Some have room for children's cots.

- *Suite*—a living room with one or more connecting bedrooms and baths, many with kitchen/bars. Most hotels have honeymoon suites (resorts in the Pocono Mountains are famous for heart-shaped bathtubs), VIP and presidential suites, which doesn't necessarily mean they're well decorated.

- *Junior suite*—a large room with a partition separating the bedroom furnishings from the living area.

- *Studio*—a one-room living area with one or two couches that convert into a bed.

- *Connecting rooms*—two or more rooms with private connecting doors to go from one room to another without going into the corridor.

- *Adjoining rooms*—two rooms next to one another without a connecting door between them.

MAKING RESERVATIONS

While it's possible to take an entire trip in high season without a single reservation, I advise you always to make reservations at least for the first night. How far you've traveled doesn't matter. First-night exhaustion is a combination of physical fatigue and emotional adjustment. If you're planning a trip gypsy-style, you may have to be flexible and willing to settle for some alternates to conventional hotels.

One summer in Corsica I was invited to stay with friends whose offer turned out to be standing room only, not the lodging I had had in mind for a vacation. I went to the main hotel to have a drink at the bar and started talking to a man who happened to be in real estate. He said he knew of a family who often rented out their extra room (with its own bath) and I gathered my belongings and moved in. I found a different, equally "by-chance" solution the time I was driving north from Naples with a girlfriend and we arrived about 9 P.M. in Assisi, the small town famous for St. Francis and for Giotto frescoes. The only sign of life was the local café and we asked the owner if he knew a place we could stay. (I spoke Italian, but a Berlitz phrase book would have sufficed.) Half an hour later we found ourselves in his sister's house.

Circumstances are not always so benign. I've slept in my car on several occasions when I couldn't get any kind of accommodations.

Tips for Making Reservations

1. If your travel agent makes the reservation, get a written confirmation (or voucher) that you can take with you. If possible, get the name of a specific person to contact at the hotel.

2. Many hotels or motels will make room reservations if you write or call ahead. If a deposit is necessary, ask under what circumstances you could get a full or partial refund.

3. Include the dates and the anticipated arrival time in your room request. For instance, "arriving Tuesday, July 5 and leaving the morning of Thursday, July 7." (See The Check-In and the Check-Out in this chapter.) If for some reason you're going to be late, call to advise, and request they hold the reservation. Always get the name of the person with whom you're speaking. Even if he/she goes on a break, or the shift changes, you'll have the name as a reference.

4. Many hotels will guarantee a reservation if you prepay the first night's lodgings: You agree to pay for the room even if you never show up. Just give your name, mailing address, and home phone number. Some establishments will make a reservation if you charge it to a major credit card.

5. Many hotels and motels in the United States have a toll-free reservations number that you can dial from anywhere in the country. Large chains like Hilton, Sheraton, Hyatt, and Holiday Inn can also make fast international reservations on computers. Some hotels have their own reservation systems, and some belong to the INRES, the Independent Reservation System. If you change travel plans, use the same toll-free number to cancel reservations.

6. Many first-class and deluxe hotels around the world are represented in the United States (principally in New York) by companies who book reservations. Ask the tourist office for the necessary information.

7. Airlines can make your hotel reservations. Many of the major airlines are hooked up with hotel chains—Hilton with TWA, Pan American with Intercontinental, United with Western International.

8. If you're going to any kind of major festival, book as far in advance as possible. It's possible that with rooms at a premium, the rates may be adjusted accordingly.

9. Don't overlook the free and efficient services of the national tourist offices. The personnel often come from the country (just make sure they've been back home recently) and are familiar with all types of accommodations. There are over twenty-five tourist offices in New York, as well as branch offices in major cities. In the countries themselves, the major cities (including airport and train stations) have tourist offices, and will have listings of smaller offices in towns and villages.

The Check-In and the Check-Out

When you arrive at your hotel, you'll first present your confirmation slip or voucher from the travel agent to the desk clerk. While he verifies your reservation, you will be asked to fill in a registration card with your name, address, telephone number, your company's address—if appropriate—and make of car and license number if you arrived by car. In some countries outside the United States you also have to leave your passport. This always makes me uneasy, even if it's a deluxe establishment. (In Czechoslovakia we even had to turn in our passports to the guard at a beer factory before we took the guided tour.) If you are at all apprehensive, make note of your passport number and date of expiration and keep it in your wallet. This number would facilitate more rapid issuance of a duplicate should that become necessary.

Check-in time is officially whenever you get there, although many hotels assume you're not coming if you haven't arrived by 6 P.M. If you reach the hotel before noon during a busy season it may be that the previous guests are still there. (Often I'll specify an early morning arrival.) The mandatory check-out time ranges from noon to three in the afternoon, so all you can do is wait, have a late breakfast or early lunch, or ask for another room until yours is ready. Ask about the check-out time. Is there an additional charge for overtime? Can you leave your bags at the front desk?

It's very easy to feel that the clerk is doing you an enormous favor just by handing you the room key. Do not fall into the trap! Your attitude affects how you're treated. I remind myself I am making a contract with the hotel and they are in the business of renting rooms, and I want to rent one. I always ask to see the room, just as a sommelier has you sample the wine. Inspect your room *before* the bags are taken up, otherwise there is a tendency to feel: "I'm here, it's too much trouble to move things around." It's important to be satisfied and feel you're being treated properly. After all, each client represents potential referral business, and no hotelier relishes bad word-of-mouth. I have rejected rooms in the nicest possible manner because:

1. They were next to the housekeeping quarters and I knew I'd be awakened by the endless chatter of the morning shift, the cleaning procedures, etc.

2. The view was great but so was the noise from the street below.

3. The discotheque was the floor below (or above) mine.

4. The restaurant in the garden was lovely for lunch but I didn't want to hear everyone's conversation when I wanted some peace and quiet.

HOW TO MAKE A HOTEL WORK FOR YOU

In my room I put out my own things, from pictures of friends, a cassette with my favorite music, to a vaseful of flowers or shampoo on the bathtub ledge. I also want the hotel environment to be as personal as possible, therefore the first order of business is to make myself known to the staff. Familiarity helps dissipate the anxiety of being a total stranger, particularly if I don't speak the language. It's comforting to know *someone* can find a good doctor or a good restaurant. The thumbnail sketches that follow will tell you who does what so you can benefit from the services that enrich your stay—or complain about their absence. The pronoun "he" is used to simplify the grammar, not to indicate there are no women on the job.

General manager—In large hotels he is in charge of the staff, with a resident manager (who often lives in the hotel) or assistant manager as the second in command. Smaller properties are often run by an owner-manager with one or more assistant managers reporting to him directly.

The front office manager—He oversees everything that goes on at the front desk. He may also inspect rooms to check upkeep and he usually handles guests' complaints. If you get nowhere with him, ask for the resident or assistant manager.

Front desk clerks—In addition to renting rooms, front desk clerks and other front office employees arrange and acknowledge advance room reservations made by computer, telephone, or mail. When you write for a reservation directly to the hotel, address your letter to this person. Front desk clerks occasionally act as cashiers or credit managers in approving checks and credit cards.

Bell captain and bellhops—The bell captain assigns work to bellhops who carry luggage, show you to the room, and may explain the finer points of your accommodations: how to use the air conditioner or heater; the curtains, the radio, the self-service bar (what you use is put on your bill); closet space; the telephones; the television.

The executive housekeeper—Call this person if the room is a disaster zone, if you step out of the shower and find no clean towels, if the bulb in the bathroom is so weak it seems to make the room darker. Housekeepers are in charge of all personnel in the housekeeping departments: maids; linen room and laundry workers; seamstresses; repair workers. (In Russia, the staff may include cobblers and tailors.) The maids keep the rooms clean and organized. They replenish supplies of linen, soap, facial tissue, stationery, laundry lists, the form that you hang on the doorknob for ordering breakfast the night before. In some hotels the maids will lay out your sleepwear and turn down the bed covers in the evening, or straighten up a disarray of cosmetics on the sink.

Valet service—The valet service deals with laundry, pressing, and dry cleaning. You generally have a laundry bag with a list (you fill it out) that you give the valet, or you can arrange for clothes to be picked up, pressed, dry-cleaned, and delivered back to the room the same day. In first class hotels, you can usually have things pressed and returned within an hour or two. I've had trousers mended and dresses shortened. Custom services cost more than taking things out yourself to the local laundry or dry cleaner.

Room service—This is my idea of heaven on earth. Most large hotels have a card in the room with the various room service menus, from breakfast to after-11 P.M. service. If there is no twenty-four-hour room service, I befriend the person on duty at night—even in the grandest hotels—so I can get a cup of tea when I come in late. It got so cozy at one Athens hotel that I'd walk in and as the night clerk handed me my key he'd say, "The usual?" Ten minutes later I'd have tea, an extra pot of water, honey, and a peach. If you are ordering at the rush hours (breakfast between seven-thirty and nine or dinner between seven-thirty and nine), ignore the promise "Right away, madame." Add a minimum twenty minutes to whatever they say. If you're going to the theater, have a plane to catch, or a meeting, notify room service well in advance. Be sure to check the prices. They can be outrageous. I once paid seventeen dollars for three tuna sandwiches.

Some deluxe hotels have staffed kitchens on each floor. I remember my parents always requested a particular floor at the Savoy Hotel in London because Charlie came from the old school of waiters who took pride in his work. He endeared himself to our family forever the time he was helping my father pack and came out into the living room holding the Waterpic. In a crisp Cockney accent he said, "And what should I do with your nosepick, sir?"

The concierge (or hall porter)—"I can't do everything, but I can do almost anything," said a concierge at London's Savoy Hotel. In my reading and travels, I've heard some unusual requests. The following achievements are absolutely true, and unembellished.

An audience with the Pope requires months of snipping endless red tape, but you've promised your daughter you'd get her wedding ring blessed, and you keep your promise thanks to the concierge; your pet leopard must be walked in the park; you lose your wallet, and before *you* know it, the police have halted your car on its way to the airport with wallet in hand; you need to borrow a diamond necklace; you want a pedigreed Yorkshire Terrier purchased in England and shipped to your husband as a surprise; you want a butler interviewed and sped along to you in two weeks; you want cassoulet shipped (in thermos bottles) from your favorite French restaurant to the movie set where you're shooting in Rome.

These are the extraordinary requests. The day-to-day functions of a concierge elude precise definition but his origins hint at the breadth of his responsibilities. The role of a concierge existed as early as the Middle Ages in France when châteaux owners had one very reliable servant who looked after everything. By the fourteenth century, this person had become so indispensable it is said reigning monarchs placed more trust in the concierge than anyone on their staff. Today the most common duties can range from dispensing the room keys, messages and mail, to answering questions p-a-t-i-e-n-t-l-y about restaurants, theater tickets, shopping, money exchange, and travel plans.

The concierge is a European tradition that is rarely found in American hotels. The network is extensive and formalized by Les Clefs d'Or—The Golden Keys—a fraternity (in this case an all-male club) whose influence is compared to the Mafia's. Each Clef d'Or member wears the insignia—two crossed golden keys—pinned to his lapel. The fraternity has an official textbook called *Le Hall,* specifying the personal requirements of a concierge, including "excellent hearing, equilibrium, keen observation, methodical reasoning, prudence, and, above all, patience." Thanks in part to the fraternity, a concierge in one hotel can book rooms (and get confirmation) at hotels in other cities, or simply pave the way for your arrival. Unknown to most guests, many hotels have cards that list a client's particular needs, from electric blankets to the number of pillows on the bed.

If you've requested nothing special during your stay, a smile of thanks will do, although some grateful guests have lavished concierges with small palaces or sports cars. A tip is appropriate if he has taken care of ordinary matters you would normally do yourself, like theater tickets, or plane reservations. In distinguished hotels the minimum tip should be about 7 to 10 percent of your daily room rate, maximum 15 percent, depending on how long you're there. I tip handsomely at the beginning of a stay, especially if I'm on business and/or don't know the city, to ensure special attention. But *you* must bring yourself to his attention.

The concierge can be particularly helpful for women. Let him be your advance man. You'll be treated better; not regarded with the raised eyebrow that often greets a woman alone. For instance, it's his business to know the maître d's at top restaurants. Ask him to make the reservations and explain that you're alone (if you are), to give you a nice corner table so you're not on display in the middle of the room. I once had to ask the concierge to be a "reprimanding" schoolmaster. At 2 A.M. in a deluxe hotel in London, I was on the phone talking to California. I finished the call and went down the narrow hall between the sitting room and the bathroom. When I got back, I noticed a white card had been slipped under my door. It was the business card of a barrister from Quebec. "Call or come visit room 603," he had written across the card. I immediately bolted the door. Should I call the front desk and complain? He hadn't actually "done anything" except invade my privacy. So with the door firmly bolted, and covers over my head, I fell asleep. The next morning, however, I told the story to the concierge. He promised to speak to the gentleman. I received a two-page handwritten letter of apology.

After giving the concierge miracle-worker status, I feel obliged to add a saddening postscript. Not all the newer ones are devoted to superb service. If you happen on the "old-timers," consider yourself lucky.

WHAT MAKES A HOTEL ABROAD DIFFERENT . . . SOMETIMES

Bidet—The word bidet means "little horse," from the French verb *bider,* to trot. The logic of the name, I assume, is that you "straddle" a bidet. It's a knee-high, relatively oval-shaped "sink" with hot and cold water that is principally used to bathe the genitals. They're also just the right height for soaking your feet if you sit in a chair. Bidets are also practical for doing laundry, or as a make-shift vase, for keeping flowers alive.

Room keys—Post offices in the United States will mail keys back to the hotel at no charge. In most hotels abroad you never even take the room key away with you, because it usually has the equivalent of a bowling ball on the end. Leave it at the reception desk. The only conceivable disadvantage is that the keys are in plain view in pigeonholes. It's obvious when you're not home.

Push-button lights on corridors—Even before energy conservation became a cause, many hotels tried to cut back on their electricity bills by installing light switches in the corridors that, when pressed, turned the lights on for a set number of seconds and then went off. God help you if you live at the far end of the hall. Just push the button and sprint.

Telephones—First of all, don't expect too much. I know first-class hotels where the entire switchboard has completely broken down. Secondly, if you think speaking or trying to speak a foreign language face to face poses a problem, wait till you get on the phone. Sometimes hotel operators hang up because they don't understand. If the success of your trip depends on contacting people by phone, there are several ways of trying to get better service. Identify yourself to the operator and explain you're expecting several important long-distance calls, preferably from overseas. The next day leave a tip ($5.00) in an envelope for the operator, thanking her (in advance) for her kind attention. If your calls are important, the few extra dollars are more than worth it. The one drawback to excessive telephoning is that calls made from your hotel room can cost anywhere from two to five times the normal rate.

Cafés in most European countries have public phones that require a token you purchase from the cashier. It is called a jeton in France, and a gettone in Italy. When you make long-distance calls, find out the local expression for "collect," take enough money (ask the hotel operator for the rates), or take a telephone credit card. To make overseas credit card calls to the United States, you must use an additional letter that's on your card. Make sure you know what it is. The local post office usually has public telephones. A clerk places the call and then tells you the amount due after you've completed the call. Most post offices close after 7 P.M.

"C" doesn't always mean cold—Hot and cold water faucets are often marked with a red and blue dot, and sometimes with "C" and "F." I once had a friend who logically deduced that her fleabag hotel had no hot water, and the letters stood for cold and freezing. In most Romance languages C stands for a variation on chaud, which means hot in French, and caldo which means hot in Italian. "F," freddo in Italian, and froid in French, means cold.

Shoes polished—It's a common sight to walk down a hotel corridor and see pairs of shoes (usually men's) outside each room. They are whisked away in the middle of the night, polished, and returned before you've had coffee. If your shoes are an unusual color, bring the polish and set it inside one of them so wine-color boots come back wine, not chestnut.

Eiderdowns and bolsters—Instead of ordinary, rectangular-shaped pillows, you'll often find round bolsters covered in sheeting that stretch the width of the bed. They're so fat that with your neck resting on the bolster, you're eye level with your toes. I can't sleep that way, so I ask the housekeeper for regular pillows, or, failing that, I roll up a towel in a pillow case. On the other hand, eiderdowns, or down-filled fluffy quilts, used instead of blankets, are marvelous. You'll find them in many Scandinavian and German hotels.

Floor and elevator numbering—The first floor is not the first floor. The second floor of the building is referred to as the first floor. If your room number is 101, you'd be on the second floor of the building. In France, rez-de-chaussée or RC means ground floor, or our first floor.

Room service—Waiters knock and let themselves in with their master key without waiting for your "Wait a minute," or "Come in, please." Knowing about this slightly annoying habit might spare you some embarrassing moments.

Chasseurs—The word chasseur in French means hunter. In deluxe hotels the chasseurs are often teenage boys who run errands, or bring up your mail on a silver tray. If you need chocolate-covered ants, aspirin, or theater tickets picked up, call the chasseur. (And tip the equivalent of $1–2.)

Washcloths—There are none. Bring your own.

HOTELS WITH LOCAL CHARACTER

One of the best methods of laying back the skin of a country is to find a hotel with such a degree of local character that it probably wouldn't exist anywhere else in the world. The food, the clientele, the setting, or the decor puts it in this special category. One of the most memorable nights I've spent was in a monastery compound on Lantao Island, a short ferry ride from Hong Kong. I watched the prayers, shared a vegetarian dinner with monks and nuns who were dressed in gray or brown robes, slept on a hard bed draped in mosquito netting, and was lulled to sleep by the whispered prayers of the nuns and the rattling of their beads. A night spent in a place like

Claridge's, where the staff dresses in morning coats, will give you the old-school English feeling.

There are castles-of-your-dreams in Ireland with salmon-smoking plants on the premises. At the other extreme are troglodyte dwellings in Tunisia that have been converted into modest lodgings. Troglodytes are cave dwellers who live in enormous pits in the ground, about thirty-five feet deep and thirty-five feet from side to side, where children play and the Berber women cook. The inside of the hole has different levels, punctuated by openings leading into little rooms where the Berbers sleep and store provisions.

Some "indigenous" hotels are newly built with respect to local architecture and customs. The designers often go into the bazaars to find decorative local crafts. The purple, magenta, and yellow color themes in the restaurant of the Bali Hyatt, for instance, are the colors of the Balinese temple sashes. Elaborately carved and painted wooden ceilings and beds with curtains sewn with gold thread fill rooms in a palace-turned-hotel in Morocco. In India masses of metal pots, which women balance on their heads to carry water, were tipped upside down to make a sculptured ceiling for a hotel coffee shop. The Middle East presents an interesting problem because the nomads lived in tents and never developed a craft industry. As one designer said, the style of the new hotels may one day be called "Petrol Modern."

Here are some examples of hotels with local character based on nothing but the fact that I've been there and loved them.

Tahiti and French Polynesia

Some names paint magical pictures. Tahiti is one of them, even though the capital of Papeete, which means the basket of waters, now has parking meters, shops that open by seven-thirty in the morning, and people riding motor scooters—even if they are wrapped in snappy pareo prints and have red ginger blossoms nestled behind one ear. The scene looks like a traffic jam of Gauguin models. The smaller islands of French Polynesia, with transporting names like Moorea, Bora Bora, and Huahine, fulfill the fantasy of an island paradise. Life there reflects the Tahitian phrase *aita peapea,* a sort of cheery "Who cares?" They are far apart in ambience from Papeete but only a short hop away by plane.

The traditional Tahitian home was the thatched-roofed *fare,* with separate living, sleeping, and cooking areas. The *fare* is the model for many hotels, especially on the outer islands. *Fares* are plunked on the beach, in gardens, or on stilts in the sea, where the water is often lit for night swimming, but beds aren't turned down with mints left on the pillow. In fact, in many places you take your lantern to dinner because the electricity goes off after a certain hour. Bathrooms are practically part of the garden, with greenery creeping over the edge of an outdoor shower.

All the hotels have the outdoor diversions one would expect: glass bottom boats, water skiing, snorkeling, spear fishing, deep-sea fishing and scuba diving. One of the most traditional aspects of life that many hotels offer is the *tamaaraa,* or feast, a word that refers to the meal and the special dances that follow.

Japan

Japanese-style hotels or inns are called *ryokans.* They have kept their character since the old samurai days, with the modern additions of running water and flush toilets. Ryokans may be the only type of accommodation available in small cities, hot spring spas and towns, but big-city chains like Hilton also have ryokan-style rooms. "Kan" means mansion, and the ryokan is built like a country house out of wood, stucco, and tile. Paper is used to cover the windows and to make the panels that separate the rooms, which in turn are decorated in traditional style with matted flooring called *tatami,* a low table with *aabuton,* or cushions, a *tokonoma,* or alcove with scroll painting, and a flower arrangement.

Your first potential embarrassment is forgetting to take off your shoes before stepping onto the polished wooden floors. You will be given a pair of slippers that are invariably too small—but never mind —and a *yukata,* or cotton kimono. (It is considered bad manners to ask you to register before you get in your room.) Most ryokans have rooms with private baths, but in some of the older inns, the facilities may be down the hall. A maid will bring you hot green tea and sweet cakes that symbolize a pleasant stay. Let the maid take care of everything. She will bring the meals, and make your bed, which doesn't have the usual mattress but is a slab of cotton or foam rubber, placed in the center of the floor, covered with a sheet and *futon,* or quilt.

Tradition decrees that guests should take a bath before dinner. The Japanese now understand a foreigner's modesty, so most ryokans have private Japanese baths. (If not, ask for one.) Your private bath will usually be a sunken, tiled tub, sometimes as large as a swimming pool. The idea of the Japanese bath is to soak, not to wash in the tub. First you soap up outside the tub, rinse yourself clean with warm water taken from the big tub in a wooden bucket, and then immerse yourself in the hot tub. This is the customary sequence of events, although some Japanese plunge right into the pool, soak themselves, emerge, sit on the little wooden stool, then soap and rinse, and get back into the pool.

The Japanese National Tourist Organization has a listing of ryokans. Some of the best inns belong to the Japan Ryokan Association. The price usually includes breakfast and dinner.

Kashmir

The Moghul emperors get credit for more than building the Taj Mahal. In the seventeenth century, they singled out this land of flowers and trees backstopped by the Himalayas as their summer retreat. Here are the famous Shalimar Gardens, and bazaars replete with carpets and sapphires. For an obscenely small amount of money (meals included) you can live in a houseboat on Lake Dal, with a kitchen boat attached and several servants. The houseboat life-style started in the 1800s when the British ordered native carpenters to make them floating bungalows. The houseboats often sport elaborate decor with crystal chandeliers and heavily carved wood furniture. You needn't budge from your perch to shop because a flotilla of *shikaras*—gondola-like water taxis—slide by selling flowers, silks, jewelry, fruit, even toothpaste. Eating out means boarding *doonga* boats, floating restaurants where you can make your way through a thirty-five-course meal.

England

It is reasonable to conclude that along with other civilized practices such as baths, the Romans get credit for the original English inn. In the century after Julius Caesar's invasion of Britain in 55 B.C., when the Romans introduced their superior road system, they understood that travelers needed a place to rest and refuel along these byways. The forebears of the inn included the *alehouse,* which provided ale and some kind of diversion, and the *tavern,* which dispensed wine, food, entertainment, and modest accommodations.

In the Middle Ages all these establishments had a large communal

room where jugglers, contortionists, acrobats, and strolling players performed. By the fifteenth and sixteenth centuries the grander inns were compounds with a courtyard, stables, and outbuildings with a privy (a small shed with a toilet inside), an oven house, a brewery, and a still room. Travelers in those days wrote about inns as a place where one could enjoy the comforts of home without the care. The redoubtable Dr. Samuel Johnson said, "There is nothing which has yet been conceived by man, by which so much happiness is produced, as a good tavern or inn."

Much of the appeal of an English inn today is its history. The list of "who slept here" is legion, from such personalities as Elizabeth I to Elizabeth Taylor. More importantly, the very same bed is still there because the decor has been unchanged for centuries. The hidden rooms and passages that secreted priests and contraband goods remain along with the timbered galleries, beamed bathrooms, four-poster beds, oak-paneled rooms. Some rooms have ghosts, and some of the ghosts even have names, like Mad Maude, the nun who was seduced and executed and is the in-residence apparition at Western

Manor Hotel. The amenities are sherry, sherry glasses, and sherry crackers instead of telephones and televisions. In many small towns, local life unfolds at the inn's public bar. (The word "pub" comes from public house, where ale is drunk and darts are thrown.) (See Cafés in the chapter, "Food.")

Many inns are converted old homes, with a dozen or so rooms (and often fewer baths) that vary enormously in style and comfort from one to another, so it helps to get a detailed description of the accommodations before booking. Weekending at an inn plays a big part in the London scene. A woman alone may be slightly uncomfortable in the potentially "for couples" atmosphere, but each inn has enough history to keep you well occupied.

The inn started as a necessity for the traveler; renting rooms in an English castle, or an earl's estate, began because the nobility needed money to keep and maintain their inherited property. Today you can be a guest of this breed, which was impeccably described in *Saturday Review* magazine: "A race of doddering great-uncles pickled in Victorian spirits. Perpetually declining, they hold down the crumbling fortress of Good Manners with the scanty armor of kid gloves and dinner jackets and elongated vowels. They're elaborately meticulous in a world where everything has gone slap-dash. They're paralyzed by propriety and devitalized by decency." You may find houses with butlers who will unpack your bags and harumph at your manners. You will probably dine with the titled owner. As one cynic once said, "You can have breakfast with them too, but that will cost extra."

ETIQUETTE FOR LIVING WITH THE BARONS AND THE EARLS

1. How much you are included in the private life of your host is really a matter of your mutual chemistry. Half the point in staying in a house is to find out about the life-style. Showing a genuine interest is usually the best way to open the door.

2. Avoid subjects conducive to controversy or dispute—like "Just how *do* you earn a living?" Safe topics might include hunting, horses, gardening, food and wine—and of course the "bloody" weather.

3. Always ask about the routine of the house—meals, tea, etc.

4. Inquire about the dress. Informal? Formal? Should you wear the equivalent of a long skirt, or will trousers do? It's fairly safe to assume you "dress" for cocktails and dinner.

The opposite of castle or estate living are places the English call "Bed and Breakfast," or simply "B and B." The British Tourist Authority has a listing of "B and B," which is usually an extra room in a private home that the owners rent to make a few extra pounds and meet new people. "B and B" is a marvelous way to sample "real" life, make travel more personal and affordable. (Breakfast is included in the room price.) Breakfasts can be wonderfully English— fried bread and grilled tomatoes and kippers, hot cross buns, marmalade made with Spanish oranges and brewed English breakfast tea. Theoretically, women should consider themselves lucky to get such a feast, for until the end of the eighteenth century, breakfast was considered a masculine meal. The men of the gentry class ate cold meats, pies, ales and claret; at ten o'clock the women ate cake and drank tea and hot chocolate.

France

The French have organized many of their castles and châteaux into an association called Relais de Campagne. The Relais has its own rating system that generally corresponds to deluxe, and four-star, but in general are less expensive than hotels in a comparable category. The choice of accommodations might be a *mas,* the word in the Provence region that means farmhouse, a chalet in the Savoie region, a former house of a king's mistress, or a "real" château like D'Artigny, where you might have to actually walk through a fireplace to get to the bathroom, or your room can well be tucked away on the floor above a three-star restaurant.

In French, *chez des amis* literally means "at home with friends." I leap at the chance to stay "at home" in a foreign country. Having lived with families in Italy and France, I know the difference between what you absorb staying in a conventional hotel, and by staying with a family. In the case of an outfit called Chez des Amis, French and American women have interviewed and selected families all over France, of different income levels, different occupations and interests who would like to share their home with Americans. You fill out an elaborate questionnaire to help Chez des Amis match you with the appropriate family. The queries can be as personal as, "Do you mind sharing a bathroom with the family?" to general questions about your interests in food, sports, or hobbies.

United States

Our history isn't long in terms of years, but some of its richest elements—the down-home, American hospitality, with a touch of the "old" country traditions—are available at a reasonable price if you stay in one of the many guesthouses, dude ranches, farms, or working dairy farms. You are giving up room service, and possibly your own bathroom, but you may be getting: huge farm breakfasts of homemade bread and jams, farm-grown eggs and bacon; the chance to see branding and calving, to camp out, river-raft; the chance to watch cows being milked, to take boat rides and hay rides, to hunt Indian artifacts, or pick berries in the woods to make blueberry pie, to share hot chili and corn muffins with wranglers at a rodeo; and, of course, there is the very personal exchange between your hosts and their family. Helpful sources for such vacations are: Country Vacations U.S.A., Adventure Guides, 36 East 57 Street, New York, N.Y. 10022, and the Tourist House Association of America's Guide to Guest Houses, Box 355A, Greentown, Pennsylvania 18426.

ALTERNATIVES TO HOTELS

You may pay less and get more atmosphere in the following alternatives to hotel living. Your choices range from university dorms and youth hostels to making someone else's home your castle (literally) or to a down-filled sleeping bag under nature's own ceiling.

1. *House swapping*—If you are going to spend your entire vacation wondering if the people are going to put your good china in the dishwasher, forget house swapping. But you may be missing a chance to live on an estate in South Carolina with its own twenty-seven-hole golf course, or an oceanfront villa in the Caribbean. House swapping is instant immersion into someone else's life that may result in life-long friendships with the neighbors or even the family themselves. Often there are bonuses like use of the car, the boat, the bicycle, or membership in sports clubs. Several home exchange clubs arrange house swapping. Generally they publish a directory that lists the houses and the facilities. (Ask your travel agent for specifics.) You can write directly to the owner. You can also list your house in the directory (with or without photograph) for a fee.

2. *House sitting*—Here you can live in splendid digs in the location of your choice with no taxes and few expenses. Essentially, you are taking care of a house while the owners are away. Usually this is a second, or vacation home, and the duties can be simply being there, or the upkeep of the garden, the grounds, and feeding the pets, etc. You must make sure you are willing to accept the responsibilities, and not just envision extensive side trips exploring the area. You can put an ad in the local paper saying "house sitter available." Offer references. You can also contact a local real estate agent who may know of homes, the local chamber of commerce for the names of agencies that handle house sitting arrangements, or write letters of inquiry to resort owners. Find out exactly what your duties are. Ask every question you can think of before you accept the position.

3. *Renting a condominium, apartment, or house*—You can rent anything from a simple one-bedroom apartment on Spain's Costa del Sol to a city hall turned into a house in France or a "barn" in Oxfordshire, England, with a batik-walled bathroom. Sometimes the houses come with servants. One of the largest companies specializing in such rentals is At Home Abroad, 136 East 57 Street, New York, N.Y. 10022, with over two thousand offerings. You can also contact the local tourist office of the country you are visiting, and a number of the international and Caribbean airlines may be able to suggest rental agents in their countries. Off-season prices are lower than "in season," just like the hotel business. (See the chapter, "Planning.")

Heed these guidelines if you decide to rent:

- Put yourself in the hands of a qualified agent whose judgment you trust and who has seen the property.
- Look at photographs. Make sure "sleeps six comfortably" doesn't mean two of the "beds" are cots in the hall.
- Ask if there's an adequate supply of hot water, heating, or air conditioning.
- Make sure the property is for your sole use. Some owners reserve a section for them or the caretaker, which is fine as long as it doesn't come as a surprise.

4. *University dorms*—Many universities in the United States, Canada, and other countries around the world offer campus accommodations to the general public during the summer and other school vacations; some colleges offer year-round lodging. The rates are

astonishingly low. The accommodations vary from single rooms to apartments, and often include access to the college's recreational and cultural activities, from lectures to a swimming pool. Cafeterias usually stay open year round.

5. *International Youth Hostels*—Don't be misled. Youth hostels are open to interested parties of all ages and located on all continents, in such unlikely dwellings as reconverted city jails, old mills, former railway stations, and churches. Many hostels have separate quarters for men and women, but some have family accommodations. The one drawback is the curfew that hostels sometimes impose, and, unlike a pension, where you can ask for a key and come home whenever you want, you must be back at the appointed time. You have to join American Youth Hostels for a minimal membership fee, which qualifies you for international travel. Write to the American Youth Hostels, National Campus, Delaplane, Va. 22025. Ask for the brochure and order form for the book listing the hostels.

Camping

People who know me as a city-dwelling adult find it amusing, even admirable, that at the age of nine I was at the stern of a canoe during a thunder-and-lightning storm on Lake Champlain; that I washed pots in a stream using pebbles mixed with sand to scrape off the charred layers left by the campfire; that I hiked a mile-high mountain in Maine with a thirty-five-pound backpack, although what I remember most about that trip was hearing over the radio that Marilyn Monroe had died.

My friends laugh about the time a park ranger said, "There's no need to pitch tents, it hasn't rained here in August in twelve years," and then it poured so heavily that twenty of us took shelter in the large outhouse and wrote a parody about our plight to the tune of "On Top of Old Smokey." Who could sleep under *those* circumstances?

I don't deny that today I build fires indoors with logs made of wax, sawdust, and a copper-based coloring agent guaranteed to burn at a heat content of some 85,000 BTUs. Nonetheless, I have wonderful memories of life outdoors from my eight years as an enthusiastic camper. I loved sudsing my hair and rinsing it squeaky clean under a waterfall; being awakened on a beach by the glow of the Northern Lights; the indelible aroma of bacon sizzling over an open fire; and s'mores, a contraction of "some more," a camper's delight as traditional as pumpkin pie on Thanksgiving, that is the unlikely combination of roasted marshmallows squished in between a graham cracker and a chocolate bar.

Intimacy with the wilderness is part of the American heritage that has been "rediscovered" with vigor. In examining the trend, *Newsweek* magazine said that "city dwellers see the wilds as a sort of drive-in therapy." Whatever the impetus, the gear, the terminology and style of the Great Outdoors has crept into everyday life. Even "Park Avenue people" talk about backpacking, L. L. Bean, four-wheel-drive Jeeps, white-water rafting, Outward Bound, cross-country skiing, canoeing, and camping out. There was such an increase in hikers at Yosemite, the park service reported, that some of the trails had to be paved to prevent erosion.

There seem to be two distinct outdoor types: the "Rugged Outdoorspersons" and the "Softies." This latter group usually invests in expensive recreational vehicles, more commonly known as RV's, that come with such "extras" as sunbathing roofs lined with artificial turfs. Softies park in campsites so urbanized there are outlets for cable television, and they scoot around the campsite in secondhand golf carts. So much for the Great Outdoors. Life for the Rugged has also become cushier (the challengers of Mount Everest notwithstanding). The Rugged Outdoorsperson might prefer the fragrance of pine and sleeping on the ground, but his expensive sleeping bag will be cushioned by a pad of closed-cell pads, the newest in mattresses for the woods.

What all this means is that the mechanics of camping have become easier—particularly important for women who might not have considered camping alone, with girlfriends, or children. The new equipment, from tents to clothing, allows you to minimize the chores and maximize outdoor pursuits. You can even become a trailpack gourmet with no effort with such items as freeze-dried beef stroganoff and freeze-dried chop suey.

My advice is to talk to people who run sporting goods stores about renting, rather than buying equipment for your first excursions, and to read the best books on the subject. I like Richard Langer's *The Joy of Camping: The Complete Four-Seasons, Five-Senses Practical Guide to Enjoying the Great Outdoors (Without Destroying It).* It was in these pages that I learned about gorp. Gorp? Gorp. Langer says that gorp is the traditional trail food combination of dried fruit, nuts, and/or chocolate. Now I ask you—is that a hardship?

6.
Traveling Companions

Relatively speaking, I've seen people select a cantaloupe with more care than they would give to choosing a traveling companion.

Consider fresh fruit at Sunday's brunch. What's in season? What's the right color, texture, size, the most refreshing? The fickle strawberry? The wanton apple? You head for the pyramids of fruit at your market; your eyes light upon a cantaloupe. You feel its weight in the palm of your hand, then slowly turn it, examining the contours, shifting it to the other hand, testing its ripeness by gentle squeezes with all five fingers. Is it too tender, too coarse, too pale? You notice the price: $2.50 a pound. *Outrageous,* but cantaloupe is so perfect. You lift one to your nose. Ah, the fragrance of summer. You waver, you ponder, you buy it.

At least that much consideration should be given to choosing the man or woman with whom you will take a trip. This chapter explains why—and suggests how. No matter whether you're with your college girlfriend or the man with whom you live, traveling together is an intimate experience. You share a physical intimacy simply because you're in the same room, not to mention the same bathroom. You develop an emotional intimacy because you turn to each other to answer myriad needs that at home would be met by a number of people. And most important, the defenses protecting your highs and lows, strengths and weaknesses are peeled away by the fact that it's tough to disguise yourself when you're virtually living together.

Pick a companion for any kind of trip—a weekend at the beach, a cruise, a whirlwind tour of Europe's capitals, a dig in the jungle—as methodically as you would plan anything in your life.

It's one thing to know your husband, from his favorite food to his wildest dream; another to think that you and your neighbor have all the world in common, a woman you don't know terribly well but like yourself is a recent divorcée at forty-two. It's obviously unrealistic and downright impossible to predict someone's behavior. You may even find that how someone *says* he behaves in a certain situation is sometimes quite different when put to the test. I know one man who always bragged about his equanimity in the face of hard-line customs officers or insolent waiters. It was very interesting the day he refused to order anything at all in a restaurant in France because of the waiter's Gallic frost. (He told me he had eaten a late lunch.)

What you *can* do is consider basic personality traits, and make an

educated guess about your compatibility. To this end, it's important to know as much as you can before you leave. You shouldn't have to get all the way to Paris to find out that you love art and your companion hates museums.

And remember, no one will change his basic character. A person with no curiosity about food at home will not make finding new eating experiences a personal "Holy Grail." A pessimist at home will probably be worse abroad. Do you want to travel with someone whose reaction to an unexpected rainstorm is, "Baloney, now the whole day is *ruined!*" and yours is, "I love to walk in the rain"?

THE PRETRIP SUMMIT CONFERENCE

Some things you learn by observation and intuition, others can be discovered through conversation. It will help to sit down before you go and discuss as many aspects of the trip as possible. During all the discussions, one rule should be canonically observed: Be honest with yourself and your partner. Don't say your college Spanish will get you by if you're too shy to say "Buenos dias" to anyone who speaks fluent Spanish.

The first question in determining whether you can travel together is obvious, but often overlooked. The *answer* should start, "I am going on this trip because . . ." Are you exhausted? Bored? Escaping? Adventuring? Do you share a common purpose—at least on the trip you're about to take? If you're in the mood to take five books, one bathing suit, and be in bed by ten, while your cohort wants to dance until dawn, you have some negotiating ahead.

There are nature lovers who savor climbing goat trails in the Pyrénées while you may consider window-shopping a prime outdoor activity. There are culture mavens who devour every museum, mosque, and tomb in town. For you, it's enough just knowing that you and the Mona Lisa are in the same town. There are night people who greet the day at three in the afternoon, but you get up so early that eleven in the morning is practically time for high tea. There is a way all this can be worked out, but it's more difficult once you're there and you each have a vested interest.

Do you have the same energy level? Will you be uncomfortable with someone who has to be on the move every minute of the day and night? Do you need to sit quietly, read, recharge, and de-

compress from the last three museums so your mind is clear and ready for a new batch of information? If someone else pushes you, you may react with aggression or petulance to things that under other circumstances wouldn't faze you.

Describe a perfect day and a perfect night. My mother, for instance, is a night person. When she was assigned to wake-up call as a camp counselor, she used to lean out the window from her bed, blow reveille on the bugle, and go back to sleep until noon. Her idea of a perfect day is sleeping until most people would be rounding off lunch with an espresso. At that point, she wants breakfast. In the late afternoon, she might go shopping, have a sandwich around six, take a stroll if she's by the sea, and go back to the hotel to relax until getting dressed for dinner. She is a superb storyteller and likes nothing better than chatting deep into the night. When we travel together, I stay up, although my perfect day begins about eight-thirty in the morning with steaming café au lait. When I travel with my mother I just program an afternoon nap so I don't miss the stories.

I like to get an early start, but not as early as my friend Carol, whose internal alarm clock rings at 6 A.M. We decided this would be her time to read, write letters, do her hair, etc. I have another close, dear friend whose wife likes to sleep late, especially on a trip. This makes him crazy. Instead of giving in to his reaction, he has breakfast and orders hers for an hour or so later. He goes out, her breakfast arrives, and when he comes back she's ready to begin and he hasn't wasted his morning. Being aware of someone's rhythms prevents rude surprises, disappointments, and allows you to make appropriate accommodations.

What kind of hotels do you like? I know people who actually seek out the ones where the paint is peeling, the maids never show up, and the name flashes in garish neon. I like atmosphere too, but not every day. If you share my views, you must clear up in advance that one or two nights in such conditions would be . . . interesting . . . but otherwise you prefer the kind of hotel that puts paper around the toilet certifying it's been sanitized.

Are your interests complementary? What kinds of people do you enjoy? Is one of you looking for bohemia and the other for tennis pros and vintage wine? How important is food? A joy? A boring necessity? Do you plan what you'd like for lunch when you're still eating breakfast? Can you tolerate his or her doing something on his own, or is it threatening? In reality, it's unimportant to agree on everything. Just avoid the temptation to prove your idea is better. The line is thin between gently prodding someone in a new direction because you want to share a passion, and pushing with the underlying message, "If you don't do this, you're going to ruin our trip."

I know one couple who went to Europe for the first time together, even though she had traveled her way through three passports and he had never left Minneapolis. Their "summit meeting" revealed that he wanted to see sporting events, and she wanted to see museums. She could easily have disparaged his activities, saying that "one goes to Europe for art and culture." But she accepted his preferences without grinding her teeth because he didn't spring them on her the first morning they awoke in Paris when she was all set to show him her favorite Monets. Instead, they regrouped happily over meals and long walks. He even went to a few museums.

What kind of organization or planning will make everyone the most comfortable? Who is responsible for making the various arrangements for hotels and transportation, restaurant reservations, et al. There are two general types of travelers: the Itinerary Traveler and the Itinerant Traveler.

It's highly unlikely that the Itinerary Traveler will decide at noon to board a plane at two that same afternoon for a place where he has neither reservations nor friends. He needs plans for the trip typed in triplicate with such predictable information as flight numbers, names of hotels and restaurants. The Itinerant thrives on the serendipity of travel: the chance meeting or the missed plane that translates as a new opportunity; the spontaneous combustion of people who make friends at the hotel bar and decide to go off together.

Most of us fall somewhere in between. I like to be flexible enough to change plans on the recommendation of someone I meet along the way, but in mid-July in the South of France, I would prefer to know I had a bed in my name.

How do you feel about money? Are you each paying your own way? Does one of you have more than the other? Are you the kind of person who must count pennies, or are you willing to split restaurant bills and figure that the few dollars' difference each time will eventually even out.

The two most important considerations are the amount you can afford to spend for the trip, and how you agree to spend it. It may be that you want to splurge on the luxury of a Ritz Hotel for one or two nights and balance the budget by eating cheaply. Your companion may prefer the exact opposite. How you resolve such a question is almost less important than the fact that you discuss it.

In any case you should:

1. Have a general idea of what things cost so that a forty-dollar dinner bill isn't a shock. (If in doubt, ask when making reservations.)

2. Not borrow from each other.

3. Consider money spent on shopping your own business.

THE QUIRK LIST

Everybody has peccadilloes. They can be terribly funny, or incredibly irritating. No matter which, it's always a good idea to know what you're up against. Each of you should make two lists: the first with all the things that drive you crazy, the second with your own habits and needs. If you don't actually write them down, then at least mention them in passing—reliably enlightening and always good for a few laughs.

Here is my personal, unedited list. Some of my quirks are reasonable, others are wildly illogical, a few would stop the Boy Scouts from ever considering me a suitable Den Mother.

I'm not suggesting that any one of them applies to you, but I offer them to show that quirks can be small, insignificant and seemingly unimportant, and that, like the pea under the princess' mattress, they can also be very disturbing. Being aware quirks exist is important to your own enjoyment and the enjoyment of your traveling companion.

1. I usually eat everything with my fingers, with the obvious exception of ice cream, soups, and things of a similar texture.

2. I've got to have breakfast. I don't need croissants and grapefruit marmalade served on bone china painted with dark pink ribbons, served on a black lacquer tray. I'm not fussy about *where* I eat, or *what* I eat. It just has to be *very* soon after I wake up.

As it happens, this particular quirk has resulted in some interesting experiences. I've had Germany's traditional breakfast of roast beef and assorted cheese (although I feel I'm eating yesterday's buffet lunch); *son jok gow yuk,* beef roll and bean curd, in Hong Kong; beignets (fritters) and café au lait in the French Market in New Orleans; hot cross buns, porridge, kippers, and eggs in England (where else?). Somerset Maugham once observed that the best way to eat well in England is to have breakfast three times a day. I'm not *that* peculiar.

3. I like to sleep in the bed near the phone.

4. I don't smoke. I don't mind sitting in the smoking section of airplanes because the smoke drifts to all corners anyway. I do mind: the odor of cigarettes left in an ashtray overnight; ashes in the sink;

cigarette butts in an unflushed john. Yet I always carry a pack of cigarettes in my bag when I travel with a smoker. It's purely selfish. I
don't want to suffer when someone invariably runs out at some un-
godly hour, and we disrupt our lives looking for nicotine in hotels,
drugstores or an all-night grocer's.

5. "You can sleep at home," or "Why did we come all this way if
you're not going to look at the . . ." Familiar? These phrases can
make you feel sufficiently guilty to do whatever is in question, and
should be eliminated from everyone's traveling vocabulary.

6. Please clean the bathroom sink, tub, and shower after shaving,
brushing hair, etc.

7. I travel light. It's just easier. I don't mind wearing the same
outfit with a different shirt five days in a row. I do mind someone

who spends an excessive period of time deciding what to wear, what not to wear, or brings clothes that always need pressing or dry cleaning. And when porters aren't available to carry the excess, either my back or my patience suffers.

8. It's important not to impose food habits on another person, whether it's a comment about the fourth order of french fries, or a reprimand like "How can you be in Japan and not eat raw fish?" If you're not on the same eating wavelength, live and let live. You're a traveling companion, not a missionary.

9. Many people feel that last-minute arrivals have a certain panache. The tension created by being late is also a fail-safe antidote for boredom. I would rather arrive at an airport two hours early and sit, rather than waste my energy being nervous that I may miss the plane. There are clearly two camps. The Chronically Late, who truly believe that if you're invited for seven-thirty, you're on time if you leave *your* house at seven-thirty (even if you have an hour's drive ahead of you). And the On-Time freaks like me. Sometimes I have no choice but to adjust. I add fifteen minutes to whatever time we agree to do anything. I shower last. I set the clock ahead.

10. I am a moderately neat person, although what I've worn for the past three days is probably piled on a chair. At least it's in one place. Hotel living is different. One pin out of place creates an imbalance, so I make an effort to use the closet instead of the chair and the bureau drawers instead of the desk top. The place looks better, but I can't find a thing.

All the discussions in the world won't prevent minor skirmishes—or even outright war. A fight en route is not like one at home where you can make a dramatic exit, and lick your wounds. It can be rather sobering to storm out of a hotel room at 3 A.M. with no place to go.

Unexpressed anger has the same property as a sauce reducing over a low flame: it gets more and more concentrated. Under the guise of not wanting to "ruin your trip" silence may do more damage. Just make sure you pick your fights in hotels with comfortable lobbies.

Traveling with someone means living together. The main difference is that the perils of cohabitation become more pronounced because you don't have the buffer of a daily routine or friends back home.

This takes on still another dimension when the demands, compromises, entreaties, and concessions of traveling are colored by an emotional relationship with a male companion. And I mean an intimate relationship, not platonic friendship.

TRAVELING WITH A MAN

Few ideas reek with as many romantic notions as traveling with a man. We all want to believe the ads that show tanned couples with perfect teeth smiling at each other. The implicit message is: "You too can find happiness when you visit . . ." Hollywood hasn't helped much, either, by leaving us the legacy that love overpowers fatigue and starvation. While plots have gotten slightly more realistic, the wish for fairy-tale romance remains. Real life isn't like that, but it must exist *somewhere*. And the best candidate for that "somewhere" seems to be a vacation.

Romance is at the core of a vacation for two. The trip is a panacea for everything that ails a relationship, with the combined healing powers of penicillin and Oral Roberts. Everything will sort itself out once you get under a coconut palm, or an eiderdown quilt on a big brass bed. Sometimes it does.

You just have to rein in overdeveloped expectations, and honeymoon fantasies. A lively imagination is priceless, but it helps to remember that the realities of travel—fatigue, disorientation—may sometimes interfere. And you may have neglected to give him your script.

Despite the women's movement, there is an expectation that stems from centuries of conditioning: a woman still dreams of being in love with a strong man who takes care of everything. She might subconsciously shift the responsibility of the trip to him by simply handing him the passports and plane tickets or, in the unfair extreme, expect him to create her good time. *While the purpose of going together is to augment each other's pleasures, it's essential that you be able to have a good time on your own as well.* This will help you handle the very real problem of too much togetherness. You are not joined irrevocably at the hip; sharing also means recounting experiences you've had by yourself. Private time at home is built in by involvements with a career, friends, even separate homes. On a trip, the need to be alone somehow seems unacceptable or threatening.

A desire to poke through a flea market at your own pace or to collect your thoughts in your room without so much as the silent presence of another person need not suggest incompatibility or rejection.

To minimize the emotional sting in expressing the need to be alone, I try to avoid sentences that begin: "You're always so impatient when we go shopping," or "You're *impossible* in museums." It's better to put the issue in a practical, commonsense framework. "We both know shopping (substitute whatever is appropriate) isn't your favorite activity, so why don't I wander around by myself and meet you later for a cappuccino?"

You are being honest and considerate, taking care of your own needs, avoiding a potentially tense situation, and at the same time saying, "We'll share something else later." There are also times when you'd just like to relax by yourself and your friend doesn't feel like going down to the café to write postcards. Assuming that most of us can't afford the sprawl of a Presidential Suite, use the terrace or the bathroom as another space. The bathroom works best when you have a tub and you can immerse yourself in a bubble bath for an hour.

A trip will usually magnify your role in the relationship. Are you the idea person, the planner, the adventurer, the nester, the Indian, the Chief? The importance of who does what may depend solely on your view of male and female roles in general. Which one of you drives or talks to the waiter could have larger implications. You may have divided the responsibilities very well at home, but a trip can bring up a few "unassigned" areas that affect the balance of power.

Before your trip to France, for instance, did it matter that your French is fluent and he only knows things like *crêpes Suzette?* It's often debilitating to be unable to communicate, especially when you think that getting anything done depends on it. I've known men who need to take charge so badly that they react to their partner's superior skill with hostility rather than appreciation. A male friend of mine once described the feeling as a combination of being alienated, afraid, and impotent. It's possible you're on sensitive ground when you're the linguist. I try to ease the feeling of dependence it creates by making my taking care of certain things a luxury, not an affront.

A subtle power struggle can also reside in the choice of who's in charge. The healthiest attitude is that it really doesn't matter, but you must know your companion well enough to pick up the small distress signals. For example: When the response to your suggestion is "Whatever you want, dear," in a patronizing tone of voice, there's trouble ahead. Watch it when something you've planned doesn't work out and he says disgustedly to no one in particular, "Whose bright idea was this, anyway?"

The subject of money and who pays for what is so personal, so fraught with psychological nooks and crannies, that suggesting any kind of formula would be irrelevant. At best, you should consider some points that color the issue. Most men have been programmed by society and their mothers to be the good provider. How ingrained the training has been will affect his attitude about your earning power, and whether it matters that you make more than he does, and how he feels about your financial contributions. I've found that it's the *exceptional* man over twenty-five who can accept a woman paying her own way without feeling slightly, if not fundamentally, emasculated.

If you are living together or married, there has certainly been *some* discussion about finances that would apply to a trip. It is sometimes more difficult for women who *feel* they have no leverage because their contributions are made in nonfinancial terms, like raising the children. In fact, I know many women who have gone back to work so money would give them a voice, or the freedom to go off on their own.

This doesn't mean that it's distasteful or antisocial for the man to pick up the tab. There are some women who'd have it no other way and, what's more, manage to bring out the urge in men to give them diamonds at breakfast. It is an art to receive graciously, and a skill to know when turning something down robs the other person of the pleasure of giving. This works both ways, but only a very secure man can accept such gifts. It's been difficult enough getting men to accept as a matter of course a business lunch paid for by a woman.

Whatever the arrangements for your trip, never leave home without your credit card, traveler's checks, and return ticket. Having them will fortify your own sense of independence and your willingness to suggest and reject ideas on an equal basis and, if need be, to go your own way. There is dignity and strength in knowing you can rely on yourself, even if you never need to.

The Tasteful Hotel Check-In

There's no problem if you're *really* married; you only feel uncomfortable (possibly) checking in when you're not. Actually, the hotel's concern is less moral than it is the fear that you'll behave unseemingly. So don't neck wildly at the front desk, or carry three vodka bottles in plain view. Dress well, stand up straight. Remember you're paying, and not being taken in as a favor to your mother.

In America, our Puritan heritage shows. Somehow it's more congenial if you check in as Mr. and Mrs. If you are terribly nervous, and can afford it, take two separate rooms. *Whatever you do, put the same name on your luggage that you use for the check-in. It helps in retrieving lost baggage . . .*

In Europe you (often) have to hand in your passports, so a Mr. and Mrs. registration is not practical. If need be I've said my legal papers are all in my professional name, or that I was just married. Be firm, and steamroll any objection with charm, not a raised voice. And in Europe, thank goodness, hoteliers are conditioned to trysts. One concierge told me that a man stayed at his hotel with his mistress and came back a week later with his wife. The concierge just had to be careful not to say, "How nice to see you again," or "The same room with the canopy bed and sunken tub you had last week, sir?"

Your Husband or the Equivalent

You have the comfort of knowing each other so very, very well. By this time you can capitalize on each other's strengths and minimize the weaknesses. He snores, so you take earplugs. You always lose your sunglasses, so he packs an extra pair in his suitcase. He can track down the quintessential french fry or the perfect sorbet; you'll find the best deal on a rent-a-car, or a chauffeured car that's even cheaper.

This trip together is not to discover one another, but to enjoy, and perhaps rediscover, those things that brought you together and to find new, mutual interests. It may even be the time to create a few "romantic" situations. Let him get dressed first; you meet him in the bar looking terrific. Order breakfast in bed, but do it the night before.

You know each other's background and share a personal history together that adds meaning to events, places, and observations. As my friend June says, "When we're in Italy I point out the best-looking women, and my husband leads me to the best *linguine alle vongole.*"

The New Acquaintance

You may have shared only one evening of candlelight and dawn, but you can tell going away together would be wonderful. You have so much in common. You both drink campari with lime, not lemon, eat salad with your fingers (and order roquefort dressing on the side), and he thinks women who work are a turn-on. Over freshly squeezed orange juice at his place the next morning, you plan the interlude, and you rush out to buy snug little T-shirts, robes slit up the side, and an extra bottle of the perfume he admired.

Since there's everything to unearth about one another, why go to a place with distractions like culture? Islands or self-contained resorts have all the essentials. Honeymoon-type hotels with heart-shaped bathtubs are good too. You are geared to do everything right; to please, charm, seduce, and entertain each other. You even keep your makeup neatly arranged. There's an energy to communicate constantly; this is the time to talk about life and religion, why your previous relationships have ended. You're at the stage when you haven't found anything wrong. The fact he spends an hour in the bathroom morning and night is still wonderful because he's doing it for you. The fact he writes his mother a postcard every day is "thoughtful, caring, even admirable." You're still thinking it indicates a healthy attitude about women. Then one morning you wake up and see this total stranger lying next to you. You feel trapped instead of secure.

It's definitely a gamble to go away with someone you don't know well. It can either be stupendous or horrific. Unfortunately, there is no guarantee. The best you can do is be as realisitic as your emotions and enthusiasm permit, and recognize the behavior patterns of infatuation. And one more thing. An island isn't *necessarily* the most desirable spot. You may need all the diversions you can get.

Someone Else's Husband and Other Variations

Remember the childhood pleasures of getting away with something? Take a minute and think back to the devilish things you did as a half-pint: slyly pocketing your sixth, still warm, chocolate chip cookie or playing possum after lights out, with a flashlight and comic book hidden under the pillow. These are some of the same emotions and pleasures you feel when you go away with someone who society says (with a wink) is off limits. We've all done it once, or at least considered it seriously. Alas, the commandment about adultery somehow self-destructs at the bedroom door.

The traditional situation has been the single woman involved with someone else's husband. Today it is just as likely that the woman will also be married, or will be the married half. You must accept the humor and intrigue of it all: telegrams signed in code names; a special post office box; hang-up calls on your phone just before and after the trip. You don't have to be a psychologist to know the danger is half the appeal. *But should the thought, "Is it all worth it?" cross your mind, you'd better reconsider the trip—and maybe the whole relationship.*

I don't mean to say that being highly neurotic isn't normal. It is. The pattern goes something like this: the better the sex, the more the guilt; the more the guilt, the more neurotic and paranoid you get. Anyone who looks at the two of you with the slightest bit of interest is a detective. I once flew with a man from Los Angeles to New York who said to me that if we were having an affair, he would never *dream* of flying on the same plane. Some people not only have guilt, they manufacture it.

The tricky part is not so much in choosing where to go, but in not leaving a trail. Remember that some people *want* to be found out to substantiate their guilt feelings, or to be rapped on the knuckles by the "wife-mother." You can expect a few gymnastics just to be together. One man I know said he told his wife he was going on a hunting trip to some isolated spot in Canada where you're dropped in by seaplane and remain incommunicado until you're picked up. He arrived at the airport with a duffle bag full of shooting gear which he promptly checked into a locker, and retrieved on his way home. Actually, he was going sailing in the Caribbean. On another occasion, he left all his belongings in a hotel room in Chicago where he was on a business trip, flew to meet his "friend" for the day in Detroit. Detroit?! Remember, being together is all that counts.

If you're set on going on "a Detroit," here are some points to keep in mind:

1. Instruct your answering service to say you're in town and will be checking in shortly. Better still, that you'll be calling in an hour.

2. Never register in the same hotel using your own name unless you have a damned good reason. Is it sheer coincidence you're both in Anchorage? There are minor problems if you use a phony name; what is your home address when you register; your identification, etc. Mr. and Mrs., using his name, is sometimes safe, unless the party is hot on your trail. Keep in mind you can be reached almost anywhere in the world by phone.

3. Never answer the phone if the room is registered in his name.

4. Avoid credit card calls. The card shows the area where it's issued, and the telephone company will often verify charges.

5. Don't use personal checks or credit cards. Pay with cash.

6. Never go to the house in the country. People in the area know you/him. And it might be just the weekend the kids/neighbors turn up as a surprise.

7. Potential clues: cocktail napkins, or slips of paper with your name (or his) written on it twenty times; tickets and receipts for anything; late-afternoon meetings on the days when offices close at noon, like Christmas Eve; fuzz from your carpet imbedded in his socks; appointments on your calendar that can be checked, or entire days marked with a big "X"; a large withdrawal from a joint account; hotel room keys; new pieces of jewelry; brochures; saying, "Oh, I was just there," in a crowd of people when your spouse can overhear; suddenly looking put together *all* the time; getting dreamy-eyed while you're making hamburgers or figuring out your company's profit and loss statement.

8. Is it worth it? Personally, I'd rather have another chocolate chip cookie.

OTHER WOMEN

While I champion the notion of women traveling alone, a trip with one or several women has substantial, if different, rewards. In recent years women have found emotional satisfaction and mutual support from one another's friendship. An unspoken bond exists from having lived with the same basic set of hopes, fears, joys, and disappointments. It's almost like being the same religion. Small things are understood without translation: why getting a two-hour hot oil treatment for your hair is worthwhile when all of Paris is at your feet; why a hotel room just doesn't "feel" right, or the need to make it a home, not a transit area, even if it involves moving furniture, buying flowers, or changing rooms. There's no need to explain the larger issues: why a mother has to get back to check on the children; why a woman is afraid to travel alone.

A Twosome

You have the same interests, the same two weeks free, you're old friends who never have enough time together, you want to share expenses, and the thought of eating dinner alone pushes you over the edge, so you decide to pair up. A partner is particularly reassuring for a trip that may be your first without a husband or friend because you are recently divorced or widowed, or you have your own money to spend. You'll probably find yourself thinking, *"He* used to do all this," but you manage, and better than you expected.

Two is a comfortable number from the practical point of hotel rooms or plane and train seats. With two of you, the fact that the taxi driver doesn't speak English can become almost humorous. You share responsibilities and disappointments and have the protection of each other's company. The flip side is that the safety of another person may reduce the chance of self-discovery. You won't be faced with dealing with your aloneness or with learning to appreciate a sunset or a temple all by yourself. Another woman can also limit the opportunities for meeting new people. You tend to talk with one another at dinner, while shopping, or sightseeing. People *feel* that you're not available. A man on the scene can bring up a whole series of problems.

More Than One Woman

I genuinely like women, but traveling with more than one often reminds me of some of the worst aspects of a quilting bee. However, you can recapture the experience of a girls school's junior year abroad when you're guided by a fearless spirit of adventure and insatiable curiosity. There is a warmth and camaraderie, and *someone* will always go to one more gargoyle, dance all night or get up at 5 A.M. to see the sunrise or the fishermen bring in their catch. You have more pairs of eyes, you can order more dishes to taste, and you can listen to a conversation rather than participate. But as part of a group, you are even more insulated from other people and if you get invitations or have friends, it's awkward to ask if you can include the whole troupe.

A word of caution if you're a threesome: one person can easily be left out, or intentionally excluded. It's tempting for two of you to gossip about her while she's in the bathroom. You'll intensify rather than alleviate the feeling. I was traveling in France with two girls I had met in a painting class in Provence. Elaine and I hit it off immediately, but we knew Cynthia was a "princess." We checked into a hotel where the only room available had one double bed and a single. Without discussing it, we knew that unless she got the single, she'd spend the next day telling us how badly she slept.

She was also afraid that even inhaling in France would add pounds so she ordered "fish, broiled dry" at every meal and gave us a calorie count for everything we ate, accompanied by a continuing monologue about the joys of the summer when she had rented a house in St. Tropez. She couldn't understand that we weren't *dying* to make a pilgrimage.

Men—When Traveling with Other Women

Conflicts over men can, and have, brought nations to war and, on a more personal level, can permanently scar or dissolve the most impregnable friendship. Competition may not be an issue if she loves the tall, dark, and handsome ones and you like Scandinavians. The problem is more likely to be how to integrate the man one of you has met into your lives. It's tempting to go to his family restaurant where Mama still makes the world's best *gnocchi verdi;* to spend a weekend in the country when the apple trees are in bloom; or to go to Istan-

bul. Whatever. You are faced with the realization of your fantasy. You have met a man, either an American living abroad or a local, who will introduce you to his way of life. *Now* you'll have espresso for breakfast because it's done that way, not because it's an affectation.

Suddenly you wish you had been traveling alone. But you're not, and you must weigh the responsibility to your original companion. You may have agreed in the pretrip discussion that either of you would be free to go off into the night, for one night, or the remainder of the trip, without recrimination. Alternatively, you might have established ground rules that you two are sticking together no matter what. If Vladimir/Pierre/Mario/Mohammed/Chauncy/Duleep is irresistible, you have several options. You ask if he has a friend. It's not incumbent on your companion, however, to find him as enchanting as you find Vladimir. It's easy, but not entirely honorable, to pressure her into a foursome to assuage your guilt. On the other hand you may be fortunate because she's delighted to have an evening by herself. Just don't expect her to sleep on the equivalent of the living-room couch. You and Vladimir either go to his place, or share the cost of a hotel room.

And if it doesn't work out, consider the encounter as a piece of jewelry you wanted but couldn't really afford. The moment you get five paces out of the shop the yearning subsides, and eventually disappears.

ANOTHER COUPLE

Absolute compatibility between two people, even clones, is highly improbable. Imagine, then, the compatibility between two *couples*. What complicates matters is that you are actually dealing with several independent but simultaneous relationships that affect the group's *ultimate* compatibility: the relationship of each individual to one another; of one couple to another; and the relationship *within* each couple. Wait! It's not irretrievably complex, but arranging the situation so that during the trip you can honestly say, "Boy, I'm delighted they came along," may require an extra shot of awareness, consideration, flexibility, and straightforward communication.

Since people can't reliably be programmed like a computer, there's no unimpeachable method of deciding whether or not the pairing will work. But you can begin to evaluate the *probabilities* by asking yourself, and the couple in question, some basics that apply to any situation involving someone else's ideas, needs, expectations, quirks, and personal habits. Why are you taking this trip? Do you enjoy each other's company? Do you share enough interests? How much money can you spend, and how do you want to spend it? Beyond these practical points, how well do you know the other couple?

In an effort to be as realistic as possible, I would add the following rider to any conclusion: unless you have lived with, or traveled together before, and consequently have "in-the-field" evidence, be prepared for a few surprises. The reactions you get in your living room may be much different than when you're actually faced with no hotel rooms, or an inedible meal.

If it works out, you will have four people contributing to make everyone's time richer, happier, and more fun. The combinations of people doing things together is greater. If you abhor gregarious breakfasts in the dining room and want coffee in the room by yourself, and your friend *loves* breakfast in the dining room, the problem may be painlessly resolved because the other couple loves the dining room too. There may be certain things men will enjoy doing themselves, as will the women. To help ensure that your particular experience will have the best, not the worst, aspects of traveling with another couple, here are some guideposts, gentle warnings, and axioms. You might be able to head off trouble at the pass.

The Leaners—These are the people who can't do anything without asking what you're doing, which is okay, unless it's because they want you to make all their decisions—and then hold you responsible.

The Competitors—Did you ever go shopping with someone who repeatedly said, "You find all the *good* things"? Her insecurity and competitiveness is showing, and the best you can do is be generous and kind. Don't rise to the bait.

The Whiners—You've gotten three blocks from the hotel, and someone's foot hurts. Don't let guilt stop you. You're not a baby-sitter. Suggest they go back to the hotel and meet you later.

Never get in the middle of the life struggle of another couple. You might find yourself in the position of interpreting one to the other for the entire trip. Their marital backwaters should be off limits. Clearly, you should never travel with a couple who is counting on the trip to patch up their differences.

If the other couple recommends a restaurant and the food is truly despicable, don't hold it over their heads for the rest of the trip. It proves nothing, and creates tension. Besides, you may find yourself in the same position. This attitude goes for other situations: side trips, shops, bars, etc.

If you have money to spend, remember the other couple may not have a comparable amount. It's embarrassing, humiliating, and unkind ever to put someone in the position of either spending more than he can afford or having to say, "I can't afford that." Your pre-trip discussion should set money matters straight. Avoid borrowing from each other.

Neither couple should feel obliged to spend every waking moment together. But out of consideration, try to give some notice. In other words, don't wait till eight o'clock, when you're supposed to meet in the lobby for dinner, to say, "Gee, we'd rather have room service."

Carry your own tickets, hotel or touring vouchers. No one should be put in the role of group leader.

Consider how you feel about the following possibilities:

1. You've been married for ages. They barely know each other.

2. He wants them to come because the other guy plays tennis, but you can't stand her.

3. You've been having your problems, and they are still billing and cooing.

4. You're madly attracted to him, and have arranged the trip for that express reason. Now be honest.

5. They swing and you don't.

If you don't genuinely *like* the other people, for heaven's sake, don't go! This is not an endurance contest. This is your vacation we're talking about.

WHO IS MOMMY? TAKING YOUR MOTHER ON A TRIP

When was the last time you spent more than three days and nights in a row with your mother? I don't mean with the whole family at your house, or hers, during the holidays, but away from familiar surroundings where both of you are starting from scratch. The answer is likely to be not since the day you moved out. And now, presumably years later, the two of you are sharing a room and three meals a day. For a whole week. Who is this person? Hardly a new acquaintance, but can you honestly say you know each other well? Most of your life together was in the past, and your ideas about one another took root and probably remain in that period. I will never forget hearing my mother introduce me to someone as her "child." I was thirty years old. Technically, of course, she was correct. I am, and always will be, her child. When I'm *fifty* I'll still be her child. That's just the way it is with mothers.

It's normal for children to grow into adulthood and welcome the transition from regarding parents as omniscient authority figures to peers whose answers—if there are any—may be wrong. It's more difficult for a parent to realize his grown-up child no longer needs "parenting," and sometimes even harder to accept the inevitable role reversal. As a result, you are dealing with someone you haven't spent a lot of time with recently, and one who probably has an outdated picture of you. It's up to you to make it work.

The reason is simple. YOU understand the whole picture. You have the patience, energy, and flexibility of youth (by comparison at least), and should have the generosity to give a little more than you might get this time around. Chances are that you will be more comfortable about traveling, being in a new place, and handling whatever problems arise—from a language barrier to just getting through the airport jungle. Your mother may need some extra looking-after, reassuring, and some organizing, especially if you want some time to yourself.

Find out what Mom would really like to do. Gently talk her out of a one-city-a-day trip if you feel she's being unrealistic about her stamina. If she's adamant, then *you* suggest taking naps each day. This advice varies with the individual, of course. My great-aunt Dorothy was taking three-month cruises on a freighter when she was eighty-two. Don't be angry if, after you've organized the entire venture from itinerary to tickets, she suddenly turns "mother" on you—if she insists on supervising your packing (and putting in "one good dress") and tells you midway through the first meal that your eating habits haven't improved since you were fifteen. My advice is that you smile, chuckle, agree with her, and go right on doing as you please. Parents never change, but you're beyond falling in the trap.

Most importantly, you must take the trip for what it is: a chance to spend some time with your mother and to get to know each other as you are today. This is not the moment for your sexual adventures, and it would be unfair to both of you if you tried to make the trip something you never meant it to be. If you're lucky, what will develop during the trip is very special: the feeling that you are friends, who just happen to be mother and daughter.

TRAVELING WITH PETS

The following is a "real-life" story. A pet monkey arrives by cargo plane at John F. Kennedy Airport. When the officials unload, they discover the monkey has gotten loose in the cabin and eludes all attempts at capture. They decide to bait him with a banana, his favorite fruit, with the slight twist that it's loaded with a tranquilizer. The monkey cheerfully takes the banana and, to everyone's astonishment, instead of taking a bite, breaks it in half and removes the pill. *Then* he eats the banana. As the vet in charge explained, "Maybe they have a sense we don't know about." The monkey was finally caught in a net.

Although this particular situation probably won't befall you, you might very well arrive at your hotel in Florida only to discover that the management won't allow dogs because they pick up sand fleas on the beach, or you might have to book a different flight in order to take airlines that allow dogs.

To help you avoid these problems, here is a checklist for predeparture and en-route care of your pet.

1. Each country, and each state in the United States has a different set of regulations for admitting pets. Some require a rabies shot given within the past year, others specify a certain time before departure. Many countries require a lengthy quarantine at the owner's expense; others don't even let animals in. Since regulations change frequently, check with the consulate, the ASPCA, or the airlines for the most up-to-the-minute information.

2. See your veterinarian well ahead of the departure date. He (or she) can give you a health and inoculation certificate—records of rabies, distemper, and hepatitis are the most commonly required. Ask about tranquilizers. Some doctors recommend injections instead

of pills because a shot acts immediately, and pills sometimes have delayed reactions. You may want to try a practice run at home if you're using pills.

3. Make sure your dog has a license. Otherwise, if he gets lost, he may be put away in the city's kennels. You might add a special tag with your hotel and your name.

4. Take an extra collar and leash. They're easy to lose.

5. Be sure to find out when you're making the reservations whether the hotels and airlines of your choice even allow pets. Etiquette for your pets at hotels: always keep a dog on a leash in public areas; ask about regulations for the pool and dining areas. (You're more likely to be able to keep pets with you in European establishments.) Don't leave a dog alone in your room. Pets often try to follow you, especially in a strange environment, which could lead to endless mischief. If you do leave a pet in a room, place a "Do Not Disturb" sign on the door and alert the front desk and the floor maid.

6. If your pet is on a special diet, take an ample supply of the food with you. A standard brand is probably available in most parts of the United States, and *may* have counterparts in other countries. (The "doggie bag" routine is fairly standard the world over.) In countries where you wouldn't drink the water, give your pet bottled water too. And be sure the toilet seat is always down in case he gets thirsty and doesn't wait for you.

7. Be careful about leaving your pet out in the sun too long to prevent possible heat stroke.

8. If your pet is unique or valuable (for reasons other than emotional) large insurance companies have policies for animals.

9. *Car Travel*

- Get the pet used to traveling in the car before you go on an extended trip. Teach him to stay in one place (not in the front seat), unless he fits in someone else's lap. Your pet may choose just the wrong moment to smother you with affection and jump on your lap, or go under your legs and step on the gas pedal.

- Keep extra drinking water in the car, or bring a Baggie of ice cubes.

- If you have a nervous animal, soothe him by calling him by name, petting, and using familiar command words.

■ If you leave your pet unattended in a car, park in a shady spot, leave the windows open an inch or so.

■ Stop frequently so the dog can run around a park area, or walk him on a leash.

■ Spare your dog the leftovers of highway dining, like hot dogs and tacos. Bring at least a beginning supply of biscuits and dry foods for the road.

10. *Bus and Train Travel*—No pets except Seeing Eye dogs are usually allowed on buses in the United States. On most trains, dogs, cats, and birds in suitable containers go in the baggage compartment and you have visiting privileges if the stop is longer than ten minutes.

11. *Air Travel*—First find out whether the airline allows pets, and if small dogs are allowed in the passenger cabin. Sometimes there is a limit to one pet in a cabin and it's first come, first served. Chances are you will have to ship your pet in the baggage or cargo compartment, and while these areas are usually pressurized, they are not air-conditioned. The hazard is that pets may be left out on a very hot or very cold airfield for hours before being moved into a terminal.

■ Crates or flight kennels should be big enough so the animal will be able to stand up straight, turn around, eat comfortably, and lie down. (Never put more than one animal in a crate.) The crate must be strong enough to withstand rough weather and turbulence, and have adequate ventilation. Ask your vet to recommend the best kind of crate and try it out at home to familiarize your pet with his temporary "home."

■ To prevent air sickness, do not feed your pet for several hours before flight time. Small sips of water suffice. (Check with your vet.)

■ If you are taking the pet as baggage and have to make a connecting flight, make the reservations separately for each flight so you can transfer him yourself. An animal should not be in a cargo compartment more than five to eight hours.

12. Almost any animal *can* be shipped by air. American Airlines once carried a four-thousand-pound performing whale that was covered with hydrous lanolin ointment and continuously sprayed with water.

7.
Traveling with Children

There's no getting around the realities of traveling with children. If you want escargots for dinner every night, one museum after another, and an iota of tranquility, plan separate vacations for you and your kids. It's hopeless to pretend you're alone on a great adventure, or in search of the perfect sunset with the perfect partner. Whether you're a single parent or a couple—even if a corner of you keeps yelling, *"Why do I have to take the kids?"*—you are dealing with a Family Vacation.

The biggest stumbling block to the success of the trip may well be your own attitude. It helps to remember that traveling is as much an adjustment for children as it is for adults. The bunting of the family will protect them from the loneliness that can plague the single traveler, but kids may miss the comforting signs of home: pancakes on Sunday morning, their own bed, or a best friend. You must prepare yourself to be extra patient, tolerant, understanding, and to put their well-being ahead of yours. Besides, the fact is that your well-being may depend on theirs.

Changing your outlook means letting go of *your* expectations of what the kids will get out of the trip. The first lesson may come when you say, for instance, "How would you like to go to Italy?" Your programming says this question should be met with wild enthusiasm.

"Do we *have* to?" is the plaintive cry. Children under nine will probably bow their heads and shuffle their feet. What kind of kids do you have?

The word "Italy" all by itself is enough to make *you* salivate, so what's wrong with them? You've had enough exposure to immediately associate it with pleasurable images: the fragrance of freshly ground coffee beans, Michelangelo's David, tables lurching under the weight of antipastos, the tight pants of Italian men, the elegance of the women, etc. The problem is, your kids haven't been clued in. You may need more than a bald announcement about the trip to

arouse their interest. Focus on something they can relate to at their particular age level: "We're going to the country that gave us spaghetti and meatballs (or Sophia Loren)."

Some parents feel that up to a certain age, children are too young to appreciate anything. *Your* notions about what kinds of activities will "teach" them the most can inhibit their learning process. I think every experience filters into the computer and will ultimately enrich their lives. A friend of mine has a four-year-old girl who woke up each morning in an Athens hotel to a view of the Acropolis. Driving through the Greek countryside a few days later, she saw a mountain and said to her mother rather wistfully, "Gee, if only that mountain had an Acropolis." Her mother said it was incredible just to hear the word "Acropolis" come out of the mouth of a four-year-old.

One of the revelations in traveling with your children is that they will find diversion in things long familiar to you. Children see things from a different physical and emotional perspective—whether it's cobblestones and skyscrapers, or the beauty and terror of the ocean—but they can't see intangibles like borders between countries. A ten-year-old I know was perplexed that on one side of the Rhine River people spoke German and spent marks, but on the other side they spoke French and spent francs. "What makes them so different if they're only separated by a river?"

Letting children learn at their own pace means allowing and encouraging their interests and enthusiasms. Don't be too pained if getting an ice cream takes precedence over seeing Mona Lisa. What *you* have to guard against is fretting that your kid will "never get culture." (See How to Get Your Children "Cultured," in this chapter.) Finding the best ice cream in Italy can be a heady and exciting pursuit to a child, so why not make it a cultural experience? One of my favorite places to eat ice cream is the Tre Scaline Café in Rome's Piazza Navona, a square with a famous Bernini fountain. Point it out *after* you've settled on the flavor of the ice cream.

In the effort to make the most of a trip you may have a single-minded vision of what children should want, and little acceptance of what they need. It helps to remember that their expectation of adventure can be quite simple. A hotel can provide unexpected treats. Some kids love taking the elevator by themselves, unpacking and arranging their things in special ways, the little packets of soap in the bathroom, and ordering from room service. Just signing the check—with a nod of approval from you to the waiter—can be a thrill.

I have a friend who agonized over "doing nothing" on her twelve-year-old daughter's first trip to Europe because life fell into a predictable rhythm in a small French beach town. She thought they should see every art museum in the area and stay at a different, quaint hotel each night. It finally occurred to her that what her daughter wanted was a sense of stability, which she got from getting chocolate ice cream at the same place every afternoon, making friends on the beach with someone her age (who didn't speak English, but came over to play catch), and seeing the same waiter each night for dinner. In fact, she was so taken with "their" waiter's genuine interest that under his tutelage she agreed to try snails.

Traveling can show children that learning isn't confined to a classroom and textbooks. Learning is also a matter of listening, watching, inhaling, wondering, and asking. What children absorb from a trip may be as simple as the lesson that people the world over have the same needs, problems, and desires, even though their patterns of daily life may be different. One child-friend of mine marveled that a clockmaker in Sorrento didn't have a regular shop but rented wall space in a narrow alleyway where every day he'd bring his card table and suitcase full of clock parts and open up for business.

Children may not remember—or care—who painted the Last Supper but they learn that stores in Mediterranean countries usually close in the afternoon because the family regroups around the midday meal, or they discover that "spaghetti" comes in a variety of sizes and shapes.

As your children move into the preteen and teenage years, a trip together can help bridge the transition from your role as parent—omnipotent and infallible—to peer and mere mortal. Daily living at home may be overwhelmed by your own priorities, and your children have their own responsibilities and interests. These distractions leave little time for appreciating or discovering one another as people, and it becomes as important for parents and children to get away together as it is for couples.

On a trip, nobody has the protective shell of "home." You have time to each learn another's curiosities, foibles, interests, and idiosyncrasies. I remember meeting my father in Paris when I was seventeen. The first night we went to the Tour d'Argent, the prototype of the grand French restaurant. Here, overlooking the Cathedral of Notre Dame, I discovered the awful truth. It seems that all the years I had heard him "speak" French, it was actually gobbledygook with a few real French words thrown in that made the overall effect totally convincing. I had to order the meal! I also realized he was proud I could speak the language.

Traveling with your kids binds you together by the adhesive of common experience. You develop a treasure chest of memories—funny stories and potential disasters—that become points of reference for the rest of your life. On a trip to Hawaii when I was seven, my mother was writing the score to *The Court Jester,* one of my father's movies, and because of her particular biological clock, she started to work when most people went to bed. The only problem was that as she sat down to compose at the piano in our hotel room, a band started playing Hawaiian music directly under the window. If we hear ukuleles—even if we're sitting in the dentist's office—we smile knowingly at each other about the music she describes as Hawaiian "sponge cake."

PLANNING

Preparing for a trip always gets less attention than it deserves. There is always one more book to read, one more film to see, one more brain to pick. Since children at best can be disinterested if not reluctant travelers, it is up to you to interest them. For that reason, advance planning is particularly important. It gives more meaning to the trip and can make life easier once you're there. (See the chapter, "Planning.")

A key to a successful vacation is to *involve* your children in the preparations. Work under the assumption that anything familiar is remembered better. Feeling that their contributions can make a richer trip reassures kids that they're not just piled onto the plane, train, or car because they can't stay home alone. The pretrip "orientation" can be fun in itself. Just be light-handed enough so that merely mentioning "the trip" doesn't scatter them in four directions.

Here are a few ideas for the weeks before your departure:

1. When you write away for literature, brochures, maps, etc., have them addressed to the kids. This will create a sense of participation and responsibility for sharing knowledge with the family. Besides, everyone loves getting mail. When requesting information from government agencies, airlines, or hotels, specify the ages of the children and ask about special programs, areas of interest, recreation areas, special meals, amusement parks.

2. Investigate the financial bargains of traveling with children. (See Hotels in this chapter and the chapter, "Transportation.")

3. If you are going someplace that has a distinctive cuisine, experiment at home with a few dishes: a gooey dessert; a spectacular-looking main course like paella; finger-food like tacos; Chinese dumplings; or pita bread filled with roast lamb; salads, etc. The *Time-Life* cookbooks have workable recipes, accompanied by superb color photographs and cultural and historical notes about the origin and traditions of the food. (See Appendix for "Indispensable Reading.")

4. The same principle applies to music. It's unnecessary to set everybody down and say, "We're going to hear a Swiss cowbell so-

nata." The lesson can be as unobtrusive as background music in the home, garden, or the car, which becomes painlessly familiar through osmosis.

5. If one of your children is gifted in languages, give him (or her) a phrase book and choose an area—whether it's shopping or restaurants—in which they can learn some of the expressions and be of real help to everyone.

6. Buy an inexpensive camera. You will be amazed how much more children will see, from the expression on people's faces, to a manhole, to a church façade. They can make a scrapbook of the pictures at home.

7. Encourage them to gather material for a presentation about the trip to their social studies, geography, or history class when they come back. It could be as simple as talking about favorite or unfavorite things. If the project becomes a burden, the purpose is lost. If there's a teacher your child or children particularly like, so much the better. If you know the teacher personally, it might help if you suggest that he or she express interest in the trip and ask to be kept informed through postcards, or stamps, coins, etc.

PACKING AND LAUNDRY

Take as many wash-and-wear items as possible. The idea of taking more tops than bottoms to change outfits doesn't hold for children, because they are just as likely to soil the pants or skirt as the top. No professional gambler would give you odds on how long a seven-year-old will keep a T-shirt or jeans clean. But you can build the wardrobe the same way in terms of colors. (See the chapter, "Packing.") My suggestions about laundry are based on the idea that it's *your* vacation too, and a few extra dollars might free you from having to watch clothes spin-dry in the laundromat when you'd rather be in a museum or on the beach.

1. If you're changing hotels frequently, inadequate time and space can make laundry a problem. Ask about "next day" service at the hotel the moment you arrive.

2. Take more clothes.

3. Have a "laundry hour" in which everybody washes underwear and clothes that drip-dry.

4. Tip the manager of the laundromat to take care of your bundles.

TRAVEL DOCUMENTS

Children need passports too. You can get individual or joint family passports. Individual passports cost more but they buy flexibility. Joint passports require that you cross borders together, which could be impractical if you have to stay behind with a sick child, or make an unexpected business detour. Your physician and public health officials have the information about required inoculations. Children get smaller doses but need the full series. You cannot get vaccinations if you're sick so be sure to plan well enough in advance. (See the chapter, "Etc.")

THE PORTABLE MEDICINE CABINET

Most supplies are available abroad, but three in the morning may not be the most convenient time to find an open drugstore. Take everything listed in the "Packing" chapter, with these additions:

1. Any medicine for specific allergies, chronic ailments, and extra prescriptions in case refills are needed.

2. Special children's medicine: aspirin, cough drops, cough syrups, etc.

Finding a competent local physician can be a worry. Most hotels out of the United States can recommend English-speaking doctors. Always take your own doctor's telephone number, and ask him to recommend a colleague where you're going. In emergencies, call the American Embassy. IAMAT (the International Association for Medical Assistance to Travelers) and Intermedic are New York-based operations that give their members a directory of English-speaking physicians in most major cities. IAMAT's head office is Empire State Building, 350 Fifth Avenue, Suite 5620, New York, N.Y. 10001. Intermedic is 777 Third Avenue, New York, N.Y. 10017.

EQUIPMENT TO TAKE OVERSEAS FOR YOUNG CHILDREN

1. A stroller that folds up like an umbrella; a baby backpack.

2. An adequate supply of disposable diapers.

3. Baby bottles. They aren't standard size, so take plenty of rubber nipples.

4. Rubber crib sheets and flannel cover that double as a makeshift bed when you have unexpected delays.

5. A supply of airsick bags.

6. Moist cleansing pads.

HOTELS

Choosing a hotel is not unlike choosing a restaurant: you have to evaluate your pocketbook as well as the maturity of your kids. It's important for them to learn to accept the world on its terms, but it's unreasonable for you to expect consistently perfect manners. You might substitute places that welcome kids (you can generally tell by what services they offer) for elegant surroundings.

The hotel industry is well aware of the power of advertising. Hotel billboards tout color TVs, double beds, Happy Hours, *and* baby-sitters. Some hotels have really zeroed in on the children's market by such gimmicks as putting pictures of your kids in their Rogue's Gallery. One hotel features a Sleepy Bear Club that issues each child a "passport" with his picture, vital statistics, and photograph. Large hotel chains often cater to children's eating habits with child-sized portions, special dishes on the menu, or entire menus designed for entertaining them and their palate. Ramada Inns once offered a coloring book as a menu and another chain named dishes to appeal to the imagination. A peanut butter and jelly sandwich became a "pur-

ple nut." Holiday Inn designed All About Ecology, and All About
Wildlife Conservation children's menus. Some hotels have youth centers that are licensed by the state as day-care centers.

Ask about the services a hotel offers through your travel agent,
writing or calling the hotel, or the toll-free 800 reservations number
used by many chains. Have a list of prepared questions. Specify how
old and how many children you have, the length of your stay, and
any special requirements.

You would like to know: 1) what equipment they supply for small
children/babies (most hotels have cribs, although when pressed you
can use a bureau drawer lined with blankets and pillows); 2) the
room service hours—can you get a glass of hot milk at two in the
morning? 3) restaurant facilities; 4) the most economical living arrangements. Many hotels have family plans in which children under
twelve stay in the same room with the adults at no extra charge. If
your budget permits, separate rooms for parents and children does
help keep the peace (and your sanity).

If you are staying at a resort hotel with a special children's camp
or youth program, these suggestions and queries can help you evaluate the program.

1. Talk with the camp director.

2. Ask for a copy of the schedule for a day (even if it's last
year's). You can get a sense of the balance between indoor and outdoor activities. It ought to give you a pause if swimming follows
lunch with no rest period in between.

3. What is the camper-counselor ratio?

4. Ask for a description of the children's facilities. You don't
want them playing all day in a drafty convention hall.

5. Are kids physically separated from the adults in the dining
room? Do you eat at different times?

THE BABY-SITTER DILEMMA

Without a baby-sitter the most practical, unflappable mother can
have visions of kidnap, illness, and fires raging through the hotel
room. The bottom line is, "If something happens to my baby (aged

eleven? . . .) I'll never forgive myself." Even *with* a sitter, it's likely that candlelit dinners will be interrupted either by your imagining what's going on, or by actually getting up and calling the baby-sitter to see if your child is still alive, with the ruse of providing essential information like, "I forgot to tell you his middle name is Stanley."

Most hotels have lists of sitters, or know of agencies which can provide English-speaking qualified people. Many sitters are bonded, which means you have legal recourse should anything go wrong. Here are some guidelines: 1) Restrain yourself from giving a crash course in child care that continues by phone. 2) It's a thoughtful gesture to have some fruit and coffee in the room or to authorize an order from room service. 3) In general, you will have to pay the sitter's transportation costs as well as a per hour rate. Assume that a reasonable fee will be anywhere from three to five dollars an hour in major cities. The truth is that you will probably be suspicious about their rates. It's part of the feeling that "you'll be taken" in a country where you don't know the customs and the language. You might ask just how far they live from the hotel and check with the desk clerk for an average bus or taxi fare.

CHILDREN'S HOTELS

Hotels for children originally started in Europe and are called *maisons d'enfants,* or children's houses. They function like camp, except kids stay the night, a weekend, or several weeks, and activities range from arts and crafts to tutors during the school year. The tourist offices of each country have information about children's hotels. Be sure to ask if the staff speaks English, and if there is medical care on the premises in case of an emergency.

TRANSPORTATION

The Airlines

My mother tells me that at the ripe age of three I passed the time on a Los Angeles to New York flight handing out peanuts to all the passengers. I was delighted to get my pilot's wings, which in those days was the airlines' major attempt to capture the children's market. Today's sophisticated marketing techniques offer something for everyone, including a stroller for your toddler, kiddie meals, and special rates, if not a free ride, if your child is under a certain age.

The common sense of the inflight crew accounts for much of the careful handling of children. In fact, there is a section in the Flight Services Handbook of many airlines that sets down specific rules. The crew are not, however, airborne baby-sitters required to change diapers. If you receive special attention, be grateful. Cabin attendants are supposed to help parents with hand luggage getting on and off the aircraft, to provide bassinets, warm baby food, and bottles shortly after takeoff. For older children there are usually coloring books, puzzles, and word games. On long flights, it's worth investing in a pair of headsets for the movie and music programs. Bring your own formula if your baby is on a bottle, moist cleansing pads, a small blanket, a change of clothes in case of air sickness or change of climate, disposable bibs, and a favorite, reasonably sized toy.

A child traveling alone is officially called an "unaccompanied minor" and usually taken by a Passenger Service agent to the Senior Purser on board who is given the necessary documents, including a form in which the parent or guardian says the child will be met by a responsible adult at the other end, who must present identification and sign for his release.

If your children have never traveled before, give them a preview of things to come. Tell them the landing gear makes noise, and the pilot may make periodic announcements, pointing out scenic highlights or warning about turbulence. What keeps an adult physically comfortable also applies to children—drink a lot of water or juice, walk up and down the aisle. Because the airlines don't pass out gum as liberally as they used to, I take my favorite gum and mints to make enough saliva so I can swallow to keep my ears open. Ever since I flew with a head cold and got a terrible ear infection, I bring nose spray to keep my sinuses clear. Small babies usually cry because changing air pressure causes physical discomfort. Try to make them drink juice or water throughout the flight, but especially on takeoff and landing, to help them swallow and relieve the pressure in their ears.

The headline for an interview I once gave about airline food read "Coffee, Tea, or Yuk!" I said that airlines should stop pretending they were airborne gourmet restaurants and should serve sandwiches and delicatessen food. A plane is clearly not the place to introduce your kids to fine dining. In fact, you might bring along nonjunk-food snacks to shorten the wait for the meal service. Another alternative is packing food baskets with items you know your kids will like. Food can be a good diversion on a plane, provided you aren't flying through the eye of a storm. If you really want to surprise them, order a cake. With ample notice, most airlines will make them, often at no extra cost.

Trains and Cars

Travel by train and travel by car share a similar advantage. You move along the ground floor of a country—particularly helpful for children who have a hard time with the abstractions of geography, movement, and distance. I remember one time my parents talked about going from Los Angeles to Honolulu for Christmas. I just wanted to know if Honolulu was as far away as Palm Springs.

TRAIN TRAVEL

Trains may be the ideal way to take kids on vacation. (It has advantages for both parents and children.) As a parent you can painlessly devote your attention to your mutual entertainment. But parents can also enjoy a relative sense of independence, because the train itself is a diversion. To a child, the train is a small community. He (or she) can explore the different cars, or have ginger ale in the club car, and "go out" for dinner by themselves in the dining car. It helps if you make arrangements for payment with the waiter and tip him nicely.

There is an element of adventure to sleeping on a train, especially if you need a ladder to get to the top berth. The different way the toilet and faucets work in the bathroom are a new experience. Assuming your kids won't run wild through the train, the idea of a community can also have a socializing effect. One friend of mine who is a veteran of four extended rail trips says, "Kids make friends easily with other kids and adults who carry chewing gum."

There are ways of trimming the budget so the advantages of train travel are not derailed by high costs. On an extended rail trip, plan to have one meal a day in the dining car, but vary it between breakfast, lunch, and dinner, so the menu choice and time of day will be different. Use "picnic" type food for the other meals: a food hamper with the basics you would take in the car, plus paper utensils and a thermos to hold boiling water from the dining car for instant drinks, soup, chocolate, oatmeal, etc.

CAR TRAVEL

You get six blocks from home and the Voice in the Back Seat says, "I have to go to the bathroom."

You left the restaurant fifteen minutes ago, and the Voice in the Back Seat pipes up, "I left my doll under my chair."

You're driving over a winding road and the Voice in the Back Seat whispers, "I'm going to throw up," and does before you can do anything.

Such is life on the road with kids. Nonetheless, piling the family in the car to go on vacation is an American ritual, like making a pig of yourself at Thanksgiving, or cheering madly at baseball games. Our nation overflows with so many hotels, motels, and outposts of "highway dining" that one could forget that the point of the whole trip is actually *getting* someplace. Life on the highway became so predictable for one family that when they drove into yet another motel, the eight-year-old remarked, "How could we have spent all day in a car and still be in the same place?"

A car *is* a means of getting from A to B, but it is also a mobile unit for the feeding and entertaining of the whole family. Traveling in a car is a lot like sharing a room. There's nowhere to go. A friend of mine with four kids, ages five to twelve, says either she or her husband sits in the back seat to create a buffer zone. Car sickness is another problem. If a child is given to queasiness, consult your physician for the appropriate medication (or take the train).

The age of your children dramatically alters how you plan. You can take children under two wherever you're going, without too much concern for their interests. Keep a handful of supplies in the back seat, from food to disposable diapers, since you may need them when it's inconvenient to pull over and open the trunk.

For children over three, it is crucial to bring an "entertainment center," with you, and to plan the trip so long stretches on the road are tolerable, even pleasant. Kids can't sit still for too long. You just have to be philosophical about stopping every two hours. Plan to do a few exercises when you stop. Bend at the waist and swing the arms like an elephant's trunk; roll the head around, raise shoulders up "to your ears" and down, and bring a ball or Frisbee. Activities organized around the meal also provide a change of scene. Picnics solve your problem of a place to let off steam, and save you the all-too-frequent trauma of restaurants.

When you are traveling on the road with more than one child, avoid restaurants at peak hours. The debate about what to order is endless; when the dish finally arrives, your adorable child might well say, "But that's not what I wanted!" Ignore this remark. As my mother once said about a period when I only wanted pickled herring, "When you got really hungry you asked for 'real food.'"

You can improvise your own "room service" on the road by stocking up on:

> individual boxes of cold cereal
> packages of instant oatmeal and soup, a thermos of
>   hot water
> packages of hot chocolate
> fruit, nuts and dried fruit
> powdered milk
> jar of honey
> individual cans of juices (and an opener)

Equipment for a Car Trip

1. Blanket and pillows for the back seat fill several needs. They enable the kids to sit high enough to see license plates and billboards for games, they cushion some of the jolts and bumps, and they make a cozy napping area. Be sure to adjust the ventilation so there is enough cool air in the back seat.

2. A roll of toilet tissue for emergency pit stops.

3. Moist cleansing pads, wet washcloths in plastic bags, paper towels.

4. Plastic bags for collecting rocks, bottle tops, etc.

5. A cooler with ice for juices, flavored yogurts.

6. An attachment to warm baby bottles that fits into the dashboard lighter.

7. A Swiss army knife.

8. A small sewing kit.

Our family car trips amounted to driving from Los Angeles to Palm Springs on weekends. When I was four years old, my big treat was driving fast on a road with so many dips that it felt like a small roller coaster. I soon outgrew that thrill and turned to license plate games and finally word games. I never read books and magazines or played auto checkers (pieces that fit in the board) because I got carsick. (Avoid toys with sharp edges and games that require little bits and pieces. One slam on the brakes, and . . .) The following suggestions for games you can play in the car come from my own memories, my friends' children, and various parents.

License plate games

Games are invented by using the numbers, colors, or letters on the plates.

1. Out-of-state plates: Which state will you see the most? The least?

2. Pick one letter in the alphabet that will not appear on a license plate. You win if your letter never appears.

3. Pick categories: Countries, flowers, dogs, cartoon characters, movie stars, heads of state, etc. If the license plate has the letters DLM, for example, and your category is flowers, you have to name a flower for each letter: daisy, lily, mum.

Word games

1. Geography. You name a place (city, country, river, etc.), Nevada, for example. The next person takes the last letter of the place, A, and names any place that begins with A.

2. One person picks a celebrity in any field. Everyone else tries to figure out who it is by asking questions. The trick is they only get yes and no answers.

3. That old standby, "Twenty questions"!

HOW TO GET YOUR CHILDREN "CULTURED"

The urge to ply your kids with culture can be as uncontrollable as reaching for your third piece of chocolate cake. In both cases, your watchword should be "moderation." Your aim is to expose them to ideas, objects, thoughts, and not to insist they swoon over the Mona Lisa for an hour. (They may like the *grounds* of the Louvre Museum better.) They should taste, study, chew, mull over, and digest. And then come back. On the other hand, don't underestimate the power of a masterpiece to carry through to kids. I've seen children walk back and forth and sideways in front of a Rembrandt in the Rijksmuseum in Amsterdam, convinced the eyes in the painting were following them.

You've got a corner of a child's interest anytime you can find special events, pageants, or festivals that make history entertaining rather than a bore. I was captivated by the spectacle of a Catholic mass in Italy with priests wearing colorful finery, or a night in Florence when the city hall, an historical building, was lit inch by inch with big torches. These are pageants that bring cities to life. The "event" can be as unexpected as seeing the guards on horseback on

their way back to Buckingham Palace. The drama that I find transporting is the *son et lumière,* a sound and light production staged on the sites of many ruins and famous buildings. The formula is to light up various parts of the ruins—for example, the Roman Forum, the Acropolis in Athens—and have narration and music tell the story of the people and the events of the time.

You can make "sight-seeing" more attractive by relating things that kids are seeing to something familiar. One friend of mine called Rome's Colosseum the Yankee Stadium of the ancient world, and explained the city of Pompeii in Italy as a thriving city which was obliterated by a volcano and is now a ghost town.

RULES OF FAMILY TRAVEL TO MAKE YOUR LIFE EASIER

1. Quit before everyone collapses, not after. It's better to see less and be happy than to see more and be miserable.

2. Throw balanced meals to the wind. Quell the "I'm hungry" routine with something to eat, not a lecture about ruining the appetite. Half the fun of traveling is succumbing to the pastry shop twenty minutes before dinner. Changing time zones accounts for part of this always-hungry tendency, and you're probably better off with de-

mand-feeding and letting the body, not the clock, set mealtimes. As someone once said, "Children behave best when their stomachs are full and their bladders are empty."

3. Establish a complaint box. All gripes must be put in writing, and then each day at a certain time all complaints will be read aloud. Even the most outraged complainer can see the humor/pet-

tiness/silliness when he or she hears her own words like, "Tommy got three more french fries than I did," or "Jane was hogging the telescope so she got to look at the stars longer than me!" etc.

4. Turn discomfort into adventure. (Just the effort to look at the brighter side will hoist you out of the doldrums, and set a positive example for dealing with unpleasant or unexpected situations.) If there is no closet space, for instance, pretend you're on a ship where the suitcase becomes the dresser drawers and the closet.

5. Establish areas of responsibility for each child. Give each an allowance in the currency of the country. He (or she) is allowed to buy anything, even if you think it's useless and ugly. Make it clear, however, that there's no more money coming when they've spent it all. It just may be that having to take responsibility for purchases might turn some reckless buyers into thoughtful shoppers.

6. Everyone should have his own in-flight bag or overnight carry-all with personal belongings. This satchel may contain games for the airplane, car, or train; souvenirs picked up along the way, an extra sweater. Consider it their own territory. *You do not care if it's a mess* and no one will/should take responsibility. If it's lost, they'll shoulder the disappointment themselves.

7. It is difficult to satisfactorily answer the question "When are we getting to . . . ?" because it's hard for younger children to relate to a number of miles, or a spell of time, and almost impossible to grasp the idea of "soon." Take maps and colored pens to trace your route, and if possible give each child a watch. They'll learn the different time zones, and won't plague you as much with the "how much longer till we get there" routine. Just give an approximate time of arrival at the beginning of each journey.

8. Nothing does more to exorcise the "I can't sit stills" than physical exercise. Keep in mind that kids sleep at odd times in odd places and just may be raring to go when you're ready for a hot tub and a double scotch. Try to find time during each day to spend in a park, or a children's playground. A tourist office or even a hotel should have some suggestions. Copenhagen's Tivoli Gardens can solve your problems for an entire day, for it contains everything from *pølse* stands (hot dog stands) and informal or fancy restaurants, to mime

theater and lakes and boats. Even Paris has the unexpected diversion of a nearby safari park. Picnics are easy to arrange and they provide a double bonus of containing exactly what the kids want to eat, and of being outside. On longer trips, you might break up a big city itinerary by stints in the country. I have friends who took their teenaged boys to Paris but went backpacking in Switzerland before they went on to Rome.

9. Give each young child an identification bracelet with his/her name and passport number. In each new city, pin a slip of paper in a pocket with the name of your hotel. Be sure to point out policemen to your children so they will recognize the uniform in each country, and will know who to ask for help.

10. Keep first class a secret.

8.

Meeting a City and the People

You've arrived. You're finally where you've pictured yourself. Now all you have to think about are the delicious discoveries that await you. But how to proceed without going in all directions? This chapter will guide you through the waters of meeting a city and the people, pointing out the rapids perhaps but cheering you on to find your own private wading pools.

WHAT IS A TOURIST?

". . . and the *best* part of the whole trip was that we were the only Americans there," seems to be a traveler's ultimate praise. "Tourist attraction" translates immediately as "tourist trap" and any place or experience is defiled by the mere presence of another camera-carrying visitor. People even apologize for doing "touristy" things like going to the top of the Empire State Building. What an irony that so much is sacrificed just to avoid being called "tourist," a label associated with being unsophisticated, unaware, gullible, an easy mark; an innocent in sensible shoes who tries to walk, read a map, look at the churches, and stay on the sidewalk all at the same time.

There is nothing embarrassing about being a tourist; there is nothing demeaning in joining the millions whose breath has been taken away by that first glimpse of the Eiffel Tower or of Venice by moonlight when the stained palaces are white again and the silent canals graced with the ghosts of plumed gallants and fair ladies. In fact, being a tourist is a state of continuous curiosity which I consider—along with breathing—one of the vital signs.

A tourist is a student who lovingly works to unlock the secrets of a city and its people. A tourist gets to know the surface characteristics and the inner soul of a city, as with a new acquaintance, by asking questions, observing, participating, and recording the impressions in the mind, on paper, or on film.

The "successful" or skilled tourist knows how to get the feeling of *living* in, rather than *visiting* a city. It's easier for a lone traveler or a couple to integrate into city life than it is for a group, which is a self-contained and usually self-sufficient unit.

No one has put the essential characteristics of the successful traveler more gracefully than Edward Gibbon, the great historian of the eighteenth century and best known as the author of *The History of the Decline and Fall of the Roman Empire.*

> He should be endowed with an active, indefatigable vigor of mind and body, which can seize every mode of conveyance, and support, with a careless smile, every hardship of the road, the weather, or the inn. It must stimulate him with a restless curiosity, impatient of ease, covetous of time, and fearless of dangers; which drives him forth, at any hour of the day or night, to drive the flood, to climb the mountain, or to fathom the mine on the most doubtful promise of entertainment and instruction. The arts of common life are not studied in the closet . . . The last virtue borders on a vice; the flexible temper which can assimilate itself to every tone of society from the court to the cottage; the happy flow of spirits which can amuse and be amused in every company and situation.

The art of making a city more personal applies in America as well as abroad. American cities may *seem* easier to plumb because you know the language and the currency, but that very familiarity may breed a complacency which makes discovering the unique character of the city even more difficult.

In a totally new environment, however, you are forced to make an effort just to survive, and in the process the city reveals itself. Part of the problem is an irrational feeling that anything simmered in centuries requires and deserves more attention. Mark Twain observed in *Innocents Abroad,* his account of a group tour through Europe, that American tourists reverentially examine the moldiest-looking objects from churches to brooches which at home would pass unnoticed.

THE AMERICAN TOURIST

People are the life force of a city. The ability to attract and get to know them requires a knowledge and sensitivity about their culture as well as an awareness of what *they* see in *you* as an American.

We are often unconscious of our habits as a nation, and how they may be interpreted in other cultures. America still reflects the frontier spirit of the risk-takers and pioneers who built the country only two-hundred-odd years ago. And in our relative youth America has retained some of the traits of a child whose instincts haven't been dampened by society. We're open, friendly, and informal.

Our informality is distinctive among nations and can both disarm and offend. We're likely to say, "Hi, everybody," rather than make individual greetings. We rarely shake hands on meeting *and* departing. We certainly don't embrace with a hand on each shoulder and kiss on both cheeks. Our habit of calling people by their first names right away is often disconcerting and sometimes regarded as an invasion of privacy.

Americans also delight in nicknames. Think of what we've called our recent presidents: Harry, Ike, Jack, Dick, Gerry, and Jimmy. Nicknames or diminutives in a foreign language can be tricky. Edmond in French reduces not to Ted or Ed, but MoMo.

Americans don't have the concept of rank, caste, or "knowing one's place," some important social delineations that are a holdover in countries raised on the feudal system and the monarchy. The closest we come to such a tradition is calling a person Judge, Governor, or Ambassador, long after the appointment has expired.

Some cultures skirt the whole problem by addressing anyone outside intimates and family as "Señora," "Madame," "Monsieur," etc. The difference in attitude is also reflected in many languages by the use of a formal and an informal word for "You."

Americans can be blunt and tend to ask personal questions. In the first five minutes of conversation, out of nothing but genuine interest, we inquire about someone's economic level, occupational status, and where their children go to school. Americans unwittingly impinge on physical space, too. We are "touchers." We poke in the ribs, slap on the back, hit on the knee. This is anathema in some cultures, particularly in Asia, where people have the idea of space around a body. They don't shake hands; they bow. They don't extend hands to make contact; they hold their palms together in front of them, as a sign of respect and preservation of the space in between.

Buddhists consider the head the resting place of the soul, for instance, so following the bent of Americans to pat children on the head is not merely unacceptable but sacrilegious. I once watched members of a Japanese family who had been separated for thirty years greet each other. They simply bowed.

Realistically speaking, we are not likely to become overnight anthropologists who can converse fluently about the folkways and mores of each destination. *Your best safeguard is to use simple courtesy and good manners that transcend oceans and cultures, and to remember that you're not in your own backyard, but in a new friend's home.*

I make a practice of finding out some of the distinguishing characteristics wrought by history and geography in the places I'm going. To take two small examples: someone from Naples considers himself a Neapolitan first and *then* an Italian; the politics of Italy is really the politics of each region (as is the cuisine). Both these ideas make sense if you know that until 1861 Italy was made up of separate, independent, and usually hostile states and the people still proudly cling to their regional identity.

I want to know about a nation's pastimes and passions, historical strengths and prides. A history book for children will often give you the basics. You'll find you can always talk with a Frenchman about food and wine, a Greek about politics, an Argentinean about soccer, a Californian about health, exercise, and the latest fad; an Italian about food and the family, a Chinese about food and business.

The art of conversation is often just knowing what questions to ask and then being a good listener. Communication doesn't necessarily require the language facility of a translator at the UN. An exchange can be nonverbal, too. I remember sitting under a fig tree in

Turkey, near the ruins of Ephesus, tired, hot, and impatient for my friends to come. I noticed a family nearby having a picnic. A young girl came over to me and said something I could only guess was Turkish and offered me some melon with the pieces already sliced, just waiting to be picked off the rind. I smiled, took the cool melon, and said thank you. She returned the smile and went back to her family.

Sometimes the mere effort to establish rapport is a form of communication. A friend of mine was having a pizza in Naples, its city of origin. The man next to him heard the order in English and said, "I have a brother in America. In Chicago." My friend was Canadian and lived in Montreal. He tried to explain but the man would hear nothing of it, possibly because he didn't understand much English. He insisted on writing out the address of his brother's restaurant in Chicago and assured my friend he would be treated like family.

The Italian was proud he knew someone in America and his way of communicating was saying in effect, "We have something in common." Sometimes it's better to nod and smile, rather than try to make the truth clear.

MEETING PEOPLE

During a periodic drought in my teenage romantic life, when I puzzled over the dearth of likely prospects, my mother analyzed the situation and came up with an answer that didn't please me at all. She blamed *me*. "They'll know when your flag is up," she used to say. My mother may have been explaining why I stayed home on Saturday nights in high school, but the theory holds true for life itself.

You transmit, and people sense and react accordingly, whether you are receptive, afraid, anxious, or approachable. The beginning of any kind of personal contact—with another couple, a woman or a man—is an attitude that projects a desire and willingness to find out about people, even if you may never see each other again, or you don't speak the same language. Within the bounds of personal safety, somewhere between the extremes of coming on like gangbusters and cloistering yourself, you must be willing to reach out.

Meeting people when you are traveling is different than in "real" or everyday life. You are more open and amenable to new experiences in general, and common sense says that people enrich most occasions. The principal saboteur is the fantasy that "people" means "men only" and unfortunately you overlook encounters with couples, other women, or entire families because no matter your age, you are lying in wait for the elusive white knight.

One summer my friend Tara embarked on her first trip alone to Sicily. It was a time of many collect calls to me in New York, lamenting her wild emotional swings, questioning why she ever made the trip. Then one day the owner of the small hotel where she was staying invited her to have lunch with some of his friends.

She sat next to a young Sicilian woman who spoke some English (Tara's Italian was rudimentary) and invited her home for lunch. The next day she found herself sitting around the kitchen table with the young woman (Nanni) and her father, who had come home from work (he owned a pasta factory), her mother, and her brother, sharing a family lunch of homemade pasta, basking in a sauce of plump clams and olive oil.

It was the first of many meals together because they became her second family. On later trips she shared a Christmas dinner, which included pasta stuffed with pureed squash and an Easter lunch of hand-turned gnocchi, the latter at their summer house, an old villa untouched by time (except for the plumbing), with private vineyards and a barrel where the workers once walked on grapes to make wine.

Relationships on the road take shape in a unique framework of time and personal needs. You share a taxi, meet at a café, on an airplane or in a bookstore; you have lunch, go to a museum, walk in the park, are lonely and both miss home. You decide to travel together. The process of getting to know people isn't confined to isolated lunches or dinners, but flows in a continuum of events. *On a trip you should welcome the twists brought on by meeting people; a glorious part of travel is being flexible enough to accommodate the unexpected.*

I once went shopping in Athens for a flokati, a famous, all-white, all-wool rug. I asked to see the owner of the store—always a good idea when the shop is clearly named for a person. He told me about the origin of the flokati, which led to a discussion about the island where it originated.

He sensed my interest and curiosity about his country, and invited me to go with his family to their hometown in the mountains for a folk dance festival. I based my decision to go on nothing more than a "good" feeling about him, that his business seemed prosperous, and that he exported to reputable stores in America. I spent three days in the mountains with his family of six (and several cats), sharing food, stories, dances, songs, and ultimately affection. We promised faithfully to correspond and when I got back home I sent small gifts of thanks. It's unimportant that I haven't been back to Greece in several years and we may never meet again.

Sometimes such friendships transcend the circumstances of their birth and endure, but it is equally possible they will fade like a summer romance. You must not be fooled into thinking that intensity means longevity, nor should you shy away from a "relationship" of any kind simply because it may only survive in the context that made it possible.

What matters is that for the time you shared, you are richer. Consider, for instance, an affair with an Italian. Perhaps there is nothing as volatile, as engaging, as passionate, as endless, but as finite, as an affair with an Italian. Luigi Barzini, the "biographer" of Italy, describes it in his book *The Italians:*

> Some men are indeed irresistible. Their charm, skill, lack of scruples, and boldness are proverbial. Most of them always feel free as birds, even the married ones, or those who are deeply in love or engaged . . . He may sincerely think he is in love but may only be a lukewarm and temporary *innamorato* carried away by emotions and his ability. Or he may have found the challenge to his skill or daring too strong to resist . . . Or he may be desperately in love. Whatever his feelings, his performance is almost always delightful, moving and tactful. Only rarely is it irritating.

My friend Adrienne was engaged to an Italian in New York and at age twenty-four went to Italy, for the first time ever, to meet his family—more accurately, to pass his mother's inspection. On the night she arrived to be with the man she was to love forever, etc., he deposited her (and then departed) in the middle of "la dolce vita" at a film star's home. Among the other events of the evening, the host threw an entire platter of spaghetti against the wall in protest over the impromptu appearance of a very pregnant woman, played homemade pornographic tapes, and showed Adrienne his bedroom decorated in black on black: black carpet, black walls, black satin sheets, etc.

When her fiancée surfaced later that evening to reclaim her (with no explanation of his past whereabouts) they sat down in a corner, together at last, to toast their future bliss. He looked deeply into her expectant, still-adoring eyes, his own orbs brimming with the appropriate emotion, and said, "Congratulations, my darling, on *your* engagement."

Needless to say, there was never any marriage, especially after she heard *two* pairs of feet padding around upstairs in his bedroom, and after he urged her to accept the actor's invitation to go to Spain. But they remained friends, and she had the invaluable lesson of what it feels like to be in love, even if she had projected her fantasies on an unlikely candidate. Years later, over lunch in New York, they spoke about their engagement, and he asked, "How long were you in love with me?" She answered sweetly, "About the same amount of time you were in love with me."

While you should proceed with an open mind and an open heart, never dismiss the realities that face women who travel alone, or in the company of other women or men, because at some point, somewhere, you are certain to be on your own. A woman alone, alas, is eternally provocative, partially because of the societal assumption that a woman alone doesn't wish to remain so.

One man put the situation in a positive light with his theory that no matter what, women have it better than men. He feels a shy man is the loneliest traveler because he will never approach a woman, and it's only remotely possible a woman will approach him. Women, at least, have the option of saying no.

At the most basic level, you are dealing with old-fashioned male-female chemistry. This natural phenomenon is somewhat complicated because you are a Westerner, and an American woman, which establishes, however exaggerated or erroneous, certain ideas about you and your behavior. Those very ideas once rescued me from a confirmed Don Juan who kept repeating, "*You!* My hotel tonight?" "In America it is not that way," I replied. "The man never asks the woman. The woman asks the man."

The women's movement is often interpreted merely as a sexual liberation rather than the development of a whole person who can create the options in her life, sexual and otherwise. An American woman traveling alone is, to some men, a sign of complete sexual availability. Foreign men rarely understand American signals of sexual access, especially in Asia, Latin America, and Islamic countries where their own desires are fanned because you are unlike local women—without family protection from father, brother, or husband. In these parts of the world, and outside the capitals of Europe, few women travel unaccompanied by family or friends. Men are naturally more cautious when brothers, mothers, etc. are nearby.

You may even be violating the social code by your independent status. Well-known writer Kate Simon once wrote about Spain:

> Women traveling without men may meet a subtle contempt from hotels, clerks, waiters, and railroad employees in Spain, still strongly ridden by machismo. According to Spaniards, a woman should be home breeding children, and if she isn't able to achieve that honorable status, kneeling in earnest prayer, preferably in her own country.

The preconceived ideas about you, combined with a not uncommon division of their own women into mothers and others, make you even more delectable. You will undoubtedly be the recipient of an overt or covert pass, executed with irresistible charm or gross vulgarity.

Sometimes the incongruity of being seduced in beginner's English can mitigate the distaste of a situation and even add some humor. A man often leapfrogs the preliminaries because he doesn't know how to say them in English and gets right to the point. A standard line is, "You sleep with me tonight?" which is then repeated with variations, depending on your response. If you say no, the riposte might be, "I want you to wife me," followed by lesser pleas like, "You hurt my heart, why you not kiss me?" or finally settling for, "Do you have five minutes?"

The approaches are as numerous as there are men. You should be aware that for all the benign flirts and genuine offers of friendship you might choose to accept, there are hustlers who make a business of attaching themselves to Western women in the guise of being helpful: hailing cabs, showing you stores with "good prices," helping you with directions; all of it with the underlying plan that you will somehow get them out of their country and into the United States. (For this reason alone, *you should never idly dispense invitations to peo-*

ple to visit you in the United States as a gesture of reciprocal hospitality. They may show up.)

Your desire to discard your mantle of suspicion in the name of discovery, new experiences, and adventure should never overshadow your common sense. Obviously, you will take some chances because there is no blueprint for the outcome of accepting any invitation.

I had a guide in Iran some years ago who was studying economics and poetry, a rather disarming combination I thought at the time, and after a long day of sight-seeing he invited me to have coffee at his parents' house. We arrived at an apartment building, not a house, and went up a flight of stairs. He opened the front door and the first thing I saw was the famous poster of Sophia Loren in the wet shirt; an odd choice of art, I thought to myself, for his parents to have in their front hall.

Still shrouded in the belief he was a nice student who could quote Omar Khayyam, I realized we were in one room, with only one place to sit down. The bed.

Looking back, of course, I was naïve not to have understood how *he* had interpreted my willingness to come to his parents' house. "Listen, Mohammed," I heard myself saying, "really, I just can't do this with someone I don't know." I went on about my emotional fragility, my sensitivity, my violated trust in him as a poet, as a man of superior awareness, etc. He apologized and deposited me safely back at the hotel.

It doesn't always work this way. I have a friend who was standing in the lobby of a first-class hotel in Beirut when a man in an elegant dinner jacket approached her and said, "I find myself without a date for a dinner party at the American Embassy. Would you care to join me?" She accepted the invitation.

They were wined, dined, and entertained in diplomatic splendor. At the end of the evening, he suggested they drive to the city's most famous lookout point, a suspect offer in retrospect, but they *had* just spent a delightful time together exactly where he had promised. So they drove to what proved to be a breathtaking vista, sat and talked in the car, and then headed back down the road.

Suddenly he pulled over to the side, stopped the car, and grabbed her. When she pulled away, he slapped her across the face, and continued his attack. At this point, concerned for her personal safety, not her morality, she said, "I'd love to make love with you, but let's not do it in the front seat of your car." He agreed and they headed back into town, presumably to his house. When they reached downtown, they stopped at a corner full of people and lights that she recognized was near the hotel. She leaped out of the car and made it back to her room without further incident.

Unfortunately, it is sometimes difficult to identify the men who assume that willingness to talk or have dinner means yes to all further requests. There is no yardstick to measure your behavior but instinct and common sense. In addition, what we consider a courteous turndown in America may be construed as a go-ahead simply on the basis that you responded at all.

Given the situation, you just have to pick your best defense, whether it's humorous, stern, or inventive; or taking refuge in a store, with a policeman or behind another woman.

One writer claims yelling in a language you think your admirer won't understand is an effective deterrent. She relies principally on her limited Russian vocabulary with phrases like, "Where is the pen of Masha?" or "Let us climb onto our tractors and make the fields strong."

On the other hand, your response to an invitation might be an unequivocal yes. Awareness of the potential problems doesn't consign you to a monastic life but arms you with a sense of reality and the fact that you do have choices and alternatives. You will attract whatever you seek in the way of relationships, whether it is being taken into the bosom of a family, or the bed of your Prince Charming.

GETTING TO KNOW A CITY

How many times have you heard the lament, "How things have changed. If only you had been here fifteen years ago." Long pause . . . several sighs . . . a look woeful enough to make a St. Bernard in repose look ecstatic.

To this school of thought, "changed" means ruined. It's offensive to find "un Big Mac" with "du ketsup, le apple pie and le milk shake" at McDonald's in Paris; to discover that many Japanese women wear Western dress; that mere mortals now can live in Peking's Forbidden City; that many French and Italian women shop once a week in supermarkets instead of buying each day from individual merchants.

The twentieth century *has* had a homogenizing effect on many aspects of life, but each country adapts within its own personal framework. The McDonald's in Paris, for instance, serves wine. Falconry and poetry have survived the onslaught of discos and television in the Middle East. Lunch at a fast-food restaurant in Italy can take two hours.

The tourist must probe beyond the natural and man-made birthmarks that identify a city, whether it's Big Ben, Diamond Head, or Copacabana Beach, to find the subtler trademarks: men taking their birds (in a cage) for a walk in Hong Kong; the personalized license plates in "Me-centered" Southern California; people walking *everywhere,* up mountains and down streets in Norway; a charcuterie window in France with curtains of sausages and mountains of cheeses; the pop art quality of the neon along the Las Vegas strip; the whistles in samba music that resound through Rio's streets.

Part of the excitement of a new city is having a different geographical frame of reference. Rome, for instance, is only a two-and-a-half-hour flight from Moscow. When I arrive at an airport, I always listen to the flights being called for destinations that seem inaccessible when I'm in my living room. From Hong Kong, Bali *is* only four hours away.

Where you stay, in terms of both location and type of accommodation, will make a difference in how you feel about a city. In deluxe hotels you pay for being coddled, from the concierge to the buttons by your bed that summon the valet, the maid, the waiter, etc. (Older hotels often have an extra button for guests who've brought along their personal servants.) At a small pension, the owners and the other guests constitute a family. A friend of mine staying in a pension in Rome had thought little about her birthday until she returned for dinner, and the dining room was decorated with crepe paper, and her birthday cake—with the correct number of candles—was dessert. The owner had noticed—and remembered—the date from her passport.

THE FIRST DAY IN A NEW CITY

The cardinal rule for the first day is moderation. *Never overdo.* Everything is different: the water, the time zone, the accents, the altitude, the climate, and the pace.

It's easy to forget in the flush of newness that you need energy to adjust not only to the physical changes, but the psychological ones as well. There's that first moment alone in the hotel, when the luggage sits like a lump in the middle of your room; you've looked at the view from the window, at yourself in the bathroom mirror, and you realize you've finally arrived.

You have voluntarily left behind everything familiar, including the people who love you. Allow yourself the ambivalence of being excited and anxious about what lies ahead. Call room service and order tea and something to eat, take a long bath, perhaps a nap, and then begin to plan your encounter with the city.

At this point, I find the at-home preparation begins to pay off. I have pared down the lore from magazines, guidebooks, and friends. I know that I haven't picked a day when the museum that interests me most is closed; I've studied the map so I have a sense of where I am in the city. Now I can turn to the next source of information: what the hotel provides.

Gathering Information

Hotels usually have packets of materials in the room detailing the services available in the hotel itself (particularly the big chains), and news about the current goings-on in town. *Read everything*. I've learned about such in-house items as an exercise class, a cedar closet for storing furs, and reciprocal arrangements with tennis, golf, or riding clubs. I ask the concierge, the desk clerk, or the newsstand for local magazines, tabloids, and newspapers. They provide the hard news as well as clues about priorities, fads, and passions of the city. Look at the subject matter of articles and whether they are important enough for the front page or relegated to the bottom corner of page nineteen.

You never know where you'll pick up practical or fanciful tidbits that piece together the portrait of a city: Hong Kong is the trading post of Asia dedicated to turning the dollar. I read in the sports section of the paper the season's winning horse was named Money Talks. A Greek newspaper played up a story about a man accused of rape who cleared himself in court by testimony supported by witnesses that he had eaten a huge salad, dressed unsparingly with olive oil. It seems that in some parts of the Middle East olive oil is believed to have aphrodisiac powers.

City magazines have proliferated in the last few years in America. In Europe, the *International Herald-Tribune,* published by the New York *Times* and the Washington *Post* is every American's link with home with helpful ads and personals for anything from escort services to apartments, and people looking to share the expense of driving, say, to Istanbul. Many cities abroad have English-language magazines and newspapers in English with current events information. I look for announcements of lectures, art gallery openings, sports events, theater, music, and dance programs, particularly those performed in "indigenous" locales like outdoor theaters, palaces, amphitheaters. I once saw a rock concert in the Roman amphitheater in Nîmes, France. You should arrange for tickets as soon as possible so you can make your other plans.

Newsstands themselves give clues about a city because their supplies include items indigenous to the area. The kiosks in Athens, for instance, not only stock newspapers and magazines but pistachio nuts (characteristic of the Middle East) and worry beads, a legacy from the Turks, strands of beads that look like rosaries but have no religious significance, that Greeks finger incessantly to ward off nerves and silence. (One large American bank makes worry beads for their employees with the company insignia.)

The selection of foreign language press on a newsstand indicates that a particular colony is significant enough to have its own newspaper, and probably has its own commercial areas in the city. In New York during one of that city's longest newspaper strikes, only the English-speaking citizens were short on news. The Spanish, Puerto Ricans, Italians, Chinese, Yiddish-speaking Jews, Hungarians, Germans, Filipinos, Greeks, Swedes, Japanese, Koreans, Russians, Poles, Iranians, Haitians, French, Estonians, and Armenians were kept well informed by their own journals.

Organizing Each Day

Organizing your day depends on what you most want to see and on how you feel. Listen to your own physical and mental rhythms, and be aware that you do have saturation points. This is admittedly a difficult assignment, especially when your time is limited and you feel you should have Michelangelo for breakfast, Degas for lunch, Picasso for dinner, and Gothic churches in between. Sometimes a change of pace is more relaxing than just quitting: follow shopping with tea; indoor museums with lunch in an outdoor café or park; walking through ruins with a pedicure; a day exploring on foot with dinner with a view; all night on the town with breakfast in bed.

The working and leisure hours of a city can also affect your plans. Some places just wake up early. To take a remote example, you can call business offices in South Africa at seven-thirty in the morning, but you'd be lucky to find anyone open for business in Rio before ten. The whole concept of *mañana* is alive and well in Latin and Central America, whereas England is ultra-punctual. You will get invitations that read "7:45 for 8" meaning you have exactly fifteen minutes leeway.

In Japan and Hong Kong, the meal is the evening's entertainment; it begins around seven-thirty and finishes by ten. (A Hong Kong resident once told me that at night people in Hong Kong are only thinking about tomorrow's deal.) Dinner is so late in Spain that you'll probably struggle to keep your head from falling into the hors d'oeuvres. There's no use bucking the system. Have a snack, take a siesta. *Anytime I say, "They sure do things different here," I remind myself that that's exactly why I came.*

The most effective way to introduce yourself to a city is taking a half-day bus tour of the general points of interest. Tours are multilingual and you'll meet other travelers, not necessarily Americans. Take a pen and pad for noting things to pursue or eliminate. It pays to go with a reputable company because inferior equipment, like worn-out tapes or headsets, can make the tour almost useless. Ask your travel agent, the hotel, or local tourist office for recommendations.

WALKING

Next, you start walking. Your resources couldn't be richer, for you have at your feet the distinctive architecture of the streets themselves and the whirlpool of life within. Not every city is branded in grandeur with the Colosseum, the Kremlin, the Prado, or the Golden Gate Bridge, parts of the world's "haute couture" collection of monuments. But every city or town does have its "prêt à porter," or ready-to-wear; the commonplace, utilitarian objects that are the earmarks of progress: shabby subway entrances, park benches, trash cans, kiosks, manholes like iron flowers in the asphalt, streetlamps and their shadows, and the cacophony of signs on shopping streets, all demanding your attention like a petulant child.

Look up, down, and sideways. Nothing is too inconsequential for your eye. You'll see that the design of streets in many cities abroad is different from the American design. Here streets are functional conduits, straight walks of business with an indelible line of demarcation between sidewalk and street, pedestrian and traffic. Elsewhere, the street is an actual stage where business, dining, wooing, politicking, trading, and ogling unfurl shamelessly—and simultaneously.

In these cities, life on the streets swells and recedes with the season, the day of the week, and the very hour of the day. A nook that is nonpareil in January will be deserted in July; in places like Italy, Argentina, Spain, or Mexico, the activity center of the piazza will shift hourly with the sun. Wherever you are, you should look at the bicycles, the signs, the policemen, the marquees, the doormen, the clouds, the food sold on the streets. Listen to your nose. Notice how people walk differently on Sunday than on Monday.

Go back to the same areas more than once and you'll begin to feel that they're your neighborhood. The sense of "knowing your way," without having to consult maps or passers-by, makes the city more personal, like the look of recognition from the waiter on your second visit to a café or restaurant.

Motor vehicles are part of the streetscape too. Are they to scale with the city? What about cars, civilian tanks that have conquered most cities? What about the proliferation of rules, posted on the streets or written in manuals, that gamely try to govern the interplay of driver and pedestrian. Guidelines aside, however, national styles of driving in such geographically distant spots as Tokyo, Rio, Rome, or New York are chillingly similar: no one looks where he is going. To be more precise, everyone looks *only* where he is going.

Consequently, a walker's life is not uneventful. Merely crossing the street can be a death-defying act. You are safe in California (usually) if you cross with the green light in the crosswalk. (I have gotten jaywalking tickets for proceeding otherwise.) In New York, getting from one side of the street to the other is one of the martial arts. In fact, my father began my initiation at the tender age of ten. At rush hour he took me by the hand to the middle of Fifth Avenue,

where we were fanned by traffic whizzing by on both sides until we
could breach the remaining gap. My reward was a Dr. Brown's Cel-
Ray Tonic and a sour pickle.

LOCAL TRANSPORT

Walking often has the same purpose of the *passeggiata* in Italy or
the *peripato* in Greece, a languid stroll with no particular destination
or time limit. There are times, however, when the destination is more
important than the process of getting there. I've watched myself take
taxis indiscriminately because I assume they're faster, and I don't
have the responsibility of finding my own way. Taxis aren't always
the best solution, and certainly not the most economical, although in
New York it's worth one ride on the chance you get a philosopher-
king, or in London because the vehicle itself is so special.

Taxi fares are usually based on a meter rate calculated on time and
mileage, or a fixed rate (with no meter at all) from one zone of the
city to another, as in Washington, D.C., and for long distances like
trips to the airport or between cities.

In these instances, settle on an amount *before* you leave. You can
always ask the hotel doorman or desk clerk for assistance, either in
negotiating the price, the language, or both. We've all heard horror
stories about being ripped off by taxi drivers who refuse, for instance,
to part with your luggage unless you fork over double the price.
There is no guarantee, although it's unlikely, that you'll face this dilemma. A precautionary measure is always to note the license number of the cab, or the driver's registration number, which should be
posted in plain view on the dashboard.

I get a satisfactory sense of self-reliance in using the public transportation systems—the bus, the subway, the bicycle, the ferry. You
are forced to come to grips with the layout of the city, you're taking
part in how that city lives, and you probably save money. Many
cities have transport passes, ticket booklets, or reduced fares for
specific time periods—a week, a weekend, a month. These items and
maps showing the bus and subway lines are often available at tourist
offices or bus, subway or train stations.

Some public transport is superefficient. You're practically taken by
the hand on the *Métro,* the subway in Paris. There is a large map at
most subway entrances, and many stations have maps with push but-

tons marked with the name of each station. You push the button that corresponds with your destination, and the quickest route lights up on the map. Other public conveyance offers more atmosphere, like the "taptaps," or minibuses in Haiti painted stem to stern with anecdotal religious and native scenes, and whimsically named things like "Mother Dear," "O.K. Zaza," and "Jesus Loves You."

The Filipinos met a taxi shortage after World War II by transforming U. S. Army and Navy jeeps into "jeepneys" capable of holding ten to twelve people. Now the jeepneys are the most popular form of public transport. They are painted bright colors—peacock blue on electric pink—with such standard accessories as gargoyles or a fringe draped from the roof along the open sides.

Many countries have group taxis that operate like buses, with planned routes and specific stop-off points. I partook in Morocco and Israel, and found them perfectly adequate. I've just never understood why the cars were usually vintage Pontiacs and Buicks.

The bus offers efficient, economical service, virtues you should weigh against two factors: the inhumanity of rush hour in the big cities when you face a seething, gesticulating crowd; and the heat of summer. Few buses are air-conditioned, unless you're lucky, or are in Rio, where they are called *frescos,* the "big fresh ones." The route is usually listed on the bus, sometimes including the major destinations along the way. The number of the route appears on the signs at bus stops. On new-model buses, you board in the front and pay the driver (most require exact change). In the older buses in London, you board through the open space at the rear, state your destination, and pay the conductor. If you are planning to return at night by bus, be sure to ask how late it runs.

When you take a bus in a country where you don't speak the language, take the name of your hotel or destination written in the language. I was once on a bus in Hong Kong and the driver didn't speak English. Fortunately I had a card from the hotel, printed in both Chinese and English. I pointed. He nodded. We smiled. Communication isn't always resolved so painlessly. In Japan, the houses are often numbered according to when they were built, not by a logical progression up (or down) the street. Number 114 might be next door to number 3. The Japanese affinity for drawing maps and intricate diagrams notwithstanding, if you can have your friends meet you first at your hotel, believe me, you're better off.

A DOZEN IMAGINATIVE WAYS TO UNEARTH A CITY

Every city in the world has its own "must see," "must do," "must taste" attractions that are listed in general guidebooks. The garland of suggestions that follows will point you off the routine avenues to different ways of approaching the city and the countryside, no matter where you are in the world. *The process of discovery is the same whether you're in Paris or New Delhi, even though the idea of Paris is more familiar.*

Sometimes having a specific *purpose* can focus your energy and lead to unexpected experiences. The purpose could be as obscure as going to the Valley of Roses in Bulgaria to see how perfume or marmalade is made with roses, or as familiar as taking in the springtime cherry blossoms in Washington, D.C., or Kyoto, Japan. Whatever you do, do it with zest and curiosity.

1. *See the city from the water*—Cable cars, mountain trams, top-floor bars, and observation decks are accepted vantage points (if fog and clouds don't interfere), but whenever possible, take a sight-seeing cruise on a lake, river, canal, harbor, coastline. If you doubt your sea legs, take a motion-sickness pill a half hour before boarding.

2. *Take an organized walk*—Many cities have both guided and do-it-yourself tours to areas of special interest, and "in-the-footsteps" tours of famous authors, politicians, fictional literary characters like Sherlock Holmes in London and Don Quixote in Spain. Norway's mountain paths are marked for "leisurely" or "vigorous" pace. Ask the local tourist offices, or chambers of commerce for information.

3. *Find an offbeat museum*—Practically everything imaginable has a museum all its own, not just the great masters. Consider museums devoted to: skiing in Oslo; bullfighting in Madrid; transport at the Smithsonian; hats in Bad Homburg (near Frankfurt), where four centuries of changing hat fashions are documented; the Museum of the Diaspora, in Tel Aviv, organized by areas of concern and interest to Jews, not by chronology; and a bread museum in Ulm.

4. *Browse (and I mean browse) through famous department stores*—Wander through Neiman-Marcus, Dallas (main store)—

famous for the original and expensive his and hers items like camels and submarines; Gump's, San Francisco—known for objets d'art, glass, jade, and silver; Bloomingdale's, New York—model rooms for interior design, trendy boutiques; Galeries Lafayette, Paris— everyday nonexotic items, a glimpse into French household habits (multilingual guides available, no purchase necessary); Harrod's, London—Europe's largest department store, with over two hundred sections, from a zoo to a food market and services including planning funerals and tuning pianos.

5. *Follow-up on a hobby*—Visit auctions, excavations, specialty shops, entire towns or regions geared to a particular interest of yours, from coins to cave exploring. To take a few examples: skilled copper craftsmen have located for centuries in the Normandy town of Vil-ledieu-les-Poêles, on the route between Caen and Mont-Saint-Michel, which is now alive with copperware shops and decorative objects to tempt cooks and collectors. Flower buffs can follow bulb and blossom routes mapped out by the Netherlands National Tourist Office, or see the most important flower auction hall in Europe in Aalsmeer, a few miles from Amsterdam's Schiphol Airport.

6. *Go backstage*—There are guided tours to behind-the-scenes on Broadway in New York, but consider backstage at the fashion houses of Paris, the kitchens of great restaurants. Some hotels offer classes in the well-known drinks and dishes of the region. Ask the local tourist office.

7. *Take the bus to the end of the line*—Anywhere (within reason).

8. *Seek out the indigenous music and dance*—"Live" performance always reveals a side of a culture in colorful, poetic, moving expression: the *fado,* in Portugal, is the sad, monotonous chant about human passions, destiny, and sentiment. The singer is often a woman, accompanied by several guitars, or university students, who serenade the town's prettiest girls. (If the young lady approves, and gives a particular young man a kiss, he tears a piece off the bottom of his black cape as a reciprocal gesture, hence the uneven hems of the student's robes); the *mariachi* music of the state of Jalisco in Mexico is still the traditional serenade of girlfriends. The word mariachi, from the French *mariage,* refers to the original function of the group —to play at weddings and balls; the *zeimbekiko,* the dance of Zorba

the Greek, traditionally danced by men only, in tavernas, or *bouzou-kii,* named for the music played on the bouzoukia; jazz in the French Quarter of New Orleans; the dances of Bali, such as the *legong,* the *kecak,* and the *barong,* that relate stories derived from the Ramayana or Mahabharata, the great epics of India. The most famous is the *kecak,* or monkey dance, with more than a hundred dancers, sitting in concentric circles, whose monkey-like hissing, and swaying of the arms, accompany the dance; etc.

9. *If you can, watch television.* I know people who have come to America, not speaking any English, and religiously tuned into cartoons, sports, and children's programs to learn simple English. Ads on TV are different, and give you an idea of the shopping mentality—what to buy, what is popular, what's being pushed, and to what age level. Imagine a foreigner coming to America and seeing an animated tiger in a black tie hawking breakfast cereal.

10. Visit the local university for an idea of the "youth."

11. *Ask the local tourist office about what's free* (practically). From tours to events: beer factories, pineapple canneries; outdoor concerts; self-guided walking tours; monuments (touring the White House is a no-cost attraction); crafts demonstrations; music recitals in churches; governments in session, from Parliament to Congress; the law courts (in England the judges still wear white wigs); market day anywhere; watch local athletes disport themselves—men in France playing boule, sandlot baseball in New York.

12. *Get lost!*

9.

Food

Fresh, warm fruit bought in an open stall; creamy goat cheese resting on a wicker tray; grapefruit ice at the end of a long meal; espresso in a sleepy café; the pain of jalapeños; the poetry of passion fruit; the oil of just-made french fries staining a paper bag; pasta tossed like a salad with fresh basil; bread crackling hot from a baker's oven; fresh vanilla; cold beer during a summer picnic; pistachio-studded pâté in an earthenware crock; the first bite of a truffle omelet; the last bite of a hot fudge sundae; the *very* last bite of a hot fudge sundae.

Every place I've ever been is connected with a food memory. Eating is one of the grand, sensual experiences of travel that will sharpen your sensitivity and enrich your recall. Tastes and aromas of food evoke memories and emotions as poignantly as a piece of music or the cologne of a man you once loved. Traveling is a wonderful way to expand the taste memories you've been storing up since childhood. Who could forget the pungency of a new piece of bubble gum; the consummate sweetness of the inside of an Oreo cookie; the perfect marriage of peanut butter and jelly. As a Chinese epicure and scholar once said, "What is patriotism but the love of good things we ate in childhood."

Christmas for me is the redolence of a dish that marked my father's informal debut as a cook: green peppers and onions burbling in butter, waiting to be caught in a swirl of eggs. The upheaval of adolescence was softened by his Italian period of linguine and marinara sauce and chicken cacciatore. The bouquet of the day's first pot of coffee floating upstairs into my bedroom meant someone was up before me, making a house a home.

Your attitude about food begins early in life, shaped by many obvious and many imperceptible things: the products available where you grew up—and visited; what you ate at home, what you were forbidden to eat; watching people react with pleasure or horror to certain foods; what your best friend's mother packed for her lunch (and what you traded).

Growing up in California taught me to consider salads a main course, not just a refreshing afterthought, but my tastes were very much influenced by the girl who moved in next door when I was eight. Her garden had avocados, oranges, lemons, kumquats, and a branch of her pomegranate tree languished over the fence into our driveway. Her parents were vegetarians, and tried to feed her as they ate, but we used to meet for lunch behind the giant oak tree in my garden and I'd give her my tuna fish sandwiches and eat her avocado and tomato salad, sliced, raw potatoes, and raw cashews. People impugn me to this day for eating like a rabbit.

Looking back, I realize that I absorbed a posture about food as a child that I've lived by since, particularly on a trip when I'm constantly exposed to new tastes: what you eat must be the best of *whatever* it is. My father would happily prostrate himself for a certain kind of hot dog on a regular hot dog bun, submerged in deli mustard and sauerkraut. And I would do the same for a bran muffin with a lot of crust, preferably burnt.

Your exploration of food should be governed by infinite curiosity. Fling open the gastronomic gates when you travel, suspend all known food prejudices. Remember the old story, "If you don't know what you're eating . . ." We have learned to order such delicacies as bird's-nest and shark's-fin soup in Chinese restaurants, but how would you feel about another savory from the East: fruit-eating wild cat (baked)? Or bear meat pâté? They *sound* appalling, but only because of our programming. Granted, these particular treats are probably beyond our culinary pastures, but the immediate negative reaction reveals the lurking prejudices of a lifetime's conditioning.

You should break through the barriers of what is called "gourmet food," a phrase that, at best, is an overworked and amorphous misnomer. The origin of the word, from Medieval French, is "groom," and meant servant, or vintner's assistant, but modern parlance and the food press has endowed it with new meaning and even mystique.

A person called "a gourmet cook," for instance, practically elicits the respect due a prelate, and "gourmet food" seems beyond the comprehension of the mortal palate. I found an article written as a parody by humorist Russell Baker in the New York *Times* as a response to an article about a $4,000 dinner for two consumed by that paper's food critic, Craig Claiborne, and his associate, Pierre Franey.

The meal opened with a 1975 Diet Pepsi served in a disposable bottle. Although its bouquet was negligible, its distinct metallic aftertaste evoked memories of tin cans one had licked experimentally in the first flush of childhood's curiosity . . . To create the balance of tastes so cherished by the epicurean palate, I followed with a *pâté de fruites de nuts of Georgia* . . . the accompanying drink was cold milk served in a wide-brimmed jelly glass . . . This is essential to proper consumption of the pâté since the entire confection must be dipped into the milk to soften it for eating. In making the presentation to the mouth, one must beware lest the milk-soaked portion of the sandwich fall onto the necktie. Thus, seasoned gourmandisers follow the old maxim of the Breton chefs and "bring the mouth to the jelly glass . . ."

At this point in the meal, the stomach was ready for serious eating, and I prepared beans with bacon grease, a dish I perfected in 1937 while developing my *cuisine du dépression* . . . For the meat course I had fried bologna à la Nutley, Nouveau Jersey. Six slices of A&P bologna were placed in an ungreased frying pan over maximum heat and held down by a long fork until the entire house filled with smoke . . . The cheese course was deliciously simple—a single slice of Kraft's individually wrapped yellow sandwich cheese, which was flavored by vigorously rubbing it over the bottom of the frying pan to soak up the rich bologna juices . . . Wine being absolutely *de rigueur* with cheese, I chose a 1974 Muscatel, flavored with a maraschino cherry, and afterwards cleared my palate with three pickled martini onions . . .

It was time for the fruit. I chose a Del Monte tinned pear, which, regrettably, slipped from the spoon and fell on the floor, necessitating its being blotted with a paper towel to remove cat hairs. To compensate for the resulting loss of pear syrup, I dipped it lightly in hot dog relish, which created a unique flavor . . .

So that words don't get between you and your food, excise the word gourmet, and consider the term "haute cuisine," which is thrown around just as recklessly, but actually, refers to a style of French cooking with specific characteristics: Sauces are the hallmark; dishes are flavored with great subtlety; and salads have a minor role. Wine is a "course" that must be harmonized into the menu plan, and truffles, the world's most famous fungus, are obligatory, although their appeal has always escaped me.

And remember, the French are equally renowned for "cuisine bourgeoise," simple home cooking that chefs sometimes call "cuisine grand-mère" or grandmother's cooking. Whatever it is called, you should go in search of the best of anything an area has to offer, no matter where you are, whether it's a chestnut toasted to perfection on a Parisian side street, a chicken fragrant with rosemary turning on a spit, the snowy peaks of a meringue, or a foreign version of an American standard. I once had a Greek interpretation of a hot fudge sundae: bittersweet chocolate sherbet, dripping in hot fudge, strewn with particles of roasted, salted almonds. Or should I say it had me?

FOOD AS A CULTURAL EXPERIENCE

Cooking is an art form that reflects a culture as much as painting and sculpture, architecture and music. The evidence of a chef's art, however, isn't a haunting refrain, does not hang on a museum wall or tower skyward to be appreciated forevermore. The art of a cook lives fleetingly in one's mouth, and is preserved only through tastememory and recipes. What you eat on a trip will not only nourish your body, but increase your understanding of a country.

A national cuisine is a product of climate, geography, religion, and the winds of trade and war. Bologna is called the food capital of northern Italy. She owes this to her location, with the rich wheat fields that provide ingredients for the world's most delicate pasta, and the grazing land for the famed cattle who also give us the glorious by-product of Parmesan cheese. Just as San Franciscans claim that the air is responsible for the unimpeachable quality of their sourdough bread, the Italians say the same about their prosciutto. A hill town near Bologna is reputed to have the best air for curing hams, and in season, hams hang in the windows of many houses to catch the breezes which sweep over pine and chestnut forests.

In Scandinavia, the harsh climate and rugged terrain color the cuisine. Fish is abundant and the herring is practically the culinary mascot. But grazing turf for cattle is so limited that the mountainsides are turned into sloping pastures—inclines so steep that the cows are tied to a tree by rope. The available beef is stretched as far as possible, and recipes emphasize braised and chopped meats, which explains why Swedish meatballs are Scandinavia's entry in the world's repertoire of meat courses.

With our pioneering days long gone, the only time we think about gathering wood is on a camping trip, but the lack of fuel in many countries has necessitated distinct styles of cooking. In China, for instance, "chowing" or stir-fry cooking involves much preparation to get the food in the thinnest possible pieces for minimum cooking time. The Chinese still steam bread, since baking ovens are considered a waste of fuel. In Italy and France, each town used to have a community baker. The husband would take the prepared but uncooked lasagne to the baker on his way to work in the morning, and bring it home for the lunch. Desserts today in Italy are still "bought."

A country's geography is not only the internal terrain, but the borders that ebb and flow with invasions, and embrace new immigrants. The cuisine of northern India reflects the taste of the Moghuls, who brought with them their love of lamb, so that New Delhi is the capital of the kebab and other lamb dishes. Southern India is principally vegetarian.

The Mongols came down from the north into China with the Mongolian barbecue. This do-it-yourself supper consists of plates of Kleenex-thin, raw ingredients, like abalone, shrimp, beef, cabbage, bean sprouts, chives, red and green peppers, and vermicelli (noodles) that surround a large round griddle in the center of a table on which you concoct your meal.

Invaders and settlers not only brought styles of cooking and eating habits, but they sometimes brought along their favorite foods. Citrus fruits and almonds grew in many places where the Arabs spread the banner of Islam. In fact, foods often associated with an area didn't necessarily originate there. Who could imagine the Mediterranean cuisine without the tomato? But tomatoes were unknown until the Spanish explorers brought them back from the New World, where the Indians had been busy cultivating the crop for hundreds of years.

Our own country may be the most recent example of how a national cuisine evolves, although the world may have been slow to recognize the emergence of—may Escoffier rest in peace—"la cuisine américaine," which is essentially a patchwork of regional kitchens. The region most strongly identified with a "style" is New Orleans. The cooking is based on classic French methods, local ingredients, spices from trade with the West Indies, turned by the hands of the Spaniards, Africans, French Acadians exiled from Canada, and Americans. Gumbo, for instance, is a close approximation of bouillabaisse; "coubouillon" is a local fish stock, just like the one made by chefs in the French courts.

Colonists in New England adopted Old World methods to native crops like corn, beans, and squash. The missionary fathers came to California from Spain with grape cuttings, vegetable seeds, and fruit tree seedlings, ingredients that still characterize California food.

In fact, prelates in many countries have had considerable influence on gastronomy. A certain melon was first grown in (and named after) the Pope's garden at Cantalupo, near Rome. Monks in France developed cheese and wine. Perhaps the most famous beverage is Dom Pérignon champagne, invented by a Benedictine monk of the same name who reportedly said after his first sip, "Come quickly! I'm drinking stars!"

The key to eating well is to try the foods that are grown, produced, or manufactured in the area you visit, even though the basic ingredients may be augmented by sophisticated methods of transportation and refrigeration.

FOOD MYTHS

Not knowing the origin of champagne won't dim your appreciation of food. What *can* impair your food discoveries is belief in the myths that surround certain cuisines, as, "All English food is inedible."

While a myth may begin with a crumb of truth, let your curiosity propel you beyond the myth, at least for one meal. Consider the following rather popular myths:

1. *Curry is Indian food.* Curry isn't even a spice. The origin of the word curry itself is unclear. It could be *kari,* a Tamil word meaning "sauce," a spice made from the kari leaf, or *kahri,* a northern Indian dish made from buttermilk and chickpea flour. Curry powder as we know it is a blend of many spices, including cumin, red peppers, coriander, fenugreek, and turmeric, and has one distinctive flavor. Spice mixtures in India are called *masalas,* which are many spices blended and cooked differently for individual and unique tastes.

A stew-like main course with many condiments is not the only star-quality dish in the Indian cuisine. India is a subcontinent and the cuisine is appropriately varied, from lamb and rice dishes in the north, to fish along the coasts, to an infinite variety of vegetarian dishes, breads, and fruits.

2. *Italian food is heavy and fattening.* Italian cooking is made of regional specialties, so you will be able to choose from dishes as varied as feather-light veal piccata, or bistecca alla fiorentina, nothing more than a large and tender grilled steak sprinkled with olive oil and salt.

Another myth is that all pasta is spaghetti. There are over six hundred varieties, from thin linguine, to the stuffed ones, like ravioli, and those named for their shape, size, or "look," like *ricci di donne,* ladies' curls; or *vermicelli,* little worms; *radiatori,* car radiator grills; *agnolotti,* little fat lambs. And the sauces range from straight-up tomato to pesto, an ambrosial mix of fresh basil, garlic, parmesan, and romano cheese and pignola nuts.

3. *You only eat Chinese food for dinner.* What about the traditional Chinese snacks served at breakfast and midmorning tea called *dim sum,* which means "heart's delight." *Dim sum* is an endless pageant of bite-sized dumplings, piled high in individual dishes and wheeled around on serving trolleys. To taste as much as possible, *dim sum* should be shared with a group of people. Tea is poured first. Then the procession begins: salty and sweet, soft, steamed, and fried crispy, including *ha gao*—minced shrimp in a bonnet shape,

steamed rice, and noodle dumplings; *char shiew bao*—a barbecued pork surprise in a fluffy bun; mandarin scallion cake, flaky sesame pastry encasing sauteed green onions; and the sweet *dim-sum*-like prune cakes—small but rich mandarin pastries filled with sweet plum paste or mandarin custard, dusted with sesame seeds and sugar and deep-fried or Dan tart, milk lemon custard. Large "cakes," as they are called, are cut with the end of the chopstick that doesn't go in the mouth.

4. *Danish pastry comes from Copenhagen.* Not so. In Denmark, pastries are Wienerbrod—Vienna bread!

FOOD AS A SOCIALIZER

Only when you fast do you realize how much of your social and business life revolves around food. Consider the following opportunities for physical and spiritual resuscitation that arise almost hourly —in any part of the world.

Breakfast, breakfast meetings, breakfast rides (out West)

Midmorning coffee breaks, danish and coffee, stopping by for a cup of coffee

Elevenses in Great Britain; tea and a little something around eleven

Zweites Frühstück in Germany, a second breakfast of small sandwiches and coffee

Dim sum in Asia, an early lunch or late morning tea

Lunch: Family-oriented or the businessperson's version

Afternoon coffee break

Tea; tea and biscuits (English for cookies)

High tea; Legendary. Sandwiches on white bread with the crusts trimmed. Pink and yellow cakes in marzipan jackets. Scones and crumpets

Cocktails: Wine, apéritif, martinis, beer and peanuts, sparkling water for the nondrinker, and for the devout, the first reviving taste of scotch

Dinner

Supper

Midnight supper

Midnight snacks

Snacks after midnight: You open the refrigerator door at 3 A.M., *praying* that since you retired at eleven, someone, ANYONE, has left you a delectable little something

There are any number of reasons that bring people together around a table other than eating. For the moment, put those aside and contemplate the sheer power of food. Our first happiness is in the mouth; it is the love expressed when a mother feeds a child. The hospitality we offer and accept as adults is merely the socialized version of mother love. Food has the ability to make strangers friends and adversaries civil. It welcomes, warms, nourishes, and comforts. Sharing a meal can be as intimate as sharing conversation, company, and love. The Chinese put it in disarmingly simple terms: Can mouth, can happy. The phrase is the literal translation of Coca-Cola, but the meaning reaches universes beyond the beverage.

Food patterns change when you travel. You always eat out and you have to make a decision several times a day about where and what you want to eat. (I have friends who discuss their itinerary in terms of how many meals per city, not how many days.) In a new locale, you are more aware of food as an organic part of the travel experience. But it's more than what you eat. The physical environment, the people around you, from waiters to clients, the presentation of the meal, fuse together for a total effect. It's like sight-seeing sitting down, like taking a bus tour with your tongue; a rest after a morning of walking, but still allowing you to experience something new. At night after a nap, dinner allows you to have a second day in each day, when you have nothing on your mind except the relaxation of food and conversation.

Wherever your travels take you, you have at your disposal a thousand food venues: some formal, with linen napery; some casual, with newspapers for tablecloths; others with newspapers just for reading. The following section introduces the delights that await you.

CAFÉS, ET AL.

Sitting in a café and watching life go by is surely one of the world's oldest pastimes. Cafés in one form or another exist all over the world as a gathering spot for congenial company (in some countries male only), a home for the artistically inclined, a place for blue bloods to dip into Bohemia, and lovers into each other. Café is a word like caviar that is larger than itself and stands for a way of life.

The quintessential café experience will be found in Paris—at least most of us have grown up thinking so because of Paris in the 1920s, when Left Bank cafés were full of character and people like Camus and Picasso. That character exists still, having nothing to do with famous people, but with the essence of a café.

Sanche de Gramont in his book *The French, Portrait of a People* said:

> The natural habitat of some fairly common french types is the kind of cafe you can spend your day in because it combines the right degree of familiarity as in home or office, and the surroundings are inviting, counterconversations start up easily and are just as easily broken off, deals are made, bets are placed, girls are picked up, someone is always waiting to use the telephone, and couples neck soundlessly for hours in corners.

Central Casting seems to have a category called "café habitués": the artist with his *café noir,* blank page, and illusions; the students planning revolutions and wiring home for money; ladies in fake fur hats who turn up at 10 A.M. every day; and lovers touching knees under the table.

How do you unearth the "right" or the "best" café? A rule of thumb is, you find them on major thoroughfares, especially ones lined with trees; in any city's equivalent of the Left Bank or student areas; near fountains and piazzas; in deluxe hotels.

It's hard to explain the popularity of one café over another. I remember an intersection in Marrakesh with a café on each corner. But my friends always took me to the same one, around eleven each morning, for late coffee and oranges in a sunny chair and to get our shoes shined for a quarter, about nine at night to sit inside on

cracked red leather banquettes around a formica table drinking Campari and soda. We'd return after dinner about 1 A.M. to a stool at the bar for the evening's last espresso. The other café always seemed alone and empty.

In Athens, on the other hand, there seems to be a different location for different times of the day. In the morning you choose between the cafés on Syntagma (Constitution) Square, the heartbeat of the city where people dash madly to work and well-heeled travelers arrive at the famous hotels, or you give your patronage to Zonar's or Floca's two blocks away, with confections enthroned on every inch of counter space. After lunch, late in the afternoon, or past midnight, the action moves to Kolonaki Square, the chic residential section, brimming with Guccied ladies and the aroma of freshly baked spinach pie.

In most societies, the café and adjacent sidewalk is an extended living room, especially in Mediterranean countries where living rooms themselves tend to be very formal and reserved for somber occasions like receptions following funerals or baptisms.

In Italy, the espresso bar is almost as holy as the Vatican, although the Roman Catholic Church once condemned coffee as an infidel drink because it was called the wine of Islam. The original word for coffee meant wine and filled the need for a stimulant among Muslims, whose religion forbade alcoholic beverages. Fortunately, Pope Clement VIII tasted coffee and reputedly said, "This Satan's drink is too delicious to let the heathens have it all. We shall baptize it and make a Christian beverage of it."

Even though the word "café" means coffee, what you order is unimportant. Socializing and observing can be pursued just as vigorously if you order ice cream, an apéritif, or a lemonade.

It's a happy circumstance for women that café etiquette permits anyone to talk to anyone else without recrimination. This uncodified rule even applies to places that may not actually be called a café, but have a similar social purpose.

- *Pubs in the British Isles.* Pub derives from public house, the community drinking hall in town. There are thousands of them, with such endearing names as The Magnet and Dewdrop, or The World Turned Upside Down. Drinks that reinforce the warmth of a pub are hard cider and a wide variety of beers, like lager, ale, stout, or porter, which are usually sold by the pint. You order "half a bitter," to get draft beer in a half-pint glass. The accompanying sustenance may be Ploughman's lunch, freshly baked bread, cheddar cheese, and a few pickled onions; Scotch eggs (hard-boiled eggs, encased in sausage meat, coated with batter, and then deep-fried); or bangers and mash (sausages and mashed potatoes).

- *Wine bars in England and France.* You can order several different types of wine (and snacks). These bars are particularly popular spots when the new Beaujolais wine arrives in the fall.

- *Heurigen in Grinzing* (a suburb outside Vienna). "Heurige" means "of this year" and Heurigen are wine gardens where the grower sells wine produced from his own vineyards. Heurigen are open year round, but not all on the same day. A green fir branch hung on the door means "open for business." Stop at a food shop in Vienna before you go and ask for a "heurigen packet," a basket of sandwiches.

▪ *Tapas bars in Spain.* The ones in Madrid have the tradition called *chateo,* snacks with wine. Chateo itself means snub-nosed, and "a chateo" is crawling through the city's bars, drinking wine out of snub-nosed glasses, and eating *tapas,* an infinite variety of hors d'oeuvres.

▪ *Coffeehouse in Vienna.* The Viennese coffeehouse has been part of the city's social life for centuries. People can sit all day, reading newspapers (provided by the owner) and sipping coffee. You generally get a fresh glass of water every thirty minutes (depending on how tradition-bound the coffeehouse is), a custom that started three centuries ago when coffee was first introduced and was very bitter. There are several ways of ordering coffee: *melange*—coffee with milk; *mazagran*—cold coffee with ice cubes and a dash of rum; *schale gold*—coffee with enough cream to make it look gold; *kapuziner*—more coffee than milk so it looks dark brown; and if you agree with Kipling, who contended "perfect coffee is black as night, strong as hell, and sweet as sin," you order *mokka.*

▪ *Kissaten.* Coffeehouses in Tokyo. Yes, coffeehouses.

RESTAURANTS

Food in a café might be considered a sideline, a quick restorative, or a pleasing afterthought, but food in a restaurant deserves considerable attention. Your mood, your palate, and your pocketbook should all conspire to help you select the appropriate place.

Certain types of restaurants invite more camaraderie between customers than others. You are not likely to strike up casual conversation in an elegant establishment that offers frosty but impeccable service. You go to these kinds of restaurants to experience that particular style, not to be chummy with your neighbor. It's just a window seat on another world that you may want to glance at once and never again.

On the other hand, I've been to family-style bistros in the hill towns of southern France, or the coasts of Spain and Italy, where you sit at long tables that are covered in butcher block paper, in the company of a dozen people you've never met before. The style is so informal in Greece, particularly on the islands, that you can walk into the kitchens and point to what you want. I've found myself having dinner with people I met while we were selecting our meal as it simmered on the stove (or swam in a sink).

Impromptu conversations are possible even in New York's trendy Sunday brunch hangouts. I once sat next to two very attractive women, both in their forties. I noticed they were listening intently as I ordered and finally they leaned over to ask for some suggestions. They explained that they were from Dallas and came to New York to go to the theater, shop, feast, and then jog off the damage in Central Park. Both of their husbands traveled extensively and, as one of them explained, "after twenty-five years of marriage, you just have to do your own thing."

Remember that you're not necessarily consigned to dinner only when you go to a restaurant. In some parts of the world breakfast is a national habit. The offerings are usually available in the hotels, and may be a radical (and enlightening) departure from bacon and eggs. Japan: *umeboshi* (sour red pickled plums), rice topped with *nori* (seaweed), *misoshiru* (broth enriched with fermented soybean paste, tofu, vegetables, green tea); the Balkans: pork chops, hot peppers, and slivovitz (high-octane plum brandy); Spain: chocolate or coffee, rolls, butter, *churros* (deep-fried batter strips, sugared); Caribbean islands: bananas, papayas, mangoes, salt fish, *escoveche* (fried sweet and sour fish), cornbread. In Israel, the buffet breakfast at most hotels and kibbutzim is unending: eggs, cheeses, sardines, herring, olives, garlic sausage with whole peppercorns, fried potatoes, salads, dark bread, halvah, blintzes, and borscht.

How to Choose a Restaurant

I once went to a fish restaurant near Tel Aviv touted as the "in" place. It was in an area that looked like a slum, with faded posters of Indian movie stars, laundry strung on lines across buildings with the paint long since peeled away, and unpaved alleyways. Selling second-hand shoes was the main business, but the most vital life signs were gaggles of men past their prime hunched over backgammon tables.

The restaurant was simply two card tables with eight chairs placed smack in the middle of the intersection of two identical alleyways, one known as the street of the money changers; the other, unnamed. The kitchen was a niche in a wall where one man had just enough room for a cauldron of bubbling hot oil to deep-fry the fish; heads of red cabbage for cole slaw and loaves of bread were piled on a newspaper on the ground. Each morning the fishermen would bring in the catch, which the owner made for their breakfast, then served the remainder to paying lunch customers. It was exquisite.

I heard about this "restaurant" from local people, an excellent method for restaurant sleuthing, but there are many official, informal, word-of-mouth, and unexpected sources to draw on for a list of eateries.

To begin, consult several sources—as suggested below—to get a cross reference of possibilities. If the same place comes up several times, chances are you're not courting disaster. Do keep in mind however, that you are trusting someone else's palate, sense of aesthetics and what makes him/her feel comfortable. No matter what advice you get: 1) You should run from restaurants that claim to specialize in several different cuisines. The sign above the door usually reads something like "Chinese-Cuban-Italo-American-Continental." 2) A dubious-sounding or dubious-looking location is not always a testimony to bad or unclean food. Trusting your source in these cases is particularly important. 3) Restaurants and cafés around local marketplaces are fairly dependable for authentic local cuisine and clientele.

The following suggestions should aid your gastronomic detective work.

1. Guidebooks should be read, not followed slavishly. Even the most authoritative guides take one to two years to be researched, printed, and distributed. That "charming, tiny inn" may have undergone several changes of management in the interim. I do read a variety of guidebooks (see Appendix for "Indispensable Reading") to get a general idea of availability, prices, location, local specialties, restaurant hours, addresses and phone numbers for reservations, which credit cards are accepted, if any.

The granddaddy of the restaurant guidebooks is Michelin, a tome of starred and unstarred hotels and restaurants in France and several other countries in Europe. (Three stars is the highest rating, but you will probably eat as well for less money in places with one or two stars.) Michelin inspectors dine anonymously a prescribed number of times in each establishment and rate everything from the food to the view. (Details often include whether or not dogs are allowed.) The

Michelin is easily comprehensible despite the fine print, symbols, and the fact it's in French because there are instructions in English for using the book.

The "Guide des Relais Routiers" might be called the blue-collar Michelin. Truck stop is an approximate English translation of *relais routiers*. The red and blue sign of Les Routiers outside an eating establishment means the place has been inspected and approved by the truck drivers' union and listed in the guide. You can't depend on English-speaking owners, but you can count on a *prix fixe* (fixed price meal) of several courses of home cooking. The guide includes a map of the "casserole" relais, where you're likely to find the specialties of the region.

2. Read local restaurant write-ups. I get the local magazines, especially the city magazines in America that have food critics' reviews, and I check the restaurant, food, and style sections of newspapers. (Bring your clips from home.) Reading these sources is particularly helpful in unfamiliar U.S. cities.

Your local library will have back issues of *Gourmet, Bon Appétit,* and other food-oriented magazines which have written about restaurants in the foreign cities you plan to visit. (See Appendix for "Indispensable Reading.")

3. Ask people wherever you go: the taxi driver, the salesperson, the stewardess. Ask the concierge where *he* goes. So many people travel with excessive concern about food that few tourist-oriented restaurants and hotels carry unedited local dishes. Make your questions specific. Is food or atmosphere more outstanding? Is a particular place better for lunch or dinner? Is it formal, informal? What is the clientele? Can they recommend any special dishes? Does the staff speak English? What is the average price of a meal? Do you have to bring your own wine? Are reservations necessary?

If your itinerary is planned around meals in well-known restaurants, ask your travel agent or the tourist office about writing in advance—in the appropriate language—and call to reconfirm (or ask your concierge or hotel operator) when you're within reasonable phone distance.

4. Visit the restaurants themselves. Posting menus on the restaurant window or near the door is more customary outside the United States, but you can always ask to see a menu. (Don't be intimidated.) Look for regional specialties (see How to Order the Best of Everything in this chapter); take the average price of the main dish, and

double it to estimate how much you would expect to pay for a full meal, including wine, the house or local brew, not the seventy-dollar variety. Does the restaurant accept credit cards? (The one you have with you . . . ?)

If you are planning to dine alone, particularly for dinner, you might want to go over in the afternoon, meet the maître d', and select a table (if possible). When you come back that evening, you'll feel more at home. (See How to Dine Alone and Love It in this chapter.) You should never feel obligated to stay someplace where you don't feel right; where you don't like the smell, the look, the price, the other clientele, or even something you can't readily identify. As a rule of thumb, I like Italian restaurants when I eat alone because the staff has an innocuously flirtatious concern for women. It's difficult not to feel welcome, and the waiters invariably send me samples of all the desserts.

5. Find out about local feasts, ceremonies, or food festivals. These traditional events may be tarnished by commercialism, but it is usually worth overlooking. Investigate, for example, a luau in Hawaii; a clambake in New England; a chili cookoff in Texas; a *tamaaraa* in French Polynesia. *Tamaaraa* means the meal and the dancing that follows. The menu may include pig, breadfruit, and big bananas cooked in an *ahimaa,* or earthen oven. Some food is wrapped in leaves and cooked on hot stones.

6. Trust your nose. One friend of mine walks down a street until he finds the most tantalizing aroma.

How to Dine Alone and Love It (Well, Almost)

There was a time when it was not considered proper or respectable for ladies to dine alone in restaurants. In fact, some people believed that women shouldn't be permitted at the table, even in private homes. *A Book About the Table,* published many years ago, says that "women were out of place in the company of feasting epicures, whose attention should not be diverted from beautiful things to lovely creatures at the table. After coffee, the fair sex might resume their rights, which fell into abeyance during a grand meal." The situation wasn't any better for royalty. Before Catherine de Medici married Henry II and brought her Florentine cooks and etiquette to the French court, ladies didn't dine with their sovereign because, as one observer put it, "the movements of the jaws deformed the contours of their faces and detracted from the ethereal appeal of their beauty."

The lone diner, male or female, still disconcerts many maître d's, waiters, and restaurant owners. But a woman alone somehow creates more of a stir. What is she *doing* alone? In the old days, the problem was solved by simply forbidding unescorted women in restaurants, as in the case of ultra-fashionable Delmonico's in New York at the turn of the century. One evening, however, two businesswomen, who had already shocked their peers by advocating free love, spiritualism, and the vote for women, calmly seated themselves at a table and ordered "tomato soup for two." A staff member asked them to leave and politely showed them to the door, whereupon they invited the driver of a hansom cab to join them at the table and ordered "tomato soup for three."

You may not actually *choose* to dine alone, but sometimes you don't have the luxury of choice. You may be between appointments, between lovers, or caught in changing plans. Your first instinct—particularly if you have a comfortable hotel room, a good book, letters to write, or work to do—is to order room service. This is perfectly acceptable, but only if your decision is one of preference, not default. To be fair, there are times when room service *is* the best answer: you've been working hard all day and have to prepare for meetings and presentations; you have been sight-seeing and shopping since dawn, and tomorrow promises more of the same; you have dined extravagantly every night, and your stomach and waistline would appreciate clear soup and black coffee.

There will be times when you really *do* feel like a sensational meal. You want to get dressed up, sit on a plush banquette, and be treated like an Empress. The proper attitude will smooth the way. Look at it this way. Eating alone in an elegant restaurant ("joints" don't seem to cause much consternation) is a new event. It is not a lifetime but a few hours, and you may never do it again. On the other hand, you may love it. Adjust the conventional purpose of the meal, which emphasizes the social aspect, to your own purpose—dining. You are not distracted by conversation, flirtation, passion, or a novel. You have the opportunity to seriously confront the sensuous pleasures of eating and drinking. It's like the difference between reading a book for the appreciation of its content and style or using it as a sleeping pill. (When you think about it, the latter is rather insulting to the author.) When you arrive with your novel, newspapers, postcards, et al., you are communicating that dining isn't your primary purpose. Small wonder you may be treated indifferently.

To be frank, it's not so much that *you* are upset you're alone; it's what you think *other* people will think. You imagine their thought pattern runs something like this: "Look at that poor woman sitting there all alone. Unwanted and by herself. Thank God I'm not in her place. Doesn't she have anyone to have dinner with?" Observers may well think any of the above. But it's equally possible they're musing: "How intriguing! Who is that assured, confident woman. Remarkable. Here she is all by herself in this fancy restaurant. And what service she's getting."

If you aren't entirely at home with the whole idea, your appearance will help you play the part. Your look, your carriage, your clothes, and your tone of voice transmit messages about you that affect how you're treated. It's essential that you *feel* good. This may take some preparation. Instead of coming in from the day's activities, throwing water on your face, and a different sweater on your back, and going right out again, take a long, hot bath. Make it an occasion and dress up.

If you're more comfortable, try this new outing at lunch. Lunch may seem less traumatic because you *think* you are on your way *from* someplace *to* somewhere else. If you are going for dinner, you might want to book the reservation for half an hour before the crowd descends. You won't feel like the center of attention when you walk in the room, and the staff will have extra time.

Let's say that you feel and look terrific, your reservations have been made and confirmed, you arrive and the maître d' seats you directly opposite the busboy station. Speak up about changing tables with grace and resolve, not defiance and aggression. It is not a meal at your folks'. You are paying for the food and the atmosphere, and are ready to compensate for good service. (See Tipping in the chapter, "Etc.") Needless to say, you have to regulate your expectations according to the restaurant. To help focus on the experience of the food and the environment, engage the waiter in a discussion about the menu, and the sommelier about the wine. (See Wines, Spirits, etc. in this chapter.) Ask questions. I have always found that *genuine* curiosity usually compensates for a lack of knowledge.

Even though you've orchestrated the perfect menu, and you're comfortably seated in a corner to watch the life of the restaurant unfold, you still may wonder what to do between courses. Eating as fast as possible is not the answer. Here are a few suggestions. Don't take the book you've brought along out of your bag. Instead:

1. Study the decor.
2. Eavesdrop.
3. Notice what everyone is wearing.
4. Relax.
5. Think about plans for the rest of the trip.
6. Ask the waiter how a dish is prepared. Ask where *he* likes to eat.
7. Befriend the sommelier.
8. Concentrate on the totality of the meal. Notice how each dish is presented. What are the garnishes? What kind of china, silverware, and crystal are used?
9. What are other people eating?
10. How do they eat? Do they hold the knife in the left hand at all times? Do they use bread as a utensil? (In Mexico, tortillas are used as plates, forks, and spoons; in the Middle East and India, eating with the fingers is considered proper. In India snowballs of rice are dipped into bowls of sauce.)

You won't even notice that the waiter has brought your chocolate soufflé to the table until the bouquet of hot chocolate reaches your nose. And then you'll forget about everything else.

How to Order the Best of Everything

Whether you are alone or with an entire platoon of people there are some common-sense rules to help ensure that you get the best wherever you are:

1. Look for words on the menu that indicate a dish is from the region (It usually is qualified by an adjective made out of the name of the town, province, region, or the country); a specialty of the house or of the chef. Menus often say many dishes depend on what's available at the market. This is a good sign.

2. Occasionally restaurants display some of the choicest products on platters near the front door. In Asia, these could be plastic replicas of the dish. Don't be put off. Point, ask, and ask again. Never feel that you have to close your eyes and blindly point to the menu, hoping your finger lands on something edible.

3. Food markets are your window on the cuisine of the area. If you have the time or the inclination, visit one or two supermarkets or open street markets to get a general idea of what is in season, what grows in the area, what is unusual. Until I went to the markets in Bologna I had never seen cranberry beans, which look like beige string beans tie-dyed with cranberry juice, or zucchini flowers.

4. Discuss everything with your waiter. (See Wines, Spirits, etc. in this chapter.) Ask him to suggest a menu. What does the chef recommend? What is the plat du jour, or the dish of the day. Is the tourist menu (usually a selection of an appetizer, a main course, salad, cheese, and a dessert) the best buy for the money? Remember that in some cuisines—notably Chinese—the meal is a composite of different tastes, textures, temperatures, usually beginning with the most delicate and proceeding to the most piquant. The Chinese often serve soup as a refresher in the middle of a multicourse meal or as a finale.

5. Ask for half portions so you can order a variety of items.

6. Throw caution to the winds and indulge yourself. Just wear something with an expandable waist. And read the next section after overindulgence.

How to Order Nonfattening Food (Relatively) and Still Feel You're In . . .

The spring before I went to live with a family in Italy, I endured a month-long diet. Lunch was two and a half saltines, four ounces of low-fat cottage cheese, and two pieces of celery. You can guess the rest. I whittled myself down to a weight even my mother thought was acceptable. In my mind, Italy was not a country but one giant kitchen, with the ultimate temptations of pasta, bread (my particular weakness), and ice cream (my other particular weakness). I had never been to Italy before and I could already reel off five different types of ice cream, from *gelato*—the fairly hard, frozen ones—to *semifreddi* or semi-frozen, foamy ones.

My mother had more stake in my being thin than I did, so she came up with an ingenious solution. "You'll just say you're allergic to pasta and milk products." I nodded and silently scratched the idea. I could picture the first night with my Italian "family": parents, grandparents, and two daughters, gathered ceremoniously around the table, trying to explain my eating habits in my sketchy Italian. All summer long I watched them eat crusty bread at every meal; I drooled and wondered why none of them got fat. I convinced my Italian "mother" she should give me a big plate of vegetables when everyone else was eating pasta. I practically lived on pears and tomatoes. I did not have one single ice cream the entire summer, and we spent one month at the beach where a gelato in the late afternoon was a ritual. I came home thinner than ever. But I will never, ever, repeat the neurotic behavior of that summer.

I have learned through successive trips to Italy and points beyond that it is entirely possible not to come home a size larger, and still partake of the food that is so much a part of a country and its way of life. First you must lose a few pounds before you go, and second, you must learn how to say "on the side," and "no" in every language you could possibly ever need.

The cardinal rule is never deprive yourself of *anything*. This is not antithetical to staying the same size. Have everything. But taste, don't eat. A few spoonfuls of chocolate mousse has no more calories than that big apple you were virtuously going to have instead. As a friend of mine once said, "A balanced diet should have a little bit of protein, a little bit of fat, a little bit of carbohydrate, and a little bit of apple pie." If you must eat more than your share, take it easy the next day. Imagine the impossibility of being in Vienna, a city dedicated to the sweet tooth, and trying to resist a Sachertorte, the national culinary monument, which consists of chocolaty spongecake, filled, coated (or both) with apricot jam, iced with bittersweet chocolate, and served with a mound of schlagobers, or whipped cream.

There is nothing worse for your traveling companion than hearing a nonstop litany about what you would *like* to eat but can't. A recently married couple I know sailed from New York to London on the *QE II*, a vessel known for its excellent kitchen. She picked at a main course, while he would begin at the beginning, with hors d'oeuvres, soup, salad, etc. She didn't drink. He loved wines. After the third day he announced that he was going to find a girlfriend who would eat and drink with him. His message was not lost. Her solution was to match him course for course, and drink (watered down, with constant ice refills) for drink. She ordered dishes that wouldn't go straight from the plate to the hips, like oysters (and she'd always feed him a few), clams, or things that *sounded* as if she were cutting loose, like caviar (only thirty-five calories a teaspoon—and who could afford more?), and they always split the dessert. Eighty/twenty. She successfully became a participant in the food experience, but not at the expense of her figure. The bevy of suggestions that follow should help. If you really want them to, that is.

1. Appetizers: fresh vegetables; seafood without the sauce; melon and a slice of prosciutto; prosciutto and a fig or two; salads with dressing on the side. But always order *something*.

2. Have pasta for the main course; not as a first course, followed by an entrée. Or ask for a half portion of pasta, followed by a light entrée, like veal piccata.

3. Order food that occupies your fingers, like lobsters or crayfish, etc.

4. Always use chopsticks in Chinese or Japanese restaurants because you're forced to take small bites. It's a good idea even if you're not adept. You'll eat less because you'll be so busy struggling with the implements. Under no circumstances should you ask for a fork.

5. Bread is not a villain in itself. Neither is the unadorned potato. Just don't load either one with butter, etc.

6. Don't drink too much before a meal. In the first place, you'll convince yourself that handfuls of peanuts and pretzels are essential accompaniments. In the second place, a few drinks make it easier to forget about watching what you eat.

7. Don't be one of those people who think that what you eat standing up doesn't count.

8. Some cuisines are made for tasting. Many Middle Eastern and Chinese dishes are served family-style on platters set in the middle of the table. This is not your chance for a free-for-all. It's your chance to take small portions.

9. Keep in mind what a hundred calories of something looks like. Practice at home. You'd be amazed how many strawberries you get for a hundred calories. Eat half, and make up for it with a glob of *crème fraiche*.

10. EAT HALF OF EVERYTHING.

11. Snack all day if you want to, but don't eat "three good meals," as well.

12. Have eggs for dinner.

13. SHARE.

14. Order sorbets, sherbets, and ices instead of ice cream.

15. Go to the ladies' room.

16. Just order dessert.

17. Order all sauces on the side.

18. Have steamed vegetables in season for a main course.

19. Never let the waiter put the entire portion on your plate.

20. Be oblivious when the waiter comes to take your plate away.

21. *Ask* the waiter to take your plate away.

PRACTICALLY NONFATTENING CUISINES

Anyone who has undergone the rigors of dieting knows the cardinal rules: fish or chicken—broiled, poached, steamed, grilled, pan-fried (dry), and vegetables—au naturel and underdone. A pale fate for the traveler. But there are some cooking methods and dishes indigenous to particular regions or countries that are equally nondestructive.

Be cheered that almost the entire Japanese cuisine is tolerably caloric. Consider *yakimono,* an umbrella name for any kind of broiled foods, like *yakitori,* chicken and scallions cooked on a skewer. You have your choice of anything *mushimono* which means steamed or *nimono,* which are foods cooked in seasoned liquids. The best known boon to dieters, of course, is sashimi, filets of raw fish, dipped or wrapped in a variety of dressings, from seaweed to soy sauce spiked with wasabi, (green horseradish), and sushi, filets of raw fish laid over bite-sized portions of vinegared rice.

The South Americans also have a variety of "raw" fish called *ceviche,* fish that is "cooked" in salted lime and lemon juice, flavored with pepper, garlic, sliced onions and chilies. After marinating three to five hours, the fish becomes opaquely white and has the texture of cooked fish.

There is an unlikely waist-watchers aid in India called the tandoor, a large clay oven shaped like a jar with a wide mouth, used for baking chicken, fish, and meat which emerge succulent and fragrant. The potential problem is that *naan,* my favorite Indian bread, is also made in the tandoor. The dough is slapped on the inside of the hot oven and crisps in minutes. I have made an entire meal of *naan* dipped in *raita,* a cool yogurt salad dressed with thin slices of cucumbers and onions.

Yogurt is a happy accompaniment to specialties of the Middle East like kebabs, bite-sized chunks of meat, onions, green peppers grilled on a skewer. Just remember that many small bites add up!

WHAT NOT TO EAT

While breaking new gastronomic ground is one of the traveler's commandments, anyone who's ever been intestinally immobilized by the last meal probably proceeds with some degree of caution. I'm not suggesting you contemplate culinary celibacy, but your philosophy about eating adventures, whether it's street food, or three-star restaurant fare, should be a happy balance between paranoia and common sense. The need to be more aware when you are traveling is greater because your system is adjusting to new input on every level. Just remember it is entirely possible to contract anything from common indigestion to a raging stomach disorder after a meal at your favorite restaurant at home.

Here are some suggestions that reflect the leavening influence of common sense without paralyzing your curiosity.

1. Avoid a place that does not look or *feel* clean. When in doubt about drinking water, choose bottled beverages, from mineral water to beer. *Do not use ice.* Order drinks that are boiled, like coffee or tea.

2. Be careful about foods that may spoil without proper refrigeration, especially milk products.

3. Peel fruits and vegetables. It's a standard precaution that I don't always observe religiously. Just keep in mind where you are.

4. Think before you buy street foods. Is the food fresh, or has it been sitting there for days? How clean is the cooking equipment (if any)? (How clean is the vendor himself?) I've talked to friends who have lived for days on street food in Singapore and felt perfectly fine. I know residents in Hong Kong and New York who would never buy from the hometown pushcart vendors but buy pølse or hot dogs in Copenhagen without thinking because the city itself is so clean. Try to be rational.

5. Don't overeat.

WINES, SPIRITS, ETC.

A meal requires an appropriate liquid accompaniment, just as clothing needs the right accessories. Drinking, of course, is not limited to the meal itself; there's the before and after: a bitter apéritif; sherry or a two-olive martini; the postprandial brandy; and the fiery codas of eau-de-vie, like poire and framboise. In some countries people drink at breakfast. Beer is often served with morning coffee in the Netherlands, and Yugoslavians belt down slivovitz, the plum brandy that could have launched the Jupiter missile.

Every region in the world has a national alcoholic drink: Mexico has tequila; the Middle East has ouzo, tasting strongly of licorice; Scandinavia has akvavit, a spirit distilled from grain or potatoes and often flavored with caraway seed so I feel that I'm drinking liquid rye bread; the Caribbean has rum, the amber, rich-bodied ones from Jamaica; and clear, white lightning made in Puerto Rico and the Virgin Islands. Vodka is indigenous to Russia and Poland; beer to Scandinavia, Germany, Japan, the British Isles (see Cafés in this chapter); sake and beer to Japan . . . ad infinitum. (See Appendix for "Indispensable Reading.")

The drink that seems to occupy most people is wine. While wine is so much a part of life that it's tucked in the refrigerator between the milk and the orange juice, no drink engenders as much mystique, snobbism, and pomposity. The parliamentary-like debates about which wine goes with what are outdone only by the descriptions of the virtues or defects of a particular wine. Food critic and novelist Gael Greene put it better than anybody:

Bacchic Bons Mots

The Grape Nut swirls, sniffs, sips, chews and spits or swallows . . . and now a comment seems appropriate. With a minimum of bravado, even the neophyte should be able to pull off these simple classic phrases to describe the wine he's tasting and properly épater his companions.

I find it acid . . . astringent, balanced, big, bitter, brilliant. Clean, isn't it. Cloudy, coarse, common, corky. But distinguished. Dull, earthy, elegant. A bit flat, also. Nicely flinty. Fruity, full, great . . . green but harsh. I'd say, hazy, heavy. No, light. Metallic, moldy, noble, nutty. Off, but absolutely. Ordinary. Piquant, poor, powerful, ripe, robust, rounded, sick, sickly, small, soapy. Soft, isn't it. And sound. Steely, stemmy, sturdy, sweet. So thin. Typical. Withered. Woody. Yeasty. And young—ah, youth.

The intermediate wineman is more daring and scholarly, announcing as if it were his exclusive knowledge: "Oh, the treacherous '64s." "Smell the roses" (raspberries, nutmeg, rot, rust). "Weak start but what a thoroughbred finish." "I like its modesty" (imprudence, breeding, ambiguity). "A wine you can almost eat." "Don't forget how much sun they had in '59." "What can you expect from a small year?" (from a fifth cru, from an Italian wine, from little Portugal).

The .advanced stylist is bilingual. Bien meublé (well furnished). Du corsage (with body). Étoffé (plenty of stuffing). Bien en chair (fleshy). Aimable (friendly, pleasant). Du feu (spirited, fiery). De la race (a thoroughbred). Séducteur (seductive). Nif (impeccable in color).

And for haute derision: mince (thin). Étriqué (skimpy), commun (ordinary). Mal fichu (badly turned out), dégingandé (awkward, ungainly), mou (flabby). Anémique. Or try frivole (shallow), a fanfreluche (a trifling wine), embêtant (a bore), grossier (coarse).

To cut through great gusts of oenophilic pedantries try a naif change of pace.

> "Celery."
> "It smells good."
> "I say it's spinach."
> "You must be kidding."
> "I love you anyway."

The truth is, few people really understand what you're supposed to be looking for when the wine is brought to the table to taste. As a friend of mine said, "My wife once asked me what the hell I was doing with the cork. 'Beats me,' I said, 'but I can't tell the guy I don't want the cork. He'll think I don't know anything." On the contrary, admitting you don't know is the best place to start. It's logical to consider the color and the aroma. The only disconcerting part of the tasting ceremony is when you are presented with the cork. To do it right, you smell the cork. What you're looking for is a "corky" or "moldy" smell. It is no reflection on the wine; it can happen to the greatest champagne, or the most expensive château-bottled Bordeaux. It simply means that there has been a deterioration in the cork that has imparted a "corky" taste to the wine and obscured the true flavor. This is the reason it becomes undrinkable.

Depending on the kind of restaurant you choose, the sommelier, or wine waiter, will be the middleman between you and your wine. The fancier restaurants usually have sommeliers, but even in the equivalent of a three-star restaurant you'll often find that the owner or the maître d'hôtel will act as the sommelier. In fact, one of the major differences between the maître d'hôtel in the States and in Europe is that the latter counsels you on both food and wine, rather than just escorting you to your table and leaving the rest to the underlings.

In the entire chain of command in a restaurant the sommelier may have had the least formal training, yet somehow, he can be the most intimidating. Usually, sommeliers learn at the coat sleeves of another sommelier. (While there is no formal sommelier school there are sommelier societies that offer courses and oenology schools.) But as wine expert Alexis Lichine said, "He might not know as much as his costume would indicate." The sommelier wears a tablier, or apron, an old tradition that presumably started because he would bring up dusty bottles from the cellar, and use his apron to wipe off the dust and the cobwebs. He may also wear a sprig of grapes made of silver or another metal on his lapel. The sommelier sometimes has a small cup—or *tastevin*—on a chain around his neck so he can taste the wine first before offering it to you.

Your first rule is never, ever be antagonized by the sommelier's attitude. I will never forget the time my father decided to put a snooty sommelier in his proper place. We were at a very fancy French restaurant in Paris, and the sommelier came over with the extensive wine list. He had an unmistakable look of scorn on his face that seemed specially reserved for Americans. My father deliberated over the selection for an inordinate amount of time, purposely not asking the sommelier's advice. The sommelier was clearly annoyed. My father finally ordered, but did so in a stream of double-talk with a perfect French accent, interspersed with some real French words to make it even more confusing, like "vin," "Bordeaux," "rouge," "pas trop sec" (not too dry). "Très bien, monsieur," said the sommelier, after listening to my father carefully, and briskly walked away. He got halfway across the room, and at a certain point he stopped cold. We knew he realized he had no idea which wine my father had ordered. He came back to the table for confirmation. My father repeated the same routine several times, getting successively more impatient. When he felt satisfied the sommelier was reduced to proper size, he ordered a very good Bordeaux.

Remember that the sommelier, the maître d'hôtel, or the owner of the restaurant can help educate your palate—if you let him. Nonetheless, here are some guidelines that I have found helpful:

1. Nothing is more subjective than taste. THERE IS NO RIGHT AND WRONG. The reason that certain kinds of wines are associated with certain foods is that their tastes are complementary to one another. The same idea governs sauces. Some are more suited to certain dishes than others, so that a vinaigrette—not tomato sauce—for instance, is served on cold asparagus. It isn't a breach of etiquette to order red wine with fish. You may—or may not—find that a dry white makes a better taste combination.

2. Try the house wine or the wine of the region. It's usually inexpensive and sold by the glass or the carafe instead of the bottle. (Note especially if you are dining alone.)

3. The most important thing to remember when you are presented with the wine list is that you should not be afraid you'll pick the wrong wine. If you don't recognize any of the names, pick a wine on the basis of a price you can afford and your preference for red or white. Ask the sommelier, the maître d' (or whomever) to describe the characteristics of several wines within your price range. You have nothing to lose in choosing an unfamiliar wine. You are building up a repertoire of different tastes. *After several outings, you will become familiar with more wines and gradually begin to find your personal favorites. This is what matters.*

NONALCOHOLIC DRINKS

After drinking countless Coca-Colas on a trip to India, when going outdoors was like walking into a steam cabinet, I decided there must be a better road to revival. It appeared when my host at lunch one day asked me if I wanted sweet or salty lime juice mixed with water. This variation on limeade is a standard beverage in the scalding season. I quickly learned that there are drinks in most parts of the world that refresh, but do not intoxicate. Here are the fruits of my searches. Some are rather exotic and esoteric; others are an acquired taste, but they all successfully quench the thirst.

1. *Spremute*—freshly pressed juice, usually found in espresso bars in Italy; freshly squeezed juices anywhere.

2. The watery liquid of a green, immature coconut. Slightly sweet in taste, it is used on many South Pacific isles instead of water.

3. Syrups of peanut, almond, rose, or mint mixed with water are popular throughout the Middle East.

4. Any mineral water, flavored with bitters, a squeeze of lemon, lime, orange, grapefruit, a sprig of mint, or a squirt of grenadine.

5. *Chicamorada*—a drink in Peru made of cherries, lemon, pineapple, and purple corn.

6. *Guarana*—a bottled soft drink in Brazil made from the seeds of a jungle plant that tastes like a tangy fruit.

7. Teas; sweetened with mint and, in Arab countries, a dash of rose water for fragrance. Iced tea.

8. Iced coffee.

9. *Lhassi*—liquid yogurt drink, originally from India.

10. *Granadilla*—or passion fruit, found in the tropics. The interior of the granadilla is packed with small seeds, each one encased in a delicate envelope full of juice. Open, and drink up.

A VERY PERSONAL LIST OF WHAT NOT TO MISS

No list could be more randomly selected than this one. It simply includes some of the tastes I would like to have again in my mouth, not just my memory. From entrées to condiments, here are my favorites:

peach mangoes in South Africa.
aceto balsamico in Italy, a vinegar cured in over a dozen different kinds of wood, and considered so valuable it used to be included in a bride's dowry.
noodles from the noodle shops in Thailand.

mozzarella al forno, cheese baked to hot runniness in Italy.

minced pigeon sauté, wrapped in cool lettuce leaves in Hong Kong.

fresh salmon in Seattle.

"health" salads in California.

sennepsild, herring with mustard sauce and chives in Norway.

briks, triangular, tissue-thin pastry pouches filled with tuna, eggs, and herbs, quickly deep-fried, in Tunisia.

thé à la menthe, accompanied by a low-keyed belly dancer and a sunset, in Morocco.

yogurt salads shot through with fresh dill seed, thin slices of cucumber, and spiced with coriander, in the Middle East.

lamb and prune tajine in Marrakesh. Tajine is the name of the actual clay stewpot, that has come to be synonymous with the stew itself.

fraises des bois with crème fraîche in the South of France— miniature strawberries, literally called berries of the woods.

baked farmer cheese on New York's Lower East Side.

sardines grilled on a fire made of twigs on the beach in Spain and Portugal.

pain de campagne, country bread, crusty and fresh from the oven—in France.

buns sweetened with a dollop of red bean paste inside, from Japan.

pesto on almost anything, a sauce usually tossed with pasta made of fresh basil, Parmesan and Romano cheese, pine nuts, garlic, and olive oil.

shepherd's pie in the British Isles.

baked crab in black bean sauce in Hong Kong.

date shakes in the California desert.

pretzels with mustard sold by vendors on the streets in Philadelphia.

fresh water chestnuts.

blue corn tortillas in Santa Fe, New Mexico.

pêches Melba, peaches on vanilla ice with a fresh raspberry purée; *pêches Eugénie,* in honor of the Empress Eugénie, peaches with wild strawberries and a zabaglione sauce; and *fraises Sarah Bernhardt,* strawberries with pineapple and Cu-raçao mousse. (It may be I have a soft spot for these dishes because they were created by Escoffier, who said, "My success comes from the fact that my best dishes were created for ladies.")

salade niçoise, a trademark in the South of France, made with chunks of tuna, boiled potatoes, thin string beans, anchovies, and hard-boiled eggs, bathed in a tangy vinaigrette.

whole crabs, steamed and doused with fiery pepper sauce, served on newspaper that is soon piled high with cracked shells and empty claws. The quintessential finger food from Georgia.

ghee, nutty-flavored clarified butter used in Indian cooking. Old Sanskrit writings suggest that ghee can improve your appearance, speaking powers, mental processes, and digestion.

open-faced sandwiches in Scandinavia, any number of delicacies, including lumpfish (their caviar), herring and tiny shrimp, spread on a thin layer of butter on a piece of dark bread, eaten with a knife and fork. The "official" name is *smørrebrød,* a Danish word meaning "buttered bread."

mezedakia, hors d'oeuvres in Greece (in my opinion, the best part of the Greek cuisine): gnarled black olives; slices of white feta, tangy goat cheese; *dolmadakia,* stuffed grape-leaves; *spanakopetas,* small triangles of spinach pie; *taramo-salata,* fish roe, creamed with onions, olive oil, and lemon juice; pickled squid; *keftadakia,* meatballs of lamb, onion, garlic, mint, oregano, white wine, and olive oil.

choucroute garni, sauerkraut steeped in white wine and cooked with a plethora of sausages in Alsace and Germany (accompanied by an icy cold beer).

feijoada, the most sophisticated bean dish, besides cassoulet, that I know. This national dish of Brazil is a thick soup made from black beans, garnished with hunks of beef, pork sausages—sometimes pigs' ears and tails—all piled on a bed of rice and dressed with couve—a bright green leaf—and orange slices.

white gazpacho in southern Spain, where it is called *ajo blanco con uvas* (white garlic with grapes) and has a base of almonds. I could have a bowl a day, but then that's not so remarkable; gazpacho is mentioned in Greek and Roman literature as "drinkable food."

an imperfectly sliced piece of cheddar cheese, balancing on a portion of still-warm apple pie, right here in the United States.

And, alas, the inevitable half grapefruit for breakfast the first morning back home . . .

10.

Shopping

There is something undeniably sexier about underwear from Paris; something soul-satisfying about a leather purse you found in Spain and saw at home for double the price; something indestructibly sane about English tweeds bought in England; something deliciously indulgent about a custom-made silk blouse from Hong Kong. These feelings not only reflect the pleasure of having the item itself, but encompass, perhaps unconsciously, the whole shopping experience.

I remember, when I was seventeen, the almost illicit feeling of going into a tiny lingerie shop in Paris that was redolent with sensuality and gardenia sachets. The uniquely French appeal of the saleswoman was enhanced by her avoirdupois and lines around the eyes. She seemed to lead me into womanhood with a single black garter stitched in red satin ribbon. I haven't forgotten the fragrance of my first visit to Gucci in Florence; it was like being encased in a newly tanned leather pouch. I remember the protocol of drinking endless cups of much-too-sweet mint tea while bargaining for a rug in the souks of Marrakesh.

While relatively small, affordable items can recall the fun, hassles, victories, and discoveries of shopping, possession is not essential. Happily, the richness of the shopping experience doesn't have to be obliterated by a prohibitive price tag. In fact, you can probably live without whatever it is you coveted—and whatever you actually bought. Once I realized that I would like to buy more than I could afford or need, I decided to expand the definition of shopping from a purely acquisitive process to a cultural experience, a study in culture as valid as churches and museums.

When you go shopping, you are really seeing how the city works because commerce is a city's sustenance. You are watching how the marketplace meets the demands and needs of every economic level in the community. It is just as instructive to walk into a luxury-item store like Tiffany's in New York, with chandeliers and private rooms for showing jewels on velvet cushions, as to go to a teeming produce market at dawn where merchants, cheek by jowl, sell the "real" necessities of life. You discover handicraft or cottage industries that tradition has kept afloat through the centuries, like the young girls I saw weaving carpet on the island of Djerba. They were all under age twelve because their fingers had to be small enough to work the particular looms.

Shopping is also a social exchange between you and the seller that usually indicates a certain national style: bargaining in the Arab world; the unparalleled rudeness in some New York (and Paris) emporia; the laid-back salesmanship in California; or the restrained concern of the British. Shopping is a way of meeting people and seeing how they live, if not in their homes, then on their business turf, because cultural habits color all areas of life. In many English shops, for example, the tea kettle, china cups, creamer and sugar and tin of biscuits occupy as strategic a post as the cash register. Most shop owners in the Middle East and South America will automatically offer you coffee as a gesture of no-strings hospitality. In fact, when I visit an old friend in Jerusalem, we never have coffee at home but at an art gallery in the old city.

Eventually, however, you will want to buy *something,* whether it's a memento that looked better there than at home, or a dubious purchase that has grown into a treasure. The point is, how do you spend your money most effectively? How do you find the "best" places to shop? How do you decide what you want to buy—and if you are paying a reasonable price? Are the clichés good buys? Should you get perfume in Paris, lace in Belgium, chocolate and watches in Switzerland, silver in Mexico, handwoven cloth in Central America? Are there eternal bargains? The following pages will unravel the story.

WHAT TO DO BEFORE YOU GO

You can eliminate some of the indecision and agony over what to buy or not to buy, what you need and what is sheer frivolity, if you do some homework before you depart. In addition to your own considerations, let me add a friendly word of caution: try to curtail your exuberant, pretrip promises to shop for your friends. I don't mean depriving yourself of happily looking for gifts *you* choose to buy, but accepting the responsibility of finding specific items at someone else's request—like a dinner plate to match a Queen Anne pattern, a sweater to complete an outfit that involves the exact color and size. Your time and trouble is rarely appreciated properly, and your efforts are likely to be rewarded with "Well, thanks, but this isn't quite what I had in mind."

1. Have some idea about the purpose of your shopping expeditions.

- *Collecting*—Whatever it is, you probably have a place in the house where you keep lots of them. You may collect teacups, ashtrays, seashells, pocket watches, ceramic owls, cookie molds, buttons, antique spoons, folk dolls, or miniatures of famous landmarks. You're in luck if you have a specific purpose that will focus your shopping energy. Your hobby could lead to a network of people with similar interests who recommend people and sources in other cities.

- *Decorating*—You may want to buy a dining-room table and chairs in Scandinavia; dinner service in England; tiles for the patio or bathroom in Portugal; hand-blown glass lamps in Venice, etc. Be sure to take the necessary measurements, color swatches, a color photo of the room, a discriminating eye. (See To Buy or Not to Buy and Shipping Home in this chapter.)

- *Gift-giving*—I have always felt that small presents from far away are as welcome as lavish purchases from local stores where everyone else shops. As a result, I keep a "gift closet," which really amounts to a shelf, or a cardboard box filled with relatively inexpensive—and portable—treasures from around the world. I divide my gift closet-shopping into three categories. There are people to whom I always give presents for anniversaries, birthdays, and even "no occasion," and I look with these particular friends and family in mind. My aunt, for instance, plays bridge, and always likes tablecloths and matching napkins to put on the bridge table for the pregame dinner. I have many women friends who love rings, bangle bracelets, tiny purses, lingerie; men who want esoteric tobaccos and accoutrements of pipe or cigar smoking; others who like exotic teas or silk ties. The second group are people who "have everything." (Like my mother.) So I look for offbeat but fairly practical items that she wouldn't think to buy at home for herself. I once bought an antique Chinese teapot, complete with the original, quilted tea cozy, on a trip to Hong Kong. I gave it to her ten months later for her birthday. The last category is gifts-in-search-of-a-recipient. I usually buy in quantity—say three or four—and they eventually go to an appropriate owner. Successful finds include worry beads from Greece, boxes of all shapes and sizes, napkins, placemats, scarves, brandy glasses, paperweights. (See A Collection of Shopping Ideas . . . in this chapter.)

2. Consider how much money you'll have to spend. Are you going to pay with traveler's checks, credit cards, cash? (See Money in the chapter, "Planning.")

3. Think about quantity and quality. Are you planning to buy $5.00 to $10 mementos at each stop, and possibly wind up with more inconsequential things for your money than you had anticipated? Or would you rather buy one or two really good items?

4. Do comparison price-shopping at home. If you are thinking about buying something expensive—cameras to jewelry to antiques—check the prices in your local department, discount or import stores, as well as the offerings in the gift catalogues. Buying in bulk can often reduce the price of the items for these stores, who then pass on the savings to you. Even if you do find the item costs less abroad, the additional shipping, U.S. duty, and handling charges, not to mention the possible waiting time, may substantially offset your savings. The one potentially deceptive aspect of preshopping at home is that some goods are made for export to the United States. I once bought a cotton caftan from Greece in a store in Newport, Rhode Island. When I went to Greece later that year I looked for another, but never even found an acceptable substitute. A friend of mine going to Lisbon thought she'd save on china she saw at Tiffany's with a made-in-Portugal stamp. She looked everywhere but never found the pattern. It was obviously just made for export.

TIPS FOR DECIDING WHAT TO BUY WHERE

A combination of research, common sense, a critical eye, and a smidgen of perseverance should guide you. At the same time, you will stumble across things you couldn't possibly have imagined. Thank goodness. Surprise is one of the best parts of traveling. The following is a set of specifics that will help you edit your shopping list to those things a region or country does best. You can apply these principles wherever you are in the world, regardless of the vagaries of price and style.

1. Check the standard sources for suggestions about what to buy wherever you are going: magazine and newspaper articles, guidebooks (see Appendix for Indispensable Reading); tourist bureau brochures and special publications; recommendations from friends, travel agents, airline or steamship personnel, the hall porter or concierge; ethnic exhibits in department stores; specialty shops, display cases in major hotels.

2. Consider the "cliché" buys. Just like a verbal cliché, there must have been some truth in it somewhere along the way. You will have to evaluate on the spot if the product is "overworked," and if the value-for-the-price still merits purchase. The quality of perfumes in France or gloves in Italy may still be as good as ever, but the rising costs of labor and materials may have brought up the price. Check the workmanship carefully on handmade items. (See "To Buy or Not to Buy" in this chapter.)

3. Look at the history of a country. Have invaders and foreign rulers brought their particular skills and established craft industries? Has isolation or vigorous trade produced a clearly defined style of art? Sometimes a quick trip to a museum, especially a folk art or crafts museum, will provide helpful clues and guidelines. Is religion a powerful force? If so, it may be reflected in the art—from paintings to jewelry and other objects—like the kachina dolls of some Indian tribes in the American Southwest.

SHOPPING HINTS GLEANED FROM HOW PEOPLE LIVE

1. Observe how people dress at home and at work, whether they wear saris, sarongs, Nehru jackets, kimonos, yukatas (short kimonos), caftans, or shawls. Is there a distinctive decoration on the clothes? The Filipinos, for instance, do needlework on the sheer piña cloth (pineapple cloth), which is used for the *barang tagalog*, the shirts men wear in the evening, and the elaborate puff-sleeved women's gowns.

2. What do people wear on their heads? Scarves tied in a distinctive manner, berets, babushkas, etc. On their feet? Espadrilles to thongs. Are there any decorative accessories for the neck, wrists, ankles, waist? (See A Collection of Shopping Ideas . . . in this chapter.)

3. Notice the utensils people use for cooking and eating. In Hong Kong I bought silver chopsticks, engraved with monograms or names; in Japan, wooden ones studded with mother of pearl. Look for antique pieces such as pearl-handled fruit knives or unusual wooden spoons. Are there any unusual (or decorative) gadgets used in the kitchen? In Mexico, chocolate is often stirred with a device invented by the Aztecs, a long-handled wooden stick that has shirred wooden tiers around the lower part. How is the food served? You can often buy attractive serving ware in houseware stores and street markets. Here are a few examples: In Japan there are various-shaped boxes: the square *bento,* the *hangetsu,* a half moon; the *koban,* a lidded box. In Scandinavia, candles, condiments, or flowers are spread along a runner, a length of material laid down the center of the table. In Morocco, stews are served in *tajines,* large clay dishes with cone-shaped tops.

4. How people carry produce or belongings, particularly in rural areas where animals are still used for transport, is another source for shopping ideas. In these places you can count on finding unusual baskets, burlap pouches, cloth satchels, handwoven bags. In the markets in Jerusalem, I once bought saddlebags used on camels—handwoven, bright-colored pouches that I separated, stuffed with foam rubber, and turned into pillows.

TO BUY OR NOT TO BUY

Why you ultimately decide to buy a particular item involves many considerations. Some people like to show friends back home how they avoid the standard "tourist" souvenirs. I've heard countless discourses about an object, in which the main virtue seems to be the circumstances of purchase. It goes something like this: the person, by *sheer* chance, found "a little place," on some side street, indubitably unknown to any other tourist, and saw some interesting-looking things. Although he had absolutely no idea what they were, the man in the store said he only made three a year, an irresistible recommendation for this kind of shopper. If nothing else, you could call one of these objects "a conversation piece."

Aside from the times when you buy because your common sense is outpaced by your emotions, the perennial shopper's question, "Should I buy it?" hinges on three main points: price, practicality, and portability. A black mark in any one of the categories should give you pause. Just remind yourself that the object is probably not vital to your existence, and consider walking out of the store. In fact, *do* walk out. Go around the block, have a cup of coffee. Think it over. Only you can really decide whether or not it's wise to buy. Salespeople, as objective and concerned as *you* try to make them, are in business to sell.

Somehow, many Americans have the feeling that everyone is going to try to take them. Clever merchants, they believe, will capitalize on the ingenuousness, lack of local market savvy, or unfamiliarity with the language. There is no question that this may happen, but the net effect is that we tend to mistrust *any* price quote. Unless the price is patently a "steal," we are suspicious, and become obsessed with "a bargain," not just a fair price.

But in reality, what *is* a bargain? The word "bargain" usually connotes paying a lower-than-market-price for an item, either because of a sale, a reduction in price, a standard discount, or your own "bargaining" skill. Some people think that within the restraining arm of your pocketbook and pragmatism, if you get what you want, it's a bargain. (See When and How to Bargain in this chapter.) But stop and think a minute. Is it still a bargain if it merely takes up precious closet space at home? I once bought a temple carving at a "bargain" price in India. There was no duty because it was classified as an antique over a hundred years old, and I shipped it economically by sea. (Who minds waiting five months for a temple carving?) It has been sitting on the floor of my coat closet since 1972.

The point is, do not be seduced by price alone. Be practical. Will the purchase fit into your life—or your house? Will you wear an Indian sari to a country club or business dinner? (Clothes and hats are particularly tempting. The truth is, you may love many styles in their indigenous surroundings but wouldn't be caught dead in them at home.) I must have a hundred yards of saris in my drawer, and the closest I've gotten to using the material was to cover a wooden chest until it was refinished. Another time I bought exquisite hand-embroidered sheets and pillow cases in Hong Kong at ridiculously low prices. I rarely use them because either they have to be hand-washed and ironed, or I have to find the impossible: a masterful dry cleaner.

Let's assume that you're happy with the price, and have at least a vague idea of what you can do with it—whatever it is. How are you going to get it home? If it's not flat or packable like clothes, perfume, or paper products, do you love it enough to carry? I wouldn't have made an effort to talk with (and eventually befriend) a woman on a flight from Hong Kong to New York if I hadn't noticed she was carrying two six-foot spears. But barring such potential social benefits, do you want to be laden with packages? If it is the beginning of your trip, the package goes with you everywhere. Will you be traveling—by car, plane, train, bicycle? Does this help or hinder taking it with you? (See Shipping Home in this chapter.)

In addition to practicality and portability, keep in mind these corollaries to the price.

1. Is there a discount if you pay in dollars, local currency, traveler's checks, or credit cards? (Some stores only take local currency for sale items.)

2. Before you tote up a large bill, ask if the store accepts credit cards, cash, traveler's checks, personal checks. It is common to have to show your passport, a driver's license, or some form of identification and a local address if you are paying with personal or traveler's checks.

3. Some countries will give you a rebate on the sales tax that is either mailed to you, or deducted from the price of the item at the time of purchase. To receive it you may be asked to fill out customs forms, and possibly present one to customs on departure.

4. It's tempting to scoop up what seem to be bargains at duty-free shops in airports and free ports, but there are two important aspects to consider: is the price of the merchandise substantially less than in retail stores in the country, or at home? Are the items duty free at *U.S.* customs? (See Customs and Duty in this chapter.)

5. Take a pocket calculator, or a slip of paper in your wallet with the equivalent in local currency of such common denominations as $10-20-50-100-500, so that you know how much you are paying, and can rely on *your* own calculations.

WHEN AND HOW TO BARGAIN

In many locales, particularly in Asia, the Middle East and Third World countries, bargaining is an accepted, even necessary business tool. Simply stated, "bargaining" is the process of arriving at a price that is low enough to be acceptable to the buyer, and high enough to satisfy the merchant. It can be a drawn-out, genteel social event, punctuated by many cups of tea or coffee, during which time you may learn that the merchant's oldest son wants to be a doctor, or where to get the best regional cooking. The exchange may be more aggressive, with barbed remarks about the quality of the products and defenses about the integrity of both the buyer and the seller.

While there are some guidelines to the art of bargaining, each situation must be assessed individually. Your attitude about the whole exercise will be determined in part by how much you actually *enjoy* the time, effort, thought, and energy required for successful bargaining. (Maybe you'd rather buy and scoot.) Do you have the nose and character for bargaining? You have to be part actor, part gambler, part psychologist. Will your position be weakened because you're more concerned that the merchant thinks you're a nice person? Of course, the bottom line is how much you *really* covet the object in question. If you do, will paying $5.00 to $10 more than you "guestimate" make such a big difference? You then have to weigh losing face, or swallowing defeat at the bargaining table, because you would be more disturbed going home empty-handed.

Just as there are restaurants where a man would automatically wear a shirt and tie, there are some places you just don't bargain. In general, these are the Big Names, be it a French couturière, a department store, famous old or famous new shops on the illustrious shopping streets, and government-sponsored centers. A second echelon of stores, such as boutiques with quality merchandise, often have signs in English, "Fixed Prices." By the same token, there will never be any official indication that bargaining is permitted, or even expected.

Bargaining is the only way to transact business in street markets, bazaars, souks, second-hand and off-the-main-shopping-axis stores. An owner who also does the selling will be more inclined to adjust the price because he has final responsibility. Here are a few things to keep in mind if you engage in this "honorable" undertaking.

1. You have to accept the fact that you will *never* know if you have gone through the whole process only to pay a price the seller had in mind all along, even if it *is* below the original asking price.

2. There is a fine line between making a reasonable offer, and one so low it's insulting to the product and the merchant. You may feel that he has no regard for *your* sense of a fair price based on the value of the item and "market conditions." On the other hand, he doesn't want to be played the fool.

3. Never walk into a place of business and telegraph that you absolutely must have a particular thing. You'll weaken your position of pleasant indifference, which is crucial to bargaining leverage. Restrain enthusiastic asides to companions, or rhapsodic facial expressions at having found, at long last, exactly what you've been looking for. *Never* flash a full wallet (and dress down).

4. You will have to concede *something* on the price. If you don't give the impression that you're willing to negotiate, which is the crux of bargaining, the seller will retrench completely. The rule of thumb is to first offer half *at most,* and then inch upward gradually in very small increments to the price you decided you'd be willing to pay at the outset.

5. At every step along the way, each party takes the measure of the other. How far to push, when to give in, when to offer a cigarette, or accept a refreshment, and when to walk out. You will just have to sense if the final offer is really final, or if there are more to come.

6. Beware of emotional ploys often reserved for women:

▪ "You're so pretty. This price is just for you."

▪ "Ah, the best price for my first customer of the day; my last customer; my first customer after lunch; my first customer after a big sale; my first sale after the birth of my first son"; etc.

▪ "Only because you're a true appreciator of art would I make such a price. Actually, I'm losing money."

7. Merchants are equally familiar with your standard rebuttals:

▪ "I'm not a tourist!"

▪ "I couldn't possibly pay this price. My husband would never understand; kill me," etc.

▪ "I'm just looking."

▪ You can politely say thank you and walk out of the store. If the script proceeds according to the movies (sometimes it does), the merchant will run after you down twisted, teeming alleyways, waving the object (unless you are buying something large like an armoire), and he will accept your final offer.

IF YOU ARE BUYING:

Clothes

1. Compare American and European sizes.

2. Bring a tape measure that shows both centimeters and inches.

3. Consider taking a garment from home to be copied, or pick out a model you can actually see, not just one in a catalogue.

4. If you are having something custom-made, have at least three fittings. Raise your arms, sit down, etc. to make sure you have enough room to move. Are the seams generous enough? How badly will that exquisite material wrinkle? (Crush in your palm.) Is it washable? How do you wash it?

5. Get extra buttons, and a few extra yards of material.

Jewelry

1. If you are buying gemstones—sapphires in Burma, diamonds in Antwerp, pearls in the Orient, emeralds in Colombia, etc.—buy only from absolutely reputable dealers. It is important to buy at the best places, not where you think you're getting a deal because you have no way of judging the quality of the stone. To take one example, a diamond is graded on four counts: color, clarity, carat weight, and cut, qualities that are not apparent to the naked eye. Smart buyers have their stones appraised by a certified gemological institute, or deal with established jewelers.

2. Fraud is possible with semiprecious stones as well. In the booming turquoise business in the American Southwest, laminated plastic masquerades as turquoise. Again, check with reputable merchants.

3. When you are buying a piece of jewelry as opposed to loose stones, remember that you are also paying for the design and workmanship. Sometimes U.S. duty is lower on unset stones.

4. Even though the workmanship may be less expensive in certain countries, the cost of the materials used, notably gold or silver, which are based on weight, may result in unexpectedly high prices.

Cameras

1. Explain your *real* picture-taking needs and skills to the dealer. You don't want to wind up with a zoom lens that makes you sound professional, but which, in actual fact, you'd never use.

2. Always buy with enough time to go back to the seller and ask any additional questions.

3. Make sure you understand the use of every lens and filter you are tempted to buy.

4. Check prices at discount stores at home. It may be less expensive in the United States.

Antiques

1. Again, anything that requires parting with a healthy sum of money merits some investigation. Unless you are very knowledgeable about antiques, find an established firm.

2. Get all the necessary shipping and customs information before you make your final decision to buy.

3. You can sometimes find what *seems* to be an antique in flea markets. If you like it enough, do you care if it's authentic? Is the price based on the fact it's a "fake"—or as if it were the genuine article?

SHIPPING HOME

If you have decided to ship home your purchases, here are some guidelines to keep in mind:

1. Use your common sense. A merchant in a small town market who can barely speak English is not going to be a very reliable shipping agent. You are better off in government shops, reputable large stores, department stores, even hotels, who are used to shipping packages to the United States. These kinds of places are also apt to be more experienced in *packing* goods for shipping, which can mean

the difference between getting a piece home intact or shattered to smithereens.

2. Ask the airlines about the cost of shipping air cargo (particularly transatlantic), and shipping packages as unaccompanied baggage, which often goes on the same airplane as you do. Ask the shop if they will send parcel post, or if they ship by sea mail, which always takes much longer. Be ready for long delays, not necessarily because of the shipping, but because of the official red tape and pileups at the docks or the other cargo depots.

3. Ask the store to quote an all-inclusive transport price. Find out how much extra the shipping will cost.

4. *Always* insure your packages.

5. Be sure to keep the bill of sale that shows the estimated date of arrival, an itemized list of what you purchased, the insured value and indication that insurance was paid.

6. If you work through a freight office, get a bill of lading. If the package gets lost, the "way bill number" is your only way of putting a tracer on the packages.

7. Call a local freight agent before you leave and ask if there are any new requirements, restrictions, or added protection for the consumer that you should know about.

CUSTOMS AND DUTY

Most everyone has a favorite story about how to outsmart customs. I've heard about putting shallots in socks (you can't bring in fruits and vegetables), sewing jewelry on the inside of coat sleeves, and replacing foreign with domestic labels. Your participation in this kind of undertaking should be strictly voyeuristic. The most intelligent way to approach the subject of customs is to be as informed as possible before you go about the pertinent rules and regulations.

The U. S. Customs Service collects revenue that is called duty, just as the Internal Revenue Service collects revenue called taxes. The amount of duty to be paid on a particular item is determined by the

customs officer, but each governmental agency, Food and Drug for
cosmetics, or Agriculture for cheese, meat, and plants, determines
what products can and cannot be brought back into the United
States.

There are some unexpected regulations. Cheeses from certain
countries are permitted, while others are not because of cattle diseases. Before you find yourself at the food counter at Harrods in
London plunking down good money for an aged wheel of cheddar
cheese, check with the Department of Agriculture (write for a brochure, or write asking specific questions) so you won't find that your
cheddar makes it to customs at the airport and no farther.

There are several "preventive" measures and useful bits of information you should know:

1. Write to the Department of Treasury (customs is under their
aegis), and ask them to send you the latest information on regulations.

2. Ask specifically about GSP, the U.S. Generalized System of
Preferences, which allows certain articles from developing countries
to enter the country duty free, with the purpose of improving their
financial or economic condition through export trade. GSP went into
effect on January 1, 1976, and will expire in 1985. Some "GSP"
countries a traveler would be likely to visit include India, Morocco,
Mexico, Brazil, Turkey, Tunisia, Hong Kong. Other destinations are
less probable, like the Wallis and Futuna Islands, or São Tomé and
Principe.

3. Many items are duty free: antiques over a hundred years old,
original paintings, sculptures of any age; some books, prints, and
maps over twenty years old.

4. There are limits to the amount of certain items you can bring
back, like liquor. Regulations are different in each state. With over
three hundred ports of entry, it is best to ask your local customs
office what is permitted.

5. If you are traveling with foreign-made cameras, tape recorders,
watches, valuable jewelry, or even clothes, register them with cus-

toms at the airport on departure so that when you return if the customs officer questions whether you purchased it abroad, you have the authorized receipt to prove that you took it with you. The same advice applies to items you might need for business purposes—samples, for instance. If you cannot register the items, then take insurance documents, or bills of sale that show reasonable proof of prior possession.

6. Iron-clad legislation has been passed in the United States and Canada that prohibits the import of all merchandise made from some four hundred endangered species of animals, like furs from the spotted cat family. Customs must seize the item, and may even press criminal charges if they are not convinced the traveler bought the item in innocence.

7. When you ship items home from abroad, they are not included in your customs declaration, and therefore not subject to duty (or exemption) on arrival. The U. S. Postal Service sends all incoming foreign mail parcels to customs for examination. If there is no duty, the package will be delivered to you by the local postman with no further charge. If you must pay, you will get a notice that a certain amount of duty is required, and either you go directly to the post office with the notice, or the postman can collect the duty from you and bring you the package for a handling fee. Mail parcels unclaimed after thirty days will be returned to the sender.

8. Some items are absolutely *verboten:* narcotics, switchblade knives, fireworks, dangerous toys, etc.

9. Stores in certain countries may report inordinately large purchases to their customs people, who in turn alert the U.S. customs service to make sure the buyer pays the appropriate duty.

10. Keep all your receipts with the retail amount you paid clearly marked so that you have proof of the value of each item. Customs may or may not ask to see the receipts.

11. Pack all the items you will have to declare in an accessible place in your suitcase, or pack them separately.

12. A word about how you dress: I would never recommend looking like a leftover of the "flower children generation." While it is impossible to say that, just because you are wearing old jeans, a sweater, and your hair needs washing, you will be suspect, that picture *does* have certain unfavorable connotations, however erroneous or outdated. On the other hand, I have a friend who, dressed to the nines, was pulled aside by a customs officer, who said, "Dressed like that you must have been able to afford a lot of shopping," intimating she was not declaring her purchases. She accused him of "reverse discrimination," and refused to pay $25 to avoid the "hassle and time" of going through her luggage, because she *wasn't* hiding anything. A half hour's debate later he finally let her go.

The Process of Going Through United States Customs

On an airplane or steamship, you will get a customs declaration form sometime prior to landing. If your purchases do not exceed the permitted amount, you will have no duty to pay, and you only need to make a verbal declaration. All other items must be listed with their approximate *retail* value. Your signature affirms you swear under penalty of law that your statement is accurate.

After you clear passport control, you claim your luggage and proceed to the row of customs officers. There are myriad theories on how to pick the "friendliest" agent. Some women only choose men, or men with beards, or young men. One woman assiduously avoids women officers because she feels they are more meticulous. No matter whom you choose, or how, remember that they've seen and heard it all. Generally they will first ask how long you have been away, or where you went, and then throw in a few apparently random questions, like what is the most expensive item you bought or what was your favorite purchase, to see if you react nervously, or in any way indicate that you haven't made a full disclosure.

Depending on your answers, how they feel that day, and other indeterminate factors, the officers might examine your luggage. I've had my bags literally emptied (you repack), and sometimes just an item or two examined. He/she will tell you if there is any duty to be paid. Presumably, you are then free to go home, enjoy what you bought and not grieve too seriously about what you left behind.

WORTH-A-STOP SHOPPING

In addition to the "classic" or famous shops and fortuitous side-street surprises, there are a host of unusual emporia. They can tempt you with products, and, at the same time, might uncover an unexpected side of the city. These kinds of places may not accept credit cards or traveler's checks. (Local currency is the best bet.)

1. *Source shopping*—The place of origin; anywhere that products are made, and often sold, usually at lower than retail prices.

▪ *Factories:* Factory outlets exist for everything from dishes to designer clothes. Sometimes there will be a separate outlet for "seconds" or goods that have imperceptible flaws, or were last year's styles. I have bought such big-name products as Dansk and Gucci at "outlet" stores. Your best source of information is the local tourist office, or the store itself. It isn't that they are being kept a secret from the consumer, but you have to make the effort to find them.

▪ *Artisans:* This very broad category can include anything from a one-man operation to an entire community devoted to a craft like a woodcarvers' town in Jogjakarta in Java, or the island in Greece where the economy seems based on making flokati rugs. Sometimes you can buy what you have watched being made. Other times you needn't buy a thing; just the process is enough. (Artisans may work in the ateliers of studios which are often located in the back of large showrooms, or stores, or sometimes in specific sections of town.) To give you a sampling: artisans make silk flowers, restore paintings, repair clocks in Paris; craftsmen on the islands of Burano and Murano in Venice fashion lace and glass; artisans handblock saris in India. Some men carry bundles of cloth on their heads, others sit cross-legged, a bolt of cloth rolled out at their feet, spraying water through their teeth to polish the cotton, while others dip wooden blocks in a thin dye and stamp the pattern on the material.

2. *National Handicraft Centers*—These government-run centers are frequently found in Third World and developing countries because they help promote the national craft industry and function as a

showplace for that country's crafts. Such centers are an excellent shopping stop because the goods are quality controlled, the prices are fixed, and shipping home is usually no problem.

3. *Auctions*—Auctions range from informal sales in the country, with goods displayed on the grass or the kitchen table, to the great international auction houses where bids for millions of dollars ring through chandelier-hung halls. Auctions can also be great social events, especially during the exhibition period when the properties up for sale are open to the general public for inspection. Here you can see exquisitely valuable jewelry, furniture, or porcelain you could never afford to buy, and have the opportunity to meet knowledgeable collectors. Whether you are going to buy or merely peruse the offerings, you can find out about auctions through the antiques, leisure, or auction pages of newspapers (especially the Sunday papers), magazines and journals specializing in the arts and antiques. Go to the exhibition and get a catalogue, which should detail an item's history and give estimated prices. If you are considering a major purchase, make sure you have done your homework: know your subject; be familiar with comparative prices at antique stores; be able to evaluate the condition of the object, and establish a maximum price. It's easy to get carried away in the tide of the bidding. (That's half the skill of an auctioneer.) If you have never bought at an auction before, you might want to go to a sale with no intention of buying, just to familiarize yourself with the proceedings. This is less important for smaller scale, "grass roots" sales. The danger here, especially when prices seem impossibly low, is that you'll buy something you'll never use. I know.

4. *Museum shops*—The information desk in the museum lobby that also had postcards has expanded into big business in museums all over the world. In special stores on the museum grounds you can buy anything from a five-cent bead to a $5,000 handcrafted rolltop desk, Indian Christmas ornaments, antique kilim rugs, art books for adults and children. Sometimes you will find reproductions or copies of the museum's permanent collection, pieces from the increasingly popular "blockbuster" theme shows, or items like tote bags, scarves, and glassware *inspired* by the works of art or based on the museum

logos. Museums also send out catalogues that are free to members, and available for a small fee to nonmembers.

5. *Stationery shops*—Here you can find everything from unusual calendars, note paper, and wrapping paper for gifts or lining closet shelves to objects covered in paper, pencils, address books, and notebooks.

6. *Art exhibits*—Posters of a current exhibit often become collector's items, and are usually inexpensive. Art centers also feature the works of the emerging artistic talent of the country at reasonable prices.

7. *Shops in hotels*—You may pay for the convenience, but in the top-quality hotels, the merchandise is usually dependable, the salespeople speak English, and, unlike buying from an unknown merchant, the hotel can be a contact if you have any problems.

8. *"Dollar" stores in Eastern Europe*—Tourists and diplomats can buy luxury goods at inexpensive prices not normally available on the local market. Check with the local tourist office or ask your guide.

9. *Centers or institutes*—For lack of a better word, these establishments specialize in the history, the art, or the preservation of a particular aspect of the culture. The Papyrus Institute in Egypt, for example, not only has a museum, but a factory that will make a cartouche for you. Some countries have opened institutes in other countries. At the Tibet Institute in New Delhi, I once bought a dozen ink drawings on rice paper. I put them in a poster tube in the side of my suitcase and gave them as Christmas presents for the next few years.

10. *Department stores*—You can get an overview of daily life, from clothes to kitchen gadgets to the latest fads, in the major department store of a big city. Some of these stores are unique, like Harrods in London or Bloomingdale's in New York, for the extraordinary services they provide. Department stores generally have good quality merchandise at reasonable prices. I always buy cotton nightgowns in Galeries Lafayette in Paris, where they also have multilingual shopper's guides, and I get marmalade at Fortnum & Mason in London. My friend swears by the "fabulous" children's underwear available in London's Marks & Spencer. In addition to the actual

merchandise, the architecture, layout of the store, and display of the goods give insight into the culture of the city, especially in the newer stores that are part of big shopping center complexes, complete with movie theaters, skating rinks, and restaurants.

MARKETS, SOUKS, BAZAARS, ETC.

You will probably have to steel yourself against the instinct to buy the glorious miscellany, bric-a-brac, castoffs from Grandma, just plain junk, Art Nouveau, Art Deco, and Art-What-Have-You furnishings, and even some real finds, on view in street markets the world over. The appropriate market attitude is that being there is often more fun than buying. You need an educated eye and/or infinite stamina to rummage through the unsorted debris. But I can think of no better place for a nosedive into local life.

The character and size of markets vary from city to countryside, and with their purpose. The merchants can range from dedicated old-timers to left-over-Sixties-type youths who may or may not speak English. Such market areas as Covent Garden in London, Les Halles in Paris, or the Faneuil Hall in Boston no longer function as a day-to-day dispensing center for produce, but have expanded into commercial centers with pockets of restaurants, boutiques, stores, and foodstalls where you eat a little bit at each one. Some refurbished markets have retained their original purpose and have added new areas of business, like Fisherman's Wharf in San Francisco or the Pikes Market in Seattle, where it is possible to buy anything from Swedish pancakes to a Muslim-world coloring book, just-cut flowers, or freshly caught crabs that vendors wave in the air like tambourines.

Markets specializing in a particular item are fascinating to visit. The jade market in Hong Kong, for instance, runs the length of one street and vendors sit shoulder to shoulder, their wares spread like loose beans on newspaper. Chances are your communication will be almost entirely in sign language. You point to what you like, they write the price on the newspaper. You either shake your head in agreement or horror, and they usually make the necessary adjustment. After all, the guy two feet away basically has the same merchandise.

There are gold markets, silver markets, and fruit and vegetable markets with produce displayed exquisitely enough to be a model for a still life painting, and small children dash about with goats swung around their necks like old sweaters. There are markets in which your nose will probably direct you to someone baking fresh bread, roasting chestnuts or lamb, or tossing pastry into sizzling fat that turns magically into airy doughnuts. Use your common sense about what to eat or not to eat. Peel the fruit, etc. (See What Not to Eat in the chapter, "Food.")

Some markets specialize in leather, straw, or antiques. Here you must be careful when buying "certified antiques." Skilled craftsmen can make impeccable "new" antiques. If you have any doubt about your knowledge, take a friend who knows. In the Middle East and Arab countries, the souks, or marketplaces, always seem to have a little too much of everything and anything. Setting up shop can be as informal as hanging a few caftans on the wall. I have sometimes allowed English-speaking teenagers to talk their way into being my "guide" in the labyrinthine souks. (Does it really matter if you are led straight to a store belonging to your guide's cousin?) It's essential to bargain in any market unless signs indicate otherwise. Just remember the shopper's cardinal yardstick (especially in markets): Do you love it enough to carry it?

A COLLECTION OF SHOPPING IDEAS AND SOME SUGGESTIONS ABOUT HOW TO USE THEM

It's possible to bypass a good buy for the simple reason you can't imagine what you'd do with it at home. Here are some general categories, with suggestions of what you might look for, and a few different ways of making them useful.

Porcelain

teacups
beakers
mugs
honeypots
jam jars

handpainted thimbles
pipes
plates, soup bowls, etc. in different patterns

Silver

pepper mills
sugar and creamers
pillboxes
miniatures fashioned after items used in the kitchen, the laundry, the
    garden: little pails, washtubs, buckets, etc.
sugar tongs
candlesnuffers
serving utensils

Such silver and porcelain items can be used in their conventional
sense, or you can fill them with: homemade chutneys, pickles, pot-
pourri, chocolates, flowers, cloves, hot butter sauce, cinnamon sugar,
tiny bay shrimps, pistachio nuts, paper clips, hairpins, straight pins,
extra buttons.

Paper and Books

first edition books
your own books tooled and encased in leather
fancy bookmarks
paper cutouts
posters
scrolls
wooden printing blocks (use as paperweights)
unusual stationery

Linens

lace handkerchiefs for baby pillow covers, sachets
monogrammed handkerchiefs
napkins
tablecloths
guest towels
fabric used as wall covering or framed like "pictures"
pillowcases

Food-Kitchen Items

You will find these products either in the local grocery store, "gourmet" shops like Fauchon in Paris, or Dallmayr in Munich, or even in a country general store that carries regional products. There is something earthy and satisfying about giving foods from the source. Just be sure to check with customs or the appropriate government agency before you leave home for a list of what cannot be brought back into this country. (See Customs and Duty in this chapter.)

mustard—Dijon and Meaux in France; Pommard in Germany

vinegars—in all different flavors; tarragon to lime, etc.

teas, tea caddies

candied fruits (especially in France and Switzerland)

spices—saffron from India (the world's most expensive spice used in paella or to color rice pale yellow); paprika from Hungary; chilies from Mexico

coffee

aprons (look for what the waiters wear)

the local candy—Lindt oversized chocolate bars in Switzerland; Perugina from Italy; Godiva from Liège in Belgium, etc.

wine—Make it a special wine, for instance a bottle of aldornetto from Italy. The aldornetto are the oldest vines in Rome. They were found pushing through the asphalt of the Grand Hotel parking lot by the hotel guardian, and named after him. Research showed that vineyards existed on that site in antiquity.

the local liqueur—Every country has one. It's become a sign of nation status, almost like a national airline or having a delegation to the United Nations.

Miscellaneous

anything that will make a base for a lamp

anything that will make a paperweight: umbrella handles, door knockers, rocks, handles of swords, daggers

any kind of box

antique dolls

Christmas tree ornaments

wood carvings—to put at the base of mirrors, under glass tables, as a piece of statuary

shells, stones, wood pieces that you put in a basket with a piece of cotton scented with sweet-smelling oil

soaps—elegant ones like soap made from violets grown in Parma, Italy; sandalwood from India; birchleaf from Sweden; apple or apricot from Germany; rose and geranium from Belgium

medicinal roots from the East—Ginseng, the emperors' ticket to longevity, the perfect gift for those you love

11.
Beauty and Health on the Road

There have always been arbitrary standards of beauty. In the 1820s, fragility was everything and women sometimes drank vinegar or stayed up all night to look pale and interesting. Today good health is a prerequisite for beauty. Feeling vital and looking alive and natural are the hallmarks of female perfection. A woman should look good straight out of the shower or just in from a stroll on a beach.

The corker is that it requires as much hard work to look natural today as it did to look pale and interesting. To get the "no lipstick" look of being "made up but natural" you need to use lip gloss, a lip liner, a dark color for the upper lip, a blender color between the liner and the dark color, another pencil to outline the lower lip, a lighter color to highlight the middle of the bottom lip for the "pout" effect, and finally more lip gloss. That's "natural"?

The whole point is that whatever the current standards, women have always spent hours primping, brushing, coloring, plucking, rubbing, manicuring, bathing, bleaching, and depilating. The process goes on whether we are at home, or on a trip, but with one important difference: at home we all have a fairly set, daily routine that involves how we work, eat, exercise, make up, and take care of our nails, hair, and skin. The basic program doesn't change, although it's often punctuated by fervent bouts of self-improvement, dedicated to more exercise, fewer late nights, and no cheating on diets.

When you travel, however, your entire pattern of living changes. You are probably getting less sleep, walking more, and eating different foods and drinks. On a trip there are greater emotional, physical, and intellectual demands on the mind and body. You are more exposed to the elements, whether you are deliberately frying yourself on a beach, shussing down a mountain of vanilla snow, or stalking ancient temples.

The vehicle for all this activity, of course, is your body. You may have spent considerable time getting your spirit ready for the trip, but how about your body? To get the most out of a trip, you have to start out, and keep yourself in good repair.

This chapter on beauty and health is about maintenance: what you can do each day, in the least amount of time, to ensure your well-being. It runs the gamut from setting up a personal routine, using natural aids from room service or a grocery store, to advice on how to go to a hairdresser in another country, and the total immersion in beauty and health—the spa vacation. This chapter is also about how to investigate, and partake of—with common sense—some of the treatments that are indigenous to different parts of the world, including walking on rocks for zonal foot therapy, warm sand packs, and massages with egg yolks and honey.

MY MAINTENANCE ROUTINE

Looking and feeling well with no effort is a luxury I lost in my early teens. The idea however is *still* appealing, and for that reason, coupled with my laziness, I have struggled to devise a practical routine for myself that I find works at home, and translates equally well on the road. Part of its success is that the products I use are simple, like baby oil; the application isn't time-consuming, and I get a "tune-up" before I go so that I embark with everything in sound working order.

The Pretrip Tune-up

1. *Rest*—I try not to get too exhausted, especially if the trip promises more than a daily progression from the beach (or pool) to the buffet table and back. Get as much sleep as possible. You will un-

consciously be drained of precious energy from excitement, nerves, and all the preparation.

2. *Diet—You* may be blessed not to have an extra five pounds as a perennial Achilles heel. This is not my good fortune, so I always try to lose a few pounds before facing a blitzkrieg of new tastes.

3. *Exercise*—Body condition is particularly important if you are going on any kind of sports vacation: tennis camps, downhill or cross-country skiing, scuba diving, or even a spa where you may be plunged into a vigorous exercise program. Enroll in ballet, swim, or dance classes at the local gym or YWCA. How much time you have to shape up will depend on how far in advance you plan your vacation. A reputable book of exercises that you can do at home in the morning or evening is a good investment.

4. *Hair*—Never get a revolutionary hairstyle—color or cut—just before you go on a trip. You don't need to add another unfamiliar item

to your travels. Your aim is to get a style that *you* can manage easily. Ask your hairdresser for one that needs the least care. Will you need rollers, a blow dryer? A good cut is the key to a trouble-free hairdo, and keeps hair healthy. Normal wear and tear destroys the protein and you may have six inches of split hair on a shoulder-length growth. (Hair should be as thick at the end as it is at the root.) If your color is done professionally ("sun" streaks, bleaching, etc.), go in about a week before your trip. If you do your own color, take the specific brand with you because products made abroad may contain different chemicals. Ask how to minister to "colored" hair soaked in salt water and chlorine. Prepare your hair by having a few conditioning treatments. The elements—sea, sun, wind—take some of the moisture out of the hair which conditioners help replenish. (See Protecting Yourself Against the Elements in this chapter.)

5. *Skin*—Talk to your doctor, dermatologist, or pharmacist about the best way to protect your skin for the appropriate weather and climate conditions. What are the most effective sun blocks?

6. *Hands and feet*—As close to departure as possible, treat yourself to a manicure and a pedicure. A trip is not the time to experiment with false nails, etc. Keep it simple. Take a bottle of your polish to touch up chipping, and a tube of bonding glue to repair broken nails. If possible, get a "European" pedicure that removes the calluses, or consider going to a podiatrist. You will probably be walking extensively and your feet should start the trip in capital condition.

7. *Medicine*—Check with your doctor about prescription medicines you might need in addition to those you take on a regular basis. (See Health Precautions in the chapter, "Etc.")

ON THE ROAD

In the "Packing" chapter I have detailed my choice of cosmetics and products, but I'll reemphasize here what I carry in my purse at all times. I find when I'm running full tilt all day, if I stop someplace —whether it's a gas station, hotel, or restaurant bathroom—for a five-minute clean-up and refurbishing job, I have more energy.

I keep the size of my travel purse (my "Pursepac") to a minimum so everything in it has to be miniature size. If the products you use don't come in "purse" sizes, look for the smallest plastic bottles, or refill the "introductory giveaway sizes" you may have collected. I also take a small Baggie with cotton balls, a plastic bottle with rose water, a tube of Vaseline, a small spray bottle or vial of cologne, and lip gloss. With just these items I can clean and remoisturize my face, dab cologne behind my ears, and start anew. You don't even need running water.

The After-a-Long-Day, Before-Dinner Pickup

I am a firm believer that, if at all possible, it's important to vary the rhythm of each day. There are times, of course, when you will be going nonstop from dawn to dinner, if not the *following* dawn. In this case my standard revitalizer is to order extra ice with a drink and hold a cube on each wrist for a few minutes. It's startlingly refreshing —and certainly a conversation piece.

Take the time, especially when the evening is practically another whole day's activity, to relax and revive yourself with some home-made remedies. (And a snooze, if possible.) In addition to your favorite preparations, room service or the local grocer can furnish "natural" supplies. I have heard of using such exotic (but impractical) treatments to rejuvenate your skin as a watercress soufflé or a mask of stiffly beaten egg whites. You may think using mayonnaise as a hair conditioner or honey as a face mask is beyond the pale, but I have used them both with success. Here are some of the more believable (and available) "natural" products.

1. *Cucumbers*—Cut oval pieces, leaving the skin and about a quarter inch of the meat, and put over your eye from the eyebrow to the bottom lid. Use half-moon shapes under your eyes. This will help reduce any puffiness, and make the area around your eyes look and feel rested.

2. *Tea bags* (preferably camomile)—Steep the tea bags in hot water (from the tap, or heated with an immersion coil), then gently squeeze out the liquid and cover your eyes with the tea bag. This routine has the same effect—with a new aroma—as the cucumbers.

3. *Oatmeal*—Uncooked oatmeal, like talcum powder, can be used as a dry shampoo. Take a handful and work it through your hair, massaging the scalp lightly with your fingertips. Vigorously brush out all the oatmeal or powder.

4. *Mayonnaise*—Take about a half cup and apply to the hair like you would a conventional cream rinse. Rinse with lukewarm water with juice of half a lemon. Rinse again with plain, cold water. Mayonnaise is also a good cleanser for the face.

5. *Vinegar*—A very good water softener (or douche) in case you have forgotten bath salts, bubble bath, or bath oil. Use cider or white wine vinegar (*never red!*).

6. *Salt*—Salt mixed with hot water makes a breath freshener and an effective gargling potion to parry a burgeoning sore throat.

7. *Bicarbonate of soda*—Put a pound of bicarbonate in a luke-warm tub and soak for fifteen to twenty minutes to relieve sunburn.

8. *Ice*—Order a bucket of ice (some hotels have ice dispensing machines). Put a piece in a handkerchief, a towel, or wad of cotton and hold gently under your eyes. Rub lightly around your face. (Ice directly on the face can sometimes break blood vessels.)

9. *Yogurt*—Apply a cup of plain yogurt to your face. Rinse off with lukewarm water after five minutes. The fat in the yogurt (as in heavy cream) is an excellent conditioner.

10. *Olive oil*—A cleanser, moisturizer, and hair conditioner.

11. *Honey*—Take about a tablespoon of honey and gingerly pat all over your face with the third finger of each hand. Be careful not to pull the skin. Leave for five minutes, then hold a steaming hot washcloth and cover your face about half an inch away from the skin, from the hairline to the chin. The steam will warm the honey so it moisturizes and tightens the skin. Rinse with tepid water. (Honey is naturally acid balanced and an excellent toner for all skin types.)

12. *Avocados or bananas*—Mash up with a fork, apply to the face and neck, leave for five minutes and rinse with tepid water. Both make a good cleanser and conditioner. The inside peel of the avocado can be used to soften rough elbows and heels. (After all, when you're in the tropics bananas seem like a logical beauty product.)

While I'm waiting for the ice to arrive or the bananas to activate, I stretch out with my back pressed flat to the floor, elevate my feet on the bed or a chair, and roll up a towel to put under my neck. Sometimes I sit in a warm tub, but I use a towel to support my neck because holding your head so your hair won't get wet doesn't aid relaxation. A tense neck impedes proper blood circulation to the head and the brain, and can make you feel tired or groggy. The ideal way to relax, of course, is to take a short nap. Do it right. Undress and get under the covers. Just set the alarm clock so you don't keep one eye open worrying you'll oversleep.

What I Bring from Home

1. *Baby oil or mineral oil*—All-purpose oils that are cleansers and lubricants for the entire body.

2. *Rich protective cream*—Moisturizers are 50 to 75 percent water, so I use a rich, nourishing cream.

3. *Deep pore cleanser*—Your local health food store or drugstore sells "natural" products, like cleansers made with a gentle abrasive—crushed apricot pits, or a honey and crushed almond mixture—that remove the surface dry skin.

4. *Cayenne pepper*—I always take a jar of cayenne pepper that I mix in plain yogurt or buttermilk for a terrific energy boost. Stir well so you don't get "ejected" in one mouthful.

5. *Baby powder*—I use it as a dry shampoo, in addition to its traditional purposes.

6. *Rose water*—With or without glycerine, rose water is an astringent that also relieves swelling around the eyes. A cotton ball dipped in rose water and patted gently over freshly applied makeup takes away the "cake pancake" look.

PROTECTING YOURSELF AGAINST THE ELEMENTS

Exposure to the elements, whether by choice, chance, or necessity, is an age-old problem. As early as 10,000 B.C. hunters and shepherds living in the valley of the Nile smeared their bodies with oil from the castor plant as a lubricant and shield against the sun. With the development of an agricultural society, cosmetics served as a barrier against evil, as well as a sun shield. Kohl, the most famous product, is still used today, mainly in the Middle East and Arab countries, and is, in fact, packaged as eye makeup by major cosmetic houses. Kohl is a composite made from lead ore that the ancients used as eyeliner to protect the eyes from the glare. Baseball and football players follow the same principle when they put a thick black line under their eyes to mitigate the glare of sunlight or stadium lights.

There will be times, of course, when you *want* to be one with the sun, wind, and water. If you participate in outdoor sports, from tennis to water skiing or snow skiing, you probably are conscious of needing some kind of protection. However, you are just as vulnerable sight-seeing in a sunswept city or lying at the beach on a hazy day. The total effect on your body, literally, from head to toe, can be drying, chapping, burning, discoloring, irritating, and ultimately aging—not to mention the attendant discomforts.

Consider these precautionary measures:

1. Never leave home without an *effective* sunscreen. Don't delude yourself by using a product like cocoa butter which helps you fry quite nicely. Most people are sun worshippers who have convinced themselves they feel "healthier" with a tan. A little bit of sun at a time over a period of a few days may well make you look and feel good. First, you have to know the sensitivity of your own skin. Then get your geographical bearings. The sun is more intense the closer you are to the equator. Even in the United States, the strength of the sun in the southern half of the country is one and a half times greater than in the northern United States, so you get more radiation per hour in Key Biscayne than on Cape Cod. You should also be aware that the hours between 10 A.M. and 2 P.M. standard time, are the maximum tanning and burning hours. I love basking in the sunshine but my mother and my dermatologist have convinced me that too much sun ages your skin faster than anything else so I use a sun-

block (as opposed to a sunscreen), which stops all the tanning rays. Check with your own dermatologist or pharmacist for the appropriate precautions. If you buy a product with PABA, a sunscreening agent, check to see how much is in the product. Reapply any sunscreen or sunblock after swimming or vigorous physical exercise.

2. When you ski, protect your eyes with goggles: dark gray for bright sunshine; yellow for hazy days, and clear for night. Most ski goggles are ventilated to prevent fogging, but you can use an antifog spray or rub a thin film of soap on the inside. Sunglasses should be dark enough so that you don't have to squint in bright sunlight.

3. Wash your hair as frequently as possible. (Think how often you wash your face.) If you are skiing or in direct sunlight put a conditioner on your hair and cover with a ski hat or scarf. The elevated body temperatures will help the conditioner do its work.

4. Rub your feet with a pumice stone to keep them soft, free of calluses and dry skin. Let your feet and the stone soak in water, then rub gingerly.

5. Use a lip moistener, a very oily lip gloss or lipstick to prevent drying and chapping.

BEAUTY SALONS IN OTHER COUNTRIES

"You're not going to believe this one," a friend of mine said in a very controlled voice over the phone, "but I have green hair." *"Green hair??!!"* I screamed. "Green hair," she said grimly. She explained that unexpectedly, her married lover had called her in London where she was visiting friends and asked if she'd meet him for a blissful twenty-four hours in Paris. She had exactly one day to get gorgeous. Her blond hair needed reblonding so she ran around the corner from where she was staying to a tiny beauty salon with flowered chintz curtains, and tea and biscuits for all the clients.

Nothing, however, could have compensated for how she felt at the first sight of her verdant locks. Suffering from shock, and rabid mistrust of the operator's promise to fix everything, she ran home and called her lover to say she'd have to come a day later. (Under the circumstances, wearing a turban would never do.) Alas, the tryst was postponed. When a married man has a day, it's usually just *that* day.

Clearly this case is an extreme, although nonfictionalized, example, to point out that you must choose a hairdresser wisely, especially if you're planning something more elaborate than a shampoo. I make a point to go to a reputable hairdresser or beauty salon with such extracurricular offerings as massage, waxing, and manicures. I find it's the ideal rainy day activity, a no-fuss means of getting my hair washed, nails done, and, equally important, a different avenue for understanding another culture.

The momentary intimacy that exists between hairdresser and client allows personal exchanges. I've discussed birth control in India, black politics in Jamaica and South Africa, herbal medicine vs. conventional treatment in Hong Kong, and the life of an Arab in Israel. I've also picked up ideas from other clients about what to do in the city as well as listened to the daily trials and tribulations of the housewife and the careerwoman.

We all want to come back from a trip to accolades of how rested, how much younger, how absolutely *wonderful* we look. Don't be tempted to find the road to such praise by getting a *total* makeover. In the interests of getting the best out of an hour or two at the local beauty salon, heed these tips:

1. Most large hotels that cater to a tourist or business trade will have a hairdresser on the premises. There is a better chance the operators here will speak English than in the charming shops around the corner (unless you have a personal recommendation).

2. If possible, go to the shop to make an appointment. Do you feel comfortable? Is the staff pleasant? Will they accept traveler's checks, cash, personal checks, etc.?

3. Consider limiting yourself to a shampoo and set or shampoo and blow dry. Anything more involved—a permanent, straightening, bleaching, dyeing, even cutting—should be reserved for your home territory. Procedures that can dramatically alter your looks should be undertaken in optimum conditions, without a language problem and unfamiliar products. This applies even if you have only two more days ahead of you. Hair is a very emotional subject. Why invite potential upset?

4. Take a phrase book with you for such basic terms as shampoo, conditioner, pin curls, etc.

5. Ask the price of everything in advance. What are the "extras"—conditioners, hair spray? You will usually find, apart from the super-luxurious or famous salons that a shampoo and set abroad is less expensive than at home.

6. Ask about other treatments, like manicures, pedicures, waxing. I wouldn't try waxing unless you do it regularly at home. But if you are a devotee, you might find interesting variations. In the beauty shop of the Athens Hilton, I discovered a cold wax called *halawa,* made from sugar, honey, and lemon. I later found out that *halawa* dates back to Cleopatra's time, and in some Middle Eastern countries today, a bride-to-be has a complete going-over with *halawa.* I now make it at home according to a recipe from a Lebanese friend. I never worry about leftovers because it is made from the same ingredients as the syrup that's used in all obscenely rich pastries in the Middle East.

7. If you plan to get a facial, be sure to go to the *best* salons. Ask the concierge in your hotel or go to a branch of a well-known firm. It's important to know if your skin is sensitive to certain products and chemicals since a trip is no time to develop a skin allergy, rash, or irritation. You might ask for creams and lotions without perfumes, and masks made from such natural sources as herb teas, fruits, or vegetables.

8. Natural or indigenous plants or roots are often used as hair conditioners. Henna, a substance that has become widely accepted in American beauty salons, is made from ground-up dried leaves and stems of a shrub found in North Africa and the Near East. The ancients mixed it with such fruits and vegetables as beets and carrots, even wine and coffee, to color hair reddish tones. Early advocates included Cleopatra and Mohammed, who allegedly used it to dye his beard. In many Middle Eastern countries henna is used instead of nail polish to paint elaborate designs on the hands and the feet. "Natural" hair conditioners from this part of the world include *zait ghar,* made from the oil of laurel or sweet bay leaves (origianlly was the base of many soaps), and *beyloun* or *traba,* a soil cake that is pulverized and mixed with water until it turns a chestnut color.

9. Tip in the local currency. The amount will probably be so small it's almost more trouble for the operator to go to the bank to change dollars. (See Tipping in the chapter, "Etc.")

10. It's not the worst fate if you don't like the hairstyle, and in the privacy of your room, you wash or brush it into oblivion. Think of the good stories you'll have to tell.

SPAS

My credentials as a devout spa-goer date back to puberty, when my mother took me along for company, and I was too uninitiated to recognize the ultimate compliment: people asked what I was doing there. Since then, I've *needed* to go to spas. I assure you that, contrary to the popular concept of being coddled to death, you don't just lie back passively. Improving yourself is hard work. Consider being buried up to your neck in jet-black, foul-smelling sulfurous earth, or having exercise teachers take you through the paces, and barely being able to walk the next day. It may be the only time in your life you salivate over a lone chicken wing completely dwarfed by a branch of parsley. Every morning at six, when I'd hear the enthusiastic voice of the person leading the two-mile, prebreakfast walk, I promised myself to never, *never* overeat again.

Through the years, I have discovered there are many reasons for going to a spa—and many different kinds of spas to accommodate each particular need. Whether you go the luxurious or shoestring route, a spa may just be the *ne plus ultra* beauty vacation: total dedication to self-improvement with no responsibilities except to your mind and body. No phones, no cares, no cars. It can be a time not just to lose weight, but to get totally away, retreat, reevaluate, and take stock of your life. My mother is a case in point. She went to Elizabeth Arden's Maine Chance, weighing in at an enviable 105 pounds (at 5'1"). The first day, when they gave her the week's exercise and activity sheet, she crossed out everything but swimming and the massage (which she scheduled after four in the afternoon). As for the menu, she requested extra sour cream for her baked potato.

Such American spas as Maine Chance, the Golden Door, or the Greenhouse are costly, luxurious places that operate on a slightly different theme than other spas, especially those outside America. Here, the basic premise is to reeducate you to nourish and care for your body beyond the time you're in residence. At the Golden Door, for instance, there are lectures about nutrition that include showing hundred-calorie portions of many foods so that your eye can count calories.

At these glamorous watering holes (the minimum stay is usually a week), the ratio of the staff to guests is almost one to one. If you don't appear for a class, someone comes to find out why. Your day is spent doing straightforward exercises or those disguised as water ballet, volleyball or tap dancing. Your rudely awakened muscles are then eased with massage and herbal wraps, in which you are encased like a mummy in warm sheets, presumably soaked in herb-flavored water. You get to relax during pedicures, manicures, facials, and makeup instruction. Mind you, your nails may look great, but from day one, your hair is slicked down with some kind of conditioner, and you wear baggy sweatsuits, somewhat redeemed by their pastel colors. After dinner, an effort is made to improve the aesthetics in all areas of your life, so you may have lectures in flower arranging, yoga, auras (the study of what "colors" you give off), and more practical pursuits like classes in low-calorie cooking.

The connecting link between the so-called glamour spas and the less expensive establishments is that the conversation in both places never gets much beyond food, constipation, and sex. The main difference is that when you pay less, the accommodations are not as spiffy (relatively unimportant), and you have to be much more self-motivated and self-sufficient. I have gone to health farms to drink juices (or fast) and, for lack of any organized distractions, have gone into town to window-shop the pastries. Many places, however, do have exercise programs supplemented by tennis, swimming, yoga, massages (usually at extra cost), and evening lectures. It's just that no one cares if you participate.

Ultimately, you have to be your own disciplinarian. A week sequestered away "being good" won't change how you live at home, although you do have a running new start. I will never forget one woman who endured a week of sweating and stretching, plotting all the while that, on the way home, she and her husband would drive an hour out of the way to stop at her favorite place for barbecued beef sandwiches.

Spas Outside the United States

In general, spas outside the United States concentrate less on restructuring your attitude toward body care. Rather, they are often organized around "cures" for specific ailments, so you might take an antistress cure or one to cleanse your liver (or your entire system), with a Buck Rogers-type device like a panthermal machine, which rids the body of toxins and oxygenates and showers the body with an algae extract. Coincidentally, it also helps dissolve fat. Some of the theories you'll encounter about weight reduction and general health are so hokey they sound made up. One place in the Alps outlaws exercise on the grounds that the climate and altitude is enough to spark weight loss. It is essential, however, to soak your palms and soles in herb water twice a day. That, too, is apparently part of the alchemy.

The second major difference between U.S. and overseas spas is that the latter generally promote passive treatment. Unlike in America, there is no attack of athletic virtue overseas. There are places in England, for instance, where you only get lemon water three times a day and a breathtaking view of a lake. (Who knows which is more effective?) Many cures involve "taking the waters" or the mud baths. You may sit in the water, drink it, get massaged under it, and sprayed with it by a sixteen-nozzle jet. In Ischia, Italy, devotees have been busy immersing themselves in radioactive mud for centuries.

On my list of Things to Do is a visit to two rather exotic-sounding spas. One involves the *abhayanga,* southern India's traditional oil bath and massage, which is routine in the life of every inhabitant of Kerala, the lush, palm-fringed, sunny coastal state at India's southern tip. *Abhayanga,* like yoga, is another branch of the Indian system of medicine and health care that dates back thousands of years. The word itself means to anoint or smear. The body is rubbed with a specific mixture of plant essence in the carrier oil, usually coconut oil or ghee (clarified butter), and then removed with a paste made of green gram flour (from lentils), which is rubbed off and followed by a hot-water bath. The method of massage, the choice of oils, and other medications are determined by the season, the temperature, and the life-style of the client. Ailments may range from high blood pressure or frigidity to more general beauty problems such as acne and problem hair. (And, one presumes, traveler's fatigue.)

The other spa that intrigues me are the sandbaths at the southern tip of Kyushu, the southernmost island of Japan. Here you are buried in dark gray sand that is heated by a volcano. In summer, when the weather is good, you can be buried right on the beach and, with patience, be rinsed off by the tide.

While you're in Japan, you might as well partake of a unique luxury: a masseuse is on call twenty-four hours a day at most hotels. It beats a glass of milk when you can't fall asleep.

12.

Business Travel

A woman vice-chairman of a New York investment firm went on a research trip to a sheikhdom in the Middle East. She was armed with the proper contacts and letters of introduction that are inordinately pivotal to successful business dealings in that part of the world. Equally important, her company status was impressive enough so that her hosts wouldn't feel she was the second string.

Additional preparation included a briefing on some of the customs of the area, notably that the pace of doing business would be much slower, and that waiting hours, even days, for appointments was routine. It is said this practice stems from the days when a visitor to the ruler or his representative was considered a guest and kept for seven days (a magic number in the Middle East), with no discussion of the true purpose of the trip.

She learned that the handshake—not firm, just a gentle clasp—is the customary greeting; that business cards printed one side in English, the other in Arabic, should be presented Arabic side up; that Islam's influence pervades both social and business life; that you should accept at all costs to your digestive tract the nonstop rounds of coffee.

It turned out that she was treated with care and respect in business. The only problem arose with an invitation for the weekend with her associate's family. A common retreat for people without second homes is taking the servants, the food, and the television and pitching tents in the desert, one for the women, and another for the men. In this case, no one could decide in which tent she belonged. The men were her associates and so-called friends, but now she was a woman in a purely social context. To break the awkward impasse, she declined the invitation.

This state of affairs shouldn't be minimized. On a state visit to Saudi Arabia, Queen Elizabeth II was invited to sit in the King's tent. In order to comply with strict Muslim edicts about women, she was, in effect, declared an "honorary man" for the evening.

The overlay of a different culture on your behavior as an independent woman, *and* a businesswoman, is likely to pose more problems for you than for a man in a comparable situation, especially in areas where "women's liberation" is a foreign term. You may be breaking new professional ground if you are in a business—particularly anything to do with finance—that is only beginning to become as standard a field for women as the arts, journalism or education. Your acceptance as a businesswoman may also be stalled by men who feel it's incumbent on them to make sexual advances. Just anticipate this eventuality, and treat it however you see fit.

Business etiquette and ethics are based on the socio-cultural environment. You are hardly expected to know every custom in detail and behave like a native-born, which may even offend your hosts. You may know, for instance, about the concept of "saving face" in the Orient, which essentially means your conduct allows another person to retain his self-respect. It's *unlikely* you'll know that in Japan you never pass food from your chopsticks to someone else's because when a person dies, this is how the bones of the deceased are passed around the table.

There are no hard and fast rules (or predictions) for how religion, politics or the role of women in the country you are visiting will affect you. In Japan female executives are a rarity, and a friend of mine representing an American bank had to spend the first fifteen minutes of every meeting explaining why she wasn't married, and why she was in a "man's" field. When she traveled to China, however, where women have always held familial and professional power, her position was never questioned. Even at home in the U.S. you may encounter some lingering misgivings (or inexperience) about doing business with women. As one man said to a friend of mine, "I don't know what we're going to do with you, Miss Collins, we're just used to secretaries and wives."

Your choice is either to challenge such customs and attitudes or adapt. To safeguard your success in business, you should adapt within reasonable boundaries and adjust your style to the point of compatibility, but not to the detriment of your goal. There's no question that as a woman this requires additional sensitivity and understanding of the other point of view. Your outlook is the all-important key. What's needed is an extra coat of patience, an unfailing sense of humor and the consideration (and courage, if necessary), to ask what is customary. (See A Miscellany of Customs in this chapter.)

You may cringe over remarks and innuendoes, but think about your response before you pass the threshold of intolerance. It helps to remember that you are representing a company, and you may even be regarded as something of a test case in parts of the world that haven't had much exposure to women in business. Just as your behavior as a tourist is often considered exemplary of all Americans, your conduct as an American businesswoman may be judged as a hallmark of that new breed.

PLANNING

Few elements of business travel fall into a predictable pattern except that you have to go someplace else to get the job done, that your time is precious—and usually pressed—and that as a glamorous perk, the business trip has been somewhat mythologized. When you're sitting at home, five days in Paris or Rome *sound* glamorous, but how glamorous is it to work around the clock so you never see more than the inside of your hotel room and an office, and sightseeing is confined to the route between the two? (See Leisure Time in this chapter.)

Your travel arrangements and daily schedule will vary according to the circumstances of the trip. You may leave without prior notice right from the office, or have two days or three weeks to plan ahead. The company travel agent may present you with tickets and an itinerary with confirmed hotel or motel reservations, or you may find

yourself on the phone with the airlines, etc. Regardless of the specific nature of your trip, here is a checklist to consider while planning your business trip. Everything that applies to *any* trip is worth remembering so there are references to other chapters in the book, but I have included areas of special concern for the business traveler, and underscored how they can affect a woman on business.

1. Religious, business, political, and legal holidays vary from city to city and country to country. Call the consulate, trade office, or tourist bureau. Check a calendar to make sure everything is open for business during the period you intend to be there the same way you would to be sure a museum is open. For example: It is impractical to plan trips to Muslim countries during Ramadan, the ninth month of the Muhammadan year that is sacred, with fasting each day from

dawn to sunset. Year round, Friday is the day of rest and Sunday is business as usual. (If you are shuttling between Israel and Arab countries, remember that Saturday is the Jewish day of rest.) Never expect to get much accomplished in Brazil during Carnival, in New Orleans during Mardi Gras, in Hong Kong during Chinese New Year, or in August in France and Italy when practically the whole population takes the month off. There are single-day holidays unknown in this country but observed elsewhere, such as banking holidays in England, the Emperor's birthday in Japan, and August 15, a red-letter day in Catholic countries.

2. If you have the luxury of time, try to arrive the night before you are scheduled for meetings, speeches, or presentations. You will be in better emotional and physical shape.

3. No matter what kind of transportation you use, the main point is to minimize the chances for delay. Nonstop flights for instance are always preferable. Ask where the plane originates. Ideally (although there is never a guarantee) you want to board the plane at the point of origin to avoid slow-downs caused by weather and mechanical problems. Check the weather conditions at your destination. I was once scheduled to speak at a meeting an hour's flight from New York during the summer when you would expect nothing but blue skies. I never got there because the airport at the other end was completely fogged in. Had I known in advance I could have taken a train. Take the phone number of your contact in case of unexpected delays. If possible, get a home number if you're traveling on a weekend or plan to arrive after business hours.

4. If you travel extensively, check the various airlines for special services offered to frequent business travelers. The amenities can include: check-in at the first-class counter; seating in the section directly behind first class (with two seats across instead of three or four; overhead lights that stay on during the movie so you can work); help with customs if you are arriving with business materials; and use of the first-class lounge. Consider membership in one of the airline clubs, a quiet setting for working, making calls, etc. (See Airplanes in the chapter, "Transportation.")

5. When you are planning departure and arrival times, consider the traffic patterns in your own city (and where you're going) that might make an off-peak travel time more practical. (I know people who schedule business meetings to avoid rush hours.) If you have a three o'clock meeting that will last an hour, for instance, don't suffer through traffic for the five-thirty flight. Go later if you can, and use the time to relax, have a drink in an attractive place, walk through a store or museum. If you are unfamiliar with the city, ask the secretary or assistant of your business associates to suggest the most convenient tranportation.

6. If you are arriving late at night or very early in the morning, arrange to have a limousine or radio cab meet you. You must weigh the possible expense against the anxiety of a woman arriving alone at off-hours in an unfamiliar airport and city. If you have to rent a car, you might want to rent in town to avoid navigating your way in from the airport and finding the hotel. In fact, carefully assess the merits of renting a car at all. You're facing one-way streets, topography, and parking spaces, with the added pressure of having to be places at a specific time. Ask your hotel or your business associates about the practicality of public transport (a subway in Manhattan is sometimes the only way to go), or the possibility of getting a car and driver. The cost is rarely prohibitive. Your choice is not an indulgence, but an intelligent business decision to help you do the best job possible with the least personal fuss.

7. When you schedule appointments in advance, try to organize them so they make logistical sense. Get a map. It's not practical to have a meeting on Wall Street at nine, one in midtown Manhattan at ten-thirty, and a lunch date back on Wall Street at noon.

8. Make a list of contacts and get letters of introduction from the appropriate people. Make a duplicate copy to keep in your hand luggage.

9. Take an adequate supply of business cards. It may be appropriate (as in Japan and the Middle East) to have one side printed in English and the other in the local language.

10. In business, everything you do contributes to the total picture of your competence (especially important for women), and can ul-

timately affect your success. In some cases it may be rather ingenuous to say, "I don't know about your city, tell me what to do." In a business context this attitude may be interpreted to mean you don't do your homework about *anything*. You'd do better to mention specific areas of interest, or sights you've heard about and ask for any other suggestions. Find out about business customs, current events, political and economic developments. While the information may seem unrelated to your particular field, it's axiomatic that the more you understand about the total environment and the concerns of colleagues, the better you will understand the factors affecting your work.

11. Giving small gifts in business circles is standard procedure in some countries even before you have consummated a deal or the relationship has become personal. The other side of this custom, particularly in the Orient and the Middle East, is that you will usually be given any object you have admired, however fleetingly. It is considered an insult not to accept graciously. Your only protection is to keep your thoughts to yourself.

Find out if small gifts are politically and socially appropriate from the consulate or trade commission of the country, the international division of your bank, or experienced associates. There are some curious traditions and taboos: certain flowers and certain colors suggest intimacy or death. You should never give chrysanthemums to a European because they are reserved for All Saints Day (November 1) and funerals; handkerchiefs are unlucky in Venezuela; if you give cutlery in West Germany, ask for a coin as a token payment so the gift won't "cut" your friendship; never give clocks in Chinese-speaking countries because the word for clock sounds like the one for "terminate." Similarly, in Japan, never give four of anything because the word for four sounds like the word meaning death. In general, a little bit of Americana, or a small token from a famous store, like Macy's or Neiman-Marcus, is appreciated as much as an extravagant gift bought wherever you are.

Traditions vary so greatly throughout the world, that you should ask about local customs before you go. Here are a few suggestions for gifts and local taboos to keep in mind:

■ A symbol of your city or state, whether it's California wine,

Virginia ham, Wisconsin cheese, or a facsimile of an apple from New York, "The Big Apple."

- Indigenous Americana: Eskimo crafts, Indian art; small carved stone statuary or wood carvings. (See Worth-a-Stop Shopping in the chapter, "Shopping.")

- Although chocolates are a fairly safe transcultural item, never give food of any kind to Muslims during Ramadan. Liquor, liqueurs, and cognacs are appropriate except in countries where the religion prohibits drinking alcohol.

- Flower etiquette: France—yellow flowers connote infidelity. Give odd numbers of flowers, but never thirteen and never a dozen; Soviet Union—yellow is a sign of disrespect for women; Mexico—yellow flowers connote death, red flowers cast spells, and white ones lift them (if you're a believer); England—white lilies suggest death; Canada and Sweden—white lilies are used at funerals; Brazil—purple flowers are out because purple is a death color. Potted plants are acceptable almost everywhere, except don't send one to an infirm person in Japan because the fear is the sickness could take root. Give odd numbers of flowers in Japan, but not white ones—it's the color of death. In China, white and yellow flowers are for funerals.

LEISURE TIME

Try to schedule a little bit of living whenever possible. At home you have the built-in respites (whether or not you use them) of lunch, the hours between a business day and a business dinner, or a weekend. On a business trip you have to carve out personal time. Women unhinge somewhat differently than men. Here are five ideas to get you thinking about what you can do:

1. Make either a business lunch or a dinner date, but not both.

2. Schedule a massage at the end of the day.

3. Take a half hour walk *anywhere*. (See the chapter, "Meeting a City and the People.")

4. Decide for yourself if quiet time alone is the most restorative break, or if another activity, even with your business associates, would be equally refreshing. Invite them to lunch in the country, to play tennis or golf, or to show you anything of particular cultural interest.

5. Plan the trip so you have a day or a weekend to explore the area, even if you pay. The cost is usually deductible.

MONEY

Traveling on an expense account means you're not *ultimately* responsible for the bills, but you still have to contend with day-to-day expenses. You should have a cash advance in traveler's checks, even if you never need to use them all, as well as personal checks and credit cards. Discuss with the company accountant if it is preferable for you to pay on a personal credit card and then get reimbursed, or to use a company card. I always take two different credit cards in case one or the other is not accepted. I'd rather charge or pay by personal check because it simplifies my record-keeping. Keep *all* the receipts for tax purposes—even more important if you are self-employed. Take a pocket calculator.

HOTELS

Quaint charm will have to wait. A business trip is the time to choose a hotel on the basis of security and location (in relation to your appointments) and the services available—from telex to twenty-four-hour room service, meeting rooms, secretaries, or hairdressers. If you don't have the use of an office, you may want to use the facilities of the hotel and the expertise of the staff to help solve whatever problems may arise—you need a translator at the last minute, for example. Consider selecting a hotel for its prestige value. In business staying in the best is just being smart, not profligate.

Ask your travel agent, or whoever makes the reservations (or inquire personally by phone or mail), to actually *check* that the hotel has the services and equipment that you need, right down to the correct voltage for your hairdryer. If you are planning to have meetings in your room, ask for a single room with a sitting area with a couch or a table and chairs, or a junior suite. Are the single rooms large enough? In Japan, for instance, one friend says the singles are so small that she always uses a double. Get as much comfort as you can afford. There is nothing restful about traveling for business.

PACKING

If ever the adage "Less is more" fits a situation like a hand in a glove, it is your business travel wardrobe. At the same time, your appearance really *does* matter. Plotting your clothes strategy should be as methodical as designing a kitchen on a submarine. Nonessentials are out of place. Each piece of clothing has to work together and suit the occasion.

Several elements distinguish business from vacation wardrobes. It's important that your clothes convey an image of responsibility and professionalism. Would you unhesitatingly sign over a large account to someone dressed in a skirt that in another life was a petticoat? An exaggeration to be sure, but looks can telegraph specific messages. How you dress on vacation is not likely to affect the bottom line, but why take such an unnecessary business risk?

In addition to looking appropriate, care and thought should be given to fabrics that can withstand the rigors of the day and translate successfully into evening wear. You may have to go from the airplane to a meeting, or dinner may follow nonstop appointments. Meanwhile, you've been wearing the same outfit since breakfast.

The psychological transition one normally makes from daytime to evening, from feminine to seductive, is totally inappropriate on a business trip. Clothes are nonverbal communication; it's unfair to send out conflicting signals. As one man said, "Women want to be treated like a man in business but they want you to remember they're ladies." A woman associate tried to clarify the point: "Women want to be part of the company but not 'one of the boys.'"

The Wardrobe

The basic considerations of weather and your activities aside (jeans are perfect for scouting fashion photography layouts), try to determine if you will be with the same people day after day or going from city to city. You'll need fewer outfits the more people you see.

I have traveled with variations on the following wardrobe for three days to two weeks. I add one more "basic" outfit for every additional week.

The principles for organizing what to take are the same as outlined in the "Packing" chapter. You take a basic outfit (or two) whose parts interchange, and you create new looks with various combinations of blouses, sweaters, and accessories.

1. One four-piece suit in any noncrushable fabric. Pick a basic color, but avoid white or pastels that quickly show dirt and wrinkles. The pieces should be a jacket, skirt, pants, and a vest. Pants are sometimes inappropriate for business but useful for your own time. Add an extra skirt if necessary.

2. Two wash-and-hang-dry blouses. I like a polyester fabric that looks like silk. For cold climates substitute (or add) one sweater and a lightweight sweater vest to wear alone or over a blouse.

3. A classic-cut two-piece dress in a jersey-like fabric that works for evening and can be turned into different-looking outfits with

scarves tied like shawls—turned around with the point in the front, tied around the hips and waist, or around the neck. Use jewelry to make the outfit more or less dressy.

4. A silk bandeau to wear under the jacket with the skirt (or pants) for evening.

5. One daytime purse or briefcase in which you carry a flat purse with the necessary cosmetics and a wallet (and an extra pair of panty hose).

6. One small flat evening purse.

7. One pair of daytime shoes. (If you are going to Japan, be careful about boots. You'll be putting them on and taking them off constantly.)

8. A pair of sandal-type shoes for evening.

Luggage

Your goal is independence from the system, and that includes porters and traveling companions. If possible, carry everything yourself. You don't want to squander precious time waiting for luggage or, at worst, losing and tracing rerouted bags. Nor do you want to take the time to buy or replenish items, an activity that's a pleasant diversion on a pleasure trip but is sheer aggravation when you're traveling on business. (See Luggage in the chapter, "Packing.")

The Ever-ready Makeup Case

The frequent business traveler (and the popular weekend guest), should always keep a complete bag of cosmetics and drug-related items (and a converter for your hairdryer or rollers) so that, if necessary, you can pack in fifteen minutes for overnight or two weeks. I keep a ten-day supply of everything in small bottles that I can refill. With this ongoing system, I never have to start from scratch or panic that I don't have time to prepare the essentials. If you often have to leave unexpectedly right from the office, keep a duplicate set of cosmetics in your desk drawer.

Taking Business Materials

1. If you take a briefcase, pick one that is practical (not suede),

and in a neutral, attractive color, like burgundy. Carrying a briefcase *and* purse can look awkward and unwieldy. I take a small flat pouch for the essentials—money, credit cards, lipstick—that fits in the briefcase.

2. If you are checking large presentations or charts, carry a letterhead-sized version in case the luggage is lost.

3. If you need to bring a large number of copies, carry a master that can be duplicated.

4. If you are shipping materials air freight, put the waybill numbers in your wallet.

5. Sift through reference materials and pare them down to the essentials.

6. Check with customs about commercial visas for taking certain supplies and samples. Ask about customs declarations on leaving this country and entering others.

TRAVELING WITH MALE ASSOCIATES

Contrary to popular opinion, there are probably fewer intramural skirmishes between men and women on the road than one is led to believe. You have to develop your own personal style to handle the man-woman situation. It may be healthier and more comfortable to deal with it openly on the acceptable basis of humor, complete with double-entendre remarks. The successful woman knows how to make a man comfortable with what might be called business sexuality, in which custom, habit, and biology all blend into a manageable degree of sexual expression.

Much of the responsibility rests with the woman to indicate what is appropriate. The point is that a business trip affords the natural opportunity for relaxed socializing together after a day's work. Your general conduct sets the tone and your best protection against *unwanted* attention is to remain the sober party in every sense.

You set the ground rules more by your behavior than your words. You might go out to drinks and dinner, but at a certain moment you should be the one to say good night. You may be saving everyone from a potentially awkward morning-after. Derek S. Newton comments aptly on the problem in his book *Think Like a Man, Act Like a Lady, Work Like a Dog:* "The management of personal warmth is perhaps the most difficult aspect of being a woman in business. It is potentially your biggest plus and your biggest minus. Too little warmth and you won't be liked. Too much warmth and you won't be taken seriously."

You have probably worked out your relationships with your male colleagues long before you travel together. But what about the chance encounters on the road? If you're not interested, start talking about your children, your pets (especially referring to them often by name), your herb garden. There is nothing like domestic responsibilities to kill a twenty-four-hour romance.

TAKING YOUR HUSBAND ALONG

Companies are programmed for men to bring their wives. There is a prevalent corporate philosophy I've heard expressed both bluntly and obliquely that goes something like this: men behave better with their wives around. As an added incentive, some companies have elaborate programs for wives during meetings, and in some cities independent organizations specialize in "spouse" activities.

To my knowledge, there are no separate programs for the accompanying husband. Inviting your husband or lover might in fact be considered too departural. I know of one situation where a woman asked to bring her live-in friend of many years and was told it was inappropriate. With a corporate okay, the decision then depends on the nature of your relationship. Presumably if you are sufficiently committed to your career to be going on extended trips and meetings, your spouse has already accepted your involvement. All the same, you have to discuss and evaluate how he will feel in a situation where you are occupied principally with others, and you will visibly be the important party. Is he self-sufficient, secure, gregarious? Will you be overly concerned about him? If the mutual decision is that he come along, ask your company if you should personally cover all the expenses and get reimbursed or vice versa. Just tell your husband/friend to take his own mad money.

A MISCELLANY OF CUSTOMS

An unexpected corollary to this husband-wife situation is your relationship with the *wives* of your associates who accompany their husbands. In your own way, you should make it clear that you are only there to do business, not to land their husbands.

Any attempts to make a definitive list of Achilles' heels or traditions relating to specialized business situations would be foolish, if not presumptuous. Knowing *how to find out* in each situation is your most valuable and timeless tool. The following observations will point the way.

1. The importance or disregard for titles in business can be a bellwether of formality, power in the company or a sign of respect. Titles have different meanings in different countries. For example: A chief operating officer in America has the last word. In Japan he is usually more of a figurehead, since decisions are made by consensus; in Germany *all* titles are taken seriously; "Dottore" in Italy is commonplace and always used in preference to a simple "signore" because it indicates a higher level of education.

2. Even if you do not speak the language, knowing something about it can provide some insight into how people relate to one another. The Romance languages have the familiar and the formal "you." Which one is used gives a clue about the status of your relationship.

3. There is a Japanese expression which means "scarching into each other's stomachs." It refers to the rapport, information, and perception about a person gleaned from social contact, rather than the kind of tangible knowledge you get from an annual report. Every country in the world has the equivalent of doing business over meals, cocktails, or the golf course. Americans and Israelis seem particularly devoted to breakfast meetings. In the United States, social events at the golf or tennis club extend the business day, while the same purpose is accomplished in Brazil by going to the polo games or the soccer matches in Argentina. One businesswoman I know said

she felt she was on a food trip in Mexico because the Mexicans have raised the business lunch and dinner to such a fine art that business was hardly discussed. In Finland, nothing could be more natural than proceeding from the office to the sauna in the home of your business associate. Sometimes there is a sauna for men and women, and sometimes only one for everyone. In this case, wrapping yourself in a towel is the only way to give the occasion some formality.

4. Questions about social etiquette ranging from who should entertain whom to what gifts are appropriate may be addressed to the secretary or assistant of your business associates. They are familiar with the habits and character of their associates, and can put them in the context of the local customs. You should be sensitive, however, to the times when it may be more offensive to insist that you pick up the dinner bill. It could be better business to accept graciously, while making it clear that you fully intend to reciprocate. Often you can overcome the objections by reminding your guests that your company is doing the inviting, not you personally. Many men still find it hard to accept a woman paying for a meal because for so long, going to a restaurant had purely social connotations.

5. Look at commercials and advertisements to get an idea of how differently the same products are marketed in different countries. The worldwide advertising campaign for diamond engagement rings, for example, shows how the character of each country requires a personally tailored approach. In Mama-dominated Italy the copy reads, "My mother says we're engaged. For us, diamonds mean we are together." For the United Kingdom the lingo was updated, "With a diamond on your finger, there's no way you're just good friends."

6. Social customs can give you an idea about the place of women, although there is usually an added distinction between urban and small towns, and different economic and social levels. The arranged marriage, for example, is still a custom of certain classes in Japan, although as a Japanese friend of mine explained, "Our marriage wasn't arranged. After four years we grew to love each other." Other clues to the status of women outside the home are found in the number of women in politics—cabinet posts to members of the legislature —the number of college graduates, the number of women in the work

force. In the Philippines, for instance, where so many businesses are owned by women, they have an equitable version of how women were created. Adam's rib had nothing to do with it. A piece of bamboo split to make a man and a woman.

13.
Etc.

My silver-haired great-aunt Dorothy is the kind of person who gladly parted with such snippets of family heritage as her secret recipe for chocolate cake, but she'd always manage to leave out an essential ingredient—the chocolate. The family never held it against her—we knew this was her way of being indispensable.

This last chapter will remedy the Aunt Dorothy syndrome and include essential miscellany not covered elsewhere in the book. The gathered loose ends range from recommendations on how to overcome the cliché travel photograph to dissecting the ever-puzzling subject of tipping to unusual types of bathrooms you might encounter.

One suggestion: read this chapter while eating a piece of chocolate cake.

OFFICIALDOM—PASSPORTS, VISAS, TOURIST CARDS, INOCULATIONS AND HEALTH CARDS

1. *Passports*—I'm not quite sure what it does psychologically to have an up-to-date passport, but it makes me feel secure to know I *could* get on a plane and head for anywhere in the world, even if money and time usually preclude such spontaneity. Getting or renewing a passport is a simple procedure whose only complication might

be the delays inherent in the peak travel season. And even then, if you live in a city with a local passport agency, you can get your passport on a day's notice, as long as you have tickets that prove your imminent departure.

Normally you apply at a passport agency. You need proof of citizenship (your birth certificate), two passport-size photographs, personal identification such as a driver's license, and the fee for the passport. If there is no local agency, some county clerks and local post offices are authorized to accept passport applications. Bring the above-mentioned material, fill in and sign the form and they mail it to the passport agency. You can expect to get your passport anywhere from ten days to three weeks after your application has been received, although you should allow extra time in the busy travel seasons.

2. *Visas*—A visa is not a separate document, but an official stamp in your passport issued by the consulate of a country and usually garnished with fancy tax stamps and signatures with *real* fountain pens. Visas are not necessary for all foreign travel, but are often required in Africa, the Middle East, and the Orient. They merely allow you to visit certain countries for a specific length of time. The required ticket out of the country shows you have no homesteading intentions. Essentially, having a visa is official testimony that you are neither a spy nor a reporter investigating government practices. When I went to South Africa to do an article about diamonds, for example, I had to sign a letter stating I wouldn't write anything about politics.

The main problem with visas is not that you won't qualify, but that they can take so long to get, particularly if you live in a city without consulates, as most of us do. Your passport must go to each consulate with the visa application, so that getting visas for several destinations can be a lengthy process. (Applications by mail take at least one week.) If a travel agent is booking your trip, he will usually handle the visa application. Two final words: It's conceivable that filling out unfamiliar government forms can be slightly anxiety-producing; once you have your visa in hand, the immigration officer at the border makes the final decision. In my experience, the smaller the country, the more elaborate the proceedings. We had to fill out visa applications at the border of a small African nation. Mine was delayed for the unlikely reason that the page corner was crumpled. It was then affixed with three stamps, two signatures, and a seal. This process sounds exaggerated, but it's well to remember that most officialdom is plagued with pomp, formality, red tape, and inexplicable delays. Always carry a book.

3. *Tourist Cards*—In a sense these are second echelon passports. They are a proof of citizenship and are required by only a few countries, primarily Mexico and in South America. To get the tourist card you must show you are a United States citizen, either with a passport or a birth certificate. The cards are available through the carrier airlines either at the airport or local ticket office, or through a travel agent.

4. *Inoculations and Health Cards*—Because vaccination requirements and suggested inoculations are subject to change, contact your state or local health department for the latest information. You can also write to the Superintendent of Documents, the U. S. Government Printing Office, Washington, D.C. 20402 for a copy of the booklet published by the Center for Disease Control in Atlanta, which operates under the aegis of the Department of Health, Education and Welfare, with information on infected areas, the water, and the food, etc.

In addition to public sources, always check with your doctor for recommendations specifically for you. If a certain inoculation is suggested as a general prophylactic—gamma globulin which protects you against hepatitis, for instance—I always take it. Be sure to do your research well in advance to allow enough time for any required waiting periods between the shots.

OTHER HEALTH PRECAUTIONS

If you have special medical problems, carry (do not pack) a set of pertinent medical records. These records should include the generic names and dosage of all the drugs you take, any known allergies, and your blood type. If you have a serious heart condition, take a copy of your latest electrocardiogram.

Take your doctor's home and office number and a number where you can reach him/her on vacation. Ask for names of doctors in the areas where you will be traveling.

Keep in mind such resources for medical emergencies as the local police, the concierge at the hotel, and the American Embassy. Although the embassy can provide a list of English-speaking doctors and their specialties, it will never recommend a particular doctor because of potential liability. If you have a medical problem complicated by language difficulties, ask to see the American consulate. According to the Department of State, American embassies have duty officers available twenty-four hours a day.

TRAVEL FOR THE HANDICAPPED

The term "handicapped" generally refers to someone who needs a wheelchair at all times, but it really should include anyone from a kidney patient in need of regular dialysis treatments to a person with a breathing malfunction. Ironically, some people travel with a *mental* handicap—fear or lack of curiosity—that can limit the travel experience as much as any physical disability! The handicapped traveler has probably overcome the standard psychological blocks about travel. He must worry about managing the major and minor *logistical* problems. It can be done. For anyone with any kind of physical disability, or anyone planning a trip with someone who is handicapped, consider these key areas:

1. Attitude is the sustaining factor. While you should not have unrealistic expectations about what you can do, don't be defeated by the answer "We've never done that before." One friend of mine is confined to a wheelchair, yet goes to Europe every year with one attendant. She says that there are numerous incidents of touching gallantry, but you must be prepared for all kinds of reactions, even hostility, which is usually a manifestation of embarrassment or of total lack of experience with the situation.

2. Access to buildings, from doorways to steps, and all types of transportation need investigation. Call the passenger service department of the airlines, steamship, or train companies to ask about steps, breezeways, hydraulic lifts, ramps, and storage space for wheelchairs. Can you take a collapsible wheelchair on the airline, or must it be checked through like baggage, with the anxiety-producing

possibility it may be lost? If you are going abroad, ask the airline or tourist office about English-speaking help. Ask museum officials, for instance, about permission to use freight elevators that exist for transporting sculpture and paintings. Inquire with the local chamber of commerce if that particular city publishes an access guide.

3. Plan ahead. Try to anticipate situations in advance. You may lose spontaneity, but you'll gain comfort. If you are booking through a travel agent, ask for hotels that cater to handicapped travelers. One friend takes the situation in her own hands and writes to the hotels for a sketch of the bathroom, including the height of the toilet. Whenever possible, she has friends in each city check out the premises and measure doorways to the room and the bathroom.

BATHROOMS

Bathrooms are a subject unto themselves, filled with humor and pathos—and infinite variety. Throughout the world, there are unusual facilities (to say the least) that call themselves bathrooms. I've stood next to the kitchen stove in a restaurant, waiting to use the john, which was part of the supply closet, and maneuvered the setup where there are two small troughs to stand in on either side of a hole in the ground—you squat and hope for the best. In many places, men and women use the same lavatory. I have a friend who went to what she thought was the ladies' room in a Tokyo hotel. She was putting on lipstick when a man came in, bowed politely, used the urinal, and bowed again on his way out.

Here are some tips to gently prepare you for some of the possibilities:

1. Wrapping a trenchcoat over a nightgown at 3 A.M. to go down a flight of stairs to the communal bathroom is one of those travel experiences that may be more amusing to tell afterward than live through. The "logic" is that you do save money when you get a room without bath (see the chapter, "Hotels"), and the rooms usually have a sink and a portable bidet that looks something like a bedpan stashed underneath the sink.

2. Toilet paper comes in unbelievable variations. Whatever it is, there never seems to be enough: pieces of torn-up newspaper hung on a nail; wax paper; paper towels; shreds of paper towels and other abrasive, nonabsorbent materials. It's in your best interest to carry a purse-sized packet of facial tissues, and take a few paper napkins with you in restaurants and café facilities.

3. The many ways of flushing may include: pulling an antiquated

chain by a wooden handle that you think will break at the slightest bit of pressure (but doesn't); pressing buttons on the wall, pushing buttons on the floor; throwing in a pailful of water; walking out as quickly as possible, and warning the next person, particularly if you're friends.

4. Many bathrooms don't have doors. Take a friend, especially in unisex facilities, and swallow your propriety.

5. The most convenient attire for the hole in the ground model is a skirt or dress, although such advance planning is often impossible. If you are wearing pants, take them off completely. Otherwise you will be busy trying to keep your balance and your clothes dry at the same time.

6. Gas stations in Europe usually have bathrooms.

7. Anything marked W.C. (water closet) usually means toilet only.

8. Many public bathrooms have attendants who keep things clean and can provide you with anything from a needle and thread to cologne or aspirin. Leave the equivalent of twenty-five to fifty cents.

9. Some bathrooms have a hot water tank with a roaring fire—they're safe.

10. Many European hotels have a shower which is literally in the middle of the bathroom. There is no curtain, and the drain is in the middle of the floor. In these cases, you do not have a conventional shower head, but what is called a telephone shower, a shower head attached to a long cord that looks something like the gadget used to wash your hair in beauty salons, only bigger. The trouble is that these cords often contort unexpectedly, drenching the entire bathroom, including you, your hair, and your one and only towel.

TIPPING

Weeks before my parents were to sail on the *Queen Mary*, my father started agonizing about who and what to tip. To quiet his fears, some friends made him a bon voyage present of Tip Packets, envelopes marked for each person he would need to tip with the appropriate amount of cash in each one.

My father's malaise is not uncommon. In fact, most travelers are thoroughly discombobulated by the whole subject of tipping, although the reasons may go beyond the sheer monetary aspect. Somehow, knowing how to take care of the maître d' in black tie or the owner-waiter-chef of a beachfront shack connotes worldliness. *Not* knowing brands you as a philistine. The added twist is that women have a reputation for being bad tippers.

Each time I find myself pondering anxiously over the correct tip, whether it's a hairdresser, bathroom attendant, theater usher, concierge, or waiter, I have the feeling I *should* know exactly the right amount, until I remind myself that each situation is different. It's easy to lose sight of the original principle of tipping, which is to give extra remuneration for particularly good service. Unfortunately, tipping has become expected procedure in some industries and bears no relation to the quality of service. New York taxi drivers think giving a tip is an automatic reflex. Other times (in other places), a simple thank you and an extra appreciative smile is sufficient. In Japan and Thailand, for instance, tipping is not customary at all.

There is one practice that might charitably be called tipping, or, more honestly, bribing. This procedure involves paying, or "greasing someone's palm," in advance in order to *get* good service. I have always found this the most awkward part of the whole tipping ritual, yet it should not be entirely dismissed, especially if you frequent a particular restaurant for business purposes when a good table and excellent service can make an important difference.

While there are no irreversible rules for tipping, these personal guidelines will help ease the confusion. (See the chapter, "Hotels" for tipping the concierge and the Cruises, Freighters, Yachts in the chapter "Transportation" for tipping on cruises.)

1. If I am unclear about the custom or the proper percentage of the bill to tip the waiter, the sommelier, the maître d', etc. I ask. (You might consult the maître d' in your own hotel.) Ask the concierge for any special tipping customs. In England, for instance, you always tip ushers in the theater.

2. Source material for the most up-to-date tipping suggestions in-

clude annually revised country and city guides, magazines and newspapers, brochures often published by the airlines, major hotel chains and large travel agents or currency exchange companies.

3. I keep single dollar bills or the equivalent of a dollar (and of fifty cents) in the local currency for airport porters, hotel bellmen and doormen. Figure fifty cents per bag, and add anywhere from twenty-five to fifty cents for what you might consider extra help. I never hesitate to give something above what is called for, particularly if I am staying in the hotel more than one night. You never know when you need some special care.

4. If you go to an internationally known beauty salon, assume you tip the same percentage of the bill, apportioned according to whoever cuts, sets, or shampoos your hair on a scale comparable to what you would do at home.

5. Inflation notwithstanding, the general rule of thumb for tipping in a restaurant is 15 percent of the bill. But there are some qualifications. Is the service included? This is usually written at the bottom of the check and means that you don't have to tip the waiter, although if the maître d' has given you a special table, or any kind of special service, you might want to give him a few dollars. In some restaurants, the maître d' will seat you, suggest dishes, and prepare them at tableside. In these cases, you should tip the maître d' the 15 percent, and the waiter who will probably clear the table and take coffee and dessert orders, about 8 percent.

Sometimes the function of the maître d' is simply to show you to the table, and the waiter takes care of the suggesting, ordering, and preparing. Tip according to who does the most for you. If you're not sure exactly who is doing what—sometimes everyone is wearing a black dinner jacket—ask. It's always better to show you would like to do the right thing, rather than blindly deciding what's right. I have consoled myself with the notion that during my lifetime all my over- and undertipping will average out to make me as equitable a tipper as humanly possible.

6. Service in a hotel is usually included in the price of the room. There is no need to tip the maid, unless you have asked for something special—like washing out underwear, cleaning the kitchenette (common in resort hotels), etc.

If you are staying in a hotel for more than a few days, you might want to give the maid a few extra dollars. Sometimes you get a fairly blatant hint. A friend of mine had an experience in a resort in the northeast in which there was an envelope on the dresser marked with the name of the maid. It's difficult to decide the right amount, but you can't go wrong leaving $5–10, based on the length of your stay, how many people in the room, and *if* you feel extra care was taken.

You are expected to give the waiter from room service a tip. You can add it to the bill when you sign for the service, or tip in cash. Use your common sense. If he simply brings breakfast, for instance, a $1–3 is sufficient. If, on the other hand, he sets up and serves a dinner $5 is more appropriate.

CAMERAS

Having photographed monuments I didn't recognize months later and raspberry sunsets that looked like a magenta smudge on a 5×7 print, I have been forced to reconsider the whole point of taking pictures. I realized that a photograph had taken on the same meaning as an autograph: it was just proof I had been there. Was I more concerned with immortalizing the moment rather than just enjoying it? Or was I afraid I wouldn't remember if I didn't have a picture? When I came to the unpleasant conclusion that there was truth in these concerns, I decided to use the camera in a new way—as a companion and as a second pair of eyes. Now, I observe everything more carefully in the process of looking for interesting shots. The process is thoughtful, instead of haphazard, and involves selecting what to record, whether it's as artsy as a manhole covered with confetti so that it looks like a stained-glass window, as corny as a spray of flowers, as creative as the juxtaposition of different styles of architecture, and as scrapbookish as a picture that a stranger took of me standing in front of the Eiffel Tower.

Since many books have been written on the subject of travel photography, I can only share with you some personal discoveries I have made through sheer luck, mistakes, and the suggestions of photographers I know:

1. Taking brand-new, borrowed, or untried equipment is as short-sighted as planning a walking tour in new shoes. If the camera is any

more complicated than an Instamatic, practice at home. Use the flash attachment. Shoot at different times of the day. Try out the different lenses. Consider a Polaroid. I'm crazy about mine.

2. I always buy postcards of famous palaces, houses, or street scenes because someone has spent a lot of time figuring out the best vantage point for the picture. Then I can make my own variations.

3. The best picture-taking light is early morning and late afternoon, especially in the summer when the bright noon sun "whitewashes" all the shadows.

4. Avoid buying film outside the United States except in an emergency. It is usually more expensive because the cost of processing is included. (Many major film manufacturers publish literature on the use and care of film overseas, which is available for a small fee by writing directly to the company.

5. Most airports have some kind of electronic devices for examining hand luggage and baggage for hidden bombs and weapons. Ideally, carry all your photographic equipment with you and request a visual inspection.

6. Common courtesy is the best policy if you sense that taking a photo might be an intrusion of privacy. Ask permission. If you don't speak the language, simply point to the camera; you'll be understood. In the eagerness to capture what is unthinkingly called local color, you forget that people at all economic levels have dignity and pride about how they live.

7. It is not uncommon to be asked for money in exchange for letting you take a picture. One couple who have stood at the lookout point to China from the New Territories are said to have made a small fortune. You have to decide if the picture is worth a few cents. It usually is.

8. Whatever the reasons that you miss, forego, or neglect to take a picture, your mind's eye will remember.

Appendix

INDISPENSABLE READING

Sharing favorite books is a very personal thing. You can only hope they will touch someone else as they have touched you. The following books are like family to me. I have read, reread, leafed through, forgotten about and then rediscovered every one. They are a mixture of mood pieces about specific cities to inspire you and make you long to be there, and practical guidebooks, although I generally don't follow any one book religiously.

Omissions and inclusions might seem incomprehensible to anyone but me, but then these lists are nothing more than a reflection of my own taste.

I should add that I am a magazine junkie as well. One of my favorite ways to spend an evening alone is to curl up with the latest issues of my favorite publications. I keep file folders handy because inevitably I find articles on destinations, food, shopping, etc. that I will want to have for that rainy day when I plan my next trip.

I read: *Travel and Leisure* (especially good on books, food, howto, personal essays and trends); *Business Week,* particularly the Personal Business section; *Cosmopolitan, Vogue, Town and Country,* and *W* (published by the company who puts out *Women's Wear Daily*) for up-to-the-minute trends in chic anything; *Architectural Digest* for an idea of interiors and gardens (some you can visit); *Bon Appétit* and *Gourmet* for food-related travel pieces and recipes; *Harper's* and *Queen* for news of the continent and Great Britain; *Newsweek* and *Time,* which sometimes have extensive special travel related sections; *Saturday Review's* travel column.

BOOKS FOR GETTING IN THE MOOD

Paris! Paris! by Irwin Shaw, illustrated by Ronald Searle. A collection of pieces and drawings about Paris so poignantly done that the description of a street, or the face of a Parisienne transports you immediately. (A Delta Book, Dell Publishing Company, New York, 1976, paperback)

The Great Railway Bazaar—By Train Through Asia by Paul Theroux. Never have I been so entranced and seduced by train travel. Both the people and the landscapes are sketched in exquisite detail—with a storyteller's hand. (Houghton Mifflin Company, Boston, 1975)

The Maharajahs by John Lord. Their wealth and life-style was incomprehensible and fascinating. Even if you never get to India, it's worth reading. (Random House, New York, 1971)

The Scandinavians by Donald S. Connery. Delicious analysis and commentary of that block of land, country by country, so that you will no longer be able to lump them conveniently together. (Simon and Schuster, New York, 1966)

The Italians by Luigi Barzini. Witty, incisive, totally delightful picture of the habits and folkways of the Italians. (Atheneum, New York, 1977, paperback)

The French: Portrait of a People by Sanche de Gramont. The best biography of the French. (G. P. Putnam's Sons, New York, 1969)

Anything by Jan Morris, who writes with the poetic sensibility of the nineteenth-century Romantics, but with a reporter's eye.

Anything by Kate Simon, who writes tart, funny, personal, refreshing, and practical books about her favorite places.

Time-Life Cookbooks. My first reference source because they give you a feeling about the food, with color pictures, recipes, and tidbits about history, literature, folklore, and customs. (Time-Life Books, New York)

The World Atlas of Food: A Gourmet's Guide to the Great Regional Dishes of the World. In one volume, this wonderful book shows you the world of food, through maps, illustrations, and recipes. (Simon and Schuster, New York, 1974)

GETTING MORE PRACTICAL

The Sunset Travel Guides. Straightforward, practical prose, but always with an angle—special trips through Europe, for instance. Sidebars on unusual things to see, eat, or do. (Lane Publishing Co., Menlo Park)

Alexis Lichine's New Encyclopedia of Wines and Spirits by Alexis Lichine. The best comprehensive, easy-to-understand, and well-organized overview of libations. (Alfred A. Knopf, New York, 1974)

Fodor's Guides. Best for the essays on each country that focus on a particular aspect of the culture.

Fielding's Guides. Though their style is too cute for my taste, these books at least give a good point of reference for the specifics.

Robert S. Kane's A to Z guides. Very factual, grounded in history, readable.

Myra Waldo's guides. Spirited and sophisticated, especially if you're going by car.

Michelin green guides. Best on history, background, superb maps, and in English. Easy-to-carry paperbacks.

Michelin red guides. Musts for restaurants and hotels.

Ian Keown's guides: Lovers' Guide to the Caribbean and Mexico and Very Special Places; Lovers' Guide to America. The best of exactly what the title implies. (Collier Books, New York, 1975; Collier Books, New York, 1974)

The Joy of Camping: The Complete Four-Seasons, Five-Sense Practical Guide to Enjoying the Great Outdoors (Without Destroying It) by Richard Langer. The title tells all. (Penguin Books, Baltimore, 1974)

Where to Eat in America: An Indispensable Guide to Finding What You Want to Eat When You Want to Eat It in the 30 Most Traveled American Cities, edited by William Rice and Burton Wolf. The only one of its kind and excellent. (Random House, New York, 1977)

How to Take Better Travel Photos by Lisl Dennis. (HP. Books, Tucson, 1979)

Around the World Weather Guide

NOTE: For most of the entries which follow, the base figure for the number of days with measurable precipitation is 0.01 inches. This will be true unless otherwise noted. But in some cases the base measure is 0.04 inches (indicated by *), or 0.1 inches (indicated by **).

Afghanistan KABUL

MONTH	Temperature (Average Daily) Max. degrees fahrenheit	Min.	Relative Humidity percent	Precipitation Average Monthly inches	Average Number Days with 0.01 inches or more
January	36	18	70	1.2	2
February	40	22	62	1.4	3
March	53	34	44	3.7	7
April	66	43	35	4.0	6
May	78	51	32	0.8	2
June	87	56	24	0.2	0.6
July	92	61	22	0.1	0.4
August	91	59	23	0.1	0.4
September	85	51	18	0.1	0.1
October	73	42	22	0.6	0.9
November	62	33	31	0.8	2
December	47	27	53	0.4	1

Algeria ALGIERS*

January	59	49	66	4.4	11
February	61	49	60	3.3	9
March	63	52	59	2.9	9
April	68	55	57	1.6	5
May	73	59	60	1.8	5
June	78	65	60	0.6	2
July	83	70	60	0.1	0.4
August	85	71	60	0.2	0.5
September	81	69	62	1.6	4
October	74	63	60	3.1	7
November	66	56	63	5.1	11
December	60	51	64	5.4	12

Argentina BUENOS AIRES

January	85	63	61	3.1	7
February	83	63	63	2.8	6
March	79	60	69	4.3	7
April	72	53	71	3.5	8
May	64	47	74	3.0	7
June	57	41	78	2.4	7
July	57	42	79	2.2	8
August	60	43	74	2.4	9
September	64	46	68	3.1	8
October	69	50	65	3.4	9
November	76	56	60	3.3	9
December	82	61	62	3.9	8

Australia MELBOURNE, VICTORIA

MONTH	Temperature (Average Daily) Max. degrees	Min. fahrenheit	Relative Humidity percent	Precipitation Average Monthly inches	Average Number Days with 0.01 inches or more
January	78	57	48	1.9	9
February	78	57	50	1.8	9
March	75	55	51	2.2	9
April	68	51	56	2.3	13
May	62	47	62	2.1	14
June	57	44	67	2.1	16
July	56	42	65	1.9	17
August	59	43	60	1.9	17
September	63	46	55	2.3	15
October	67	48	52	2.6	14
November	71	51	52	2.3	13
December	75	54	51	2.3	11

PERTH, WESTERN AUSTRALIA

MONTH	Max.	Min.	Humidity	Monthly	Days
January	85	63	44	0.3	3
February	85	63	43	0.4	3
March	81	61	45	0.8	5
April	76	57	49	1.7	8
May	69	53	58	5.1	15
June	64	50	63	7.1	17
July	63	48	63	6.7	19
August	64	48	61	5.7	19
September	67	50	58	3.4	15
October	70	53	55	3.2	12
November	76	57	49	0.8	7
December	81	61	47	0.5	5

PORT DARWIN, NORTHERN TERRITORY

MONTH	Max.	Min.	Humidity	Monthly	Days
January	90	77	71	15.2	20
February	90	77	72	12.3	18
March	91	77	67	10.0	17
April	92	76	54	3.8	6
May	91	73	47	0.6	1
June	88	69	47	0.1	1
July	87	67	44	0.1	1
August	89	70	45	0.1	1
September	91	74	49	0.5	2
October	93	77	52	2.0	5
November	94	78	58	4.7	10
December	92	78	65	9.4	15

MONTH	Temperature (Average Daily) Max. degrees fahrenheit	Min.	Relative Humidity percent	Precipitation Average Monthly inches	Average Number Days with 0.01 inches or more
January	78	65	64	3.5	14
February	78	65	65	4.0	13
March	76	63	65	5.0	13
April	71	58	64	5.3	14
May	66	52	63	5.0	14
June	61	48	62	4.6	13
July	60	46	60	4.6	12
August	63	48	56	3.0	12
September	67	51	55	2.9	11
October	71	56	57	2.8	12
November	74	60	60	2.9	12
December	77	63	62	2.9	12

Austria VIENNA

January	34	24	72	1.5	15
February	37	27	66	1.7	14
March	46	34	57	1.7	13
April	59	42	49	1.8	13
May	66	50	52	2.7	13
June	73	57	55	2.6	14
July	77	59	54	3.3	13
August	75	59	54	2.8	13
September	68	51	56	1.6	10
October	57	44	64	2.3	13
November	44	37	74	2.0	14
December	37	30	76	1.7	15

Bahamas NASSAU*

January	77	65	64	1.4	6
February	77	64	62	1.5	5
March	79	66	64	1.4	5
April	81	69	65	2.5	6
May	84	71	65	4.6	9
June	87	74	68	6.4	12
July	88	75	69	5.8	14
August	89	76	70	5.3	14
September	88	75	73	6.9	15
October	85	73	71	6.5	13
November	81	70	68	2.8	9
December	79	67	66	1.3	6

Barbados BRIDGETOWN

MONTH	Temperature (Average Daily) Max. degrees fahrenheit	Min.	Relative Humidity percent	Average Monthly inches	Average Number Days with 0.01 inches or more
January	83	70	71	2.6	13
February	83	69	66	1.1	8
March	85	70	64	1.3	8
April	86	72	65	1.4	7
May	87	73	67	2.3	9
June	87	74	70	4.4	14
July	86	74	71	5.8	18
August	87	74	72	5.8	16
September	87	74	73	6.7	15
October	86	73	76	7.0	15
November	85	73	78	8.1	16
December	83	71	73	3.8	14

Belgium BRUSSELS

January	38	30	86	2.6	21
February	44	33	81	2.3	17
March	51	36	74	2.1	17
April	58	41	71	2.3	18
May	65	46	65	2.1	16
June	72	52	65	3.0	15
July	73	54	68	3.7	17
August	72	54	69	3.1	18
September	69	51	69	2.4	13
October	60	45	77	3.2	17
November	48	37	85	3.0	20
December	43	32	86	3.4	19

Benin (formerly Dahomey) COTONOU*

January	80	74	68	1.3	2
February	82	77	70	1.3	2
March	83	79	69	4.6	5
April	83	78	70	4.9	7
May	81	76	74	10.0	11
June	78	74	78	14.4	13
July	78	74	77	3.5	7
August	77	73	76	1.5	3
September	78	74	76	2.6	6
October	80	75	75	5.3	9
November	82	76	74	2.3	6
December	81	76	71	0.5	1

Bermuda HAMILTON*

MONTH	Temperature (Average Daily) Max. degrees	Min. fahrenheit	Relative Humidity percent	Precipitation Average Monthly inches	Average Number Days with 0.01 inches or more
January	68	58	70	4.4	14
February	68	57	69	4.7	13
March	68	57	69	4.8	12
April	71	59	70	4.1	9
May	76	64	75	4.6	9
June	81	69	74	4.4	9
July	85	73	73	4.5	10
August	86	74	69	5.4	13
September	84	72	73	5.2	10
October	79	69	72	5.8	12
November	74	63	70	5.0	13
December	70	60	70	4.7	15

Bolivia CONCEPCIÓN

January	85	60	63	7.6	15
February	86	66	74	6.1	13
March	85	65	71	4.6	12
April	86	62	65	2.4	5
May	83	59	61	3.1	6
June	80	56	61	0.9	4
July	81	54	55	1.1	2
August	87	56	47	0.6	4
September	91	61	49	2.3	4
October	88	66	58	3.0	8
November	88	62	61	8.1	11
December	86	65	69	5.2	15

LA PAZ

January	63	43		4.5	21
February	63	43		4.2	18
March	64	42		2.6	16
April	65	40		1.3	9
May	64	37		0.5	5
June	62	34		0.3	2
July	62	33		0.4	2
August	63	35		0.5	4
September	64	38		1.1	9
October	66	40		1.6	9
November	67	42		1.9	11
December	65	42		3.7	18

Brazil BELEM

MONTH	Temperature (Average Daily) Max. degrees fahrenheit	Min.	Relative Humidity percent	Precipitation Average Monthly inches	Average Number Days with 0.01 inches or more
January	87	72	88	12.5	27
February	86	72	91	14.1	26
March	87	73	90	14.1	28
April	87	73	89	12.6	27
May	88	73	87	10.2	24
June	88	72	85	6.7	22
July	88	71	86	5.9	19
August	88	71	85	4.4	16
September	89	71	83	3.5	16
October	89	71	80	3.3	15
November	90	71	81	2.6	12
December	89	72	84	6.1	19

RIO DE JANEIRO

January	84	74	70	4.9	13
February	85	74	71	4.8	11
March	83	74	74	5.1	12
April	80	74	73	4.2	10
May	77	72	70	3.1	10
June	76	71	69	2.1	7
July	75	69	68	1.6	7
August	76	69	66	1.7	7
September	75	70	72	2.6	11
October	77	71	72	3.1	13
November	79	72	72	4.1	13
December	82	73	72	5.4	14

SALVADOR

January	86	73	70	2.6	14
February	86	73	71	5.3	17
March	86	72	74	6.1	19
April	84	69	73	11.2	22
May	82	66	79	10.8	24
June	80	64	79	9.4	23
July	79	63	78	7.2	25
August	79	64	76	4.8	20
September	81	65	74	3.3	17
October	83	66	74	4.0	14
November	84	68	73	4.5	15
December	84	71	72	5.6	15

Bulgaria SOFIA

MONTH	Temperature (Average Daily) Max. degrees fahrenheit	Min.	Relative Humidity percent	Precipitation Average Monthly inches	Average Number Days with 0.01 inches or more
January	35	25	78	1.4	9
February	40	27	69	1.1	10
March	51	31	56	1.6	10
April	60	42	50	2.4	12
May	69	50	52	3.4	13
June	76	55	51	2.8	12
July	81	60	46	2.6	10
August	79	60	46	2.5	9
September	72	52	51	1.6	7
October	63	46	59	2.5	11
November	48	36	72	1.9	10
December	38	28	77	1.9	12

Burma MANDALAY

January	82	55	52	0.1	0.1
February	88	59	41	0.1	0.3
March	97	66	31	0.1	0.5
April	101	77	33	1.2	2
May	98	79	52	5.8	8
June	93	78	64	6.3	7
July	93	78	66	2.7	6
August	92	77	72	4.1	8
September	91	76	74	5.4	9
October	89	73	78	4.3	7
November	85	66	74	2.0	3
December	80	57	66	0.4	0.8

RANGOON

January	89	65	52	0.1	0.3
February	92	67	52	0.2	0.3
March	96	71	54	0.3	0.6
April	97	76	64	2.0	2
May	92	77	76	12.1	14
June	86	76	85	18.9	23
July	85	76	88	22.9	26
August	85	76	88	20.8	25
September	86	76	86	15.5	20
October	88	76	77	7.1	10
November	88	76	72	2.7	3
December	88	67	61	0.4	0.6

Canada CALGARY, ALBERTA

MONTH	Temperature (Average Daily) Max. degrees fahrenheit	Min.	Relative Humidity percent	Precipitation Average Monthly inches	Average Number Days with 0.01 inches or more
January	24	2	69	0.5	7
February	28	6	70	0.5	8
March	37	14	61	0.8	10
April	53	27	49	1.0	8
May	63	36	47	2.3	11
June	69	43	55	3.1	12
July	76	47	50	2.5	10
August	74	45	44	2.3	10
September	64	37	54	1.5	8
October	54	29	60	0.7	7
November	38	17	68	0.7	5
December	29	9	69	0.6	5

HALIFAX, NOVA SCOTIA

January	32	15	69	5.4	17
February	31	15	63	4.3	14
March	38	23	60	4.9	15
April	47	31	60	4.5	15
May	59	40	62	4.1	14
June	68	48	63	4.0	14
July	74	55	64	3.8	14
August	74	56	65	4.4	13
September	67	50	65	4.1	12
October	57	41	66	5.4	12
November	46	32	71	5.3	13
December	35	21	68	5.4	14

MONTREAL, QUEBEC

January	21	6	73	3.8	15
February	23	8	69	3.0	14
March	33	19	62	3.5	14
April	50	33	56	3.6	12
May	64	47	54	3.1	12
June	74	57	55	3.4	13
July	78	61	52	3.7	12
August	75	59	54	3.5	11
September	67	51	57	3.7	12
October	54	40	60	3.4	13
November	39	27	70	3.5	14
December	26	13	75	3.6	15

ST. JOHN'S, NEWFOUNDLAND

MONTH	Temperature (Average Daily) Max. degrees	Min. fahrenheit	Relative Humidity percent	Average Monthly inches	Precipitation Average Number Days with 0.01 inches or more
January	29	18	76	5.3	15
February	28	16	77	4.9	15
March	33	22	79	4.6	15
April	41	30	81	4.2	15
May	50	35	79	3.6	15
June	61	44	77	3.5	13
July	68	51	79	3.5	13
August	69	53	80	3.7	13
September	62	47	80	3.8	14
October	53	40	78	5.3	16
November	42	32	80	5.9	17
December	34	24	79	5.5	17

TORONTO, ONTARIO

January	30	16	70	2.7	16
February	30	15	67	2.4	12
March	37	23	62	2.6	13
April	50	34	56	2.5	12
May	63	44	55	2.9	13
June	73	54	58	2.7	11
July	79	59	56	2.8	10
August	77	58	58	2.7	9
September	69	51	60	2.9	12
October	56	40	62	2.4	11
November	43	31	68	2.8	13
December	33	21	71	2.6	13

VANCOUVER, BRITISH COLUMBIA

January	41	32	85	8.6	20
February	44	34	78	5.8	17
March	50	37	70	5.0	17
April	58	40	67	3.3	14
May	64	46	63	2.8	12
June	69	52	65	2.5	11
July	74	54	62	1.2	7
August	73	54	62	1.7	8
September	65	49	72	3.6	9
October	57	44	80	5.8	16
November	48	39	84	8.3	19
December	43	35	88	8.8	22

WINNIPEG, MANITOBA

MONTH	Temperature (Average Daily)		Relative Humidity percent	Precipitation	
	Max.	Min.		Average Monthly inches	Average Number Days with 0.01 inches or more
	degrees fahrenheit				
January	7	−13	83	0.9	12
February	12	−9	83	0.9	11
March	28	5	78	1.2	9
April	48	27	57	1.4	9
May	65	39	52	2.3	10
June	74	50	60	3.1	12
July	79	55	53	3.1	10
August	76	51	53	2.5	10
September	65	43	61	2.3	9
October	51	31	62	1.5	6
November	30	13	79	1.1	9
December	15	−3	85	0.9	11

Canary Islands LAS PALMAS

January	70	58	71	1.4	8
February	71	58	72	0.9	5
March	71	59	72	0.9	5
April	71	61	62	0.5	3
May	73	62	72	0.2	1
June	75	65	74	0.1	0.9
July	77	67	76	0.1	0.8
August	77	70	76	0.1	0.8
September	79	69	75	0.2	1
October	79	67	74	1.1	5
November	76	64	74	2.1	7
December	72	60	73	1.6	8

Chile SANTIAGO*

January	85	53	38	0.1	−
February	84	52	40	0.1	−
March	80	49	41	0.2	1
April	74	45	46	0.5	1
May	65	41	58	2.5	5
June	58	37	64	3.3	6
July	59	37	60	3.0	6
August	62	39	58	2.2	5
September	66	42	55	1.2	3
October	72	45	50	0.6	3
November	78	48	41	0.3	1
December	83	51	38	0.2	−

People's Republic of China   CANTON*

MONTH	Temperature (Average Daily)		Relative Humidity percent	Precipitation	
	Max.	Min.		Average Monthly inches	Average Number Days with 0.01 inches or more
	degrees fahrenheit				
January	63	49	51	1.8	5
February	63	52	63	2.7	8
March	69	55	70	3.6	11
April	77	66	68	5.9	12
May	86	74	68	9.9	15
June	88	76	63	10.6	17
July	91	78	62	9.9	16
August	91	78	63	9.6	13
September	89	76	55	5.4	10
October	83	67	50	2.3	4
November	77	60	46	1.6	3
December	69	54	51	1.4	5

PEKING

January	34	17	42	1.2	5
February	36	20	47	1.4	4
March	45	29	46	1.9	5
April	59	40	49	2.8	6
May	69	50	50	3.5	7
June	75	59	62	4.9	9
July	80	67	72	10.8	14
August	81	68	73	12.5	13
September	74	58	65	7.0	9
October	65	47	53	3.0	6
November	51	34	50	2.6	5
December	38	23	49	1.2	3

SHANGHAI

January	46	33	58	1.9	6
February	47	34	60	2.3	9
March	55	40	53	3.3	9
April	66	50	58	3.7	9
May	77	59	56	3.7	9
June	82	67	66	7.1	11
July	90	74	66	5.8	9
August	90	74	65	5.6	9
September	82	66	63	5.1	11
October	74	57	53	2.8	4
November	63	45	55	2.0	6
December	53	36	62	1.4	6

Colombia BOGOTÁ

MONTH	Temperature (Average Daily)		Relative Humidity percent	Precipitation	
	Max.	Min.		Average Monthly inches	Average Number Days with 0.01 inches or more
	degrees fahrenheit				
January	67	48	51	2.3	6
February	68	49	53	2.6	7
March	67	50	54	4.0	13
April	67	51	57	5.8	20
May	66	51	58	4.5	17
June	65	51	56	2.4	16
July	64	50	56	2.0	18
August	65	50	54	2.2	16
September	66	49	54	2.4	13
October	66	50	61	6.3	20
November	66	50	64	4.7	16
December	66	49	56	2.6	15

Cook Islands MANIHIKI

January	86	78	76	13.1	17
February	86	78	81	12.4	16
March	86	78	77	7.5	13
April	86	78	78	6.9	12
May	86	78	78	7.9	12
June	85	78	79	5.7	10
July	84	77	80	7.9	12
August	84	78	82	5.3	10
September	84	78	80	4.8	10
October	85	77	77	8.6	11
November	86	78	79	9.1	13
December	86	78	78	8.5	13

Costa Rica SAN JOSÉ

January	75	58	63	0.6	3
February	76	58	57	0.2	1
March	79	59	55	0.8	2
April	79	62	60	1.8	7
May	80	62	70	9.0	19
June	79	62	74	9.5	22
July	77	62	74	8.3	23
August	78	61	73	9.5	24
September	79	61	76	12.0	24
October	77	60	78	11.8	25
November	77	60	71	5.7	14
December	75	58	67	1.6	6

Cuba HAVANA

MONTH	Temperature (Average Daily) Max. Min. degrees fahrenheit		Relative Humidity percent	Precipitation Average Monthly inches	Average Number Days with 0.01 inches or more
January	79	65	64	2.8	6
February	79	65	61	1.8	4
March	81	67	58	1.8	4
April	84	69	58	2.3	4
May	86	72	62	4.7	7
June	88	74	65	6.5	10
July	89	75	62	4.9	9
August	89	75	64	5.3	10
September	88	75	66	5.9	11
October	85	73	68	6.8	11
November	81	69	65	3.1	7
December	79	67	64	2.3	6

Cyprus NICOSIA

January	59	42	66	3.0	14
February	61	42	61	1.7	10
March	66	45	55	1.4	8
April	75	50	46	0.2	4
May	86	57	41	0.8	1
June	93	65	37	0.3	1
July	97	70	34	0.0	0
August	97	70	35	0.8	1
September	91	65	38	0.4	1
October	82	58	45	0.9	4
November	72	51	53	1.3	6
December	63	45	63	2.6	11

Czechoslovakia PRAGUE

January	50	8	73	0.7	13
February	53	10	67	0.7	11
March	64	18	55	0.7	10
April	73	28	47	1.4	11
May	82	36	45	1.8	13
June	87	45	46	2.1	12
July	91	48	49	3.7	13
August	90	47	48	2.1	12
September	84	38	51	1.2	10
October	72	28	60	1.3	13
November	57	23	70	0.8	12
December	50	16	78	0.8	13

Denmark COPENHAGEN

MONTH	Temperature (Average Daily) Max. degrees fahrenheit	Min.	Relative Humidity percent	Average Monthly inches	Precipitation Average Number Days with 0.01 inches or more
January	36	28	85	1.9	17
February	36	27	83	1.5	13
March	41	31	78	1.1	12
April	51	37	68	1.5	13
May	61	46	59	1.6	11
June	66	56	60	1.8	13
July	72	57	62	2.9	14
August	70	56	64	2.6	14
September	63	51	69	2.4	15
October	54	45	76	2.3	16
November	45	38	83	1.8	16
December	40	31	87	1.9	17

Dominica ROSEAU

January	84	68	65	5.2	16
February	85	67	62	2.9	10
March	87	68	59	2.9	13
April	88	69	61	2.4	10
May	90	71	61	2.8	11
June	90	73	65	7.7	15
July	89	72	69	10.8	22
August	89	73	69	10.3	22
September	90	73	67	8.9	16
October	89	72	70	7.8	16
November	87	71	70	8.8	18
December	86	69	67	6.4	16

Dominican Republic SANTO DOMINGO (Ciudad Trujillo)*

January	84	66	64	2.4	7
February	85	66	58	1.4	6
March	84	67	60	1.9	5
April	85	69	62	3.9	7
May	86	71	65	6.8	11
June	87	73	66	6.2	12
July	88	72	66	6.4	11
August	88	73	66	6.3	11
September	88	72	66	7.3	11
October	87	72	66	6.0	11
November	86	70	66	4.8	10
December	85	67	66	2.4	8

Ecuador GUAYAQUIL

MONTH	Temperature (Average Daily) Max. degrees fahrenheit	Min.	Relative Humidity percent	Precipitation Average Monthly inches	Average Number Days with 0.01 inches or more
January	88	70		9.4	20
February	87	71		9.8	25
March	88	71		10.4	24
April	89	71		4.6	14
May	88	68		1.1	9
June	87	68		0.3	4
July	84	67		0.2	2
August	86	65		0.0	0
September	87	66		0.1	2
October	86	68		0.3	3
November	88	68		0.1	4
December	88	70		2.0	10

QUITO

MONTH	Max.	Min.	Relative Humidity percent	Average Monthly inches	Average Number Days with 0.01 inches or more
January	72	46			16
February	71	47			17
March	71	47			20
April	70	47			22
May	70	45			21
June	71	44			12
July	72	45			7
August	73	45			9
September	73	46			14
October	72	45			18
November	72	46			14
December	72	45			16

Egypt CAIRO*

MONTH	Max.	Min.	Relative Humidity percent	Average Monthly inches	Average Number Days with 0.01 inches or more
January	65	47	40	0.2	1
February	69	48	33	0.2	1
March	75	52	27	0.2	0.8
April	83	57	21	0.1	0.4
May	91	63	18	0.1	0.2
June	95	68	20	0.1	0.1
July	96	70	24	0.0	0
August	95	71	28	0.0	0
September	90	68	31	0.1	0
October	86	65	31	0.1	0.3
November	78	58	38	0.1	0.8
December	68	50	41	0.2	1

England LONDON

MONTH	Temperature (Average Daily) Max. degrees	Min. fahrenheit	Relative Humidity percent	Precipitation Average Monthly inches	Average Number Days with 0.01 inches or more
January	43	35	85	2.0	15
February	45	35	82	1.5	15
March	49	36	79	1.4	14
April	55	40	75	1.8	13
May	62	45	73	1.8	12
June	68	51	73	1.6	12
July	71	54	73	2.0	13
August	70	54	76	2.2	13
September	65	49	80	1.8	12
October	56	44	85	2.3	16
November	49	39	86	2.5	16
December	45	36	86	2.0	16

PLYMOUTH

MONTH	Max.	Min.	Humidity	Monthly	Days
January	47	40	81	3.9	19
February	47	38	78	2.9	15
March	50	40	74	2.7	4
April	54	43	69	2.0	12
May	60	47	71	2.4	12
June	64	52	73	2.0	12
July	66	55	74	2.7	14
August	67	55	75	3.0	14
September	64	53	75	2.0	15
October	58	49	77	3.5	16
November	52	44	79	4.4	17
December	49	41	82	4.3	18

Ethiopia ADDIS ABABA*

MONTH	Max.	Min.	Humidity	Monthly	Days
January	75	43	33	0.5	2
February	76	47	39	1.5	5
March	77	49	37	2.6	8
April	77	50	44	3.4	10
May	77	50	43	3.4	10
June	74	49	59	5.4	20
July	69	50	73	11.0	28
August	69	50	72	11.8	27
September	72	49	64	7.5	21
October	75	45	39	0.8	3
November	73	43	37	0.6	2
December	73	41	29	0.2	2

Finland HELSINKI

MONTH	Temperature (Average Daily) Max. degrees fahrenheit	Min.	Relative Humidity percent	Precipitation Average Monthly inches	Average Number Days with 0.01 inches or more
January	26	17	87	2.2	20
February	25	15	82	1.6	18
March	32	19	70	1.4	14
April	44	30	66	1.7	13
May	56	40	58	1.6	12
June	65	49	59	2.0	13
July	71	54	63	2.6	14
August	68	53	67	2.8	15
September	59	46	72	2.7	15
October	46	37	79	2.8	18
November	37	30	86	2.6	19
December	31	23	89	2.6	20

France BORDEAUX

MONTH	Max.	Min.	Humidity	Monthly	Days
January	49	35	80	3.5	16
February	51	36	73	2.9	13
March	59	39	64	2.4	13
April	63	43	60	1.9	13
May	69	49	60	3.4	14
June	75	54	62	2.6	11
July	78	57	61	2.2	11
August	78	56	60	2.8	12
September	74	54	67	3.3	13
October	65	47	71	3.2	14
November	55	40	80	3.8	15
December	49	36	83	4.3	17

MARSEILLE

MONTH	Max.	Min.	Humidity	Monthly	Days
January	50	35	68	1.7	8
February	53	36	60	1.2	6
March	59	41	57	1.7	7
April	64	46	54	1.6	7
May	70	52	54	1.7	8
June	79	59	50	0.9	4
July	84	63	45	0.4	2
August	83	63	49	1.3	5
September	77	59	54	2.3	6
October	68	51	61	3.0	8
November	59	43	66	2.7	9
December	52	37	68	2.6	10

PARIS

MONTH	Temperature (Average Daily) Max. degrees fahrenheit	Min.	Relative Humidity percent	Precipitation Average Monthly inches	Average Number Days with 0.01 inches or more
January	43	34	80	2.0	17
February	45	34	73	1.8	14
March	54	38	63	1.3	12
April	60	43	54	1.6	13
May	67	40	55	2.2	12
June	73	55	58	2.1	12
July	76	58	57	2.3	12
August	75	58	61	2.4	13
September	70	54	65	2.1	13
October	60	46	71	1.9	13
November	50	40	79	2.0	15
December	44	36	82	1.9	16

Germany BERLIN

January	35	26	82	1.8	17
February	36	26	78	1.5	15
March	45	31	67	1.3	12
April	55	39	60	1.6	13
May	66	47	57	1.9	12
June	71	56	58	2.5	13
July	74	56	61	2.8	14
August	73	55	61	2.7	14
September	68	49	65	1.8	12
October	55	42	73	1.9	14
November	44	36	83	1.8	16
December	37	30	86	1.6	15

FRANKFURT

January	38	29	77	2.2	17
February	41	34	70	1.7	15
March	51	35	57	1.5	12
April	60	42	51	1.7	14
May	68	49	50	2.1	14
June	73	55	52	2.8	14
July	77	58	53	2.7	14
August	75	57	54	2.9	14
September	69	51	60	2.2	13
October	57	43	68	2.0	14
November	47	35	77	2.1	16
December	39	31	81	2.1	16

MONTH	Temperature (Average Daily) Max. degrees fahrenheit	Min.	Relative Humidity percent	Precipitation Average Monthly inches	Average Number Days with 0.01 inches or more
January	36	27	84	2.2	18
February	37	27	80	1.8	16
March	44	31	68	1.9	13
April	54	38	61	2.0	14
May	63	44	57	2.2	14
June	69	50	59	2.4	14
July	72	55	63	3.2	17
August	71	54	63	3.1	16
September	65	49	65	2.4	15
October	55	42	74	2.3	17
November	45	36	83	2.2	18
December	39	31	86	2.2	18

MUNICH

January	35	22	77	2.3	16
February	37	23	71	2.0	16
March	47	30	61	1.8	13
April	56	37	55	2.4	15
May	64	44	57	4.3	15
June	70	51	58	4.7	17
July	73	55	57	5.5	16
August	72	53	58	3.9	16
September	67	48	61	3.3	13
October	55	39	68	2.6	13
November	43	32	78	2.2	15
December	35	25	82	1.8	15

Ghana ACCRA

January	87	73	61	0.6	1
February	88	75	61	1.3	2
March	88	76	63	2.2	4
April	88	76	65	3.2	6
May	87	75	68	5.6	9
June	84	74	74	7.0	10
July	81	73	76	1.8	4
August	80	71	77	0.6	3
September	81	73	72	1.4	4
October	85	74	71	2.5	6
November	87	75	66	1.4	3
December	88	75	64	0.9	2

Greece ATHENS

MONTH	Temperature (Average Daily) Max. degrees fahrenheit	Min.	Relative Humidity percent	Precipitation Average Monthly inches	Average Number Days with 0.01 inches or more
January	55	44	62	2.4	16
February	57	44	57	1.5	11
March	59	49	54	1.5	11
April	68	52	48	0.9	9
May	77	60	47	0.9	8
June	85	68	39	0.5	4
July	92	73	34	0.2	2
August	91	73	34	0.3	3
September	84	66	42	0.9	4
October	74	59	52	2.0	8
November	65	53	61	2.2	12
December	58	46	63	2.8	15

CORFU

January	57	43	66	7.9	15
February	59	43	51	6.1	14
March	60	45	63	3.9	12
April	66	50	63	2.7	10
May	73	55	60	1.5	6
June	82	61	54	0.5	3
July	88	67	50	0.1	1
August	88	67	48	0.8	2
September	81	63	58	3.7	6
October	73	57	62	7.0	11
November	66	51	66	9.4	15
December	60	46	68	10.2	17

Guatemala GUATEMALA CITY

January	73	53	69	0.3	4
February	77	54	62	0.1	2
March	81	57	51	0.5	3
April	82	58	51	1.2	5
May	84	60	55	6.0	15
June	81	61	70	10.8	23
July	78	60	67	8.0	21
August	79	60	72	7.8	21
September	79	60	71	9.1	22
October	76	60	72	6.8	18
November	74	57	71	0.9	7
December	72	55	70	0.3	4

Haiti PORT-AU-PRINCE

MONTH	Temperature (Average Daily)		Relative Humidity percent	Precipitation	
	Max.	Min.		Average Monthly inches	Average Number Days with 0.01 inches or more
	degrees fahrenheit				
January	87	68	44	1.3	3
February	88	68	44	2.3	5
March	89	69	45	3.4	7
April	89	71	49	6.3	11
May	90	72	54	9.1	13
June	92	73	50	4.0	8
July	94	74	43	2.9	7
August	93	73	49	5.7	11
September	91	73	54	6.9	12
October	90	72	56	6.7	12
November	88	71	54	3.4	7
December	87	69	48	1.3	3

Hawaii HONOLULU, OAHU

January	76	69	66	4.1	14
February	76	67	67	2.6	11
March	77	67	65	3.1	13
April	78	68	64	1.9	12
May	80	70	64	1.0	11
June	81	72	63	0.7	12
July	82	73	63	0.9	14
August	83	74	64	1.1	13
September	83	74	65	1.4	13
October	82	72	66	1.9	13
November	80	70	67	2.5	13
December	78	69	68	4.1	15

Hong Kong

January	64	56	66	1.3	4
February	63	55	73	1.8	5
March	67	60	74	2.9	7
April	75	67	77	5.4	8
May	82	74	78	11.5	13
June	85	78	77	15.5	18
July	87	78	77	15.0	17
August	87	78	77	14.2	15
September	85	77	72	10.1	12
October	81	73	63	4.5	6
November	74	65	60	1.7	2
December	68	59	63	1.2	3

Hungary BUDAPEST

MONTH	Temperature (Average Daily) Max. degrees fahrenheit	Min.	Relative Humidity percent	Average Monthly inches	Precipitation Average Number Days with 0.01 inches or more
January	34	31	76	1.5	13
February	39	28	68	1.8	12
March	50	29	55	1.5	11
April	62	43	48	1.8	11
May	71	52	49	2.9	13
June	78	58	49	2.8	13
July	82	62	47	2.2	10
August	81	60	47	1.9	9
September	74	53	49	1.3	7
October	61	44	60	2.2	10
November	47	37	76	2.8	14
December	38	30	81	1.9	13

Iceland REYKJAVÍK

January	35	28	79	3.5	20
February	36	28	75	2.5	17
March	39	30	72	2.4	18
April	43	34	73	2.2	18
May	50	39	67	1.6	16
June	45	54	72	1.6	15
July	57	48	72	1.9	15
August	56	47	71	2.2	16
September	52	43	73	2.7	19
October	45	38	78	3.7	21
November	39	32	80	3.0	18
December	36	30	80	3.1	20

Ireland DUBLIN

January	45	35	80	2.8	11
February	46	35	76	2.0	10
March	50	38	72	2.0	9
April	54	40	67	1.6	10
May	58	44	69	2.4	10
June	64	49	69	2.1	10
July	66	52	70	2.6	12
August	65	51	72	3.1	12
September	62	49	73	3.0	12
October	56	45	75	2.6	10
November	50	40	79	2.6	12
December	47	48	81	3.0	14

SHANNON

| MONTH | Temperature (Average Daily) | | Relative Humidity percent | Precipitation | |
| | Max. | Min. | | Average Monthly inches | Average Number Days with 0.01 inches or more |
	degrees fahrenheit				
January	46	35	84	3.7	15
February	47	36	78	2.6	11
March	52	38	72	2.2	11
April	56	41	67	2.0	11
May	61	44	66	2.4	11
June	65	50	69	2.2	11
July	66	53	71	3.0	14
August	67	53	72	3.1	14
September	63	50	74	3.3	14
October	58	45	78	3.3	14
November	51	40	82	3.7	15
December	48	38	85	4.5	18

India AGRA

January	73	43	35	0.5	1
February	78	46	28	0.5	1
March	89	55	15	0.3	1
April	101	67	11	0.2	1
May	107	77	14	0.5	1
June	105	83	34	2.3	4
July	94	80	60	9.1	11
August	91	79	68	8.1	10
September	93	75	58	4.1	5
October	92	61	30	0.8	1
November	85	48	28	0.1	0.3
December	76	43	39	0.3	1

BOMBAY

January	83	67	61	0.1	0.2
February	83	67	62	0.1	0.2
March	86	72	65	0.1	0.1
April	89	76	67	0.1	0.1
May	91	80	68	0.7	1
June	89	79	77	19.1	14
July	85	77	83	24.3	21
August	85	76	81	13.4	19
September	85	76	78	10.4	13
October	89	76	71	2.5	3
November	89	73	64	0.5	1
December	87	69	62	0.1	0.1

CALCUTTA

MONTH	Temperature (Average Daily) Max. degrees fahrenheit	Min.	Relative Humidity percent	Precipitation Average Monthly inches	Average Number Days with 0.01 inches or more
January	80	55	52	0.4	0.8
February	84	59	45	1.2	2
March	93	69	46	1.4	2
April	97	75	56	1.7	3
May	96	77	62	5.5	7
June	92	79	75	11.7	13
July	89	79	80	12.8	18
August	89	78	82	12.9	18
September	90	78	81	9.9	13
October	89	74	72	4.5	6
November	84	64	63	0.8	1
December	79	55	55	0.2	0.3

MADRAS

January	85	67	67	1.4	2
February	88	68	66	0.4	0
March	91	72	67	0.3	0
April	95	78	72	0.6	0
May	101	82	67	1.0	1
June	100	81	61	1.9	4
July	96	79	62	3.6	7
August	95	78	66	4.6	8
September	94	77	70	4.7	7
October	90	75	75	12.0	11
November	85	72	75	14.0	11
December	84	69	72	5.5	5

NEW DELHI

January	70	44	41	0.9	2
February	75	49	35	0.7	2
March	87	58	23	0.5	0.6
April	97	68	19	0.3	0.5
May	105	79	20	0.5	0.6
June	102	83	36	2.9	9.3
July	96	81	59	7.1	5.1
August	93	79	64	6.8	7.0
September	93	75	51	4.6	6.5
October	92	65	32	0.4	2.2
November	84	52	31	0.1	0.1
December	73	46	42	0.4	1.3

Indonesia JAKARTA*

MONTH	Temperature (Average Daily) Max. degrees fahrenheit	Min.	Relative Humidity percent	Average Monthly inches	Precipitation Average Number Days with 0.01 inches or more
January	84	74	75	11.8	18
February	84	74	75	11.8	17
March	86	74	73	8.3	15
April	87	75	71	5.8	11
May	87	75	69	4.5	9
June	87	74	67	3.8	7
July	87	73	64	2.5	5
August	87	73	61	1.7	4
September	88	74	62	2.6	5
October	87	74	64	4.4	8
November	86	74	68	5.6	12
December	85	74	71	8.0	14

Iran TEHRAN**

MONTH	Max.	Min.	Humidity	Monthly	Days
January	45	27	75	1.8	4
February	50	32	59	1.5	4
March	59	39	39	1.8	5
April	71	49	40	1.4	3
May	82	58	47	0.5	2
June	93	66	49	0.1	1
July	99	72	41	0.1	0.5
August	97	71	46	0.1	0.2
September	90	64	49	0.1	0.3
October	76	53	54	0.3	1
November	63	43	66	0.8	3
December	51	33	75	1.2	4

Iraq BAGHDAD

MONTH	Max.	Min.	Humidity	Monthly	Days
January	60	39	51	0.9	4
February	64	42	42	1.0	3
March	71	48	36	1.1	4
April	85	57	34	0.5	3
May	97	67	19	0.1	1
June	105	73	13	0.1	0
July	110	76	12	0.1	0
August	110	76	13	0.1	0
September	104	70	15	0.1	0
October	92	61	22	0.1	1
November	77	51	39	0.8	3
December	64	42	52	1.0	5

Israel JERUSALEM

MONTH	Temperature (Average Daily) Max. degrees fahrenheit	Min.	Relative Humidity percent	Precipitation Average Monthly inches	Average Number Days with 0.01 inches or more
January	55	41	66	5.2	9
February	56	42	58	5.2	11
March	65	46	57	2.5	3
April	73	50	42	1.1	3
May	81	57	33	0.1	0.6
June	85	60	32	0.1	0.1
July	87	63	35	0.0	0
August	87	64	36	0.0	0
September	85	62	36	0.1	0.1
October	81	59	36	0.5	1
November	70	53	50	2.8	4
December	59	45	60	3.4	7

Italy MILAN

January	38	32	82	1.7	6
February	46	35	73	2.2	7
March	56	43	65	3.0	7
April	65	50	57	3.7	8
May	74	57	59	3.0	8
June	80	63	56	4.5	9
July	84	67	61	2.5	6
August	82	66	58	3.6	7
September	75	61	63	2.7	5
October	63	52	73	4.8	8
November	51	43	80	4.7	10
December	43	35	89	3.0	7

PALERMO

January	60	46	67	2.8	12
February	62	47	63	1.7	8
March	63	48	60	1.9	8
April	68	52	60	1.9	6
May	74	58	58	0.8	3
June	81	64	54	0.3	2
July	85	69	52	0.8	0
August	86	70	52	0.8	2
September	83	66	53	1.6	4
October	77	60	61	3.0	8
November	71	54	64	2.8	8
December	64	49	65	2.4	10

ROME

MONTH	Temperature (Average Daily)		Relative Humidity percent	Precipitation	
	Max.	Min.		Average Monthly inches	Average Number Days with 0.01 inches or more
	degrees fahrenheit				
January	52	40	68	2.8	8
February	55	42	64	2.4	9
March	60	45	56	2.2	8
April	66	50	54	2.0	6
May	74	54	56	1.8	5
June	81	63	48	1.4	4
July	87	67	42	0.6	1
August	86	67	43	0.8	2
September	80	63	50	2.5	5
October	71	55	59	4.0	8
November	61	49	66	5.1	11
December	55	44	70	3.7	10

VENICE

January	42	33	76	1.4	6
February	46	35	76	1.9	6
March	53	41	68	2.4	7
April	62	49	67	3.0	9
May	70	56	69	2.5	8
June	73	63	65	2.7	8
July	81	66	64	2.0	7
August	80	65	63	2.7	7
September	75	61	64	2.3	5
October	65	53	68	3.0	7
November	53	44	75	3.7	9
December	45	37	79	2.4	8

Jamaica KINGSTON*

January	86	67	61	0.9	3
February	86	67	62	0.6	3
March	86	68	62	0.9	2
April	87	70	66	1.2	3
May	87	72	68	4.0	4
June	89	74	68	3.5	5
July	90	73	65	1.5	4
August	90	73	70	3.6	7
September	89	73	70	3.9	6
October	88	73	73	7.1	9
November	87	71	68	2.9	5
December	87	69	62	1.4	4

Japan OSAKA*

MONTH	Temperature (Average Daily) Max. Min. degrees fahrenheit		Relative Humidity percent	Precipitation Average Monthly inches	Average Number Days with 0.01 inches or more
January	47	32	56	1.7	6
February	48	33	56	2.3	6
March	54	37	56	3.8	9
April	65	47	56	5.2	10
May	73	55	57	4.9	10
June	80	64	63	7.4	11
July	87	74	63	5.9	9
August	90	74	59	4.4	7
September	83	67	61	7.0	11
October	72	55	58	5.1	9
November	62	44	57	3.0	7
December	52	37	57	1.9	6

TOKYO*

MONTH	Max.	Min.	Humidity	Monthly	Days
January	47	29	48	1.9	5
February	48	31	48	2.9	6
March	54	36	53	4.2	10
April	63	46	59	5.3	10
May	71	54	62	5.8	10
June	79	63	68	6.5	12
July	83	70	69	5.6	10
August	86	72	66	6.0	9
September	77	66	68	9.2	12
October	69	55	64	8.2	11
November	60	43	58	3.8	7
December	52	33	51	2.2	5

Jordan AMMAN*

MONTH	Max.	Min.	Humidity	Monthly	Days
January	54	39	56	2.7	8
February	56	40	52	2.9	8
March	60	43	44	1.2	4
April	73	49	34	0.6	3
May	83	57	28	0.2	0.8
June	87	61	28	0.0	0
July	89	65	30	0.0	0
August	90	65	30	0.0	0
September	88	62	31	0.1	0.1
October	81	57	31	0.2	1
November	70	50	40	1.3	4
December	59	42	53	1.8	5

Kenya   NAIROBI

| MONTH | Temperature (Average Daily) | | Relative Humidity percent | Precipitation | |
| | Max. | Min. | | Average Monthly inches | Average Number Days with 0.01 inches or more |
	degrees fahrenheit				
January	79	54	44	1.5	6
February	75	55	40	2.5	5
March	77	57	45	4.9	11
April	75	58	56	8.3	16
May	72	56	62	6.2	17
June	70	53	60	1.8	9
July	70	51	58	0.6	6
August	69	52	56	0.9	7
September	75	52	45	1.2	6
October	76	55	43	2.1	8
November	74	56	53	4.3	15
December	74	55	53	3.4	11

Korea   SEOUL*

January	32	15	51	1.2	8
February	37	20	47	0.8	6
March	47	29	46	1.5	7
April	62	41	46	3.0	8
May	72	51	51	3.2	10
June	80	61	54	5.1	10
July	84	70	67	14.8	16
August	87	71	62	10.5	13
September	78	59	55	4.7	9
October	67	45	48	1.6	7
November	51	32	52	1.8	9
December	37	20	52	1.0	9

Kuwait   KUWAIT CITY

January	61	49	61	0.9	2
February	65	51	61	0.9	2
March	72	59	61	1.1	2
April	83	68	55	0.2	1
May	94	77	55	0.1	0
June	98	82	72	0.0	0
July	103	86	41	0.0	0
August	104	86	46	0.0	0
September	100	81	51	0.0	0
October	91	73	60	0.1	0
November	77	62	43	0.6	1
December	65	63	65	1.1	3

Lebanon BEIRUT

MONTH	Temperature (Average Daily) Max. degrees fahrenheit	Min.	Relative Humidity percent	Precipitation Average Monthly inches	Average Number Days with 0.01 inches or more
January	62	51	70	7.5	15
February	63	51	70	6.2	12
March	66	54	69	3.7	9
April	72	58	67	2.2	5
May	78	64	64	0.7	2
June	83	69	61	0.1	0.4
July	87	73	58	0.1	0.1
August	89	74	57	0.1	0.1
September	86	73	57	0.2	1
October	81	69	62	2.0	4
November	73	61	61	5.2	8
December	65	55	69	7.3	12

Liberia MONROVIA

January	86	73	78	1.2	5
February	85	73	76	2.2	5
March	87	74	77	3.8	10
April	87	73	80	8.5	17
May	86	72	79	20.3	21
June	85	73	82	38.3	26
July	80	72	83	39.2	24
August	80	73	84	14.7	20
September	81	72	86	29.3	26
October	83	72	84	30.4	22
November	85	73	80	9.3	19
December	86	73	79	5.1	12

Libya TRIPOLI

January	61	47	59	3.2	11
February	63	49	60	1.8	7
March	67	52	57	1.1	5
April	71	57	57	0.4	2
May	76	61	62	0.2	3
June	81	67	70	0.1	1
July	85	71	72	0.1	0.2
August	86	72	69	0.1	0.3
September	85	71	67	0.4	2
October	80	65	59	1.6	5
November	73	57	53	2.6	7
December	64	49	55	3.7	11

Luxembourg LUXEMBOURG CITY

MONTH	Temperature (Average Daily) Max. degrees fahrenheit	Min.	Relative Humidity percent	Precipitation Average Monthly inches	Average Number Days with 0.01 inches or more
January	36	30	86	2.4	20
February	40	31	78	2.5	16
March	49	35	64	1.6	14
April	57	40	58	1.8	13
May	65	46	59	2.5	15
June	70	52	61	2.5	14
July	73	55	61	2.3	14
August	71	54	63	3.2	15
September	66	50	67	2.8	16
October	56	43	76	2.0	15
November	44	37	86	2.6	19
December	39	33	91	3.1	20

Malawi LILONGWE

MONTH	Max.	Min.	Relative Humidity	Average Monthly	Average Number Days
January	80	63	64	8.2	19
February	80	63	66	8.6	18
March	80	61	60	4.9	13
April	80	57	50	1.7	5
May	77	51	41	0.1	1
June	74	47	38	0.1	0.1
July	74	45	33	0.1	0.1
August	77	47	31	0.1	1
September	81	53	30	0.1	0.6
October	86	59	28	0.1	1
November	85	63	42	2.1	7
December	82	64	58	4.9	15

Malaysia KUALA LUMPUR

MONTH	Max.	Min.	Relative Humidity	Average Monthly	Average Number Days
January	90	72	60	6.2	14
February	92	72	60	7.9	14
March	92	73	58	10.2	17
April	91	74	63	11.5	20
May	91	74	66	8.8	16
June	90	73	63	5.1	13
July	90	73	63	3.9	12
August	90	73	62	6.4	14
September	90	73	64	8.6	17
October	89	72	65	9.8	20
November	89	72	66	10.2	20
December	89	73	61	7.5	18

Mali TIMBUKTU*

MONTH	Temperature (Average Daily) Max. degrees fahrenheit	Min.	Relative Humidity percent	Average Monthly inches	Average Number Days with 0.01 inches or more
January	87	55	22	0.1	0.1
February	93	58	19	0.1	0.2
March	100	66	18	0.1	1
April	107	72	15	0.1	0.3
May	110	78	18	0.2	2
June	109	80	71	0.9	5
July	103	77	45	3.1	9
August	97	75	57	3.2	9
September	103	76	45	1.5	5
October	104	73	23	0.1	2
November	98	65	17	0.1	0.1
December	89	56	19	0.1	0.1

Malta VALLETTA

January	58	50	67	3.5	12
February	58	51	66	2.3	8
March	61	52	65	1.5	5
April	65	56	64	0.6	2
May	71	61	63	0.5	2
June	79	67	60	0.0	0
July	84	72	59	0.0	0
August	85	73	62	0.3	1
September	81	71	64	1.1	3
October	74	66	65	2.4	6
November	67	66	67	3.6	9
December	61	54	68	4.3	13

Martinique FORT-DE-FRANCE

January	83	69	77	4.7	19
February	84	69	73	4.3	15
March	85	69	72	2.9	15
April	86	71	71	3.9	13
May	87	73	74	4.7	18
June	86	74	77	7.4	21
July	86	74	78	9.4	22
August	87	74	78	10.3	22
September	88	74	79	9.3	29
October	87	73	80	9.7	19
November	86	72	81	7.9	20
December	84	71	79	5.9	19

Mexico ACAPULCO

MONTH	Temperature (Average Daily) Max. degrees fahrenheit	Min.	Relative Humidity percent	Precipitation Average Monthly inches	Average Number Days with 0.01 inches or more
January	78			0.4	
February	78			0	
March	79			0	
April	80			0	
May	83			2.1	
June	83			17.2	
July	83			8.6	
August	83			9.8	
September	82			14.3	
October	82			6.7	
November	81			1.2	
December	79			0.4	

MÉRIDA

MONTH	Max.	Min.	Relative Humidity	Average Monthly inches	Average Number Days
January	83	62	53	1.0	8
February	85	63	48	0.7	6
March	89	66	46	1.1	6
April	92	69	41	1.1	5
May	94	72	45	3.1	10
June	92	73	58	6.8	19
July	91	73	56	4.8	20
August	90	73	58	5.3	19
September	87	73	62	6.1	20
October	85	71	62	4.0	17
November	85	67	55	1.3	12
December	82	64	53	1.2	9

MEXICO CITY

MONTH	Max.	Min.	Relative Humidity	Average Monthly inches	Average Number Days
January	66	42	34	0.5	4
February	69	43	28	0.2	5
March	75	47	26	0.4	9
April	77	51	29	0.8	14
May	78	54	29	2.1	17
June	76	55	48	4.7	21
July	73	53	50	6.7	27
August	73	54	50	6.0	27
September	74	53	54	5.1	23
October	70	50	47	2.0	13
November	68	46	41	0.7	6
December	66	43	37	0.3	4

MONTH	Temperature (Average Daily) Max. degrees fahrenheit	Min. degrees fahrenheit	Relative Humidity percent	Precipitation Average Monthly inches	Average Number Days with 0.01 inches or more
January	68	48	60	0.6	6
February	72	52	59	0.7	5
March	76	57	45	0.8	7
April	84	62	53	1.3	7
May	87	68	51	1.3	9
June	90	71	57	3.0	8
July	91	71	49	2.3	8
August	92	72	57	2.4	7
September	86	70	66	5.2	10
October	80	64	67	3.0	9
November	71	55	60	1.5	8
December	65	50	55	0.8	6

Monaco   MONACO

January	54	47	67	2.4	5
February	55	47	69	2.2	5
March	57	50	73	2.8	7
April	61	54	72	2.5	5
May	66	60	78	2.5	5
June	73	66	75	1.3	4
July	78	71	71	0.9	1
August	78	71	72	0.9	2
September	75	67	71	2.6	4
October	68	61	71	4.4	7
November	61	54	72	4.8	7
December	56	50	72	3.9	6

Morocco   MARRAKECH*

January	65	40	63	1.0	7
February	68	43	58	1.1	5
March	74	48	53	1.3	6
April	79	52	47	1.2	6
May	84	57	42	0.6	2
June	92	62	41	0.3	1
July	101	67	36	0.1	1
August	100	68	37	0.1	1
September	92	63	40	0.4	3
October	83	57	45	0.9	4
November	73	49	49	1.2	3
December	66	42	57	1.2	7

MONTH	Temperature (Average Daily) Max. degrees	Min. fahrenheit	Relative Humidity percent	Precipitation Average Monthly inches	Average Number Days with 0.01 inches or more
January	60	47	68	4.5	7
February	61	48	69	4.2	7
March	63	50	69	4.8	8
April	65	51	65	3.5	7
May	71	56	62	1.7	5
June	76	60	62	0.6	3
July	80	64	61	0.1	0.6
August	82	65	61	0.1	1
September	78	63	63	0.9	3
October	72	59	67	3.9	5
November	65	52	68	5.8	6
December	61	48	70	5.4	8

Mozambique MAPUTO*

January	86	71	66	5.1	9
February	87	71	65	4.9	8
March	85	69	67	4.9	9
April	83	66	63	2.1	5
May	80	60	61	1.1	3
June	77	56	46	0.8	2
July	76	55	59	0.5	2
August	78	57	60	0.5	2
September	80	61	63	1.1	3
October	82	64	66	1.9	5
November	83	67	67	3.2	7
December	85	69	66	3.8	9

Nepal KATMANDU**

January	65	35	70	0.6	1
February	67	49	68	1.6	5
March	77	45	53	0.9	2
April	83	53	54	2.3	6
May	86	61	61	4.8	10
June	85	67	72	9.7	15
July	84	68	82	14.7	20
August	83	68	84	13.6	21
September	83	66	83	6.1	12
October	80	56	81	1.5	4
November	74	45	78	0.3	1
December	67	37	73	0.1	0.2

New Guinea PORT MORESBY

| MONTH | Temperature (Average Daily) | | Relative Humidity percent | Precipitation | |
| | Max. | Min. | | Average Monthly inches | Average Number Days with 0.01 inches or more |
	degrees fahrenheit				
January	89	76	69	7.0	8
February	87	76	72	7.6	7
March	88	76	73	6.7	9
April	87	75	74	4.2	5
May	86	75	77	2.5	2
June	84	74	77	1.3	3
July	83	73	78	1.1	2
August	82	73	77	0.7	2
September	84	74	77	1.0	2
October	86	75	76	1.4	2
November	88	76	73	1.9	3
December	90	76	69	4.4	6

New Zealand AUCKLAND

January	73	60	62	3.1	10
February	73	60	61	3.7	10
March	71	59	65	3.2	11
April	67	56	59	3.8	14
May	62	51	70	5.0	19
June	59	48	73	5.4	19
July	56	46	74	5.7	21
August	58	46	70	4.6	19
September	60	49	68	4.0	17
October	63	52	66	4.0	16
November	66	54	64	3.5	15
December	70	57	64	3.1	12

CHRIST CHURCH

January	70	53	59	2.2	10
February	69	53	60	1.7	8
March	66	50	69	1.9	9
April	62	45	71	1.9	10
May	56	40	69	2.6	12
June	51	36	72	2.6	13
July	50	35	76	2.7	13
August	52	36	66	1.9	11
September	57	40	69	1.8	10
October	62	44	60	1.7	10
November	66	47	64	1.9	10
December	69	51	60	2.2	10

WELLINGTON

MONTH	Temperature (Average Daily) Max. degrees fahrenheit	Min.	Relative Humidity percent	Precipitation Average Monthly inches	Average Number Days with 0.01 inches or more
January	69	56	67	3.2	10
February	69	56	71	3.2	9
March	67	54	69	3.2	11
April	63	51	76	3.8	13
May	58	47	77	4.6	16
June	55	44	78	4.6	17
July	53	42	76	5.4	18
August	54	43	74	4.6	17
September	57	46	75	3.8	15
October	60	48	74	4.0	14
November	63	50	69	3.5	13
December	67	54	69	3.5	12

The Netherlands AMSTERDAM

January	40	31		2.0	
February	41	31		1.4	
March	47	34		1.3	
April	54	39		1.6	
May	62	45		1.8	
June	67	51		1.8	
July	70	55		2.6	
August	70	55		2.7	
September	66	51		2.8	
October	57	45		2.8	
November	48	38		2.6	
December	42	34		2.2	

Norway BERGEN

January	38	31	77	5.6	20
February	38	30	74	5.6	17
March	43	33	67	4.3	16
April	48	37	68	5.6	19
May	57	44	64	3.2	15
June	61	49	71	4.8	17
July	66	54	73	5.6	20
August	65	54	73	6.7	20
September	60	49	74	9.0	21
October	46	43	76	9.1	23
November	46	38	77	8.2	21
December	41	34	79	7.9	22

MONTH	Temperature (Average Daily)		Relative Humidity percent	Precipitation	
	Max.	Min.		Average Monthly inches	Average Number Days with 0.01 inches or more
	degrees fahrenheit				
January	28	19	82	1.9	15
February	30	20	74	1.3	12
March	39	25	64	1.0	9
April	50	31	57	1.7	11
May	61	41	52	1.7	10
June	68	50	55	2.7	13
July	72	55	59	3.2	15
August	70	54	61	3.7	14
September	60	46	66	3.1	14
October	48	27	72	3.0	14
November	38	31	83	2.7	16
December	32	25	85	2.4	17

Nigeria   LAGOS

January	88	74	65	1.1	2
February	89	77	69	1.8	3
March	89	78	72	4.0	7
April	89	77	72	5.9	10
May	87	76	76	10.6	16
June	85	74	80	18.1	20
July	83	73	80	11.0	16
August	82	73	76	2.5	10
September	83	74	77	5.5	14
October	85	74	76	8.1	16
November	88	75	72	2.7	7
December	88	75	68	1.0	2

Northern Ireland   BELFAST

January	43	35	87	3.1	20
February	44	35	80	2.0	17
March	49	37	74	1.9	16
April	53	39	69	1.9	16
May	59	43	66	2.0	15
June	63	49	71	2.7	16
July	65	52	73	3.7	19
August	65	51	75	2.7	17
September	61	49	78	3.1	18
October	55	44	80	3.2	19
November	48	39	85	2.8	19
December	45	37	89	3.5	21

Pakistan KARACHI**

MONTH	Temperature (Average Daily) Max. degrees fahrenheit	Min.	Relative Humidity percent	Precipitation Average Monthly inches	Average Number Days with 0.1 inches or more
January	77	55	45	0.5	1
February	79	58	49	0.4	1
March	85	67	57	0.3	1
April	90	73	62	0.1	0
May	93	79	68	0.1	0
June	93	82	69	0.1	1
July	91	81	73	3.2	2
August	88	79	74	1.6	2
September	88	77	71	0.5	0
October	91	72	57	0.1	0
November	87	64	49	0.1	1
December	80	57	45	0.2	0

Panama PANAMA CITY (BALBOA HEIGHTS) CANAL ZONE*

January	88	71	84	1.0	4
February	89	71	81	0.4	2
March	90	72	78	0.7	1
April	90	74	81	2.9	6
May	87	74	88	8.0	15
June	86	74	90	8.4	16
July	87	74	91	7.1	15
August	87	74	91	7.9	15
September	86	74	91	8.2	16
October	85	73	92	10.0	18
November	85	73	92	10.2	18
December	87	73	89	4.8	12

Paraguay ASUNCION

January	95	71	56	5.5	8
February	94	71	55	5.1	6
March	92	69	55	4.3	6
April	84	65	59	5.2	7
May	77	58	62	4.6	6
June	72	53	61	2.7	6
July	74	53	56	2.2	5
August	78	57	53	1.5	4
September	83	60	48	3.1	7
October	86	62	50	5.5	8
November	90	65	53	5.9	8
December	94	70	50	6.2	7

Peru   LIMA*

MONTH	Temperature (Average Daily) Max. degrees fahrenheit	Min.	Relative Humidity percent	Average Monthly inches	Average Number Days with 0.01 inches or more
January	82	66	69	0.1	0.5
February	83	67	66	0.1	0.1
March	83	66	64	0.1	0.1
April	80	63	66	0.1	0.2
May	74	60	76	0.2	0.8
June	68	58	80	0.2	1
July	67	57	77	0.2	1
August	66	56	78	0.3	2
September	68	57	76	0.3	1
October	71	58	72	0.1	0.2
November	74	60	71	0.1	0.2
December	78	62	70	0.1	0.1

Philippines   MANILA

	Max.	Min.	Humidity	Monthly	Days
January	86	69	63	0.9	6
February	88	69	59	0.6	4
March	91	71	55	0.7	4
April	93	73	55	1.3	4
May	93	75	61	5.1	12
June	91	75	68	10.0	17
July	88	75	74	17.0	24
August	87	75	73	16.6	23
September	88	75	73	14.0	22
October	88	74	71	7.6	19
November	87	72	69	5.7	14
December	86	70	67	2.6	11

Poland   WARSAW

	Max.	Min.	Humidity	Monthly	Days
January	31	22	84	1.0	15
February	31	21	80	1.2	14
March	42	28	70	1.0	11
April	53	37	61	1.4	13
May	67	48	56	1.8	11
June	74	52	59	2.7	13
July	75	48	63	3.7	16
August	73	56	63	2.5	13
September	66	49	64	1.6	12
October	55	41	73	1.5	12
November	42	30	83	1.2	12
December	35	27	87	1.7	16

Portugal   LISBON

MONTH	Temperature (Average Daily) Max. Min. degrees fahrenheit		Relative Humidity percent	Precipitation Average Monthly inches	Average Number Days with 0.01 inches or more
January	57	46	71	4.3	15
February	57	46	64	3.0	12
March	62	50	64	4.3	14
April	67	52	56	2.1	10
May	69	55	57	1.7	10
June	76	59	54	0.6	5
July	81	62	48	0.1	2
August	81	62	49	0.1	2
September	78	61	54	1.3	6
October	72	57	59	2.4	9
November	62	51	68	3.6	13
December	58	49	72	3.9	15

Puerto Rico   SAN JUAN

	Max.	Min.	Humidity	Monthly	Days
January	80	70	75	4.3	20
February	80	70	74	2.7	15
March	81	70	74	2.9	15
April	82	72	75	4.1	14
May	84	74	75	5.9	16
June	85	75	77	5.4	17
July	85	75	78	5.7	19
August	85	76	77	6.3	20
September	86	75	77	6.2	18
October	85	75	76	5.6	18
November	84	73	76	6.3	19
December	81	72	77	5.4	21

Rhodesia   SALISBURY

	Max.	Min.	Humidity	Monthly	Days
January	78	60	57	7.7	18
February	78	60	53	7.0	15
March	78	58	52	4.6	13
April	78	55	44	1.1	5
May	74	49	37	0.0	2
June	70	44	36	0.0	1
July	70	44	33	0.0	1
August	74	47	28	0.0	1
September	79	53	26	0.0	1
October	83	58	26	1.1	4
November	81	60	43	3.8	11
December	79	60	57	6.4	16

Romania BUCHAREST

MONTH	Temperature (Average Daily) Max. degrees fahrenheit	Min.	Relative Humidity percent	Precipitation Average Monthly inches	Average Number Days with 0.01 inches or more
January	34	11	87	1.09	11
February	38	23	84	1.0	9
March	50	30	73	1.1	9
April	60	41	63	2.3	11
May	74	51	63	3.0	13
June	81	51	62	4.7	12
July	86	60	58	2.0	10
August	86	59	59	1.8	7
September	78	52	63	1.8	5
October	65	43	73	1.1	7
November	50	35	85	1.3	12
December	39	27	89	1.0	10

Samoa (Western and American) APIA

January	86	75	79	17.9	22
February	85	76	78	15.2	19
March	86	74	78	14.1	19
April	86	75	76	10.0	14
May	85	74	76	6.3	12
June	85	74	73	5.1	7
July	85	74	75	3.2	9
August	84	75	73	3.5	9
September	84	74	75	5.2	11
October	85	75	76	6.7	14
November	86	74	75	10.5	16
December	85	74	77	14.6	19

Saudi Arabia JIDDA/MECCA

January	84	66	54	0.2	0.8
February	84	65	52	0.1	0.3
March	95	67	52	0.1	0.3
April	91	70	56	0.1	0.5
May	95	74	55	0.1	0
June	97	75	50	0.1	0
July	99	79	51	0.0	0
August	99	80	61	0.1	0
September	96	77	61	0.1	0
October	95	73	59	0.1	0
November	91	71	54	1.0	2
December	86	67	55	1.2	1

RIYADH

MONTH	Temperature (Average Daily) Max. degrees fahrenheit	Min.	Relative Humidity percent	Precipitation Average Monthly inches	Average Number Days with 0.01 inches or more
January	70	46	44	0.1	1
February	73	48	37	0.8	1
March	82	56	34	0.9	3
April	89	69	34	1.0	4
May	100	72	31	0.4	1
June	102	77	31	0.1	0
July	107	78	19	0.0	0
August	107	75	19	0.1	0
September	102	72	24	0.0	0
October	94	61	25	0.0	0
November	84	55	33	0.1	0
December	79	49	52	0.1	0

Scotland EDINBURGH

January	42	34	84	2.2	17
February	43	34	83	1.5	15
March	46	36	81	1.5	15
April	51	39	75	1.5	14
May	56	43	76	2.1	15
June	62	49	75	1.9	15
July	65	52	78	3.2	17
August	64	54	80	2.0	16
September	60	49	80	2.2	16
October	54	44	82	2.6	17
November	48	39	83	2.4	17
December	44	36	84	2.2	18

Senegal DAKAR*

January	79	64	45	0.1	0.1
February	80	63	45	0.1	0.1
March	80	64	51	0.1	0.1
April	81	65	55	0.1	0
May	84	68	59	0.1	0
June	88	73	62	0.7	2
July	88	76	66	3.5	7
August	87	76	74	10.0	13
September	89	76	72	5.2	11
October	89	76	65	1.5	3
November	86	73	50	0.1	1
December	81	67	46	0.3	0.1

Sierra Leone FREETOWN

MONTH	Temperature (Average Daily) Max. degrees fahrenheit	Min.	Relative Humidity percent	Average Monthly inches	Precipitation Average Number Days with 0.01 inches or more
January	85	75	67	0.5	0.8
February	86	76	67	0.1	0.7
March	86	77	69	0.5	2
April	87	77	71	2.2	6
May	86	77	74	6.3	15
June	87	75	76	11.9	23
July	85	74	81	35.2	27
August	82	73	82	35.5	28
September	83	74	81	24.0	25
October	85	74	77	12.2	23
November	85	75	75	5.2	12
December	85	76	71	1.6	4

Singapore SINGAPORE

January	86	73	78	9.9	17
February	88	73	71	6.8	11
March	88	75	70	7.6	14
April	88	75	74	7.4	15
May	88	75	73	6.8	15
June	89	75	73	6.8	13
July	88	75	72	6.7	13
August	88	75	72	7.7	14
September	87	75	72	7.0	14
October	87	75	72	8.2	16
November	87	75	72	10.0	18
December	87	74	75	10.1	19

South Africa CAPETOWN*

January	78	60	54	0.6	3
February	79	60	54	0.3	2
March	77	58	57	0.7	3
April	72	53	60	1.9	6
May	67	49	65	3.1	9
June	65	46	64	3.3	9
July	63	45	67	3.5	10
August	64	46	65	2.6	9
September	65	49	62	1.7	7
October	70	52	58	1.2	5
November	73	55	56	0.7	3
December	76	58	54	0.4	3

JOHANNESBURG*

MONTH	Temperature (Average Daily) Max. degrees fahrenheit	Min.	Relative Humidity percent	Precipitation Average Monthly inches	Average Number Days with 0.01 inches or more
January	78	58	50	4.5	12
February	77	58	53	4.3	9
March	75	55	50	3.5	9
April	72	50	44	1.5	4
May	66	43	36	1.0	3
June	62	39	33	0.3	1
July	63	39	32	0.3	1
August	68	43	29	0.3	1
September	73	48	30	0.9	2
October	77	53	37	2.2	7
November	77	55	45	4.2	10
December	78	57	47	4.9	11

Soviet Union KIEV

January	24	14	81	2.2	18
February	28	17	75	2.8	18
March	36	25	69	1.9	16
April	56	41	56	1.7	11
May	69	51	50	1.9	13
June	75	56	51	2.1	11
July	77	59	53	3.5	13
August	76	57	55	3.5	12
September	68	50	54	1.1	7
October	56	43	65	1.3	10
November	42	34	82	2.2	15
December	30	22	84	2.2	19

LENINGRAD

January	19	8	84	1.4	21
February	22	14	73	1.2	17
March	32	18	70	1.2	14
April	46	33	65	1.4	12
May	60	42	57	1.8	13
June	68	51	53	1.9	12
July	70	55	61	2.9	13
August	69	54	61	3.0	14
September	60	47	68	2.5	17
October	48	39	78	3.0	18
November	35	28	85	1.9	18
December	26	18	86	1.6	22

MOSCOW

MONTH	Temperature (Average Daily) Max. Min. degrees fahrenheit		Relative Humidity percent	Precipitation Average Monthly inches	Average Number Days with 0.01 inches or more
January	15	3	77	1.6	18
February	22	8	66	1.5	15
March	32	18	64	1.4	15
April	50	34	54	1.5	13
May	66	46	43	2.0	13
June	70	51	47	2.3	12
July	73	55	54	3.4	15
August	72	54	55	2.8	14
September	61	45	59	2.3	13
October	48	37	67	1.8	15
November	35	26	79	1.9	15
December	24	15	83	2.1	23

VLADIVOSTOCK

January	13	0	58	0.3	2
February	22	6	55	0.4	2
March	33	19	56	0.7	4
April	46	34	59	1.2	5
May	55	43	65	2.1	8
June	63	52	76	2.9	10
July	71	60	79	3.3	10
August	75	64	74	4.7	9
September	68	55	64	4.3	7
October	55	41	53	1.9	5
November	36	24	55	1.2	4
December	20	8	56	0.6	3

Spain   BARCELONA

January	55	43	61	1.2	5
February	57	45	58	1.5	5
March	60	48	60	1.9	8
April	65	52	59	1.7	9
May	71	57	59	2.0	8
June	77	65	59	1.4	6
July	82	70	59	1.0	4
August	82	70	63	1.9	6
September	77	65	66	2.9	7
October	69	58	64	3.4	9
November	61	51	64	2.9	6
December	56	46	62	1.8	6

GRANADA

MONTH	Temperature (Average Daily) Max. Min. degrees fahrenheit		Relative Humidity percent	Precipitation Average Monthly inches	Average Number Days with 0.01 inches or more
January	54	36	69	2.1	8
February	58	37	58	1.0	8
March	62	41	58	2.4	10
April	67	45	54	2.0	10
May	73	56	49	1.7	8
June	85	58	38	0.3	2
July	93	63	33	0.1	1
August	91	63	38	0.3	1
September	84	58	42	0.1	4
October	72	50	53	1.9	7
November	63	43	59	1.9	8
December	55	38	70	2.8	10

MADRID

January	47	35	71	1.5	8
February	52	36	62	1.3	7
March	59	41	56	1.7	10
April	65	45	49	1.9	9
May	70	25	49	1.9	10
June	80	58	41	1.0	5
July	81	63	33	0.4	2
August	85	63	35	0.6	3
September	77	57	46	1.2	6
October	65	50	58	2.0	8
November	55	41	65	1.9	9
December	48	36	70	1.9	10

Sudan KHARTOUM*

January	90	59	20	0.1	0
February	93	61	15	0.1	0
March	100	66	11	0.1	0
April	105	72	10	0.1	0
May	107	77	13	0.1	1
June	106	79	18	0.3	1
July	101	77	33	2.1	5
August	98	76	41	2.8	6
September	102	77	30	0.7	2
October	104	75	21	0.2	1
November	97	68	19	0.1	0
December	92	62	21	0.0	0

Sweden STOCKHOLM

MONTH	Temperature (Average Daily) Max. degrees fahrenheit	Min.	Relative Humidity percent	Precipitation Average Monthly inches	Average Number Days with 0.01 inches or more
January	30	23	83	1.7	16
February	30	22	77	1.1	14
March	37	26	68	0.1	10
April	47	34	60	1.2	11
May	58	43	53	1.3	11
June	66	51	55	1.8	13
July	72	57	59	2.3	13
August	68	56	54	3.0	14
September	60	49	69	2.3	14
October	49	41	76	1.9	15
November	40	34	85	2.1	16
December	35	29	86	1.9	17

Switzerland GENEVA

January	38	29	78	2.5	11
February	42	30	71	2.2	9
March	51	36	62	2.1	9
April	59	42	56	1.9	9
May	66	49	58	2.7	11
June	73	53	58	3.5	11
July	77	58	56	2.5	9
August	76	52	59	3.7	11
September	69	53	65	3.9	10
October	52	45	71	2.8	10
November	47	37	76	3.9	11
December	40	31	79	2.3	10

ZURICH

January	36	26	74	3.0	14
February	41	28	65	2.7	13
March	51	34	55	2.5	12
April	39	40	51	2.9	13
May	67	47	52	3.9	14
June	73	53	52	5.1	15
July	76	56	52	5.3	14
August	73	56	53	4.8	14
September	69	51	57	3.09	12
October	57	42	64	3.0	12
November	45	35	73	2.8	12
December	37	29	76	2.5	13

Syria DAMASCUS

MONTH	Temperature (Average Daily) Max. Min. degrees fahrenheit		Relative Humidity percent	Precipitation Average Monthly inches	Average Number Days with 0.01 inches or more
January	53	36	57	1.7	7
February	57	39	53	1.7	6
March	65	42	42	0.3	2
April	75	49	32	0.5	3
May	84	55	26	0.1	1
June	91	61	22	0.1	1
July	96	64	19	0.1	0
August	99	64	21	0.0	0
September	91	60	24	0.7	2
October	81	54	31	0.4	2
November	67	47	46	1.6	5
December	56	40	59	1.6	5

Tahiti

January	89	72	77	9.9	16
February	89	72	77	9.6	16
March	89	72	78	6.9	17
April	89	72	78	5.6	10
May	87	70	78	4.0	10
June	86	69	79	3.0	8
July	86	68	77	2.1	5
August	86	68	78	1.7	6
September	86	69	76	2.1	6
October	87	70	76	3.5	9
November	88	71	77	5.9	13
December	88	72	78	9.8	14

Taiwan TAIPEI*

January	66	54	71	3.4	9
February	65	53	75	5.3	13
March	70	57	69	7.0	12
April	77	63	71	6.7	14
May	83	69	68	9.1	12
June	89	73	68	11.4	13
July	92	76	62	9.1	10
August	91	75	64	12.0	12
September	88	73	66	9.6	10
October	81	67	65	4.8	9
November	75	62	66	2.6	7
December	69	57	69	2.8	8

Thailand BANGKOK

MONTH	Temperature (Average Daily) Max. degrees fahrenheit	Min.	Relative Humidity percent	Precipitation Average Monthly inches	Average Number Days with 0.01 inches or more
January	89	68	53	0.3	1
February	91	72	55	0.8	1
March	93	75	56	1.4	3
April	95	77	58	2.3	3
May	93	77	64	7.8	9
June	91	76	67	6.3	10
July	90	76	66	6.3	13
August	90	76	66	6.9	13
September	89	76	70	12.0	15
October	88	75	70	8.1	14
November	87	72	65	2.6	5
December	87	68	56	0.2	1

Trinidad ST. CLAIR (BOTANIC GARDENS)

January	87	69	68	2.7	14
February	88	68	65	1.6	10
March	89	68	63	1.8	9
April	90	69	61	2.1	9
May	90	71	63	3.7	12
June	89	71	69	7.6	19
July	88	71	71	8.6	22
August	88	71	73	9.7	23
September	89	71	73	7.6	19
October	89	71	74	6.7	18
November	89	71	76	7.2	18
December	88	69	71	4.9	17

Turkey ISTANBUL

January	46	37	75	4.3	18
February	48	36	72	3.6	14
March	51	38	67	2.8	14
April	60	45	62	1.8	9
May	70	53	61	1.5	8
June	77	60	58	1.3	6
July	81	65	56	1.3	4
August	82	66	55	1.1	4
September	76	61	59	2.2	7
October	68	55	64	3.1	11
November	59	48	71	4.0	14
December	51	41	74	4.7	18

Uruguay MONTEVIDEO*

MONTH	Temperature (Average Daily) Max. degrees fahrenheit	Min.	Relative Humidity percent	Precipitation Average Monthly inches	Average Number Days with 0.01 inches or more
January	83	62	53	2.9	6
February	82	61	55	2.6	5
March	78	59	57	3.9	5
April	71	53	61	3.9	6
May	64	48	66	3.3	6
June	59	43	69	3.2	5
July	58	43	69	2.9	6
August	59	43	67	3.1	7
September	63	46	65	3.0	6
October	68	49	62	2.6	6
November	74	54	56	2.9	6
December	79	59	52	3.1	7

Venezuela CARACAS

January	75	56		0.9	6
February	77	56		0.4	2
March	79	58		0.6	3
April	81	60		1.3	4
May	80	62		3.1	9
June	78	62		4.0	14
July	78	61		4.3	15
August	79	62		4.3	15
September	80	61		4.2	13
October	79	61		4.3	12
November	77	58		3.7	13
December	78	60		1.8	10

Vietnam HANOI*

January	68	56	68	0.7	7
February	69	58	70	1.1	13
March	74	63	76	1.5	15
April	82	69	75	3.2	14
May	90	74	69	7.7	15
June	92	78	71	9.4	14
July	91	78	72	12.7	15
August	90	78	75	13.5	16
September	88	76	73	10.0	14
October	84	71	69	3.9	9
November	78	64	68	1.7	7
December	72	59	67	0.8	7

Wales CARDIFF

MONTH	Temperature (Average Daily) Max. degrees fahrenheit	Min.	Relative Humidity percent	Average Monthly inches	Precipitation Average Number Days with 0.01 inches or more
January	45	35	89	4.2	18
February	45	35	87	2.8	14
March	50	38	82	2.4	13
April	56	41	74	2.5	13
May	61	45	74	3.0	13
June	67	51	73	2.4	13
July	69	54	76	3.5	14
August	69	54	78	3.8	15
September	64	51	81	3.9	16
October	58	45	85	4.3	16
November	51	41	88	4.8	17
December	46	38	89	4.3	18

People's Democratic Republic of Yemen PERIM ISLAND (ADEN)

January	84	75	63	0.2	0.6
February	85	75	64	0.1	0.9
March	87	77	65	0.2	1
April	90	79	65	0.1	0.7
May	95	83	60	0.1	0.1
June	98	85	59	0.1	0.2
July	99	85	56	0.1	0.4
August	98	86	57	0.2	1
September	97	84	61	0.5	0.9
October	92	81	61	0.1	0.2
November	88	78	63	0.1	0.2
December	85	76	65	0.1	0.9

Yugoslavia BELGRADE

January	37	26	75	1.9	14
February	42	32	67	1.8	13
March	52	36	56	1.8	12
April	64	45	49	2.1	13
May	72	54	51	3.0	14
June	79	60	51	3.8	13
July	83	63	47	2.4	9
August	83	62	46	2.1	9
September	76	56	47	1.9	8
October	64	47	58	2.1	11
November	51	39	71	2.3	14
December	42	32	76	2.1	14

Zaire KINSHASHA*

MONTH	Temperature (Average Daily) Max. degrees fahrenheit	Min.	Relative Humidity percent	Precipitation Average Monthly inches	Average Number Days with 0.01 inches or more
January	87	70	72	5.3	11
February	88	71	71	5.7	11
March	89	71	71	7.7	12
April	89	71	70	7.7	16
May	88	71	73	6.2	12
June	81	67	71	0.3	1
July	81	64	67	0.1	0
August	84	65	61	0.1	0
September	87	68	61	1.2	5
October	88	70	66	4.7	11
November	87	71	71	8.7	16
December	86	70	73	5.6	15

Zambia LUSAKA

MONTH	Max.	Min.	Relative Humidity	Average Monthly	Average Number
January	79	63	71	9.1	21
February	78	63	70	7.5	17
March	79	62	56	5.6	15
April	78	59	47	0.7	3
May	77	54	37	0.0	1
June	73	50	32	0.0	0
July	73	49	28	0.0	0
August	77	53	26	0.0	0
September	84	59	19	0.0	0
October	88	64	23	0.4	3
November	84	64	46	3.6	11
December	80	63	61	5.9	17

U. S. Cities

Alabama BIRMINGHAM

MONTH	Temperature (Average Daily) Max. degrees fahrenheit	Min.	Relative Humidity percent	Precipitation Average Monthly inches	Average Number Days with 0.01 inches or more
January	54	34	63	4.8	12
February	58	36	55	5.3	10
March	65	42	54	6.2	11
April	75	51	52	4.3	9
May	82	66	56	3.7	9
June	88	66	57	4.0	10
July	90	69	62	5.2	13
August	90	69	62	4.3	10
September	85	63	62	3.7	8
October	76	51	56	2.6	6
November	64	40	59	3.8	9
December	55	35	63	5.2	11

Alaska ANCHORAGE

January	20	3	71	0.8	7
February	27	9	68	0.8	9
March	33	14	58	0.5	8
April	44	27	56	0.5	7
May	55	37	50	0.5	6
June	63	46	57	1.0	8
July	65	50	61	2.0	11
August	64	48	65	2.3	12
September	56	40	65	2.3	14
October	42	28	65	1.4	12
November	28	14	73	1.0	9
December	20	5	75	1.0	11

Arizona PHOENIX

January	65	38	30	0.7	3
February	70	41	25	0.6	4
March	74	45	22	0.7	3
April	83	52	15	0.3	2
May	93	60	13	0.1	1
June	101	68	12	0.1	1
July	105	78	20	0.7	4
August	102	76	23	1.2	5
September	99	70	23	0.6	3
October	87	57	22	0.4	3
November	74	45	27	0.4	2
December	67	38	34	0.8	4

TUCSON

MONTH	Temperature (Average Daily) Max. degrees fahrenheit	Min.	Relative Humidity percent	Precipitation Average Monthly inches	Average Number Days with 0.01 inches or more
January	63	38	32	0.7	4
February	67	40	26	0.7	3
March	71	43	22	0.6	4
April	81	50	16	0.3	2
May	90	57	12	0.1	1
June	98	66	13	0.2	1
July	98	74	29	2.3	10
August	95	72	33	2.3	9
September	93	67	27	1.3	5
October	84	56	25	0.6	3
November	72	45	28	0.5	3
December	65	40	34	0.9	4

Arkansas LITTLE ROCK

January	50	29	61	4.2	10
February	53	32	57	4.4	9
March	61	38	56	4.5	11
April	73	50	56	5.2	10
May	81	58	56	5.3	10
June	92	67	54	3.5	8
July	92	70	58	3.3	9
August	92	68	56	3.0	7
September	85	60	60	3.5	7
October	76	48	51	3.0	6
November	62	38	57	3.8	8
December	52	31	62	4.0	9

California LOS ANGELES

January	66	47	50	3.0	6
February	67	48	52	2.7	5
March	68	50	52	2.1	6
April	70	53	54	1.2	4
May	73	56	55	0.1	1
June	76	60	56	0.0	1
July	83	63	53	0.0	1
August	84	64	55	0.0	1
September	82	63	54	0.1	1
October	78	59	56	0.2	2
November	73	52	49	2.0	3
December	68	48	50	2.1	5

PALM SPRINGS

MONTH	Temperature (Average Daily) Max. degrees fahrenheit	Min.	Relative Humidity percent	Precipitation Average Monthly inches	Average Number Days with 0.01 inches or more
January	69	39	32	1.1	2
February	73	43	28	0.66	1
March	78	45	26	0.63	1
April	87	52	22	0.24	1
May	94	58	21	0.04	0
June	102	64	17	0.00	0
July	108	73	20	0.24	0
August	107	72	22	0.24	1
September	102	66	22	0.26	1
October	92	57	22	0.26	1
November	79	41	35	0.68	1
December	70	40	41	1.1	2

SACRAMENTO

January	53	37	69	3.7	10
February	60	40	60	2.6	9
March	64	42	51	2.1	8
April	71	45	42	1.5	6
May	79	50	36	0.5	3
June	86	55	31	0.1	1
July	93	58	28	0.0	1
August	91	57	29	0.0	1
September	88	55	31	0.1	1
October	77	50	39	0.1	3
November	64	42	59	2.1	7
December	53	38	71	3.1	9

SAN DIEGO

January	65	46	54	1.8	6
February	67	48	58	1.4	6
March	66	50	58	1.5	7
April	68	54	58	0.8	5
May	70	57	64	0.1	2
June	71	60	67	0.0	1
July	75	64	66	0.0	1
August	78	65	66	0.0	1
September	76	63	65	0.1	1
October	74	59	62	0.0	0
November	70	51	61	1.2	1
December	66	48	58	1.7	0

SAN FRANCISCO

MONTH	Temperature (Average Daily) Max. Min. degrees fahrenheit		Relative Humidity percent	Precipitation Average Monthly inches	Average Number Days with 0.01 inches or more
January	56	46	63	4.5	11
February	59	48	63	2.0	10
March	60	48	61	2.7	10
April	61	49	61	1.6	6
May	62	51	68	0.5	3
June	64	53	71	0.1	1
July	64	53	74	0.0	1
August	65	54	73	0.0	1
September	69	55	66	0.1	1
October	68	54	60	1.0	4
November	63	51	63	2.6	8
December	57	47	63	4.1	10

Colorado ASPEN

January	34	7		1.6	6
February	37	9		1.4	6
March	42	15		1.8	6
April	52	24		1.7	5
May	63	32		1.5	4
June	73	38		1.2	4
July	79	44		1.4	5
August	77	43		2.0	6
September	69	36		1.6	5
October	59	28		1.6	4
November	44	17		1.5	5
December	34	8		1.8	6

VAIL

January	24	4		2.4	7
February	25	4		1.9	7
March	29	6		2.0	7
April	37	14		2.5	8
May	47	25		1.7	5
June	57	33		1.5	5
July	65	38		2.3	6
August	61	37		2.5	8
September	55	31		1.5	4
October	45	22		1.2	4
November	52	11		1.6	5
December	26	6		2.0	6

DENVER

MONTH	Temperature (Average Daily) Max. Min. degrees fahrenheit		Relative Humidity percent	Precipitation Average Monthly inches	Average Number Days with 0.01 inches or more
January	43	16	44	0.6	6
February	46	19	43	0.6	6
March	50	24	41	1.2	8
April	61	34	38	1.9	9
May	70	44	38	2.6	10
June	80	52	37	1.9	9
July	87	58	36	1.8	9
August	85	57	36	1.3	8
September	77	48	39	1.1	6
October	66	37	35	1.1	5
November	53	25	44	0.7	5
December	46	19	44	0.4	5

Connecticut NEW HAVEN/MYSTIC

	Max.	Min.			
January	33	16	57	1.9	12
February	36	18	45	1.5	7
March	47	32	63	4.6	13
April	61	40	54	1.6	8
May	66	47	62	4.4	17
June	73	57	77	4.5	12
July	82	64	64	1.1	9
August	80	62	62	3.0	14
September	75	56	56	2.3	5
October	65	49	58	1.2	6
November	50	36	64	6.5	22
December	39	23	54	6.6	13

Delaware WILMINGTON

	Max.	Min.			
January	40	24	60	2.8	11
February	42	25	58	2.7	10
March	51	32	53	3.7	11
April	63	41	50	3.3	11
May	73	52	53	3.2	11
June	82	61	54	4.3	11
July	85	66	54	3.9	9
August	84	64	56	3.4	9
September	78	57	55	2.6	9
October	68	46	54	3.4	8
November	55	36	56	3.3	7
December	43	26	60	3.2	9

Florida KEY WEST

MONTH	Temperature (Average Daily) Max. degrees fahrenheit	Min.	Relative Humidity percent	Precipitation Average Monthly inches	Average Number Days with 0.01 inches or more
January	75	65	69	1.6	6
February	76	66	67	1.8	5
March	79	69	66	1.5	5
April	82	73	63	2.1	4
May	85	76	65	2.5	8
June	87	79	68	4.5	12
July	89	80	66	4.1	13
August	85	79	67	4.4	15
September	87	78	70	7.3	16
October	84	75	69	5.5	12
November	79	70	69	2.6	7
December	76	66	69	1.5	7

MIAMI

MONTH	Max.	Min.	Relative Humidity	Average Monthly	Average Number Days
January	75	58	60	2.1	7
February	76	59	57	1.9	6
March	75	63	57	2.0	6
April	82	67	54	3.6	6
May	85	70	61	6.1	11
June	88	73	67	9.0	15
July	89	75	65	6.9	16
August	89	75	74	6.7	17
September	88	75	68	8.7	17
October	84	71	65	8.1	15
November	79	64	61	2.7	8
December	76	60	59	1.6	7

ORLANDO

MONTH	Max.	Min.	Relative Humidity	Average Monthly	Average Number Days
January	70	50	57	2.2	6
February	71	51	51	2.9	7
March	76	55	50	3.4	8
April	81	61	45	2.7	5
May	86	66	49	2.9	9
June	89	71	56	7.1	14
July	89	72	59	8.2	17
August	90	73	60	6.7	16
September	87	72	60	7.2	14
October	82	66	56	4.7	10
November	76	56	54	1.5	8
December	71	51	56	1.9	6

PALM BEACH

MONTH	Temperature (Average Daily) Max. degrees fahrenheit	Min.	Relative Humidity percent	Precipitation Average Monthly inches	Average Number Days with 0.01 inches or more
January	75	55	59	2.6	7
February	76	56	56	2.6	7
March	79	60	54	3.3	7
April	82	64	52	3.5	7
May	86	68	57	5.1	11
June	88	72	66	8.1	14
July	89	74	64	6.5	15
August	90	74	64	6.9	16
September	88	74	66	9.8	17
October	84	70	62	8.7	13
November	79	62	58	2.4	8
December	76	57	57	2.2	8

Georgia ATLANTA

January	51	33	60	4.3	11
February	54	35	54	4.4	10
March	61	41	52	5.8	12
April	71	50	51	4.6	9
May	79	59	55	3.7	9
June	84	66	58	3.6	10
July	86	69	63	4.9	12
August	86	68	62	3.5	9
September	81	63	61	3.1	7
October	72	52	53	2.5	6
November	61	40	54	3.4	8
December	52	34	59	4.2	10

SAVANNAH

January	61	38	55	2.9	9
February	63	40	49	2.8	9
March	69	46	48	4.4	10
April	77	54	47	2.9	9
May	84	61	52	4.2	9
June	89	68	56	5.8	11
July	90	71	60	7.8	15
August	90	70	63	6.4	12
September	85	66	61	5.5	10
October	78	55	53	2.8	6
November	69	44	50	1.9	6
December	62	38	44	3.2	8

Idaho BOISE

MONTH	Temperature (Average Daily) Max. degrees fahrenheit	Min.	Relative Humidity percent	Precipitation Average Monthly inches	Average Number Days with 0.01 inches or more
January	36	21	74	1.4	12
February	43	27	68	1.6	10
March	51	30	55	1.0	9
April	61	36	47	1.1	8
May	70	44	45	1.3	8
June	78	51	42	1.8	7
July	90	58	33	0.1	2
August	87	56	34	0.3	3
September	77	48	39	0.4	4
October	64	39	49	0.8	6
November	48	30	65	1.3	10
December	39	25	74	1.3	12

SUN VALLEY

MONTH	Max.	Min.		Average Monthly inches	Average Number Days
January	30	1		2.6	6
February	36	4		1.5	4
March	40	9		1.1	4
April	52	21		1.0	3
May	64	30		1.6	5
June	71	34		1.8	5
July	82	38		0.71	2
August	81	37		0.84	2
September	72	30		0.81	3
October	61	22		0.90	3
November	44	14		1.6	4
December	32	4		2.7	7

Illinois CHICAGO

MONTH	Max.	Min.	Relative Humidity	Average Monthly inches	Average Number Days
January	31	17	65	1.8	11
February	34	20	62	1.5	10
March	44	29	59	2.7	13
April	59	40	55	3.7	13
May	70	49	53	3.4	12
June	80	60	54	3.9	10
July	84	65	54	4.9	9
August	83	64	56	3.1	8
September	75	56	56	3.0	9
October	65	45	55	2.6	8
November	48	32	64	2.2	10
December	35	21	71	2.1	11

SPRINGFIELD

MONTH	Temperature (Average Daily)		Relative Humidity percent	Precipitation	
	Max.	Min.		Average Monthly inches	Average Number Days with 0.01 inches or more
	degrees fahrenheit				
January	34	18	69	1.7	9
February	38	21	67	1.7	9
March	48	30	64	2.7	12
April	63	42	55	4.1	12
May	74	52	53	3.5	11
June	83	62	53	4.1	10
July	86	65	55	3.8	9
August	85	63	59	2.7	8
September	78	55	57	3.2	9
October	68	45	54	3.0	7
November	51	32	64	2.1	9
December	38	22	73	1.9	10

Indiana INDIANAPOLIS

January	36	19	69	2.8	11
February	39	21	66	2.3	10
March	49	30	63	3.7	13
April	62	41	55	3.8	12
May	72	51	56	4.8	12
June	82	61	58	4.1	10
July	85	64	60	3.6	9
August	84	62	61	2.8	8
September	77	54	60	2.8	8
October	67	44	57	2.5	8
November	50	32	67	3.1	10
December	38	23	73	2.7	12

Iowa DES MOINES

January	27	11	69	1.1	7
February	32	15	67	1.5	7
March	42	25	63	2.3	10
April	59	39	57	2.9	10
May	70	50	56	4.2	11
June	79	61	56	4.9	11
July	84	65	56	3.2	9
August	83	63	58	3.3	9
September	74	54	60	3.7	9
October	64	43	55	2.1	7
November	46	29	63	1.4	6
December	32	17	70	1.0	7

Kansas WICHITA

MONTH	Temperature (Average Daily) Max. degrees fahrenheit	Min.	Relative Humidity percent	Average Monthly inches	Precipitation Average Number Days with 0.01 inches or more
January	41	21	63	0.8	5
February	46	25	59	0.9	5
March	55	32	53	1.7	7
April	68	45	52	2.9	8
May	77	55	53	3.6	11
June	86	65	53	4.4	9
July	91	69	49	4.3	8
August	91	68	50	3.1	7
September	81	59	56	3.6	8
October	71	47	53	2.5	6
November	55	33	56	1.1	5
December	44	24	61	1.1	6

Kentucky LOUISVILLE

January	42	24	64	3.5	12
February	45	26	62	3.4	11
March	54	34	58	5.0	13
April	66	44	53	4.1	12
May	73	53	55	4.2	11
June	83	62	58	4.0	10
July	87	66	58	3.7	11
August	86	64	58	2.9	7
September	80	57	60	2.9	8
October	70	45	55	2.3	7
November	54	35	61	3.3	10
December	44	27	65	3.3	11

Louisiana NEW ORLEANS

January	62	43	67	4.5	10
February	65	46	53	4.8	9
March	70	56	61	5.4	9
April	78	58	60	4.1	7
May	84	65	60	4.2	7
June	89	71	62	4.7	10
July	90	74	66	6.7	15
August	90	73	66	5.2	13
September	86	69	66	5.5	10
October	79	59	59	2.2	6
November	70	49	61	3.8	7
December	64	45	67	5.1	10

Maine CARIBOU

MONTH	Temperature (Average Daily) Max. degrees fahrenheit	Min.	Relative Humidity percent	Average Monthly inches	Average Number Days with 0.01 inches or more
January	19	1	67	2.0	14
February	23	2	64	2.1	13
March	32	14	61	2.2	13
April	45	27	57	2.4	13
May	60	39	53	2.9	13
June	70	48	57	3.4	14
July	75	54	58	3.9	14
August	73	51	59	3.7	13
September	64	43	61	3.4	13
October	52	34	62	3.3	12
November	38	24	72	3.5	14
December	23	8	71	2.6	14

PORTLAND

January	31	11	62	3.3	11
February	33	12	60	3.5	10
March	40	22	59	3.6	11
April	52	32	55	3.3	12
May	63	41	58	3.3	13
June	73	51	61	3.1	11
July	79	56	60	2.6	9
August	77	55	59	2.6	9
September	69	47	61	3.0	8
October	60	38	59	3.3	9
November	47	29	63	4.8	12
December	34	16	62	4.0	12

Maryland BALTIMORE

January	41	24	58	2.9	10
February	43	25	55	2.8	9
March	53	32	51	3.6	11
April	65	42	49	3.0	11
May	74	52	52	3.6	11
June	83	61	53	3.7	9
July	86	66	53	4.0	9
August	85	64	53	4.2	10
September	79	57	56	3.1	7
October	68	46	54	2.8	7
November	56	36	54	3.1	9
December	43	26	59	3.2	9

Massachusetts BOSTON

MONTH	Temperature (Average Daily)		Relative Humidity percent	Precipitation	
	Max.	Min.		Average Monthly inches	Average Number Days with 0.01 inches or more
	degrees fahrenheit				
January	35	22	57	3.6	12
February	37	23	57	3.5	11
March	44	31	57	4.0	12
April	56	40	53	3.4	11
May	67	50	57	3.4	11
June	76	59	60	3.1	11
July	81	65	56	2.7	9
August	79	63	57	3.6	10
September	72	56	61	3.1	9
October	64	47	57	3.0	9
November	51	38	61	4.5	11
December	39	26	61	4.2	12

CAPE COD

January	38	22		4.0	8
February	38	22		3.9	7
March	44	28		3.9	8
April	53	37		3.2	8
May	63	46		2.9	7
June	72	56		2.6	6
July	78	62		4.0	5
August	77	61		3.5	5
September	71	54		3.6	5
October	62	45		4.1	6
November	52	36		3.5	7
December	42	26		3.6	7

NANTUCKET

January	38	24		3.9	8
February	38	25		4.1	7
March	42	30		4.2	8
April	50	37		3.6	7
May	59	45		3.4	6
June	68	54		2.0	4
July	74	60		2.8	4
August	74	60		3.7	6
September	69	55		3.6	5
October	61	47		3.3	6
November	52	39		4.3	8
December	42	29		4.4	8

Michigan DETROIT

MONTH	Temperature (Average Daily) Max. degrees fahrenheit	Min. degrees fahrenheit	Relative Humidity percent	Average Monthly inches	Average Number Days with 0.01 inches or more
January	31	19	68	1.9	13
February	33	20	65	1.8	12
March	43	27	60	2.3	13
April	57	38	52	3.0	12
May	68	48	51	3.4	12
June	79	59	53	3.0	11
July	83	63	51	2.9	9
August	81	62	53	3.0	9
September	74	54	55	2.3	9
October	63	45	55	2.5	9
November	47	34	64	2.3	11
December	35	23	69	2.1	13

Minnesota MINNEAPOLIS-ST. PAUL

	Max.	Min.	Humidity	Monthly	Days
January	21	3	67	0.7	9
February	25	7	65	0.8	7
March	36	19	64	1.6	10
April	55	34	54	2.0	10
May	67	46	53	3.2	12
June	77	56	54	3.9	12
July	82	61	54	3.6	10
August	80	59	55	3.0	10
September	70	49	60	2.7	9
October	60	39	58	1.7	8
November	40	24	66	1.2	8
December	26	10	70	0.8	9

Missouri ST. LOUIS

	Max.	Min.	Humidity	Monthly	Days
January	39	22	65	1.8	8
February	44	26	61	2.0	8
March	53	33	58	3.0	11
April	67	46	54	3.9	11
May	76	55	56	3.8	11
June	84	67	57	4.4	9
July	88	68	57	3.6	9
August	87	67	57	2.8	9
September	80	59	61	2.8	9
October	69	48	55	2.7	8
November	54	35	62	2.4	8
December	42	26	69	2.0	10

Montana HELENA

MONTH	Temperature (Average Daily) Max. degrees fahrenheit	Min.	Relative Humidity percent	Average Monthly inches	Average Number Days with 0.01 inches or more
January	28	7	64	0.5	8
February	35	14	62	0.3	6
March	41	19	54	0.6	8
April	55	30	48	0.9	8
May	64	39	44	1.7	11
June	71	46	46	2.3	12
July	83	52	39	0.9	7
August	82	50	41	0.9	8
September	70	40	48	0.9	7
October	58	31	52	0.5	6
November	42	20	62	0.6	7
December	32	13	67	0.5	8

Nebraska OMAHA

January	32	12	65	0.7	7
February	38	17	61	0.9	7
March	47	26	57	1.5	9
April	64	40	53	2.9	9
May	74	51	54	4.1	12
June	83	61	55	4.9	11
July	88	65	56	3.7	9
August	87	64	59	3.9	9
September	78	54	61	3.2	8
October	69	42	56	1.9	6
November	50	29	62	1.1	5
December	37	18	67	0.8	6

Nevada LAS VEGAS

January	55	32	28	0.4	3
February	61	36	25	0.3	2
March	67	41	19	0.3	2
April	77	50	15	0.2	2
May	87	59	13	0.1	1
June	97	67	11	0.0	1
July	103	75	14	0.4	3
August	101	73	17	0.4	3
September	94	65	16	0.2	2
October	81	53	19	0.2	2
November	65	40	27	0.4	2
December	56	33	32	0.3	2

MONTH	Temperature (Average Daily) Max. degrees	Min. fahrenheit	Relative Humidity percent	Precipitation Average Monthly inches	Average Number Days with 0.01 inches or more
January	45	18	50	1.2	6
February	51	23	39	0.8	5
March	56	24	32	0.7	6
April	64	29	28	0.5	4
May	72	37	25	0.7	5
June	80	42	24	0.4	3
July	91	47	19	0.2	3
August	89	44	21	0.2	2
September	81	38	21	0.2	2
October	70	30	26	0.4	3
November	56	24	40	0.7	5
December	46	20	51	1.0	6

New Hampshire CONCORD

January	31	9	74	2.6	11
February	33	11	75	2.4	10
March	42	22	57	2.7	11
April	56	31	46	2.9	11
May	68	41	49	3.0	12
June	77	51	56	3.3	11
July	82	56	53	3.1	10
August	80	54	54	2.8	10
September	72	46	58	3.0	9
October	62	36	54	2.6	8
November	47	28	62	3.9	11
December	34	14	66	3.2	11

New Jersey ATLANTIC CITY

January	41	24	57	3.5	11
February	42	24	56	3.3	10
March	50	31	55	4.3	11
April	62	41	50	3.3	11
May	72	50	56	3.5	10
June	80	59	58	3.3	9
July	84	65	58	4.3	9
August	83	63	57	4.9	9
September	77	56	58	2.9	8
October	67	45	56	3.4	7
November	55	36	57	4.2	9
December	44	26	59	4.0	10

New York BUFFALO

MONTH	Temperature (Average Daily) Max. degrees fahrenheit	Min.	Relative Humidity percent	Precipitation Average Monthly inches	Average Number Days with 0.01 inches or more
January	29	17	73	2.9	20
February	31	17	70	2.5	17
March	39	25	67	2.8	16
April	53	36	58	3.1	14
May	64	45	56	2.9	13
June	75	56	57	2.2	10
July	79	60	55	2.9	10
August	77	59	58	3.5	11
September	70	52	60	3.2	11
October	60	42	61	3.0	11
November	46	33	71	3.7	16
December	33	22	75	3.0	20

NEW YORK CITY

January	38	25	60	2.7	11
February	40	26	58	2.9	10
March	48	33	55	3.7	12
April	60	43	51	3.3	11
May	71	53	53	3.4	11
June	80	62	55	2.9	10
July	85	68	55	3.6	11
August	83	66	57	4.0	10
September	76	59	57	3.2	8
October	66	50	55	2.8	8
November	55	40	59	3.7	9
December	41	29	61	3.5	10

North Carolina ASHEVILLE

January	48	27	60	3.3	10
February	50	28	55	3.6	9
March	58	33	53	4.6	12
April	69	42	50	3.5	9
May	76	50	57	3.3	12
June	82	58	60	3.9	12
July	84	62	64	4.8	13
August	83	61	64	4.5	13
September	78	55	65	3.5	10
October	69	44	59	3.2	9
November	58	34	56	2.9	9
December	49	28	60	3.5	10

CAPE HATTERAS

MONTH	Temperature (Average Daily) Max. degrees fahrenheit	Min.	Relative Humidity percent	Precipitation Average Monthly inches	Average Number Days with 0.01 inches or more
January	52	38	68	4.2	11
February	53	38	64	4.1	10
March	57	43	62	3.8	10
April	66	51	60	3.0	9
May	73	60	66	3.2	11
June	80	68	69	4.8	10
July	83	72	70	5.9	12
August	83	71	70	6.7	11
September	79	67	67	5.7	9
October	71	59	63	4.7	10
November	63	48	63	4.4	9
December	54	40	67	4.5	10

RALEIGH

January	51	30	55	3.2	10
February	53	31	48	3.3	10
March	61	37	48	3.4	10
April	72	46	44	3.0	9
May	79	55	55	3.3	10
June	85	63	57	3.6	9
July	87	67	59	5.0	11
August	86	66	61	4.9	10
September	81	59	59	3.7	8
October	72	48	54	2.8	7
November	62	37	49	2.8	8
December	51	30	56	3.0	9

North Dakota BISMARCK

January	19	−2	73	0.5	8
February	24	2	76	0.4	7
March	35	14	78	0.7	8
April	54	31	79	1.4	8
May	67	41	79	2.1	10
June	75	51	84	3.5	12
July	84	57	82	2.2	9
August	85	54	81	1.9	8
September	71	43	82	1.3	7
October	60	33	78	0.8	5
November	39	18	79	0.5	6
December	26	5	76	0.4	8

Ohio CINCINNATI

MONTH	Temperature (Average Daily)		Relative Humidity percent	Precipitation	
	Max.	Min.		Average Monthly inches	Average Number Days with 0.01 inches or more
	degrees fahrenheit				
January	39	22	67	3.3	12
February	42	23	62	3.0	11
March	51	31	60	4.0	13
April	65	42	43	3.6	12
May	74	51	53	3.7	12
June	83	61	55	3.8	11
July	86	64	57	4.1	10
August	85	63	57	2.6	9
September	79	55	59	2.5	8
October	68	45	55	2.1	8
November	53	34	63	3.0	11
December	42	25	69	2.8	12

CLEVELAND

January	33	20	69	2.5	16
February	35	20	68	2.1	15
March	44	28	65	3.0	16
April	58	38	67	3.4	14
May	68	48	58	3.4	13
June	78	57	59	3.2	11
July	81	61	58	3.4	10
August	80	59	60	3.0	9
September	74	63	61	2.8	10
October	63	43	60	2.5	11
November	48	34	67	2.7	13
December	36	24	71	2.3	16

Oklahoma OKLAHOMA CITY

January	47	26	60	1.1	5
February	52	30	54	1.3	6
March	59	36	52	2.0	7
April	71	49	52	3.4	8
May	78	57	57	5.2	10
June	87	66	56	4.2	9
July	92	70	50	2.6	7
August	92	69	51	2.5	6
September	84	61	57	3.5	7
October	74	50	52	2.5	6
November	60	37	54	1.4	5
December	50	29	57	1.2	5

TULSA

MONTH	Temperature (Average Daily) Max. Min. degrees fahrenheit		Relative Humidity percent	Precipitation Average Monthly inches	Average Number Days with 0.01 inches or more
January	47	26	59	1.4	6
February	52	30	54	1.7	7
March	60	34	52	2.5	8
April	71	50	52	4.1	9
May	80	58	57	5.1	11
June	87	67	59	4.7	9
July	92	71	54	3.5	7
August	92	70	54	3.0	7
September	84	61	61	4.0	8
October	75	51	53	3.2	6
November	61	38	57	1.8	6
December	50	30	61	1.6	7

Pennsylvania   PHILADELPHIA

January	40	24	59	2.8	11
February	42	25	56	2.6	9
March	51	32	53	3.6	11
April	63	42	48	3.2	11
May	74	52	52	3.3	11
June	83	61	55	3.7	10
July	86	66	54	4.0	9
August	84	64	55	4.1	9
September	78	57	56	3.0	8
October	67	46	53	2.5	7
November	55	36	55	3.3	9
December	43	27	60	3.3	10

PITTSBURGH

January	37	23		2.6	15
February	39	24		2.2	14
March	48	31		3.5	15
April	62	42		3.4	13
May	72	52		3.5	13
June	81	61		3.7	12
July	84	65		3.7	11
August	82	63		3.1	9
September	76	56		2.5	9
October	66	45		2.7	10
November	51	36		2.4	11
December	39	26		2.5	14

Rhode Island NEWPORT

MONTH	Temperature (Average Daily) Max.	Min. degrees fahrenheit	Relative Humidity percent	Precipitation Average Monthly inches	Average Number Days with 0.01 inches or more
January	38	19		2.9	7
February	39	20		3.3	6
March	46	27		4.0	7
April	56	35		4.0	7
May	67	44		3.3	7
June	75	53		2.7	6
July	80	59		2.8	5
August	79	58		4.4	6
September	72	50		3.5	5
October	64	40		3.2	5
November	52	32		4.5	7
December	41	22		3.8	7

PROVIDENCE

MONTH	Max.	Min.	Relative Humidity	Average Monthly	Average Number Days
January	36	20	56	3.5	11
February	37	21	55	3.4	11
March	44	29	54	3.9	12
April	56	36	47	3.7	11
May	66	46	51	3.4	11
June	76	56	67	2.6	11
July	81	63	57	2.8	9
August	79	61	55	3.9	10
September	73	53	57	3.2	9
October	63	43	54	3.2	8
November	52	34	58	4.5	11
December	39	23	70	4.2	12

South Carolina CHARLESTON

MONTH	Max.	Min.	Relative Humidity	Average Monthly	Average Number Days
January	59	37	56	2.9	10
February	61	39	51	3.2	9
March	67	45	50	4.7	11
April	76	53	49	2.9	7
May	83	61	54	3.8	9
June	87	68	59	6.3	11
July	89	71	63	8.2	14
August	88	70	63	6.4	13
September	84	65	63	5.1	9
October	77	55	55	3.0	6
November	68	44	51	2.1	7
December	60	37	55	3.1	9

South Dakota   PIERRE

MONTH	Temperature (Average Daily) Max. degrees	Min. fahrenheit	Relative Humidity percent	Precipitation Average Monthly inches	Average Number Days with 0.01 inches or more
January	25	5		0.41	1
February	32	11		0.72	2
March	41	20		0.80	2
April	58	33		1.9	4
May	70	45		2.9	6
June	80	55		3.8	6
July	90	61		2.0	4
August	88	60		1.8	4
September	75	48		1.3	3
October	63	37		1.0	2
November	45	23		0.49	1
December	31	11		0.62	2

Tennessee   GATLINBURG

MONTH	Max.	Min.	Relative Humidity	Average Monthly	Average Number
January	51	27		4.8	9
February	54	29		4.7	9
March	61	34		5.3	9
April	71	42		4.5	8
May	79	50		4.5	9
June	86	58		5.2	9
July	88	59		5.6	10
August	87	60		5.2	10
September	83	54		2.9	5
October	72	43		3.1	6
November	61	33		3.4	7
December	52	28		4.4	8

MEMPHIS

MONTH	Max.	Min.	Relative Humidity	Average Monthly	Average Number
January	49	31	64	4.9	10
February	53	34	59	4.7	10
March	60	41	56	5.1	11
April	72	52	53	5.4	10
May	81	60	55	4.3	9
June	88	68	56	3.4	8
July	91	71	57	3.5	9
August	90	70	56	3.5	8
September	84	62	56	3.0	7
October	74	51	51	2.5	6
November	61	40	55	3.9	8
December	51	33	62	4.7	10

NASHVILLE

MONTH	Temperature (Average Daily) Max. degrees	Min. fahrenheit	Relative Humidity percent	Average Monthly inches	Precipitation Average Number Days with 0.01 inches or more
January	47	29	65	4.7	11
February	50	31	58	4.4	11
March	59	38	59	5.0	12
April	71	48	52	4.1	11
May	79	57	56	4.1	11
June	87	65	56	3.3	10
July	90	69	59	3.8	10
August	89	67	60	3.2	9
September	83	60	62	3.8	8
October	73	48	56	2.1	7
November	59	37	59	3.4	9
December	46	31	64	4.5	11

Texas DALLAS-FORT WORTH

MONTH	Max.	Min.	Relative Humidity	Average Monthly	Days with 0.01 or more
January	55	35	60	1.8	7
February	59	37	56	2.3	6
March	66	43	57	2.5	7
April	76	54	59	4.3	9
May	82	62	61	4.4	8
June	90	70	56	3.0	6
July	95	74	50	1.8	5
August	96	73	52	2.2	5
September	89	66	60	3.1	7
October	79	56	56	2.6	6
November	67	44	56	2.0	6
December	58	37	58	1.8	6

EL PASO

MONTH	Max.	Min.	Relative Humidity	Average Monthly	Days with 0.01 or more
January	57	30	42	0.3	4
February	62	34	34	0.4	3
March	68	40	28	0.3	2
April	78	49	22	0.2	2
May	87	57	52	0.3	2
June	94	65	24	0.6	3
July	94	69	39	1.5	8
August	92	68	40	1.7	7
September	87	61	44	1.1	5
October	78	48	36	0.7	4
November	66	37	37	0.3	2
December	57	30	43	0.5	4

HOUSTON

MONTH	Temperature (Average Daily) Max. Min. degrees fahrenheit		Relative Humidity percent	Precipitation Average Monthly inches	Average Number Days with 0.01 inches or more
January	62	41	64	3.5	11
February	66	44	55	3.5	6
March	71	49	61	2.6	10
April	79	59	60	3.5	10
May	85	65	61	5.1	8
June	91	70	59	4.5	7
July	93	72	58	4.1	10
August	94	72	61	4.3	11
September	90	68	65	4.6	10
October	83	58	59	4.0	8
November	73	49	60	4.0	8
December	65	43	62	4.0	9

SAN ANTONIO

January	61	39	60	1.6	8
February	65	43	57	2.0	8
March	72	49	53	1.5	7
April	80	58	56	2.5	8
May	86	65	58	3.0	8
June	92	72	56	2.7	6
July	95	73	51	1.6	4
August	95	73	51	2.4	5
September	89	68	55	3.7	7
October	81	59	54	2.8	6
November	71	48	55	1.7	6
December	64	41	57	1.4	7

Utah SALT LAKE CITY

January	37	18	67	1.2	10
February	43	23	57	1.1	9
March	50	28	44	1.6	10
April	61	36	39	2.1	10
May	72	44	31	1.4	8
June	81	51	26	1.3	6
July	92	60	20	0.7	4
August	90	58	22	0.9	5
September	80	49	27	0.6	5
October	66	38	40	1.1	6
November	50	28	58	1.3	7
December	39	21	71	1.3	9

Vermont MONTPELIER/STOWE

MONTH	Temperature (Average Daily) Max. Min. degrees fahrenheit		Relative Humidity percent	Precipitation Average Monthly inches	Average Number Days with 0.01 inches or more
January	25	5		1.9	5
February	27	7		2.5	6
March	36	18		2.4	6
April	50	30		2.5	7
May	64	40		3.0	7
June	73	50		3.2	8
July	78	54		3.0	7
August	75	52		3.1	6
September	67	45		2.5	6
October	57	35		2.6	6
November	42	26		3.0	7
December	28	12		2.9	7

Virginia WILLIAMSBURG

	Max.	Min.			
January	50	28		3.2	10
February	52	30		3.4	10
March	60	36		3.6	11
April	71	45		2.8	10
May	79	55		3.8	10
June	85	62		4.1	9
July	88	67		5.3	12
August	86	66		4.7	10
September	81	60		3.7	8
October	72	49		2.8	7
November	62	39		2.9	8
December	51	30		3.1	6

Washington, D.C.

	Max.	Min.			
January	43	27	54	2.6	10
February	46	28	51	2.4	9
March	55	35	49	3.3	11
April	67	45	47	2.8	10
May	76	55	51	3.6	11
June	84	64	52	3.4	9
July	88	69	52	4.1	10
August	86	67	54	4.6	12
September	80	61	51	3.0	7
October	69	49	51	2.6	12
November	57	38	52	2.9	8
December	45	29	57	3.0	16

Washington SEATTLE

MONTH	Temperature (Average Daily) Max. degrees fahrenheit	Min.	Relative Humidity percent	Precipitation Average Monthly inches	Average Number Days with 0.01 inches or more
January	43	33	75	5.7	19
February	48	36	66	4.1	16
March	51	36	63	3.6	18
April	57	40	58	2.4	14
May	64	45	54	1.7	10
June	69	50	53	1.5	9
July	73	53	49	0.7	5
August	73	53	53	1.0	7
September	68	50	58	1.9	9
October	59	44	68	3.9	14
November	50	38	74	5.8	18
December	45	35	77	5.9	20

SPOKANE

January	31	19	77	2.4	15
February	39	25	68	1.6	11
March	46	28	54	1.5	11
April	57	35	43	1.1	8
May	66	42	40	1.4	9
June	73	49	35	1.3	8
July	84	55	25	0.5	4
August	81	54	28	0.5	5
September	72	46	34	0.8	6
October	58	37	49	1.4	8
November	41	29	74	2.2	12
December	33	24	81	2.3	16

Wisconsin MILWAUKEE

January	27	11	68	1.6	11
February	30	14	67	1.1	9
March	39	23	65	2.2	12
April	54	34	62	2.7	12
May	65	43	62	2.8	12
June	75	53	62	3.5	11
July	80	59	60	3.4	10
August	79	58	62	3.6	9
September	71	50	63	3.0	9
October	61	40	63	1.9	9
November	44	28	67	2.0	10
December	31	16	73	1.7	11

Wyoming YELLOWSTONE NATIONAL PARK

MONTH	Temperature (Average Daily)		Relative Humidity percent	Precipitation	
	Max.	Min.		Average Monthly inches	Average Number Days with 0.01 inches or more
	degrees fahrenheit				
January	27	8		1.1	4
February	32	11		0.9	3
March	40	16		1.2	5
April	51	26		1.2	5
May	60	34		1.7	5
June	68	40		2.2	6
July	80	46		1.1	4
August	77	45		1.3	4
September	67	37		1.2	4
October	55	30		1.1	4
November	38	20		1.0	3
December	31	14		1.1	4